Praise fo
Free, Fair anc

If you want a truly exciting glimpse into what the world after this one might look like, this book is for you. When we move past "markets solve all problems" into a more mature approach, it will incorporate precisely the insights in this lively and engaging volume!
— Bill McKibben, author, *Falter* and founder, 350.org

David Bollier and Silke Helfrich don't just establish that commoning can work, and work well. They've analysed the contours of successful experiments in how humans have come together to make their worlds freer, fairer and more alive. This book is an expansive, thorough, and deeply thoughtful guide to a possible future politics. All that remains is for us to take up their call: not to do it ourselves, but to do it together.
— Raj Patel, author, *The Value of Nothing* and *Stuffed and Starved*

Wiki has confused educators and economists, but not our authors. They explain how and why its social system allows people to make things that couldn't have been made any other way. You will find here a handbook for tackling seemingly intractable problems by sidestepping the mistakes that make them hard.
— Ward Cunningham, inventor of the wiki

Free, Fair and Alive is an inspiring treatise for our troubled times. It presents a passionate argument for commoning and lays out thoughtful rules to follow to enact a commoned world. Its insurgent worldview is bold, caring, exciting, and challenging all at once. This book offers hope as well as down to earth strategies to all who care for the future of this planet.
— J.K. Gibson-Graham, Jenny Cameron and Stephen Healy, authors, *Take Back the Economy: An Ethical Guide for Transforming Our Communities*

Free, Fair and Alive shows the path to respond to the ecological emergency and the polarisation of society, economically, socially, culturally. The recovery and co-creation of the commons offers hope for the planet and people. Through commoning we sow the seeds of Earth Democracy and our future.
— Vandana Shiva, activist and author, *Earth Democracy*

Like a medieval cathedral this book is both philosophically lofty and as down-to-earth as a gargoyle. Its structure is encompassing and harmonious, buttressed by psychology, cybernetics, and social science. Magnificent windows let insights illuminate a new world of common facts and a new paradigm of understanding. Major ideas such as the Nested-I or Ubuntu Relationality infuse the whole, tentatively at first but with mounting conviction as this edifice of our future is constructed block by block of example and of reasoning to become a place of refuge from the destructive elements of neoliberalism and a place of collectivity against the fears it instills. Common sense and the sense of the commons are united at last, so, men and women of the commons, let us be up and doing.

— Peter Linebaugh, author, *Red Round Globe Hot Burning*

[*Free, Fair, and Alive*] is grounded in the contemporary practices of commoning and present the transformative potential of commons. With great enthusiasm and a thoughtful attitude the authors introduce the commons as set of practices, believes and values for politicizing the needed societal transformation for a fairer and more sustainable world. If you aim to initiating commoning actions or you are already entangled in a networks of commons, this is the right book for you; after reading it you will have new sparks, new ideas, new energies and the right dose of bravery to (re)launch again and again the counter-hegemonic logic of commons and enjoy the performative power of the everyday commoning.

— Giacomo D'Alisa, Center of Social Study,
University of Coimbra, Portugal

Free, Fair, and Alive eloquently describes a worldview that is both old and new. Old, because it is based on an accurate conception of human nature and society. New, because it provides a robust alternative to individualism, which has dominated social science and public policy for over a half-century. A must-read for all who are working toward an ethics for the whole world.

— David Sloan Wilson, President, Evolution Institute,
and author, *This View of Life*

DAVID BOLLIER & SILKE HELFRICH

FREE, FAIR AND ALIVE

THE INSURGENT POWER OF THE COMMONS

new society
PUBLISHERS

Cover design by Diane McIntosh.
Cover image: "Deepen Communication with Nature" by Mireia Juan Cuco.
Textbox image: © MJ Jessen

Printed in Canada. First printing July 2019.

Inquiries regarding requests to reprint all or part of *Free, Fair and Alive* should be addressed to New Society Publishers at the address below. To order directly from the publishers, please call toll-free (North America) 1-800-567-6772, or order online at www.newsociety.com

Any other inquiries can be directed by mail to:
New Society Publishers
P.O. Box 189, Gabriola Island, BC V0R 1X0, Canada
(250) 247-9737

LIBRARY AND ARCHIVES CANADA CATALOGUING IN PUBLICATION

Title: Free, fair, and alive : the insurgent power of the commons / Silke Helfrich & David Bollier.
Names: Helfrich, Silke, author. | Bollier, David, author.
Description: Includes bibliographical references and index.
Identifiers: Canadiana (print) 20190121823 | Canadiana (ebook) 20190121831 | ISBN 9780865719217
   (softcover) | ISBN 9781550927146 (PDF) | ISBN 9781771423106 (EPUB)
Subjects: LCSH: Commons.
Classification: LCC HD1286 .H45 2019 | DDC 333.2—dc23

Funded by the Government of Canada   Financé par le gouvernement du Canada

New Society Publishers' mission is to publish books that contribute in fundamental ways to building an ecologically sustainable and just society, and to do so with the least possible impact on the environment, in a manner that models this vision.

Contents

Introduction

THIS BOOK IS DEDICATED TO OVERCOMING an epidemic of fear with a surge of reality-based hope. As long as we allow ourselves to be imprisoned by our fears, we will never find the solutions we need to help us build a new world. Of course, we have plenty of good reasons to be fearful — the loss of our jobs, authoritarian rule, corporate abuses, racial and ethnic hatred. Looming above all else is the warming of the Earth's climate, an existential threat to civilization itself. We watch with amazement as space probes detect water on Mars while authorities struggle to find drinking water for people on Earth. Technologies may soon let people edit the genes of their unborn children like text on a computer, yet the means for taking care for the sick, old, and homeless remain elusive.

Fear and despair are fueled by our sense of powerlessness, the sense that we as individuals cannot possibly alter the current trajectories of history. But our powerlessness has a lot to do with how we conceive of our plight — as individuals, alone and separate. Fear, and our understandable search for individual safety, are crippling our search for collective, systemic solutions — the only solutions that will truly work. We need to reframe our dilemma as *What can we do together? How can we do this outside of conventional institutions that are failing us?*

The good news is that countless seeds of collective transformation are already sprouting. Green shoots of hope can be seen in the agroecology farms of Cuba and community forests of India, in community Wi-Fi systems in Catalonia and neighborhood nursing teams in the Netherlands. They are emerging in dozens of alternative local currencies, new types of web platforms for cooperation, and campaigns to reclaim cities for ordinary people. The beauty of such initiatives is that they meet needs in direct, empowering ways. People are stepping up to invent new systems that function outside of the capitalist mindset, for mutual benefit, with respect for the Earth, and with a commitment to the long term.

1

In 2009, a frustrated group of friends in Helsinki were watching another international climate change summit fail. They wondered what they could do themselves to change the economy. The result, after much planning, was a neighborhood "credit exchange" in which participants agree to exchange services with each other, from language translations and swimming lessons to gardening and editing. Give an hour of your expertise to a neighbor; get an hour of someone else's talents. The Helsinki Timebank, as it was later called, has grown into a robust parallel economy of more than 3,000 members. With exchanges of tens of thousands of hours of services, it has become a socially convivial alternative to the market economy, and part of a large international network of timebanks.

In Bologna, Italy, an elderly woman wanted a simple bench in the neighborhood's favorite gathering spot. When residents asked the city government if they could install a bench themselves, a perplexed city bureaucracy replied that there were no procedures for doing so. This triggered a long journey to create a formal system for coordinating citizen collaborations with the Bologna government. The city eventually created the Bologna Regulation for the Care and Regeneration of Urban Commons to organize hundreds of citizen/government "pacts of collaboration" — to rehabilitate abandoned buildings, manage kindergartens, take care of urban green spaces. The effort has since spurred a Co-City movement in Italy that orchestrates similar collaborations in dozens of cities.

But in the face of climate change and economic inequality, aren't these efforts painfully small and local? This belief is the mistake traditionalists make. They are so focused on the institutions of power that have failed us, and so fixated on the global canvas, that they fail to recognize that real forces for transformational change originate in small places, with small groups of people, beneath the gaze of power. Skeptics of "the small" would scoff at farmers sowing grains of rice, corn, and beans: "You're going to feed humanity with ... seeds?!" Small gambits with adaptive capacities are in fact powerful vehicles for system change.

Right now, a huge universe of bottom-up social initiatives — familiar and novel, in all realms of life, in industrialized and rural settings — are successfully addressing needs that the market economy and state power are unable to meet. Most of these initiatives remain unseen or unidentified with a larger pattern. In the public mind they are patronized, ignored, or seen as aberrational and marginal. After all, they exist outside the prevailing systems of power — the state, capital, markets. Conventional minds always rely on proven things and have no courage for experiments even though the supposedly winning formulas of economic growth, market fundamentalism, and national bureaucracies have become blatantly dysfunctional. The question is not whether an idea or initiative is big or small, but whether its premises contain the germ of change for the whole.

To prevent any misunderstanding: the commons is not just about small-scale projects for improving everyday life. It is a germinal vision for reimagining our future together and reinventing social organization, economics, infrastructure, politics, and state power itself. The commons is a social form that enables people to enjoy freedom without repressing others, enact fairness without bureaucratic control, foster togetherness without compulsion, and assert sovereignty without nationalism. Columnist George Monbiot has summed up the virtues of the commons nicely: "A commons ... gives community life a clear focus. It depends on democracy in its truest form. It destroys inequality. It provides an incentive to protect the living world. It creates, in sum, a politics of belonging."[1]

This is reflected in our title, which describes the foundation, structure, and vision of the commons: *Free, Fair and Alive.* Any emancipation from the existing system must honor freedom in the widest human sense, not just libertarian economic freedom of the isolated individual. It must put fairness, mutually agreed upon, at the center of any system of provisioning and governance. And it must recognize our existence as living beings on an Earth that is itself alive. Transformation cannot occur without actualizing all of these goals simultaneously. This is the agenda of the commons — to combine the grand priorities of our political culture that are regularly played off against each other — freedom, fairness, and life itself.

Far more than a messaging strategy, the commons is an insurgent worldview. That is precisely why it represents a new form of power. When people come together to pursue shared ends and constitute themselves as a commons, a new surge of coherent social power is created. When enough of these pockets of bottom-up energy converge, a new political power manifests. And because commoners are committed to a broad set of philosophically integrated values, their power is less vulnerable to co-optation. The market/state has developed a rich repertoire of divide-and-conquer strategies for neutralizing social movements seeking change. It partially satisfies one set of demands, for example, but only by imposing new costs on someone else. Yes to greater racial and gender equality in law, but only within the grossly inequitable system of capitalism and weak enforcement. Or, yes to greater environmental protection, but only by charging higher prices or by ransacking the Global South for its natural resources. Or, yes to greater healthcare and family-friendly work policies, but only under rigid schemes that preserve corporate profits. Freedom is played against fairness, or vice-versa, and each in turn is played off against the needs of Mother Earth. And so the citadel of capitalism again and again thwarts demands for system change.

The great ambition of the commons is to break this endless story of co-optation and beggar-thy-neighbor manipulation. Its aim is to develop an independent, parallel social economy, outside of the market/state system, that enacts a different logic and ethos. The Commonsverse does not pursue freedom, fairness, and eco-friendly provisioning as separate goals requiring tradeoffs among them. The commons seeks to integrate and unify these goals as coeval priorities. They constitute an indivisible agenda. Moreover, this agenda is not merely aspirational; it lies at the heart of commoning as an insurgent social practice.

Not surprisingly, the vision of the commons we set forth here is quite different from that image presented (and derided) by modern economics and the political right. For them, commons are unowned resources that are free for the taking and therefore a failed management regime — an idea popularized by Garrett Hardin's famous essay on the "Tragedy of the Commons." (More about this later.) We disagree. The commons is a robust class of self-organized social practices for meeting needs in fair, inclusive ways. It is a life-form. It is a framing that describes a different way of being in the world and different ways of knowing and acting.

The market/state system often talks about how it performs things *for* the people — or if participation is allowed, working *with* the people. But the commons achieves important things *through* the people. That is to say, ordinary people themselves provide the energy, imagination, and hard work. They do their own provisioning and governance. Commoners are the ones who dream up the systems, devise the rules, provide the expertise, perform the difficult work, monitor for compliance, and deal with rule-breakers.

As this implies, the commons involves an identity shift. It requires that people evolve into different roles and perspectives. It demands new ways of relating to other people. It requires that we reassess who matters in our economy and society, and how essential work gets done. Seen from the inside, the commons reveals that we can create value in new ways, and create meaning for ourselves in the process. We can escape from capitalist value chains by creating value networks of mutual commitment. It is by changing the micropatterns of social life, on the ground, with each other, that we can begin to decolonize ourselves from the history and culture into which we were born. We can escape the sense of powerless isolation that defines so much of modern life. We can develop healthier, fair alternatives.

Not surprisingly, the guardians of the prevailing order — in government, business, the media, higher education, philanthropy — prefer to work within existing institutional frameworks. They are content to operate within parochial patterns of thought and puny ideas about human dignity, especially the narrative of progress through economic growth. They prefer that political power be consolidated into centralized structures, such as the nation-state, the corporation, the bureaucracy. This book aims to shatter such presumptions and open up some new vistas of realistic choices.

However, this book is not yet another critique of neoliberal capitalism. While often valuable, even penetrating critiques do not necessarily help us imagine how to remake our institutions and build a new world. What we really need today is creative experimentation and the courage to initiate new patterns of action. We need to learn how to identify patterns of cultural life that can bring about change, notwithstanding the immense power of capital.

For those activists oriented toward political parties and elections, legislation, and policymaking, we counsel a shift to a deeper, more significant level of political life — the world of culture and social practice. Conventional modes of politics working with conventional institutions simply cannot deliver the kinds of change we need. Sixteen-year-old Swedish climate activist Greta Thunberg has shrewdly observed, "We can't save the world by playing by the rules." We need to devise a new set of rules. The old system cannot be ignored, to be sure, and in fact it can often deliver necessary benefits. But we must be honest with ourselves: existing systems will not yield transformational change. That's why we must be open to bracing winds of change from the periphery, from the unexpected, neglected places, from the zones without pedigree or credentials, from the people themselves.

Accordingly, we refuse to assume that the nation-state is the only realistic system of power for dealing with our fears and offering solutions. It isn't. The nation-state is, rather, an expression of a fading era. It's just that respectable circles decline to consider alternatives from the fringe lest they be seen as fuzzy-minded or crazy. But these days, the structural deficiencies of the nation-state and its alliance with capital-driven markets are on vivid display, and can hardly be denied. We have no choice but to abandon our fears — and start to entertain fresh ideas from the margins.

A note of reassurance: "going beyond" the nation-state doesn't mean "*without* the nation-state." It means that we must *seriously alter* state power by introducing new operational logics and institutional players. Much of this book is devoted to precisely that necessity. We immodestly see commoning as a way to incubate new social practices and cultural logics that are firmly grounded in everyday experience and yet capable of federating themselves to gain strength, cross-fertilizing to grow a new culture, and reaching into the inner councils of state power.

When we describe commons and commoning, we are talking about practices that go beyond the usual ways of thinking, speaking, and behaving. One could, therefore, regard this book as a learning guide. We hope to enlarge your understanding of the economy as something that goes beyond the money economy that sets *my* interest against *our* interests, and sees the state as the only alternative to the market, for example. This is no small ambition because the market/state has insinuated its premises deep within our consciousness and culture. If we are serious about escaping the stifling logic of capitalism, however, we must probe this deeply. How else can we escape the strange logic by which we first exhaust ourselves and deplete the environment in producing things, and then have to work heroically to repair both, simply so the hamster wheel of the eternal today will continue to turn? How can politicians and citizens possibly take independent initiatives if everything depends on jobs, the stock market, and competition? How can we strike off in new directions when the basic patterns of capitalism constantly inhabit our lives and consciousness, eroding what we have in common? Our aim in writing this book is not just to illuminate new patterns of thought and feeling, but to offer a guide to action.

But how do you begin to approach such a profound change? Our answer is that we must first unravel our understanding of the world: our image of what it means to be a human being, our conception of ownership, prevailing ideas about being and knowing (Chapter 2). When we learn to see the world through a new lens and describe it with new words, a compelling vision comes into focus. We can acquire a new understanding of the good life, our togetherness, the economy, and politics. A semantic revolution of new vocabularies (and the abandonment of old ones) is indispensable for communicating this new vision. That is why, in Chapter 3, we introduce a variety of terms to escape the trap of many misleading binaries (individual/collective, public/private, civilized/premodern) and name the experiences of commoning that currently have no name (Ubuntu rationality, freedom-in-connectedness, value sovereignty, peer governance).

Insights are one thing, meaningful action is another. How then shall we proceed? We regard the "how to do it" section — Part II, consisting of Chapters 4, 5, and 6 — as the heart of the book. The Triad of Commoning, as we call it, systematically describes how the world of the commons "breathes" — how it lives, what its culture feels like. The Triad offers a new framework for understanding and analyzing the commons. The framework itself emerged through a methodology associated with "pattern languages," in which a process of "patterns mining" is used to identify recurrent patterns of social practice that exist across cultures and history.

This is followed by Part III, which examines the embedded assumptions of property (Chapter 7) and how a new sort of relationalized property can be developed (Chapter 8) to support commoning. We quickly realized that such visions — or other patterns of commoning — tend to run up against state power if they become successful. States are not shy about using law, property rights, state policies, alliances with capital, and coercive practices to advance their vision of the world — which generally frowns upon the realities of commoning. In light of these realities, we outline several general strategies for building the Commonsverse nonetheless (Chapter 9). And we conclude with a look at several specific approaches — commons charters, distributed ledger technologies, commons-public partnerships — that can expand the commons while protecting it against the market/state system (Chapter 10).

As a book that seeks to reconceptualize our understanding of commons, we realize that we point to many new avenues of further inquiry that we simply cannot answer here. The greater the shoreline of our knowledge, the greater the oceans of our ignorance. We would have liked to explore a new theory of value to counter the unsatisfactory notions of value, the price system, used by standard economics. The long history of property law contains many fascinating legal doctrines that deserve to be excavated, along with non-Western notions of stewardship and control. The psychological and sociological dimensions of cooperation could illuminate our ideas about commoning with new depth. Scholars of modernity, historians of medieval commons, and anthropologists could help us better understand the social dynamics of the contemporary commons. In short, there is much more to be said about the themes we discuss.

Some of the most salient, understudied big issues involve how commons might mitigate familiar geopolitical, ecological, and humanitarian challenges. Migration, military conflict, climate change, and inequality are all affected by the prevalence of enclosures and the relative strength of commoning. Commoners with stable, locally rooted means of subsistence naturally feel less pressure to flee to wealthier regions of the world. When industrial trawlers destroyed Somali fishery commons, they surely had a role in fueling piracy and terrorism in Africa. Could state protection of commons make a difference? If such provisioning could supplant global market supply chains, it could significantly reduce carbon emissions from transportation and agricultural chemicals. These and many other topics deserve much greater research, analysis, and theorizing.

We wish to call attention to four appendices of interest. Appendix A explains the methodology used to identify the patterns of commoning in Part II of the book. Appendix B describes the conceptualization process used by Mercè Moreno Tárres to draw the twenty-eight beautiful patterns images in Part II. Appendix C lists sixty-nine working commons and tools for commoning mentioned in this book. And Appendix D lists Elinor Ostrom's eight renowned design principles for effective commons.

Part I:

The Commons as a
Transformative Perspective

1

Commons and Commoning

C AN HUMAN BEINGS REALLY LEARN TO COOPERATE with each other in routine, large-scale ways? A great deal of evidence suggests we can. There is no innate, genetic impediment to cooperation. It's quite the opposite. In one memorable experiment conducted by developmental and comparative psychologist Michael Tomasello, a bright-eyed toddler watches a man carrying an armful of books as he repeatedly bumps into a closet door. The adult can't seem to open the closet, and the toddler is concerned. The child spontaneously walks over to the door and opens it, inviting the inept adult to put the books into the closet. In another experiment, an adult repeatedly fails to place a blue tablet on top of an existing stack of tablets. A toddler seated across from the clumsy man grabs the fallen tablets and carefully places each one neatly on the top of the stack. In yet another test, an adult who had been stapling papers in a room leaves, and upon returning with a new set of papers, finds that someone has moved his stapler. A one-year-old infant in the room immediately understands the adult's problem, and points helpfully at the missing stapler, now on a shelf.

For Tomasello, a core insight came into focus from these and other experiments: human beings instinctively want to help others. In his painstaking attempts to understand the origins of human cooperation, Tomasello and his team have sought to isolate the workings of this human impulse and to differentiate it from the behaviors of other species, especially primates. From years of research, he has concluded that "from around their first birthdays — when they first begin to walk and talk and become truly cultural beings — human children are already cooperative and helpful in many, though obviously not all, situations. And they do not learn this from adults; it comes naturally."[1] Even infants from fourteen to eighteen months of age show the capacity to fetch out-of-reach objects, remove obstacles facing others, correct an adult's mistake, and choose the correct behaviors for a given task.

Of course, complications arise and multiply as young children grow up. They learn that some people are not trustworthy and that others don't reciprocate acts of kindness. Children learn to internalize social norms and ethical expectations, especially from societal institutions. As they mature, children associate schooling with economic success, learn to package personal reputation into a marketable brand, and find satisfaction in buying and selling.

While the drama of acculturation plays out in many different ways, the larger story of the human species is its versatile capacity for cooperation. We have the unique potential to express and act upon shared intentionality. "What makes us [human beings] really different is our ability to put our heads together and to do things that none of us could do alone, to create new resources that we couldn't create alone," says Tomasello. "It's really all about communicating and collaborating and working together." We are able to do this because we can grasp that other human beings have inner lives with emotions and intentions. We become aware of a shared condition that goes beyond a narrow, self-referential identity. Any individual identity is always, also, part of collective identities that guide how a person thinks, behaves, and solves problems. All of us have been indelibly shaped by our relations with peers and society, and by the language, rituals, and traditions that constitute our cultures.

In other words, the conceit that we are "self-made" individuals is a delusion. There is no such thing as an isolated "I." As we will explore later, each of us is really a *Nested-I*. We are not only embedded in relationships; our very identities are *created* through relationships. The Nested-I concept helps us deal more honestly with the encompassing reality of human identity and development. We humans truly are the "cooperative species," as economists Samuel Bowles and Herbert Gintis have put it.[2] The question is whether or not this deep human instinct will be encouraged to unfold. And if cooperation is encouraged, will it aim to serve all or instead be channeled to serve individualistic, parochial ends?

Commoning Is Everywhere, but Widely Misunderstood

In our previous books *The Wealth of the Commons* (2012) and *Patterns of Commoning* (2015), we documented dozens of notable commons, suggesting that the actual scope and impact of commoning in today's world is quite large. Our capacity to self-organize to address needs, independent of the state or market, can be seen in community forests, cooperatively run farms and fisheries, open source design and manufacturing communities with global reach, local and regional currencies, and myriad other examples in all realms of life. The elemental human impulse that we are born with — to help others, to improve existing practices — ripens into a stable social form with countless variations: a commons.

The impulse to common plays out in the most varied circumstances — impoverished urban neighborhoods, landscapes hit by natural disasters, subsistence farms in the heart of Africa, social networks that come together in cyberspace. And yet, strangely, the commons paradigm is rarely seen as a pervasive social form, perhaps because it so often lives in the shadows of state and market power. It is not recognized as a powerful social force and institutional form in its own right. For us, to talk about the commons is to talk about freedom-in-connectedness — a social space in which we can rediscover and remake ourselves as whole human beings and enjoy some serious measure of self-determination. The discourse around commons and commoning helps us see that individuals working together can bring forth more humane, ethical, and ecologically responsible societies. It is plausible to imagine a stable, supportive post-capitalist order. The very act of commoning, as it expands and registers on the larger culture, catalyzes new political and economic possibilities.

Let us be clear: the commons is not a utopian fantasy. It is something that is happening right now. It can be seen in countless villages and cities, in the Global South and the industrial North, in open source software communities and global cyber-networks. Our first challenge is to name the many acts of commoning in our midst and make them culturally legible. They must be perceived and understood if they are going to be nourished, protected, and expanded. That is the burden of the following chapters and the reason why we propose a new, general framework for understanding commons and commoning.

The commons is not simply about "sharing," as it happens in countless areas of life. It is about sharing *and* bringing into being durable social systems for producing shareable things and activities. Nor is the commons about the misleading idea of the "tragedy of the commons."

This term was popularized by a famous essay by biologist Garrett Hardin, "The Tragedy of the Commons," which appeared in the influential journal *Science* in 1968.[3] Paul Ehrlich had just published *The Population Bomb*, a Malthusian account of a world overwhelmed by sheer numbers of people. In this context, Hardin told a fictional parable of a shared pasture on which no herdsman has a rational incentive to limit the grazing of his cattle. The inevitable result, said Hardin, is that each herdsman will selfishly use as much of the common resource as possible, which will inevitably result in its overuse and ruin — the so-called tragedy of the commons. Possible solutions, Hardin argued, are to grant private property rights to the resource in question, or have the government administer it as public property or on a first-come, first-served basis.

Hardin's article went on to become the most-cited article in the history of the journal *Science*, and the phrase "tragedy of the commons" became a cultural buzzword. His fanciful story, endlessly repeated by economists, social scientists, and politicians, has persuaded most people that the commons is a failed management regime. And yet Hardin's analysis has some remarkable flaws. Most importantly, he was not describing a commons! He was describing a free-for-all in which nothing is owned and everything is free for the taking — an "unmanaged common pool resource," as some would say. As commons scholar Lewis Hyde has puckishly suggested, Hardin's "tragedy" thesis ought to be renamed "The Tragedy of Unmanaged, Laissez-Faire, Commons-Pool Resources with Easy Access for Non-Communicating, Self-Interested Individuals."[4]

In an actual commons, things are different. A distinct community governs a shared resource and its usage. Users negotiate their own rules, assign responsibilities and entitlements, and set up monitoring systems to identify and penalize free riders. To be sure, finite resources can be overexploited, but that outcome is more associated with free markets than with commons. It is no coincidence that our current period of history, in which capitalist markets and private property rights prevail in most places, has produced the sixth mass extinction in Earth's history, an unprecedented loss of fertile soil, disruptions in the hydrologic cycle, and a dangerously warming atmosphere.

As we will see in this book, the commons has so many rich facets that it cannot be easily contained within a single definition. But it helps to clarify how certain terms often associated with the commons are not, in fact, the same as a commons.

What Is and Is Not a Commons: Some Clarifications

Commons are living social systems through which people address their shared problems in self-organized ways. Unfortunately, some people incorrectly use the term to describe unowned things such as oceans, space, and the moon, or collectively owned resources such as water, forests, and land. As a result, the term *commons* is frequently conflated with economic concepts that express a very different worldview. Terms such as common goods, common-pool resources, and common property misrepresent the commons because they emphasize objects and individuals, not relationships and systems. Here are some of the misleading terms associated with commons.

Common goods: A term used in neoclassical economy to distinguish among certain types of goods — common goods, club goods, public goods, and private goods. Common goods are said to be difficult to fence off (in economic jargon, they are "nonexcludable") and susceptible to being used up ("rivalrous"). In other words, common goods tend to get depleted when we share them. Conventional economics presumes that the excludability and depletability of a common good are inherent in the good itself, but this is mistaken. It is not the good that is excludable or not, it's *people* who are being excluded or not. A social choice is being made. Similarly, the depletability of a common good has little to do with the good itself, and everything to do with how we choose to make use of water, land, space, or forests. By calling the land, water, or forest a "good," economists are in fact making a social judgment: they are presuming that something is a resource suitable for market valuation and trade — a presumption that a different culture may wish to reject.

Common-pool resources or CPRs: This term is used by commons scholars, mostly in the tradition of Elinor Ostrom, to analyze how shared resources such as fishing grounds, groundwater basins or grazing areas can be managed. Common-pool resources are regarded as common goods, and in fact usage of the terms is very similar. However, the term common-pool resource is generally invoked to explore how people can use, but not overuse, a shared resource.

Common property: While a CPR refers to a resource as such, *common property* refers to a system of law that grants formal rights to access or use it. The terms CPR and *common good* point to a resource itself, for example, whereas *common property* points to the legal system that regulates how people may use it. Talking about property regimes is thus a very different register of representation than references to water, land, fishing grounds, or software code. Each of these can be managed by any number of different legal regimes; the resource and the legal regime are distinct. Commoners may choose to use a common property regime, but that regime does not constitute the commons.

Common (noun). While some traditionalists use the term "the common" instead of "commons" to refer to shared land or water, cultural theorists Antonio Negri and Michael Hardt introduced a new spin to the term "common" in their 2009 book *Commonwealth*. They speak of *the common* to emphasize the social processes that people engage in when cooperating, and to distinguish this idea from *the commons* as a physical resource. Hardt and Negri note that "the languages we create, the social practices we establish, the modes of sociality that define our relationships" constitute *the common*. For them, the common is a form of "biopolitical production" that points to a realm beyond property that exists alongside the private and the public, but which unfolds by engaging our affective selves. While this is similar to our use of the term *commoning* — commons as a verb — the Hardt/Negri uses of the term "common" would seem to include all forms of cooperation, without regard for purpose, and thus could include gangs and the mafia.

The common good: The term, used since the ancient Greeks, refers to positive outcomes for everyone in a society. It is a glittering generality with no clear meaning because virtually all political and economic systems claim that they produce the most benefits for everyone.

Commons in Real Life

The best way to become acquainted with the commons is by learning about a few real-life examples. Therefore, we offer below five short profiles to give a better feel for the contexts of commoning, their specific realities, and their sheer diversity. The examples can help us understand the commons as both a *general* paradigm of governance, provisioning, and social practice — a worldview and ethic, one might say — and a *highly particular* phenomenon. Each commons is one of a kind. There are no all-purpose models or "best practices" that define commons and commoning — only suggestive experiences and instructive patterns.

Zaatari Refugee Camp

The Zaatari Refugee camp in Jordan is a settlement of 78,000 displaced Syrians who began to arrive in 2012. The camp may seem like an unlikely illustration of the ideas of this book. Yet in the middle of a desolate landscape, people have devised large and elaborate systems of shelters, neighborhoods, roads, and even a system of addresses. According to Kilian Kleinschmidt, a United Nations official once in charge of the camp, the Zaatari camp in 2015 had "14,000 households, 10,000 sewage pots and private toilets, 3,000 washing machines, 150 private gardens, 3,500 new businesses and shops."A reporter visiting the camp noted that some of the most elaborate houses there are "cobbled together from shelters, tents, cinder blocks and shipping containers, with interior courtyards, private toilets and jerry-built sewers." The settlement has a barbershop, a pet store, a flower shop and a homemade ice cream business. There is a pizza delivery service and a travel agency that provides a pickup service at the airport. Zaatari's main drag is called the Champs-Élysées.[5]

Of course, Zaatari remains a troubled place with many problems, and the Jordanian state and United Nations remain in charge. But what makes it so notable as a refugee camp is the significant role that self-organized, bottom-up participation has played in building an improvised yet stable city. It is not simply a makeshift survival camp where wretched populations queue up for food, administrators deliver services, and people are treated as helpless victims. It is a place where refugees have been able to apply their own energies and imaginations in building the settlement. They have been able to take some responsibility for self-governance and owning their lives, earning a welcome measure of dignity. You might say that Zaatari administrators and residents, in however partial a way, have recognized the virtues of commoning. The Zaatari experience tells us something about the power of self-organization, a core concept in the commons.

Buurtzorg Nederland

In the Dutch city of Almelo, nurse Jos de Blok was distressed at the steady decline of home care: "Quality was getting worse and worse, the clients' satisfaction was decreasing, and the expenses were increasing," he said. De Blok and a small team of professional nurses decided to form a new homecare organization, Buurtzorg Nederland.[6] Rather than structure patient care on the model of a factory conveyor belt, delivering measurable units of market services with strict divisions of labor, the home care company relies on small, self-guided teams of highly trained nurses who serve fifty to sixty people in the same neighborhood. (The organization's name, "Buurtzorg," is Dutch for "neighborhood care.") Care is holistic, focusing on a patient's many personal needs, social circumstances, and long-term condition.

The first thing a nurse usually does when visiting a new patient is to sit down and have a chat and a cup of coffee. As de Blok put it, "People are not bicycles who can be organized according to an organizational chart." In this respect, Buurtzorg nurses are carrying out the logic of "spending time" (in a commons) as opposed to "saving time" to be more efficient competitors. Interestingly, the emphasis on spending more time with patients results in them needing *less* professional care-time. If one thinks about it, this is not really a surprise: care-givers basically try to make themselves irrelevant in patients' lives as quickly as possible, which encourages patients to become more independent. A 2009 study showed that Buurtzorg's patients get released from care twice as fast as competitors' clients, and they end up claiming only 50 percent of the prescribed hours of care.[7]

Nurses provide a full range of assistance to patients, from medical procedures to support services such as bathing. They also identify networks of informal care in a person's neighborhood, support his or her social life, and promote self-care and independence.[8] Buurtzorg is self-managed by nurses. The process is facilitated through a simple, flat organizational structure and information technology, including the use of inspirational blog posts by de Blok. Buurtzorg operates effectively at a large scale without the need for either hierarchy or consensus. In 2017 Buurtzorg employed about 9,000 nurses, who take care of 100,000 patients throughout the Netherlands, with new transnational initiatives underway in the US and Europe.[9]

It turns out Buurtzorg's reconceptualization of home healthcare produces high-quality, humane treatment at relatively low costs. By 2015, Buurtzorg care had reduced emergency room visits by 30 percent, according to a KPMG study, and has reduced taxpayer expenditures on home care.[10] Buurtzorg also has the most satisfied workforce of any Dutch company with more than 1,000 employees, according to an Ernst & Young study.[11]

WikiHouse

In 2011, two recent architectural graduates, Alastair Parvin and Nicholas Ierodiaconou, joined a London design practice called Zero Zero Architecture, where they were able to experiment with their ideas about open design. They wondered: What if architects, instead of creating buildings for those who can afford to commission them, helped regular citizens design and build their own houses? This simple idea is at the heart of an astonishing open source construction kit for housing. Parvin and Ierodiaconou learned that a familiar technology known as CNC — computer numerical control fabrication — would enable them to make digital designs that could be used to fabricate large flat pieces from plywood or other material. This led them to develop the idea of publishing open source files for houses, which would let many people modify and improve the designs for different circumstances. It would also allow unskilled labor to quickly and inexpensively erect the structural shell of a home. They called the new design and construction system WikiHouse.[12]

Since its modest beginnings, WikiHouse has blossomed into a global design community. In 2017 it had eleven chapters in countries around the world, each of which works independently of the original WikiHouse, now a nonprofit foundation that shares the same mission. Simply put, WikiHouse participants want to "put the design solutions for building low-cost, low-energy, high-performance homes into the hands of every citizen and business on earth." They want to encourage people to PRODUCE COSMO-LOCALLY, a pattern described in Chapter 6. And they want to "grow a new, distributed housing industry, comprised of many citizens, communities and small businesses developing homes and neighborhoods for themselves, reducing our dependence on top-down, debt-heavy mass housing systems."

The WikiHouse Charter, a series of fifteen principles, sets forth the basic elements of the technologies, economics, and processes of open source house building. The Charter is one of many examples of how commoners DECLARE SHARED PURPOSE & VALUES in developing Peer Governance (see Chapter 5). It includes core ideas such as design standards to lower the thresholds of time, cost, skill, and energy needed to build a house; open standards and open source ShareAlike licenses for design elements; and empowering users to repair and modify features of their homes. By inviting users to adapt designs and tools to serve their own needs, WikiHouse seeks to provide a rich set of "convivial tools," as described by social critic Ivan Illich. Tools should not attempt to control humans by prescribing narrow ways of doing things. Software should not be burdened with encryption and barriers to repair. Convivial tools are designed to unleash personal creativity and autonomy.[13]

Community Supported Agriculture

On any Saturday morning in the quiet Massachusetts town of Hadley, you will find families arriving at Next Barn Over farm to pick beans and strawberries from the fields, cut fresh herbs and flowers, and gather their weekly shares of potatoes, kale, onions, radishes, tomatoes, and other produce. Next Barn Over is a CSA farm — Community Supported Agriculture — which means that people buy upfront shares in the farm's seasonal harvest and then pick up fresh produce weekly from April to November. In other words, CSA members pool the money, before production, and divide up the harvest among all members. This practice, used in thousands of CSAs around the world, inspired us to identify "Pool, Cap & Divide Up" as an important feature of a commons economy (see Chapter 6).

A small share for two people in Next Barn Over costs US$415 while a large share suitable for six people costs US$725. By purchasing shares in the harvest at the beginning of the season, members give farmers the working capital they need and share the risks of production — bad weather, crop diseases, equipment issues. One could say they FINANCE COMMONS PROVISIONING.

A CSA is not primarily a business model, however, because chasing profits is not the point. The point is for families and farmers to mutually support each other in growing healthy food in ecologically responsible ways. All the crops grown on Next Barn Over's thirty-four acres are organic. Soil fertility is improved through the use of cover crops, organic fertilizers, compost, and manure, with regular crop rotation to reduce pests and disease. The farm uses solar panels from the barn roof. Drip irrigation systems minimize water usage. Next Barn Over also hosts periodic dinners at which families can socialize, dance to local bands' music, and learn more about the realities of farming in the local ecosystem.

Since the founding of the first CSA in 1986, the idea has grown into an international movement, with more than 1,700 CSAs in the United States alone (2018) and hundreds of others worldwide. While some American CSAs behave almost like businesses, the original philosophy behind CSAs remains strong — to try to develop new forms of cooperation between farmers, workers, and members who are basically consumers. Some are inspired by *teikei*, a similar model that has been widely used in Japan since the 1970s (The word means "cooperation" or "joint business."). Here, too, the focus is on smallholder agriculture, organic farming, and direct partnerships between farmers and consumer. One of the founding players in *teikei*, the Japan Association for Organic Agriculture, has stated its desire "to develop an alternative distribution system that does not depend on conventional markets."[14]

The CSA experience is now inspiring a variety of regional agriculture and food distribution projects around the world, with the same end — to empower farmers and ordinary people, strengthen local economies, and avoid the problems caused by Big Agriculture (pesticides, GMOs, additives, processed foods, transport costs). The socio-economic model for CSAs is so solid that the Schumacher Center for a New Economics, which helped incubate the first CSA, is now developing the idea of "community supported industry" for local production. The idea is to use the principles of community mutualization to start and support local businesses — a furniture factory, an applesauce cannery, a humane slaughterhouse — in order to increase local self-reliance.

Guifi.net

Most people assume that only a large cable or telecommunications corporation with political connections and lots of capital can build the infrastructure for Wi-Fi service. The scrappy cooperative Guifi.net of Catalonia has proven that wrong. The enterprise has shown that it is entirely possible for commoners to build and maintain high-quality, affordable internet connections for everyone. By committing itself to principles of mutual ownership, net neutrality, and community control, Guifi.net has grown from a single Wi-Fi node in 2004 to more than 35,000 nodes and 63,000 kilometers of wireless connectivity in July 2018, particularly in rural Catalonia.

Guifi.net got its start when Ramon Roca, a Spanish engineer at Oracle, hacked some off-the-shelf routers. The hack made the routers work as nodes in a mesh network-like system while connected to a single DSL line owned by Telefonica serving municipal governments. This jerry-rigged system enabled people to send and receive internet data using other, similarly hacked routers. As word spread, Roca's innovation to deal with scarce internet access quickly caught on. As recounted by *Wired* magazine, Guifi.net grew its system through a kind of improvised crowdfunding system: "'It was about announcing a plan, describing the cost, and asking for contributions,' Roca says. The payments weren't going to Guifi.net, but to the suppliers of gear and ISP [Internet Service Provider] network services. All of these initiatives laid the groundwork not just for building out the overall network, but also creating the array of ISPs." What Guifi.net did was simply to POOL & SHARE (see Chapter 6) — it pooled resources and shared internet access.

In 2008 Guifi.net established an affiliated foundation to help oversee volunteers, network operations, and governance of the entire system. As *Wired* described it, the foundation "handled network traffic to and among the providers; connected to the major data 'interchange' providing vast amounts of bandwidth between southern Spain and the rest of the world; planned deployment of fiber; and, crucially, developed systems to ensure that the ISPs were paying their fair share of the overall data and network-management costs."[15]

Guiding the entire project is a Compact for a Free, Open and Neutral Network, a charter that sets forth the key principles of the Guifi.net commons and the rights and freedoms of users:

- You have the freedom to use the network for any purpose as long as you don't harm the operation of the network itself, the rights of other users, or the principles of neutrality that allow contents and services to flow without deliberate interference.
- You have the right to understand the network and its components, and to share knowledge of its mechanisms and principles.
- You have the right to offer services and content to the network on your own terms.
- You have the right to join the network, and the obligation to extend this set of rights to anyone according to these same terms.

Anyone who uses the Guifi.net infrastructure in Catalonia — individual internet users, small businesses, government, dozens of small internet service providers — is committed to "the development of a commons-based, free, open and neutral telecommunications network." This has resulted in Guifi.net providing far better broadband service at cheaper prices than, say, Americans receive, who pay very high prices to a broadband oligopoly (a median of US$80 month in 2017) for slower connectivity and poor customer service. ISPs using Guifi.net were charging 18 to 35 euros a month in 2016 (roughly US$20–$37) for one gigabit fiber connections, and much lower prices for Wi-Fi. Commons are highly money efficient, as Wolfgang Sachs once pointed out. They enable us to become less reliant on money, and therefore more free from the structural coercion of markets.

Moreover, the Guifi.net experience shows that it is entirely possible to build "large-scale, locally owned, broadband infrastructure in more locations than telco [telephone company] incumbents," as open technology advocate Sascha Meinrath put it.[16] The mutualizing of costs and benefits in a commons regime has a lot to do with this success.

Understanding Commons Holistically in the Wild

How to make sense of these very different commons? Newcomers to the topic often throw up their hands in confusion because they cannot readily see the deeper patterns that make a commons a commons. They find it perplexing that so many diverse phenomena can be described by the same term. This problem is really a matter of training one's perception. Everyone is familiar with the "free market" even though its variations — stock markets, grocery stores, filmmaking, mining, personal services, labor — are at least as eclectic as the commons. But culturally, we regard the diversity of markets as normal whereas commons are nearly invisible.

The strange truth is that a popular language for understanding contemporary commons is almost entirely absent. Social science scholarship on the topic is often obscure and highly specialized, and the economic literature tends to treat commons as physical resources, not as social systems. But rather than focus on the resource that each depends on, it makes more sense to focus on the ways in which each is similar. Each commons depends on social processes, the sharing of knowledge, and physical resources. Each shares challenges in bringing together the social, the political (governance), and the economic (provisioning) into an integrated whole.

Every commons is based on natural resources.
Every commons is a knowledge commons.
Every commons depends on a social process.

So a big part of our challenge is to recover the neglected social history of commons and learn how it applies to contemporary circumstances. This requires a conceptual framework, new language, and stories that anyone can understand. Explaining the commons with the vocabulary of capital, business, and standard economics cannot work. It is like using the metaphors of clockworks and machines to explain complex living systems. To learn how commons actually work, we need to escape deeply rooted habits of thought and cultivate some fresh perspectives.

This task becomes easier once we realize that there is no single, universal template for assessing a commons. Each bears the distinctive marks of its own special origins, culture, people, and context. Yet there are also many deep, recurrent patterns of commoning that allow us to make some careful generalizations. Commons that superficially appear quite different often have remarkable similarities in how they govern themselves, divide up resources, protect themselves against enclosure, and cultivate shared intentionality. In other words, commons are not standardized machines that can be built from the same blueprint. They are living systems that evolve, adapt over time, and surprise us with their creativity and scope.

The word "patterns" as we use it here deserves a bit of explanation. Our usage derives from the ideas developed by architect and philosopher Christopher Alexander in his celebrated 1977 book *A Pattern Language* — ideas that are further elaborated on in his four-volume masterwork, *The Nature of Order*, the result of twenty-seven years of research and original thinking. Alexander and his co-authors brilliantly blend an empirical scientific perspective with ideas about the formative role of beauty and grace in everyday life and design, resulting in what we would call "enlivenment."[17]

In Alexander's view, a pattern describes "a problem that occurs over and over again in our environment, and then describes the core of the solution to that problem, in such a way that you can use this solution a million times over, without ever doing it the same way twice."[18] In other words, patterns-thinking and solutions based on it are never decontextualized, nor disconnected from what we think and feel. We suggest looking closely at the underlying patterns of thriving social processes for inspiration while keeping in mind that a successful commons cannot be copied and pasted. Each must develop its own appropriate localized, context-specific solutions. Each must satisfy practical needs and deeper human aspirations and interests.

In this volume, we attempt to identify the patterns that are building a growing constellation of commons around the world — the Commonsverse. In our account of this realm, we are both descriptive and aspirational — descriptive in assessing how diverse commons function, and aspirational in trying to imagine how the known commoning dynamics could plausibly grow and become a distinct sector of the political economy and culture. We draw on the social sciences to discuss important aspects of the commons. But we also draw upon our own extensive firsthand experiences in talking with commoners and learning about their remarkable communities. We wish to describe a rich, textured field of human creativity and social organization that has been overlooked for too long, while reassuring the reader that commons are not so complicated and obscure that only professionals can grasp them. In fact, they arise from common people doing fairly common things that only seem uncommon in market-oriented societies.

In the course of our travels, we have been astonished at the remarkable range of circumstances in which commoning occurs. This has led us to wonder: Why do so many discussions about commons rely on economic categories of analysis ("types of goods," "resource allocation," "productivity," "transaction costs") when commons are primarily social systems for meeting shared needs? This question propelled us on a process to reconceptualize in its fullest sense what it means to engage in commoning.

We think that such a perspective contributes to a broader paradigm shift. It helps us to redefine the very idea of the economy and enlarge the functional scope of democratic action. Commons meet real needs while changing culture and identity. They influence our social practices, ethics, and worldviews and in so doing change the very character of politics. To understand these deeper currents, we need a richer framework for making sense of the commons. We need it to better explain the internal dynamics of peer governance and provisioning — and also the ways in which commoning connects the larger political economy and our inner lives. In short, we must see that the commons requires a new worldview.

2

The OntoShift to the Commons

I F COMMONING HAS PLAYED SUCH A LONG and prominent role in the history of the human species, why is it generally ignored in modern life? Why does it remain a *terra incognita* that is routinely mischaracterized and misunderstood? Over the years, as we talked with commoners in countless different contexts, we gradually came to realize that the problem isn't commoning; it's the flawed categories of thought used by mainstream economics, law, politics, and policy. Their vocabularies and logics presume a world based on individualism, economic growth, and the human mastery of "nature" (a term that implies a sharp separation of humanity from the nonhuman world). They presume an omnipotent market/state to remake the universe around these mythopoetic ideas. No wonder pockets of successful commoning seem like strange creatures from another planet!

One day, after pondering this curious mismatch between mainstream thought and the realities we have seen in our research and travels, we needed a break. We decided to stroll through the nearby Beneski Museum of Natural History, at Amherst College. It proved to be a serendipitous detour. While browsing impressive displays of dinosaur skeletons and fossilized footprints, we had a shared epiphany: *Sometimes new truths can be revealed only by making a shift in ontological perspective* — what we have come to call an *OntoShift*. We will explain this idea further in a moment, but first, our experience at the museum.

While most natural history museums in major cities have a penchant for the grand and spectacular, the modest, well-appointed Beneski Museum in western Massachusetts is a working space for teaching undergraduates how to make sense of geological mysteries. Many of the exhibits showcase the research of Edward Hitchcock, a leading geologist of the 1830s who discovered thousands of strange marks in rocks at local quarries and farms. At the museum, we saw numerous dinosaur skeletons and bones, including a fearsome Tyrannosaurus rex head, and dozens of slabs of sedimentary rock artfully displayed on the walls. Each set of marks presented a mystery from 270 million years ago. Were they "turkey tracks," as many locals once called them, or perhaps the footprints of "Noah's Raven," a gigantic bird from Noah's Ark? It was difficult to speculate, because no fossilized bones had been found at the time.[1]

For Hitchcock, a serious scientist and devout Christian, the frame of reference for theorizing about this mystery was his own eyes and the Bible. When he encountered deposits of gravel, loam, sand, and boulders on Cape Cod, he found it entirely logical to call them Diluvium, a reference to the great flood described in the Bible. As later scientists concluded, however, the deposits were in fact moraine, the rocky debris left by glaciers during the Ice Age. Even though Hitchcock corresponded with the likes of Robert Owen, Charles Darwin, and Charles Lyell, he remained convinced that the "footmarks" (as he called them), now preserved in sedimentary rock, had been created by large ancient birds.

And why not? The prehistoric world was only then being discovered. The word "dinosaur" was not coined until 1841 by British geologist Robert Owen, and the first dinosaur fossils in the US were not discovered until 1858. Charles Darwin's *On the Origin of the Species* was not published until 1859, and some of the most significant fossil discoveries were not made until the 1890s. For the Bible-believing Hitchcock, the idea of enormous lizard-like creatures roaming a very different life-world 273 million years ago was literally *unthinkable*.

In her 2006 book about Hitchcock, science writer Nancy Pick professed her admiration for his scientific achievements, but ruefully concluded in a fanciful letter to him: "I must tell you that most of your strongest convictions turned out to be mistaken. You were wrong to doubt the existence of an Ice Age. You were wrong to deny the theory of evolution. And, most painful of all, you were wrong about the animals that made your beloved fossil footprints. They were not gigantic ancient birds after all, but dinosaurs."

It is tempting for posterity to condescend to previous generations because of what they didn't or couldn't know at the time. That is not our purpose here. What we find so interesting is the way in which a worldview frames and limits what we see. We can never really see the world "as it is" because our minds are too busy *constituting and creating* it. We naturally believe that the reality we perceive is self-evident and universal — "common sense" — but, in truth, any view of reality is based on some underlying presuppositions about the nature of the world. Our beliefs are shaped by invisible assumptions affected by culture, history, and personal experience.

Language is also critical in shaping our consciousness. The language used by a political economy and culture names certain phenomena that they regard as significant and imbues them with a moral content, while leaving other phenomena nameless and ignored. This establishes a mental picture, a frame for perceiving and *not* perceiving, an insight that politicians have found quite useful. For example, conservatives like to call for "tax relief," implying that taxes are an unfair affliction and obscuring the truth that "taxes are the price we pay for a civilized society."[2] In his classic study of "THE FOLKLORE OF CAPITALISM," Thurman Arnold described how corporations are mischaracterized as persons possessing civil freedoms that would otherwise be denied them. Businesses and other organizations are described "in the language of personally owned private property, when as a matter of fact the things which were described were neither private, nor property, nor personally owned."[3] Cognitive scientists often point to the "ideologically selective character" of frames — a highly effective filter on perception.[4]

This helps explain why new truths often hide in plain sight. When John Maynard Keynes was struggling to reinvent economics in the 1930s, he wrote: "The ideas which are here expressed so laboriously are extremely simple and should be obvious. The difficulty lies not in the new ideas, but in escaping from the old ones, which ramify, for those brought up as most of us have been, into every corner of our minds."[5] Hitchcock tried, but could not escape his inherited worldview. Owen, Darwin, and Lyell also tried (with some trepidation about the explosive theological implications), and for the most part succeeded. Such is the power of a dominant worldview: it invisibly organizes phenomena into a tidy mental frame that suppresses other, potentially important ways to see the world.

In our time, the great problem is not just that the institutions of the liberal state and capitalism are crumbling. It's that our ways of perceiving and representing the world — the foundational stories that we tell about capitalism — are failing as well. These two problems are intimately connected, of course. Sometimes when political systems no longer work, it's because they rely on old narratives about existence that no longer work or command respect. Cherished stories and categories of thought fail to recognize that realities have changed. Guardians of the prevailing order generally don't *want* to acknowledge other possibilities — and so they cling to archaic language to validate their viewpoints. Sometimes new realities are not recognized because there is simply no vocabulary and logic to make them legible to the culture. Consider how the word "dinosaur" and Darwin's theory of evolution opened up new ways of seeing, challenging Bible-based perspectives of the world.

As we tried to explain the phenomena of commoning, we experienced a similar frustration with a deficient discourse. We came to realize that the discourse of conventional politics and economics cannot properly express what we have witnessed. There is a lacuna in the contemporary vocabulary which serves to keep certain realities and insights shrouded in darkness. In the words of historian E. P. Thompson, "It was always a problem to explain the commons with capitalist categories. There was something uncomfortable about them. Their very existence prompted questions about the origin of property and about historical title to land."[6]

Our point is that deeper registers of perception matter every bit as much as daily political polemics. Or even more. German philosopher Hans-Georg Gadamer once pointed out that it is a mistake to believe that one has to talk about politics to change politics. He was right. We need to talk first about our deepest presuppositions about the character of the world.

The Window Through Which We See the World

The study of the nature of reality and how it is structured — the windows through which we see the world — is called ontology. While we are not eager to plunge into these deep metaphysical waters — the topic can get very complicated and abstruse — a brisk swim is inescapable.

One's basic assumptions about reality determine what is seen as normal and desirable — what is good or bad, what is right or wrong. They amount to the "constitutional framework" of any belief-system, one that directly shapes our ideas of what types of political economy and governance structures are possible. A vision of reality that sees everyone as disconnected individuals, for example, is likely to lead to a social order that privileges individual liberty at the expense of collaborative institutions. A vision of reality that sees everyone as interconnected and dependent on each other and the Earth, opens up very different possibilities. Such a vision also requires different categories of analysis and different metaphors and vocabularies to describe the world.

You could say that one's ontological premises create different *affordances* — i.e., capacities and potential uses that have larger political implications. A bicycle creates certain affordances for personal transportation (vigorous exercise, cheap mobility) that are different from those created by an automobile (faster, safer, smoother). Pen and paper offer different affordances for communication (cheap, easy to use) than smartphones (interactive, versatile). So it is with ontologies: they have different affordances for the type of world one can build. When talking about a vision of reality, one must always ask: What does it claim about how individuals relate to each other and to groups? Does it require that things and phenomena embody fixed essences? Is a person's character fixed and given, or does it change through relationships? How does change occur — through individual agents that cause effects as a machine might, or through complicated, subtle, and long-term interactions among multiple agents in a larger environment? Are any of the phenomena that we observe historically and culturally invariant — i.e., universal — or are they variable and context-dependent?

Generally, these sorts of questions about reality are not seen as relevant to the practical, rough-and-tumble world of politics and governance. But given the institutional instability of our times, we believe that nothing is more strategic than to reassess the fundamental ways in which we perceive reality. Such an inquiry might be called *onto-political*, because our different premises about reality have enormous implications for how we conceptualize the social and political order. If we believe that God exists as an omnipotent force and is the source of truth and meaning in all human affairs, we will construct a societal order that is different from ones in which humans see themselves as entirely on their own, without divine guidance and protection. Because perspectives on reality affect how we build social and political institutions, we cannot just look at the world *through* a window — as if it were the only self-evident way of perceiving. We need to pause and start to look *at* the window.[7] Margaret Stout, an administrative theorist, puts it simply: "Ontology is important to political theory *because it frames presuppositions about all aspects of life and what is good and right.*"[8] (emphasis in original)

The OntoStory of the Modern West

The moment is ripe for those of us in the secular West to ponder the general belief system developed during the Renaissance and expanded in the eighteenth and nineteenth centuries by the capitalist societies that arose from it. We moderns live within a grand narrative about individual freedom, property, and the state developed by philosophers such as René Descartes, Thomas Hobbes, and John Locke. The OntoStory that we tell ourselves sees individuals as the primary agents of a world filled with inert objects that have fixed, essential qualities. (Most notably, we have a habit of referring to "nature" and "humanity," as if each were an entity separate from the other.) This Western, secular narrative claims that we humans are born with boundless freedom in a prepolitical "state of nature." But our imagined ancestors (who exactly? when? where?) were allegedly worried about protecting our individual property and liberty, and so they supposedly came together (despite their radical individualism) to forge a "social contract" with each other.[9] As the story goes, everyone authorized the establishment of a state to become the guarantor of everyone's individual liberty and property.[10]

Today we are heirs to this creation myth explaining the origins of the liberal, secular state. The story transfers theological notions about omnipotence (God, monarchs) to the sovereign state (presidents, parliaments, courts).[11] The Leviathan state acts with sovereign power to privilege individual liberty over all social affiliations or identities based on history, ethnicity, culture, religion, geographic origins, and so on. The primary elements of society are the individual and the state. As one commentator notes, liberalism assumes a human nature "that causes self-interested, atomistic individuals with independent, static preferences to compete in an effort to maximize their own benefits with little or no regard for the implications for others. In this political form, representation is won through competition among sovereign individuals and majority rule."[12]

This story is also the basis for capitalism, which presumes a social order based on individual autonomy and fulfillment to explain why we have market competition and hierarchies. The Nobel laureate economist James Buchanan once identified autonomy, rationality of choice, and the spontaneous coordination of people in the "free market" as the fundamental principles of his discipline.[13] In modern times, these presumptions have become ordering principles for much of everyday life. Individual freedom of choice — to choose our favorite TV channels, brand of beer, and political parties — is celebrated, with little thought given to the ways in which the spectrum of choices is determined in the first place.

To probe our presuppositions about the world is not merely an academic exercise. It is immensely consequential in practical ways. Different presuppositions affect how we perceive the world and therefore what types of political systems we regard as realistic and desirable. In a metaphor often used by German physicist Hans-Peter Dürr, fishermen who use nets with a mesh of five centimeters may understandably conclude that there are no fish in the sea smaller than five centimeters. After all, three-centimeter fish never show up in the nets. If you are committed to certain presuppositions about reality, it will be difficult to escape the larger ramifications of your nets of perception. The linkage between ontology and the larger polity and political economy might not be self-evident to ordinary people or policymakers, but the idea is not so complicated. Imagine you build a house and you lay a small, weak foundation. How can the structure possibly last? Or you install a certain number of pillars that can carry, say, ten tons of weight. A few years later you want to add a new floor that would weigh fifteen tons. The house would collapse. Does it really make sense to invest in a heavy addition to the structure if the foundation itself is flawed?

This scenario arguably describes the problem with modern capitalism. It relies on faulty premises about human beings and therefore it can no longer support the grand edifice of the global modern market/

state. Its institutional forms are increasingly ineffective, harmful, and distrusted, as seen in the rise of voter alienation and anger in the US and many European countries. When our commitment to "individual freedom" is conflated with the legal "personhood" of globe-spanning corporations, and when climate-changing capital investments are regarded as "private property," it should not be surprising that the resulting economic system is highly disruptive and literally lethal to the planet. Mainstream critics may attack "capitalism" and "the state," but they are less prone to inquire into the onto-political premises that undergird their vision of reality. That's because most of us have internalized those norms. The "prevailing life-motif" of modern capitalism and the liberal state, writes Greek social critic Andreas Karitzis:

> promotes the idea that a good life is essentially an individual achievement. Society and nature are just backdrops, a wallpaper for our egos, the contingent context in which our solitary selves will evolve pursuing individual goals. The individual owes nothing to no one, lacks a sense of respect for the previous generations or responsibility to future ones — and indifference is the proper attitude regarding present social problems and conditions.[14]

The visible pathologies of capitalism — ecological destruction, social precarity, inequality, exclusion, etc. — do not stem only from soulless corporations and cynical politicians. They derive from a deeper, more fundamental problem — a fallacious understanding of reality itself. Facing up to this issue seems to be asking a lot. It's difficult to truly see the onto-foundations of our socio-economic and political order, let alone do something meaningful to change them. Our cultural norms are subtle, subliminal, and not usually recognized.

However, there is a way forward: we can begin to cultivate a different, deeper sense of reality by looking closely at the language and metaphors that we use, and the stories we tell. The self-awareness that results, when combined with our actual experiences and practices in commoning, can point the way to a new onto-political order based on different presuppositions. The first step is to recognize the hidden beliefs that shape our perceptions and political culture. We must learn to see that everything is interdependent, and that our individual well-being depends upon collective well-being. Our polity must be "attuned to the relational dimension of life," as Arturo Escobar puts it.[15]

OntoStories as a Hidden Deep Dimension of Politics

Many public debates that are ostensibly disagreements about policy or process are, in fact, disagreements about the nature of reality and how it should be. They presume certain human ideal-types and existential realities that frame the dominant discourse. Take the idea of the "self-made man" in capitalist societies. It expresses the cultural fantasy that individuals can truly become successful all by themselves, without help from others. That story then becomes a frame for public discussion. Our presupposition that the Earth is a separate, nonliving thing existing apart from humanity, leads to a perception of land and water as "resources" that can be appropriated and marketized.

The very categories of thought inaugurated by the early modern philosophers established standard ways of thinking that modern societies now regard as self-evident. As men like Francis Bacon, Thomas Hobbes, René Descartes, and John Locke first articulated, the world is supposedly a clash of dualities such as the individual and the collective, humanity and nature, and matter and spirit. The public realm is seen as separate from the private realm. The objective is cast against the subjective. This dualistic habit of thought, as a way of registering reality, leads us to believe that some realms of life are wholly separate and distinct from others, and indeed, diametrically opposed to each other. Modern capitalist societies have built entire cultures around such presuppositions. They reflect what scholars call an OntoStory about reality.

OntoStories can have countless forms that are expressed in many different ways. But at the end of the day they can be classified according to a few traits. There are stories based on the idea that "being simply *is*" (static) and stories in which existence is a constant *becoming* (dynamic). In a static world, the present is experienced as a reality that always is and always will be, much as members of the caste system in India regard their world as "just the way things are." Such a static view of reality is likely to find political expression in theocracy, monarchy, or similar authoritarian rule. In a dynamic world, by contrast, the present reality is always unfolding and becoming something new.

There are OntoStories predicated on the idea of a single, unitary source of existence, which is likely to find expression in political forms such as socialism and collectivism. Or conversely, stories that posit many sources of existence are more likely to support a political order of modern liberalism and social anarchism. In some OntoStories, truth and meaning come from a transcendent source (God, a king, a pope), and in others from an immanent space of lived experience (the divine within each human or all beings).[16]

In any case, OntoStories always reflect a vision of the world and establish the affordances of the system — its structured fields of possibility. The narratives give respectability to certain archetypes of existence and human striving. Human energies are channeled in culturally acceptable ways. The ubiquitous world of advertising and marketing, for example, is not just about selling products; it is about reinforcing an ideal of human satisfaction through individual consumption. It tells an OntoStory about how the world is and should be. Our identity in the world is defined by what we buy or should buy. Nowadays, large corporations are increasingly devising elaborate OntoStories to define reality and thereby advance their political and economic interests. Based on vast quantities of user data, Twitter has devised a classification system of humanity — people who buy cooking supplies, people who live within five miles of a Walmart, etc. — in order to sell those datasets to advertisers.[17] The insurance industry has developed complicated classifications of human disease and injury to determine what medical expenses will be reimbursed. Many courts rely on data analytics about criminals (race, age, neighborhood, income) to predict their likelihood of committing another crime and thereby set "appropriate" jail sentences.[18] Such categories of thought reflect a vision of human existence, social behavior, and causality.

US national security agencies have actually contrived an OntoStory to advance their political interests, as Brian Massumi chillingly describes in his book *Ontopower*.[19] Rather than try to deter or prevent terrorist attacks based on known, provable facts — the historical standard for military intervention — the US Government now declares its own version of time and causation. The asserted possibility of a terrorist threat, as unilaterally determined by security experts, is used to justify lethal state aggression against "terrorists" *before* anything has happened.

Notional threats are defined as provocations. Future possibilities are declared to be actionable facts in the here-and-now. It is a subtle way to redefine time and causation. By spinning a "threat-o-genic" narrative, writes Massumi, the US military redefines reality, seeking to legitimate the state violence and mass surveillance that follows.

These stories help us see the role that ontologies play as a subterranean force in political struggle. Once we accept the idea of the self as an indivisible, bounded unit of autonomous agency, everything else naturally follows: the way we approach the world, the mental frameworks that scientists use to analyze phenomena ("methodological individualism"), the way we act in the world and conceive of leadership, the way we build institutions and policies. One might argue that the most significant field of political contention these days is not taking place in legislatures or courts, but at this level of "reality-definition." After all, what better way to advance one's long-term political goals than to propagate a self-serving version of "reality"? It preemptively marginalizes alternative visions of the future while fortifying the existing political and economic order.

Ah, but there is a rub: no ontology, however widely accepted, is guaranteed to work or command respect. An ontology may not persuade or live up to its own claims. Hitchcock's theory that fossilized footprints were evidence of ancient birds could not credibly explain the discovery of dinosaur fossils. Darwin's new narrative about evolution could. In similar fashion, today the ontological foundations that undergird capitalism are looking more antiquated than ever. The idea that individuals are born free and sovereign — the cornerstone of the liberal state and "free markets" — has always been something of a fable. But nowadays the credibility of this story is starting to fray as people realize that they inhabit a highly interconnected world. The slow-motion collapse of various ecosystems is also discrediting the idea that humanity stands apart from "nature" and that we are wholly autonomous individuals.

While countless angry political confrontations around the world are ostensibly about state policies or laws, many such battles are in fact OntoClashes. They reflect profound disagreements about the nature of reality. Clashes between Indigenous peoples and state power are perhaps the most common example. Typically, the nation-state regards some element of nature as a market resource to be exploited — an idea that many Indigenous communities see as a gross violation of their cosmovision. In New Zealand, for example, the Maori have fought the government's approval of oil drilling in ancestral fishing waters, in violation of the Waitangi treaty with Queen Victoria signed in 1840. In her studies of this conflict, anthropologist Anne Salmond noted that the state and Maori have "fundamentally different onto-logics about human relations with oceans."[20] The state approaches the ocean as a nonliving resource. As such it can be divided up into quantified, bounded units and exploited with an abstract market logic. Oil extraction is perfectly logical to the New Zealand state, whose legal system is constructed to privilege such activity. By contrast, the Maori see the ocean as a living being that has intense, intergenerational bonds with the Maori people. The ocean is imbued with *mana*, ancestral power, that must be honored with spiritual rituals and customary practices. (If this sounds *ir*rational to you, consider this: such a worldview has worked remarkably well to protect both the oceans and human societies.)

OntoClashes between the nation-state and commoners are obviously not confined to premodern cultures. Geographer Andrea Nightingale has studied Scottish fishermen who object to "rational" fishing policies and practices that regulators seek to impose.[21] In crafting catch policies, for example, the state presumes that fishermen are competitive individualists seeking to maximize their personal catch. But the state fails to see the many nonrational subjectivities that define the lives of Scottish fishermen. Working on small fishing vessels in the ocean is dangerous, difficult work, and so fishermen have learned the importance of cooperation and interdependence. Fishermen's lives are deeply entwined with "community obligations, the need to preserve kinship relationships [with fellow villagers], and an emotive attachment to the sea," writes Nightingale. State policies presume a very different reality of life and "rationality" than that experienced by fishermen.

Despite the prevalence of such OntoClashes, modern capitalism and the liberal nation-states remain obsessively committed to their vision of reality. It constitutes a kind of "riverbed"[22] of the polity through which everything flows. But increasingly, the state's OntoStories seem like relics from a different period of human history — a tattered, ill-fitting suit of clothes that is not functional or attractive. It is time to consider the question: how might one imagine and design a different suit of clothes?

The Nested-I and Ubuntu Rationality:
The Relational Ontology of the Commons

The world of commoning represents a profound challenge to capitalism because it is based on a very different ontology. This is not widely appreciated because many people continue to view the commons through archaic ontological perspectives — which is to say, through the normative lens of modern, Western culture. They have internalized the language of separation and methodological individualism. They view objects as having fixed, essential attributes and being disconnected from their origins and context. Commoning has a different orientation to the world because its actions are based on a *deep relationality* of everything. It is a world of dense interpersonal connections and interdependencies. Actions are not simply matters of direct cause-and-effect between the most proximate, visible actors; they stem from a pulsating web of culture and myriad relationships through which new things emerge.

For those of us acculturated by Euro-American cultures, it is not so easy to recognize the ontology that underlies the commons. Our very language contains all sorts of hidden biases that point us in different directions and fail to name the webs of relationality. That's why, in order to truly see the commons, we need to shed inappropriate old concepts and invent new ones. English itself as a dominant world language filters out many insights about commoning that are often better expressed in other languages and cultural experiences.[23]

We deal with this issue in greater depth in the next chapter, but for now, we wish to illustrate how basic presuppositions about reality are so powerfully consequential. In trying to communicate the realities of commoning, we kept coming up against the duality of the concepts *I* and *we* in English. The very words assert an opposition that commoning transcends. But seeing the world through a binary choice of *I* or *we* inhibits a real understanding of commoning. Language itself is a problem in communicating a different OntoStory. As we pondered this quandary, one day a solution occurred to us: the term *Nested-I*. It is an expression that helps us describe the practices and identity of a *commoner*. It overcomes the deeply rooted assumptions about individual identity and agency being opposed to collective goals. The *Nested-I* is an attempt to make visible the subtle, contextual social relationships that integrate "me" and "we." Even if our Western mindset does not easily acknowledge the idea, that reality is everywhere.

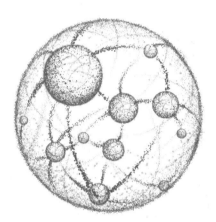

Nested-I concept.

Despite the void in our language, anthropology confirms that we humans are inescapably Nested-I's. In many non-Western cultures, according to British social anthropology professor Marilyn Strathern, "… the singular person can be imagined as a social microcosm … Indeed, persons are frequently constructed as the plural and composite site of the relationships that produced them."[24] For Strathern, an individual does not achieve autonomy by counterposing his or her self-interests to societal interests, but rather by "celebrating his/her own self-contained sociality."[25] People's identities are "multiply constituted" through an "enchainment of relations."[26] Or as the poet Walt Whitman famously put it, "I am large, I contain multitudes." Johann Wolfgang Goethe, the celebrated polymath of Enlightenment culture, regarded his life as a synthesis of myriad relationships:

> Everything I have seen, heard, and observed I have collected and exploited. My works have been nourished by countless different individuals, by innocent and wise ones, people of intelligence and dunces. Childhood, maturity, and old age all have brought me their thought … their

perspectives on life. I have often reaped what others have sowed. My work is the work of a collective being that bears the name of Goethe.[27]

One of the great unexamined truisms of our time — in pointed contrast to Goethe — is that a person can make a fortune through his or her individual efforts and become "self-made." To think that anyone can truly exist or develop apart from friends, family, colleagues, or society is absurd — a "pliable, pernicious, and irrepressible myth," as one observer has put it.[28] Developmental psychologists will tell you that an individual can only come into being through engagement with others. "It takes a village to raise a child," as the saying goes. And vice-versa: the collective can only come into being through the contributions and voluntary cooperation of individuals. Anthropologist Thomas Widlok suggests that perhaps we should talk about all of us as having "entangled identities," "joined lives," and an "extended self."[29] In other words, individuals and collectives are not incompatible opposites like oil and water. They are conjoined and interdependent. Just as the terms "I" and "we" only have meaning in relation to each other, the very terms individual and collective are *relational* — they can only convey meaning *through one another*. Using the term Nested-I helps us get beyond the idea — prevalent in the most respectable intellectual precincts of economics, evolutionary science, biology, and various other social sciences — that the individual is a self-evident category of thought.[30]

Another term that we came up with to express the relationality of commoning is *Ubuntu Rationality*. In various Bantu languages in South Africa, the relationship between "me" and "the other" is expressed by the word *Ubuntu*.[31] We use Ubuntu Rationality to refer to a way of thinking that seeks to align individual and collective well-being. The Kenyan Christian religious philosopher and writer John Mbeti translated the word Ubuntu in this way: "I am because *we* are and, since we are, therefore I am."[32] The individual is part of a "we" — and, in fact, of many "we's." The two are deeply intertwined.[33]

In Western languages, we have no synonym for Ubuntu, but we do have social practices that reflect its spirit. To be sure, there are tensions between the individual and the collective, but if people strive to develop deep, honest relationships and ongoing dialogue, such tensions are minimized and the supposed duality recedes. And we have many reasons to do so: if we reflect on social reality, we can see that Ubuntu is a source of identity and a social safety net. The individual achieves meaning and identity *through* the social context of communities and society — and society constitutes itself *through* the flourishing of the individual.

These ideas have been developed in different contexts by feminist political theorists, ecophilosophers, Indigenous peoples, traditional cultures, theologians, and religious seers. Rabindranath Tagore, the Indian poet and philosopher, wrote, "Relationship is the fundamental truth of this world of appearance."[34] The central point of philosopher Martin Buber's classic of existential philosophy, *I and Thou*, is that life is relational. We find meaning in direct encounters with other living presences, whether with other humans, nature, or God — and we encounter separation when we regard others as objects, expressed as an attitude of *I-It*.[35] Other visionaries have expressed similar ideas in their own ways. Martin Luther King, Jr., argued that "we are caught in an inescapable network of mutuality, tied in a single garment of destiny."[36] Rachel Carson, in her first major essay, "Undersea," in 1937, and later in *Silent Spring*, described life as a profoundly interwoven web.[37]

In later chapters, we will introduce other terms that name the relational phenomena of commoning more precisely. For now, it is enough to note that philosophers would call our perspective a *relational ontology*. In a relational ontology, the idea is that *relations between entities* are more fundamental than the entities themselves. Let this idea sink in. It means that living organisms develop and thrive *through* their interactions with each other. That is the basis for their identity and biological survival. That is the basis for their aliveness. As a living social organism, a commons embodies a relational ontology that is expressed through recurrent behavioral patterns such as the RITUALIZING OF TOGETHERNESS and TRUST IN SITUATED KNOWING. Commoners strive to PRESERVE RELATIONSHIPS IN ADDRESSING CONFLICTS and REFLECT ON THEIR PEER GOVERNANCE.

While scholars have theorized many different sorts of relational ontologies, they disagree about what specific "relations" between entities actually matter and what they mean. In general, relations are seen as conveying *meaning* or expressing *value* — e.g., the relationship between people and a shared symbol, such as a flag, is often associated with collective identity and pride. But there are so many conceivable types of relations that it is impossible to propose a unified philosophical account of relational ontologies. People may have relationships to the land that they cultivate, subjective or spiritual relationships, biological relationships to parents and extended families, circumstantial relationships with friends and work partners, and transient connections to people on the internet, among many others.

While one could explore many types of relational ontologies, we wish to focus on two general types and highlight how they differ. Each tells us incompatible stories about the nature of being, and each has different political ramifications. One type is called *undifferentiated relational ontology*. Here, the source of being lies within all living beings as a transcendent force. One can imagine it as a matryoshka, or Russian nesting doll, in which the largest doll encompasses and absorbs all the smaller ones within its embrace. When "the whole" incorporates everything that is "within it," the pieces might be called "undifferentiated" in that all parts are defined by the whole. No element encompassed by the whole necessarily has its own individual agency or differentiated character. All elements are more or less equal, and are considered so. Politically, such an ontology implies a forced collectivism or a centralized monoculture because every individual and thing is regarded as an undifferentiated part of the whole.

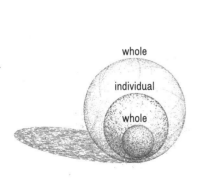
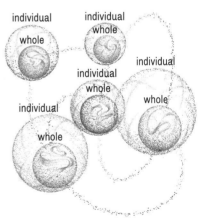

UNDIFFERENTIATED   **DIFFERENTIATED**

Differentiated and undifferentiated relational ontology.

In contrast, the realities of commoning and a commons-based society can be expressed only by a different ontology, one that recognizes the inherent diversity and differentiation of living systems within the whole. This ontology must allow space for every individual to unfold their unique self. People are born with different talents and desires in different circumstances and upbringings, and everyone faces unique circumstances. A realistic ontology should not attempt to flatten out actual individual differences and reduce them to a universal standard.

The type of ontology that best describes the realities of commoning is therefore a *differentiated relational* type in which the source of being arises from all living individuals and manifests in very different, situational ways. At the same time, each living being is connected to others and shares certain elemental aspects of life and consciousness — just as blood flows through all human bodies and yet every human being is unique. In a differentiated ontology, individuals are individuated and yet related to each other and part of a larger whole at the same time. Every living thing is "in a constant state of mutual becoming," as Margaret Stout puts it, in dynamic engagement with the whole. Since each living element is constantly evolving and affected by multiple influences, the world has no singular definition or representation. We do not live in a "One-World World," as Arturo Escobar puts it, but rather in a *pluriverse*. A diversity of life-forms are conjoined by our common humanity and engagement with life on Earth.

Complexity Science and Commoning

It is tempting to regard this entire discussion as an abstract distraction of little practical value. But let us suggest how a shift towards a relational ontology has created a new paradigm of discovery, complexity science, which is revolutionizing biology, chemistry, evolutionary sciences, physics, economics, and social sciences, among other fields. Complexity science has important things to say about the commons, too, because it sees the world as a dynamic, evolving set of living, integrated systems.[38] While individual organisms may have important degrees of agency, they can only be understood in the context of their myriad relationships and constraints by larger structures. The kidney in the human body is not an autonomous unit, for example. It is nested within a larger set of physiological systems within which it must adapt — and the human body in turn must dynamically coexist within a still larger environment.

By viewing the world through this window — a relational ontology that moves beyond mechanical metaphors and individualism — it becomes possible to offer much better explanations for all sorts of human and ecological phenomena. We can begin to understand a commons as a *life-form*, not as a "resource," and as an organic, integrated system, not a collection of discrete parts. The window on reality that a commons expresses is more encompassing and real (in our estimation!) than ontologies that consign relational dynamics to the background as "exogenous variables."[39]

Complexity science offers a more coherent way of explaining how functional design can emerge without a designer. Design happens as adaptive agents (such as commoners) interact with each other. The self-organization of agents — what we call "peer organization" in a commons — gives rise incrementally to complex organizational systems.[40] There is no master blueprint or top-down, expert-driven knowledge behind the process. It emerges from agents responding to their own local, bounded circumstances.[41] As people experiment, regularize, and refine the ways in which they engage with each other, they find solutions to problems. The kernel of solutions that work well can be described as patterns. A pattern is not a blueprint; it is a template that includes many variations that are similar but not identical. That's because each variation reflects a particular time, context, set of actors, etc.

The principles of complex adaptive systems are seen in the self-organization of microbes as they adapt to host organisms, ants as they build their nests, and other living creatures that somehow self-coordinate to generate an overall order for their collective. Biologist Stuart Kauffman, a pioneering theorist of complexity science, has identified key principles of autocatalysis that can occur when one form of matter comes into contact with another.[42] Based on experimental insights, he has proposed a theory for the origins of molecular reproduction — a dynamic that others have confirmed in biological metabolisms, chemical networks, and physics, among other realms. The rise of spontaneous order, as it is sometimes called, occurs through the interactions of local agents without any outside supervision or control. It tends to be driven by positive feedback loops within a system that reinforces constructive, order-creating behaviors. Self-ordering and self-healing properties are woven into systems and their constituent elements at a very deep level, making them unusually resilient in the face of disruptions.

This is obviously a more complicated story than we can delve into here. For our purposes, it is enough to note that the dynamics of self-organization[43] can generate a stable, living order within a sea of chaotic, random entropy. The Second Law of Thermodynamics posits that the universe is in a state of constant, increasing entropy that is always moving toward disorder. But according to some novel scientific theories, living organisms — cells, plants, animals (and commons?) — are able to temporarily capture and structure the use of entropic energy flows to sustain life. Aliveness and order spontaneously arise from chaotic disorder. A living organism relies on semi-permeable membranes to allow it to access what is useful in the external environment and filter out what is harmful, all in ways congruent with its particular context.[44] "Identity and environment are thus reciprocally defined and determined with respect to each other," writes biological anthropologist Terrence Deacon, author of *Incomplete Nature*.[45] There is no divine watchmaker or external force imposing order. Rather it emerges through an organism's internal systems for metabolizing energy and creatively adapting to its environment. The parallels between this biological process and commoning are highly suggestive and worth pondering.

Conventional scientists scoff at many of these ideas, to be sure, but numerous biologists, chemists, evolutionary scientists, and physicists have embraced complexity theory precisely because it explains things that standard science, operating within a more mechanical, individualist, and agent-based framework, cannot. A relational ontology enables scientists to see the world in more dynamic, holistic terms. It lets us become more self-aware of the reality that we are personally immersed in living phenomena. While economists have generally resisted this idea (it would shatter too many foundational principles of standard economics!), Kate Raworth, in her brilliant book *Doughnut Economics*, has proposed a real-world economic framework that recognizes a new ontology — that people are social and relational (not rational and individualistic); that the world is dynamically complex (not mechanical and tending toward equilibrium); and that our economic systems must be regenerative by design.[46]

The philosopher and biologist Andreas Weber has expressed the view of being that we take in this book: "The world is not populated by singular, autonomous, sovereign beings. It is comprised of a constantly oscillating network of dynamic interactions in which one thing changes through the change of another. The relationship counts, not the substance."[47] Weber's book *Matter and Desire* is an extended reflection on this theme, that life on Earth is about "'reciprocal specification' — an act of mutual engendering. Only through a moment of encounter does one's own character come fully to fruition. The world is not an aggregation of things, but rather a symphony of relationships ..."[48]

Making an OntoShift to the Commons

If the world is truly relational, it should be clear the one reason why Garrett Hardin, in his famous "Tragedy of the Commons" essay, could not really see the commons as a viable social system. He could see the world only through the lens of an individualist ontology. Living within this framework, he literally could not comprehend commoning or imagine a set of political affordances based on dynamic relationships.

So to truly understand the dynamics of the commons, one must first escape the onto-political framework of the modern West. One must make what we call an "OntoShift" — a recognition that relational categories of thought and experience are primary. This is not merely about looking at interactions among independent individuals. It is about *intra*-actions, a term used by physicist and philosopher Karen Barad to describe how *relationships themselves* are a force of change, transformation, and emergence. As one Barad commentator puts it: "When bodies intra-act, they do so in co-constitutive ways. Individuals materialize *through* intra-actions, and the ability to act emerges *from within* the relationship, not outside of it."[49] Seen from this perspective, relational categories are not simply cause-and-effect interactions among independent objects, such as billiard balls bouncing around a pool table. They are interactions that engage the *inner dimensions* of living organisms, and *in this way* generate change and value. Furthermore, there is no single, essentialist individual, but rather many dynamic "I's," each of which is implicated in many communities and thus a part of "many we's."

You might ask yourself, how can these ideas actually work? For people accustomed to thinking in an individualist ontology and in dualities, it's a big challenge to see the world as relational. It requires developing a different sense of reality. No one can simply announce that he/she is adopting a new perspective. A new orientation must be learned and practiced. Saying goodbye to old habits of thought requires practice. Like giving up smoking, it requires willpower, attention, and the deliberate learning of new habits. That's what the next several chapters are meant to do for those who want to "think like a commoner" and make an OntoShift.

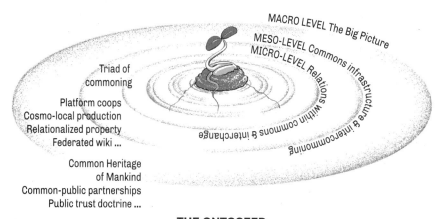

THE ONTOSEED

OntoSeed at center of galaxy of commoning practices.

So far, we have cast a foundation for a different understanding of reality. In the remainder of the book, we supply the materials for constructing the house. The new structure can help us envision different sorts of community, social practices, and economic institutions — and above all, a new culture that honors cooperation and sharing.

The first step in this journey is language. We must reflect on how the words and logic of our everyday language convey old habits of thinking and limit our sense of what is possible. So let us train ourselves to see the world in a new way through new words, relationships, and social practices.

3

Language and the Creation of Commons

Pencil, nail, and paper.

I F YOU ASK SOMEONE WHO SPEAKS ENGLISH which two of the three items above belong together, most will say the pencil and paper. But ask someone who speaks Bora, a language from the Northwest Amazonian region, and you will get a different answer. Bora speakers have "... around seventy terms for the shape of things: One for long and thin things, another for round things, and yet another for flat things with a straight edge, and so on."[1] When ethnolinguist Frank Seifart conducted a "relating-things" empirical test with Bora speakers and compared their results to those of English and Spanish speakers, he found that Bora speakers in one hundred percent of the cases answered that "pencil and nail" belonged together. To them, the relationship among things that are similar in shape seemed self-evident.

As this small experiment suggests, language profoundly shapes perception. Words, terms, and categories of thought isolate and emphasize only certain aspects of reality. They determine what we notice about a given phenomenon or thing — and marginalize other aspects. Terms and especially analytical categories point us to what "really matters," according to a certain cultural outlook or theory. They subtly direct how we perceive the world. If the words in a given language focus on shapes over function, then no wonder the speakers of that language prefer to group things according to their shape rather than their function.

So, even if we like to believe that our everyday language faithfully expresses the actual realities we experience, this is simply not the case. We not only inhabit distinct worlds; we not only describe our worlds in different idioms; consciously or unconsciously, we inhabit and create

Words, Terms, and Categories

A word is a particular symbol — usually a speech sound or combination of characters — that enables us to communicate a specific meaning. By combining one word with another and yet another in countless permutations through syntax, human communication is astonishingly versatile.

A term is a word or a phrase used to express a more abstract notion or concept. Since it originates in a specific historical and cultural context, a term is a signifier in the history of ideas and culture, much as "horseless carriage" reflects a pre-automobile culture and the "four elements" (air, water, earth, fire) points to the pre-scientific era of ancient Greece.

A category is a basic *analytical term*, that makes visible a certain dimension of a phenomenon. A category is generated through an explicit, systematic methodology. It determines what we get to see. The scope of our cognition is quite different, for example, if we use the term *homo economicus* as an analytical category instead of the *Nested-I*.

A relational category is a category based on a relational understanding of the world as explained in Chapter 2. In modern societies, the economy, diseases, and the state are treated as *things* when in fact they are relational phenomena. A person does not *have* tuberculosis or cancer, but rather is part of a dynamic vector of living cells, viruses, bacteria, etc. Similarly, the terms "the economy" and "the state" objectify a vast set of social and political relationships.

distinct worldviews *through* language. "Pencil and paper" may seem automatically to go together, but as any anthropologist will testify, the social order that we inherit or construct for ourselves is quite artificial.

Our words, terms, and idioms subtly determine what we see as pertinent and what logical relations matter. The absence of words and terms indirectly signals what we regard as unimportant — after all, we have declined to name it. In sum, we may think that the meanings of our words are self-evident and our way of life is normal, but in fact both are highly circumstantial and context-based. Consider how the simple hand gesture of an upturned palm with fingertips joined together means different things in different cultures: Egyptians use the gesture to say, "Be patient!" Italians use it to ask, "What exactly do you mean?" And Greeks are exclaiming, "That's just perfect!"[2] Again, the reality we each inhabit may feel solid and self-evident, but in fact, our symbols of meaning that we ultimately use — be they gestures or words — are somewhat arbitrary.

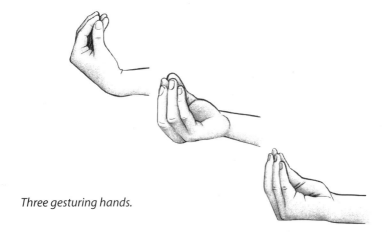

Three gesturing hands.

We ended the last chapter by noting that seeing the commons as a general paradigm requires that we learn a new orientation toward reality — an OntoShift. In this chapter, we want to explain why this orientation can only be expressed through new sorts of language.

In the course of writing this book, we often felt the desperate need for terms that more adequately describe the realities of the commons. For example, we found that the term "resource" as used by economists and policymakers implies a certain type of social relationship — impersonal, instrumental, market-oriented — that doesn't really apply in a commons. We found that the duality of "private" and "public," which implies a world divided into markets and the state, fails to acknowledge the distinct realities of the commons. On countless occasions, we found ourselves imprisoned by the language of mainstream culture and frustrated by the absence of words, terms, and relational categories that could give voice to the commons. We came to realize that if we aspire to social and political transformation but try to do so using the language of market economics, state power, and political liberalism, we will fail. Somehow we had to escape the powerful gravitational pull of old paradigm language and come up with words that name a different order of social reality! Relationships and ways of being and doing that are barely visible in the general culture have to be made explicit through language.

The Tenacity of Systems of Opinion; The Harmony of Illusions

Throughout history, problems have arisen when the language used to represent reality, fails to meet the needs and aspirations of people. An old framework of thought fails when it cannot properly name phenomena that people need to see to collectively manage their affairs. This is not just a matter of accurate analysis and representation; it is also a matter of conveying values, feelings, and relationships. In Chapter 2, we saw how Edward Hitchcock was unable to formulate and assert new facts because he was so immersed in a Biblical worldview. Nor did he have the terminologies to imagine and interpret a prehistoric world of dinosaurs. Others such as Darwin and Lyell did. They reinterpreted reality by providing new terminologies, providing a durable cognitive scaffolding for future generations. This is a recurrent experience in the history of science: the iconoclast who breaks the hammerlock of a conventional framework of understanding by offering a different one that — despite its novelty — is nonetheless recognized by enough people as more explanatory and "true."

In his 1962 book *The Structure of Scientific Revolutions*, Thomas Kuhn famously described the way that old frameworks of thought crumble in the face of new interpretations and ideas. He argued that breakthrough discoveries in science tend to arrive when upstarts challenge an underlying framework of rules and assumptions. They supplant a constellation of group commitments about how to interpret the world, and offer new assumptions, rules, and explanations. This paves the way towards a *paradigm shift*.[3] While the idea of a paradigm shift is open to wide interpretation and has become a bit of a cliché, our sense of it is described in Chapter 2 as an *OntoShift*. A real paradigm shift occurs when our fundamental presuppositions about reality change. The challenge that political changemakers rarely address is how to step outside of entrenched worldviews and question unexamined assumptions built into our cognition.

Ludwik Fleck — a Polish microbiologist and philosopher of science who in 1935 prefigured Kuhn with an even more radical approach — noted the inherent conservatism of "thought collectives." Fleck wrote: "When a conception permeates a thought collective strongly enough, so that it penetrates as far as everyday life and idiom and has become a viewpoint in the literal sense of the word, any contradiction appears unthinkable and unimaginable."[4] Fleck recalled how Columbus's idea that the world was round was too crazy for people to imagine. Who could believe that people on the other side of the world walked around on their heads, with their legs in the air?

A thought collective acts like the immune system of a body, relentlessly prowling the world for viruses and other threats to the received wisdom while authorizing access by entities deemed to be "friendly outsiders." "What does not fit into the system remains unseen," wrote Fleck. "Alternatively, if it is noticed, either it is kept secret, or laborious efforts are made to explain an exception in terms that do not contradict the system."[5] Of course, some thought collectives are far more closed and fearful than others. Some have designs and methodologies that are closed and hostile to change; others are structurally more open to heterodox opinion, dissent, evolutionary change, and methodologies that allow for integrating different ways of knowing. Galileo faced a buzz saw of religious denial when he questioned Copernicus's view of the cosmos with the Earth at its center. But eventually, the new paradigm overcame the counterclaims of orbital "epicycles" that sought to preserve the Copernican system. The tendency to interpret phenomena in ways that affirm one's own priorities — confirmation bias —

is all part of what Fleck called "the tenacity of systems of opinion and the harmony of illusions."[6] The prevailing order must be defended, insurgent views rebutted, and dissenters denigrated or even persecuted.

The arrival of a new paradigm is usually announced by new categories of thought, new terms, and new words that illuminate neglected or unimagined dimensions of reality, making them available to the culture. The idea that even empirical facts are relative, that worldviews and cultural frames are contingent, is a difficult pill for enlightened moderns to swallow. And this is why a closer look at language discloses how our sense of reality, as mediated through language, is *filled* with artificial markers of meaning. Remember the paper-pencil-nail example above.

Any society is likely to have a dominant framework of perception and meaning. This is surely one reason why humanity has succeeded so well as a species. While an individual can acquire only tiny fragments of a culture's vast storehouse of knowledge, consensus frameworks can enable indirect access to a society's collective knowledge. The cognitive framework amounts to a kind of operating system of the body/mind, with both strengths and limitations. It preordains only certain affordances of permissible perception and thought, some of which are aggressively reinforced by powerful institutions and leaders. When the methodologies and convictions of one thought collective become suffocating or harmful, the question arises: how can a new "thought style" be introduced to challenge and supplant the old one? We believe a vital strategy, though certainly not the only one, is the use of a new language with fresh, more spacious affordances.

Language and World-Making

We've seen how language is an indispensable force for imagining the world — and for socially constructing what counts as a fact. It is even more: language is a means for co-creating the world. It has only been in the past two hundred years, for example, that land and certain forms of human work have been regarded as "capital"[7] — a term of rather central importance to modern history. A whole vocabulary of economics has made the social relations of capitalism more real and normative than primary experience. As capitalists have sought greater productivity from their property, terms such as "human capital" and "natural capital" have been adopted to express relations toward people and nature.

Similarly, the internet and digital culture have given rise to entirely new vocabularies to describe the salient realities of online life – "spam," "phishing," "flame wars," emoticons, and acronyms like LOL. Bora speakers in the Northwest Amazon have developed their own highly specific terms to name what matters to them and to navigate through their social and physical terrain. The same with the Jahai people in the untouched rainforests of northern Malaysia, who have a dozen different words for odors that permeate their landscape: one for the smell of boiled onions, another for the aroma of meats, others for burnt rubber and "blood that attracts tigers."[8] Speakers of English or German don't have much need for such concepts, which is why it takes an elaborate analogy ("smell of boiled onions") simply to make a rough translation.

In his book *Landmarks*, nature writer Robert Macfarlane compiled hundreds of words that local communities have invented to name distinctive aspects of their local landscapes. On the Isle of Lewis in Ireland, for example, the word *èit* names the "practice of placing quartz stones in moorland streams so that they would sparkle in the moonlight and thereby attract salmon to them in the late summer and autumn."[9] In Hertfordshire, England, prehistoric arrowheads are known as *fairy darts*. In the Cotswolds, decayed wood is called *droxy*.[10] The countless words used by hyperlocal populations have a "compressive precision" and the capacity to make "ultra-fine discriminations," writes Macfarlane.[11] For centuries, these vocabularies "have spilled their poetry into everyday life. They have anthologized local history, anecdote, and myth, binding story to place. They have been functional — operating as territory markers and ownership designators" — helping people to name landmarks, navigate the landscape, and connect to their ancestors' history. The words function as "memory maps." As Alec Finlay puts it, the world is "lit by the mnemonics of words."[12]

A prominent ethnographer of landscape and language, Keith Basso, noted that the Apache people of western Arizona regard their special words as much more than referents. They are ways to express themselves aesthetically, ethically, and musically. They offer powerful ways to connect people to their own geographies, cultures, and histories. In our time, marketers have used the expressive power of words to advance their sales and brand identities, to the extent of buying "naming rights" for sports arenas and urban landmarks, for example.[13] When commoners replace commodified place names and branded culture with their own nomenclatures, they restore the expressive power of language and re-enchant the commons. The culture itself becomes a commons because the words resonate in people's hearts and experience; they are not just marketing totems that a wealthy corporation has paid for.

Given this role of language, the accelerating extinction of languages as the monoculture of global capitalism intensifies is troubling. Biolinguistic diversity has enabled humans to understand the nonhuman world in discerning, insightful ways. Now that crucial element of human culture is being lost. Most of Australia's 250 aboriginal languages have vanished, depriving humankind of some of our ability to imagine and name different possible human relationships to nature.[14] "Without a name made in our mouths, an animal or a place struggles to find purchase in our minds and in our hearts," as one ethnographer put it.[15]

Frames, Metaphors, and the Terms of Our Cognition

As these examples suggest, some of the most important ways of worldmaking go through language. Language is not only powerful as a tool by which we communicate and coordinate with each other. It organizes our cognition and self-awareness. Language is our most important vehicle for expressing shared concepts and asserting what we consider relevant; it is, thus, essential for creating culture. The question is, what concepts, facts, and perspectives shall we declare to be relevant? What type of shared knowledge and culture do we want to propagate?

This question brings us to the importance of *frames* and *metaphors*. As sociolinguist George Lakoff has written in his many books, the frames embedded in our language literally enact our cognition.[16] With self-congratulation, the corporate world refers to itself as "job creators," celebrating its power while marginalizing the actual work that real people do. Retailers like to frame the act of spending money on sales items as "saving money" because one is supposedly paying less than the regular price. The point of frames and metaphors is to preprogram our field of vision and subtly instill emotional meanings and values in our perceptions and thoughts. Framing predetermines the answers that can be given to questions by presuming what is important and permissible to ask in the first place. Because frames powerfully transmit the ontologies upon which they are based, we hardly notice how they silently infiltrate our brains. Even if we negate the prevailing discourse ("capitalism sucks"), we still enact it unconsciously through our semantic structures and terms. Frames in this way shape policies. In fact, they *are* policies.

To a great extent, framing works through metaphors that function at neural levels. We end up internalizing the ideas of frames in our minds as normal. It makes a difference if we imagine and talk about ourselves as "reverent guests of nature" (as in the Taoist tradition) or as "conquerors of nature" (as in the modern Western tradition).[17] Metaphors often have powerful moral associations that affect how we position ourselves toward a given topic. For example, economist Joseph Schumpeter's metaphor that capitalism is all about "creative destruction" has been used to valorize "innovation" as something fresh, modern, and progressive — not stodgy and backward-looking.[18] The word carries an implicit judgment and moral accounting. Taken together, the metaphors and frames of our language weave a web of cultural associations and attitudes. In a market culture, it's no wonder that the prevailing frames and metaphors fail to capture the realities of commons and commoning!

Paradigms and their assumptions, metaphors and the frames they create, categories and the terms that explain them — these ingredients all come together to express a "thought style," as Fleck calls it. A standard approach to perceiving the world produces "*a readiness for stylized (that is, directed and restricted) perception and action*, until an answer becomes largely pre-formed in the question, and a decision is confined merely to 'yes' or 'no,' or perhaps to a numerical determination, until methods and apparatus automatically carry out the greatest part of our mental work for us."[19] (emphasis in original) Answers are correct only insofar as the thought collective regards the discourse itself as permissible and true. To stay within the boundaries of the thought collective, most commentary and research amounts to elaborating on fundamental premises. Ideas that defy the prevailing thought collective (such as the commons and commoning) do not compute. They are avoided, rejected, and denied. Their proponents are ignored and sometimes persecuted.

Many things can be done to surmount restrictive thought frames and inaugurate new ones that can supplant them. First, one must deconstruct the dominant frames and metaphors of the dominant discourse — along with their implicit logic, values, and emotional associations. The whole chain of ontology, frame, and terms must be eliminated root and branch, and replaced — a task that obviously can only occur over time, and not in one fell swoop. This is necessary because using the same frames, concepts, and metaphors as previously will simply revivify the old worldview that we are trying to transcend. For example, the normative language about work as something that you do at a (paid) job conjures up the entire worldview that people must earn money through their commodified labor in order to survive and develop in the world. An entire worldview and social system are embedded in our everyday language and internalized in how we interpret social reality.

We therefore need to become not only more self-aware of the concepts and terms that re-entrench the existing order of thought. We also need to teach ourselves new vocabularies that point to more liberating ways of being. We need to learn a language that will help us make an OntoShift and think in relational terms about a new world that is possible. To sensitize us to the loaded words in our daily lexicon, we offer a collection of *Keywords of a Fading Era*, including a selection of *Misleading Binaries*. To help us learn to name, see, and understand commoning more clearly, we also offer a *Glossary of Commons-Friendly Terms*. You may wish to browse through these glossaries and come back to them later.

Language Evokes and Sustains a Worldview

This is our attempt to identify terms whose embedded meanings point in the wrong direction. They subtly direct our attention to old-paradigm ways of perceiving and thinking while blocking more constructive forms of cognition and communication. Many utterly familiar terms in modern societies evoke realities that are actually breaking down and decaying. We might call them keywords from a fading era — once-salient terms that are increasingly stale and archaic.

Why do we need such a glossary? John Patrick Leary, a cultural historian of capitalism and its language, explains that the keywords we use reveal a lot about the logic, values, and sensibilities of a people. They "bind together ways of seeing culture and society," he notes. Citing Raymond Willliams's classic book on keywords from 1976,[20] Leary states that the words that command our attention today "relate to affinity for hierarchy and a celebration of the virtues of competition, 'the marketplace,' and the virtual technologies of our time."[21]

This is exactly what we experienced in writing these pages. We faced a special challenge: trying to communicate the subtle realities of commons and commoning with words whose meanings are deeply embedded in a different, market-focused culture. There was no way! The words themselves are perfectly fine, but we always felt that they could not really express certain truths about commons. Many terms are slyly misleading simply because they suggest solid, trustworthy ideas, while in fact the referents are disappearing realities. The words are becoming empty husks. Think about the word *sustainability*. Today it is used to describe business models rather than the mindful use of shared natural wealth to ensure its capacity for regeneration. Certain terms signal one's belief in a worldview that is problematic. When talking about *human capital*, you endorse a world in which the primary role of human beings is to be *resources* for the labor market. When you talk about *economic growth*, you invite listeners to believe in the faux-egalitarian narrative that growth raises all boats even though the reality is quite different.

In this sense vocabulary is a living universe of meaning communicated through discrete words; it is not a mere classification system such as a taxonomy. Vocabulary is often described as a "field of words with explanations" (*vocabularium* in Latin). A look at how vocabularies actually function reveals that they are more like open, evolving collections of words and terms that reflect a hidden web of logic and relationships. A consistent, shared vocabulary illuminates the multi-fold relationships between words and helps us share experiences and knowledge with others. (That is the reason for these glossaries!)

Keywords from a Fading Era

Citizen, also called "a national," identifies a person in relation to the nation-state and implies that this is a person's primary political role. The term "citizen" is often used to imply that noncitizens are somehow less than equal peers or perhaps even "illegal."[22] A more universal term is Commoner.

Development is a term of political economy used by the US and European nations to prod "undeveloped" countries to embrace global commerce, resource extractivism, and consumerism along with improvements in infrastructure, education, and healthcare. The harmful side-effects of "development" typically include ecological destruction, inequality, political repression, and cultural dispossession. German ecologist Wolfgang Sachs has called development a mindset that puts the political economies of all nations on a single track: "The lead-runners show the way; they are at the forefront of social evolution, indicating a common destination even for countries which had highly diverse trajectories in the past. Many different histories merge into one 'master history,' many different time scales merge into one master time scale. The imagined time is linear, only allowing for progressing or regressing."[23]

Governance refers to multiple arrangements of guiding and controlling human behavior. Like the term *government*, it derives ultimately from the Greek *kubernaein* [κυβερνάω], which literally means *to steer*. The question is: Who steers whom and by which techniques? The term, as re-minted by economists and political scientists since the early 1990s, implies that a separate class, power group, or institutional apparatus stands over others and governs them — in other words, that the government and governed are separate. The term *governance* in its standard usage does not encompass the idea of collective coordination and control by people themselves. Our provisional alternative to the term *governance* is PEER GOVERNANCE.

Incentives describe the use of something, usually money, to motivate people and to direct their actions in a desired way. In the context of a system of rewards, incentives are usually meant to encourage harder work. (No wonder it was popularized in 1943 in the context of the US war economy.) While external incentives surely have a role to play, studies find that money and other incentives often crowd out instinctual motivations to create and contribute. The introduction of money in a setting signals that impersonal, self-serving social protocols are the norm, which in turn deters people from CONTRIBUTING FREELY. "[M]oney is extraordinarily unfit for addressing needs with Care," writes Miki Kashtan.[24]

Innovation refers to ideas, tools, or devices that are new, and, by implication, more original, beneficial, progressive, and effective than that which already exists. The so-called disruptive force of innovation on society and markets is celebrated even through the change is often of negligible value, antisocial, or ecologically harmful. In the end, "innovation" is seen as an engine for competitive market advantage and return on capital investment. Hence the positive aura of the word, especially when it is cast against its binary opposite, "static, traditional, and old," which implies a lack of imagination. The alternative to "innovation" is not this binary opposite, however, but creative adaptation to ever-changing needs in ways that are shared and convivial.

Leadership is a term that implies a single leader — bold, courageous, insightful — who mobilizes followers to achieve collective goals that might otherwise be unattainable. There is no question that some individuals are inspiring and catalytic. But understanding "leadership" as it happens in most organizational contexts switches on and validates a hierarchical structure in our minds. Leadership is then associated with gaining power over processes and people. It obscures the potential of commoning to actualize change and organize our lives — or, as Miki Kashtan puts it, "to inhabit an intentionality of leadership without having power."[25] Catalytic change can be achieved through processes of distributed power and shared purpose, as seen in Sociocracy,[26] the holacracy approach,[27] Theory U.,[28] and PEER GOVERNANCE practices.

Nonprofit implies that an organization is virtuous and socially minded — presumably the opposite of a self-interested for-profit corporation. But a nonprofit is primarily a legal status for organizations that grants them certain tax exemptions. The term *nonprofit* is somewhat misleading because it suggests that there is a way to participate in a capitalist economy in socially minded ways without making a profit; it is more accurate to say that nonprofits are reinvesting profits into social purposes. They ultimately depend, directly or indirectly, upon profit-making from the larger economy and do not offer structural emancipation from the imperatives of capitalism itself.

Organization usually refers to an institution or association whose members coordinate with each other to pursue shared goals and speak with one voice. This meaning is now being subverted by the power of open networks, which is rendering the idea of a stable organization with identifiable participants and boundaries archaic. Conventional organizations such as government and CORPORATIONS are discovering that as the boundaries around organizations become more porous, collaborations with "outsiders" are becoming more routine, and interactions more fluid and dynamic. Interestingly, the term *organization* stems from Greek *órganon* [ὄργανον], which translates as a tool to "compose into a viable, vital whole," as our body *organs* do. Rather than focusing on organizations as a form, we find it more useful to focus on the *quality* of organizing within an institution: conscious self-organization, networking, and PEER GOVERNANCE.

Corporations are forms of ORGANIZATIONS that business scholar Ronald Coase famously argued were a more efficient solution to high transaction costs. This analysis is now being subverted by sharing on open platforms and in COMMONS, which enable people to minimize transaction costs through collaborations within communities of trust. Flexible improvisation through COMMONING can begin to compete with corporate structures and markets, although this approach usually suffers from inadequate infrastructure and financing.

Participation is a term often used to describe CITIZEN involvement in government, community life, and organizations. Today the term is usually invoked in a positive way to imply that citizen participation (in hearings, decision-making, or participatory budgeting programs) fulfills democratic ideals and confers popular legitimacy on the outcomes. This is precisely the deficiency of the term "participation," however: it is often confined within a predetermined, top-down set of policy options and implementation strategies. The public does not really initiate and show sovereign political agency in a fuller sense. It merely "participates" in public debates and processes on terms that politicians, regulators, and other state officials have already found acceptable, giving the ultimate decisions a veneer of legitimacy. By contrast, COMMONING is a more robust, independent act of political agency.

(To) scale: "How do we scale [up] this idea?" is often another way of asking how to make it significant or consequential. The term implies some sort of verticality (bottom-up, top-down), as if centralized hierarchies were needed to expand the operationality of an idea or practice. But as we explain in our term *Emulate & Then Federate* (pp. 202–203), local projects can expand through voluntary participation, peer organization, and federation, without the ministrations of centralized systems of control. Enabling infrastructure is often helpful, but projects taken to scale invariably generate new complications and fixed overhead expenses while reducing the possibility of elegant solutions, local flexibility, and human judgment.[29] At a certain point, large-scale systems require increasing energy supplies and workloads to keep them running ("regrettable necessities," as David Fleming calls them), which can siphon away resources for meeting real needs. Large scale is fundamentally disempowering: "It is like a wave: you can ride it, but not steer it," notes Fleming.[30] The wisdom of designer Thomas Lommée is apt: "The next big thing will be a lot of small things."[31]

Scarcity in its popular understanding points to insufficiency that can be solved by the market economy through invention, INNOVATION, and economic growth. The "scarcity" of oil, land, and water may seem self-evident, but, in fact, the term does not reflect any inherent property of a resource. Oil, land, or water are merely finite. The term *scarcity* reflects the worldview of a social system that uses a resource. Something is regarded as "scarce" if there is not enough supply to meet actual or potential demand. Within a capitalist context, scarcity is even *created* when there is plenty of supply, as in the case of knowledge, software code, and information. That is the precise purpose of copyright and patent law — to prevent knowledge and creative works from being shared. "If we experience scarcity," writes Alan Rosenblith, "the problem is with our systems, not the universe."[32] The Bushmen of the Kalahari in Africa experience "affluence without abundance," as the title of a book about them puts it.[33] Dealing with limited resources is one of the core challenges a COMMONS faces. For finite resources such as land, this challenge usually happens through a CAP approach that establishes limits on the use of shared wealth. The manufactured scarcity of software code is addressed through free, libre, and open source software [FLOSS] communities.

Pluralism is often taken as social virtue because of its claims to tolerate and accept different races, ethnicities, genders, religions, etc. But pluralism within a liberal market state has normative expectations about social aspirations and attitudes toward capitalism and GOVERNANCE. For example, when individuals climb within the corporate world it is seen as proof of racial and feminist emancipation. This is very different than welcoming a PLURIVERSE, which implies a recognition of multiple ways of being in the world. Pluralism is important so far as it goes, but it generally means that "diversity" must fundamentally accept the idea of a "One-World World," as anthropologist Arturo Escobar puts it.[34]

Misleading Binaries

When using binary, or polar, opposites, a person implies that each pole exhibits a very different logic from the other and that each is essentially incompatible. But the experience of commoning in a given situation dissolves or transcends many presumed binaries. For example, people who participate in a collaborative endeavor such as a blood donation system or an academic discipline may have the experience of being a NESTED-I, which transcends the polarity of the individual and collective. As we enter the world of the COMMONS, therefore, we begin to leave the world of "misleading binaries." Here are a few of them.

Collective/Individual. This binary is often used to suggest that the interest of an individual is positioned against the interests of a collective body. Such conflicts can exist, to be sure, and can be addressed in their contexts. Problems arise, however, when the idea of "I" is pitted against the "we" (or "I" is asserted in denial of "we"). The individual is considered utterly separate and distinct from others — for example, the "self-made man." This is an illusion because an individual can develop talents and identity only through his/her participation in a larger collective. And vice-versa: the collective can only come into being through individuals. In other words, the two are conjoined and interdependent, not polar opposites and separate. We try to underscore this idea through the idea of the NESTED-I and UBUNTU RATIONALITY.

Cooperation/Competition. These two terms are often posed as opposites. But evolutionary scientists and anthropologists note that they are often quite interrelated: species tend to have symbiotic relationships that entail both competition and cooperation, depending upon the circumstances. Even economists have noted such dynamics in various market settings as people and businesses simultaneously compete and cooperate. On assembly lines, workers routinely share their tools and help each other. It is therefore misleading to state or imply that "competition is bad, and cooperation is good." They both happen everywhere, all the time. The real question is whether the fruits of cooperation can accrue to the cooperators, or whether they will be primarily captured by investors and CORPORATIONS, as in the so-called sharing economy.

Consumer/Producer. Standard economics generally sees consumers and producers as a dyad relationship: a business produces, an individual consumes. But as commons and open networks empower people to self-provision (individually and collectively), the duality of these two functions is blurring. Some observers have tried to acknowledge this fact by talking about "prosumers" who blend production and consumption in one process. This coinage has its value, but it still places the discussion on an economic, materialistic plane — production and consumption of goods through resource extraction, modification, and distribution.

Objective/Subjective. In modern life, these two modes of perception and understanding are taken as opposites. The "objective" is seen as physical, verifiable, and measurable, whereas the "subjective" is given a lesser status as merely one person's feelings, mood, and intuition, and therefore less real and true. Objectivity points to hard, immutable facts that are "scientific" while subjectivity is seen as unreliable and transient. However, neurologists, behavioral scientists, and economists have shown that the separation between objective and subjective is largely a fiction because it assumes that rationality is only cognitive and conscious — and that subjectivity is by definition irrational. In reality, the objective and subjective are utterly integrated. Non-cognitive, embodied insights and feelings can also be quite reliable and true.

Rational/Irrational. A variant of the "objective" vs. "subjective" divide noted above. The "rational" is supposedly objective, while the "irrational" is merely personal and subjective. The presumption is that non-rational modes of understanding (i.e., qualitative, emotional, spiritual, intuitive) are not to be trusted. Indeed, the irrational has been associated with women and girls, and considered more appropriate to private spheres of life (family, personal relationships) whereas the rational is associated with public life (and men and boys). This elemental distinction is often the foundation for institutions that claim to be making rational decisions by ignoring non-scientific, non-quantifiable factors and feelings.

Public/Private. This familiar binary reflects the premise of modern industrial societies that government and markets are separate and somewhat oppositional. The government is supposedly the force for "public," collective purposes, and the market is supposedly a realm of "private" choice and freedom (even though free marketers deftly reposition "private choices" as the engine of public purpose, the so-called Invisible Hand). This framing is largely a fiction. Contemporary politics has demonstrated just how closely intertwined state power and capitalist markets truly are. Any disagreements between the public and private sectors pale in comparison to their strong mutual commitments to each other, their allegiance to a worldview based on market capitalism, and the market economy's structural dependence on public financing, civil infrastructure, regulatory oversight, and so on. Political debates that revolve around an opposition between "public" and "private" rely on a shallow, specious framing that fails to acknowledge commons and other noncapitalist forms of order.

Self-interest/Altruism. The presumption that a person's behavior is either self-interested or altruistic reflects another aspect of the deeply rooted idea that people are essentially "Isolated-I's" separate from larger social collectives. In a world of Isolated-I's, it is functional to a certain extent to make calculated, rational choices. But the binary of self-interest and altruism is specious when one considers that self-care is a prerequisite for care of others and vice-versa. Self-interest and altruism are in fact blended. Showing great concern for others is also a way to advance one's own interests; caring for one's self develops an identity that enables one to care for others. The binary of self-interest and altruism dissolves.

How Commoning Moves Beyond the Open/Closed Binary

When the internet opened up a new world of instantaneous information sharing, a familiar binary was quickly called into service — open versus closed. This framing tends to be reassuring because it simplifies the choices that one apparently faces. It is often invoked in debates about territorial borders and property rights — something must either be open (accessible) or closed (restricted). It's all very black-or-white. But in fact, open and closed are just two extreme ends of a rich spectrum of possible access rules that can be applied.

In digital spaces, open versus closed refers to the general legal status or practical accessibility of information and creative works. A work is "closed" if its owner has restricted access to it by invoking copyright law or using encryption or a paywall on a website. A closed work is generally proprietary because its owner has made it exclusive and artificially scarce — a prerequisite to selling it as a product in the market.

By contrast, an "open" work is one that anyone can freely access and use, such as open source software, writing, photos licensed under Creative Commons licenses, or works that copyright law defines as in the public domain (owned by no one). So-called open platforms are routinely used to let people share their work. Scientists often use open databases for sharing data, and professors sometimes use open textbooks to make instructional content freely available to students. To make academic research more widely available, more than 12,800 open access scholarly journals have arisen over the past ten years,[35] using Creative Commons licenses to make the work accessible at no cost in perpetuity.

The term "open" suggests a binary opposition of open set against "closed," which is generally taken to mean proprietary, private, or not freely shared. In subtle ways, this framing is problematic. When we talk about an "open" or "closed" database, for example, the focus is solely on the database, as if *it* embodied this characteristic. The framing doesn't allow us to talk about the interests of the people who generated the database in the first place. That community might wish to allow limited uses of the data to trusted colleagues, for example. Or perhaps it wants to share the database for some purposes but demand payment when outsiders use it.

When the conversation is about "open" versus "closed," unfortunately, these possibilities cannot even be raised. The only options are said to inhere in the work itself (the database), and those options are crudely binary. The whole open/closed framing renders the agency of the creative community invisible. The work is conceptually separated from the community that made it in the first place.

The language of open versus closed also ignores the social dynamics by which a community generates a work — the collaborative process, the logic for creating, the social role of money in production, etc. The framing makes these factors irrelevant — and therefore we cannot see a whole social ecosystem of creativity and sharing. We don't see the community of citizen-scientists who make a shared database or the writers contributing to a wiki or photo enthusiasts sharing their images online, all of whom may wish to control and manage access to their works, as commoners. Sharing in a commons can be situational, time-specific, and related to whom exactly commoners wish to share with. This is something that the open/closed framing cannot express. It offers no way to acknowledge peer governance through commoning or articulate intermediate ways of sharing works that go beyond absolutely open or closed.

In practice, there are many possible ways to deal with access and use rights. Creative Commons licenses — today used on more than 1.1 billion works, including this book[36] — represent an ingenious attempt to deal with this problem. They offer copyright holders simple and standardized options for giving permission in advance to share and use creative work. The licenses can allow others to create their own derivative works, such as translations or textbook summaries. The licenses can allow others to copy, distribute, display, and perform their work if the work is not used for commercial purposes, or if the work is not altered when re-used, or if the copied work is also made shareable to others.

In this manner, Creative Commons licenses allow for greater freedom than closed content. The problem with the Creative Commons approach, however, is that all these decisions are only made by individuals. This reflects the dominant worldview that we create things as separate individuals, all alone, as if in an isolated cell, without drawing from the commons or sharing larger interests. It also implies that we should express our individual interests through property claims. Despite being a legal hack around copyright law, the CC licenses implicitly accept these premises. Legally, there is no recognition that creativity emerges from an indivisible group — a commons — and that commoners ought to have the legal agency to make such choices as a group. This is precisely the complaint that so many Indigenous communities have with Western copyright and patent law, often imposed on them by international trade regimes. The law does not acknowledge that any content is always influenced, to greater or lesser degrees, by social collectives, both contemporary and from the past (RELATIONALIZED PROPERTY). The open/closed binary gives us only two choices — to give it away or retain private ownership (usually for the sake of making money).

Given this binary, it is not surprising that many people conflate "openness" with the commons, and conclude that its general, defining feature is that everything is free for the taking, at no cost. This is absolutely not true. The point of a commons is to maximize shared control and benefits, a goal that requires thoughtful rules for access and use. Openness can work only when the resource being used is nonrivalrous — i.e., it is not depleted when used and shared, such as digital information. (And even such resources need to be stewarded in order to be available at no cost.) But for rivalrous natural resources that can be used up, successful commons set limits on usage, restrict access at certain periods of time, or for certain people, etc.

The point of going beyond this binary opposition is to recognize the vital role that a group may play in generating value (shared code, information, creative works) and assert some measure of curation and control. The commons discourse lets us recognize the collective agency and ethos of a group.[37] Making this shift in perspective is important because, in a world defined by "open versus closed," the act of giving away your work is regarded as altruistic, foolish, or both. Only a sucker or idealist gives away a scientific discovery or beautifully written book that could be sold for money. In the economic and cultural context of capitalism, it becomes difficult even to imagine that a book could be freely shared *and* sold at the same time.[38]

But this is precisely what we need to understand — that it is possible! Certain complications must be addressed, however, among them money (as we explore in a section on financing commons, pp. 159–161). If access to a work is to be regulated by the market — "pay this price!" — then people who have money will automatically have greater access and control (even though knowledge, information, and code tend to become *more* valuable when shared). Commoners have learned to bypass this problem by choosing to SHARE KNOWLEDGE GENEROUSLY — and then developing other ways of paying for any associated costs (e.g., POOL, CAP & DIVIDE UP, in-kind support, selective market sales, cross-subsidies, etc.). Commoners embrace such strategies precisely because they benefit *both* the individual *and* the group over the long term (for instance, more readers and users). Getting beyond the open/closed binary opens us up to these possibilities.

But this orientation requires a new vocabulary, one that recognizes the collective agency and value-stewardship of commoning. We propose *Share & Steward*. This term overcomes the narrow focus on the work itself that the open/closed framing imposes. It also gets beyond the idea that making works shareable is a silly choice of giving things away, as if forfeiting their value. But commoning makes perfect sense: if a group has generated certain forms of value (open source software, wiki contributions, cosmo-local design networks, etc.), then of course it should be able to protect and enhance that value over time. *Share & Steward* helps us express the fact that commoning creates new value and affordances by making works more useful and accessible for everyone. The "open" or "closed" binary is blind to these possibilities.

Glossary of Commons-Friendly Terms

Beating the Bounds describes the process by which COMMONERS monitor the boundaries of their commons to protect against ENCLOSURE while celebrating their identity as a community. The term derives from an ancient English custom in which members of a community, old and young, walked the boundaries of their COMMONS to familiarize everyone with their land, and destroy any hedges or fences enclosing it. The perambulation was often followed by a feast.

Capping means setting an absolute limit to determine how much people can take from finite and depletable wealth such as land, timber, and water. Setting a cap alerts people that they may not take as much as they want, which helps avoid harm to the wealth of nature upon which a group depends. CAPPING was used in medieval English COMMONS (STINTS) as well as in contemporary global governance (the "cap-and-share" proposal as outlined in Sky Trust).[39]

Care is a disposition and empathetic engagement that manifests in how someone undertakes an activity, including economic ones. CARE also describes elemental human activities that signify an awareness of interdependency, neediness, and relatedness as basic human conditions [See NESTED-I and UBUNTU RATIONALITY]. It can be seen in raising children, nursing family members and friends, PEER GOVERNANCE and provisioning, stewarding nature, and working for the common good, among other activities. The term, which has a long history in feminist studies, recognizes the importance of decommodified work and intrinsic value, which are generally ignored or undervalued by market culture. Care is sometimes incorrectly conflated with "care jobs," which in market contexts emphasize productivity over genuine human care. In fact, care involves a generous spending of time whereas care jobs tend to apply a time-saving logic for economic reasons.

Care-Wealth. When people take care of forests, farmland, water, or urban spaces, these become part of their shared memory, culture, social lives, and identities. Thus when COMMONERS provision for themselves and interact with the world with their whole being, they are enacting a different cosmovision. They do not produce goods or commodities as rational individuals, in the manner that economists would describe. They become stewards of CARE-WEALTH — things, living systems, and relationships that are the focus of affection, care, shared experiences, and emotional attachments. The term *resource* invites us to regard shared wealth as something to be used, extracted, and turned into an element of an economic calculation. CARE-WEALTH consists of affective relations with one's everyday life and culture.

Collaborative Finance describes ways of financing COMMONS and providing structural support for COMMONING while shielding these activities from the harmful influences of money and debt. A primary goal is to decommodify relationships among people and with the non-human world. COLLABORATIVE FINANCE uses money and credit in such a way that commons institutions are strengthened and people feel secure and free as they become less dependent on markets. Important aspects of collaborative finance include MONEY-LITE COMMONING, PEER-TO-PEER credits, a GENTLE RECIPROCITY in the use of money, and new PUBLIC/COMMONS CIRCUITS OF FINANCE. Historically, COLLABORATIVE FINANCE has included such models as mutual credit societies and insurance pools, cooperative finance, community-controlled microfinance, and local currencies. [See CROWDFUNDING]

Commons – Commoning – Commoner. A brief excursion into the etymology of these terms: each word connects the Latin words *cum* and *munus*. *Cum* (English "with") denotes the joining of elements. *Munus* — which is also found in the word "municipality" — means service, duty, obligation, and sometimes gift. All terms that conjoin *cum* and *munus*, such as communion, community, communism, and, of course, communication, point to a co-obligation — a linkage between use rights, benefits, and duty. As Pierre Dardot and Christian Laval write, commons "not only designate what is pooled," but also the commoners themselves — "those who have 'duties in common.'"[40]

Commons are a pervasive, generative, and neglected social lifeform. They are COMPLEX, ADAPTIVE, LIVING PROCESSES that generate wealth (both tangible and intangible) through which people address their shared needs with minimal or no reliance on markets or states. A commons arises as people engage in the social practices of COMMONING, participate in PEER GOVERNANCE, and develop collaborative forms of PROVISIONING in the course of using a resource or care-wealth. While every commons is different, all ultimately depend on the physical gifts of nature, and on sharing, collaboration, mutual respect and GENTLE RECIPROCITY. A commons is constantly becoming.

> **Every Commons arises through Commoning, which has three symbiotic aspects: Everyday Social Habits, Peer Governance, and Provisioning. This is the Triad of Commoning.**

Commoner is an identity and social role that people acquire as they practice COMMONING. It is associated with actual deeds, not an assigned legal or social title. Anyone is potentially a commoner. The more that a person aligns with a COMMONS practice and worldview, the more they *become* a commoner.

Commoning is the exploratory process by which people devise and enact situation-specific systems of PROVISIONING and PEER GOVERNANCE as part of a larger process of unfolding our humanity. It occurs as ordinary people decide for themselves how to identify and meet shared needs, manage common wealth, and get along with each other. As people draw upon their SITUATED KNOWING in assessing their problems, they are empowered to show creative agency in developing solutions that seem fair and effective to them. They also learn to live with ambiguities and uncertainties, and to respect the mysteries of the human condition. COMMONING is the only way to become a COMMONER. The power of commoning is not limited to interpersonal relations in groups but extends to the organizing of larger society as well.

> **There is no Commons without Commoning and there is no Commoning without Peer Governance.**

Commons-Public Partnership (CPP). An agreement of long-term cooperation between commoners and state institutions to meet specific needs. Either may initiate a CPP, but commoners retain control over the process. State institutions provide vital legal, financial, and/ or administrative support to commoners, and commoners provide services to each other and the broader public. Examples include community-driven Wi-Fi systems, care such as nursing and eldercare, and neighborhood-managed projects implemented with government support. A CPP enables commoners to create convivial organizational structures that empower them to make their own decisions and bring about customized solutions.

Commonsverse describes the loosely connected world of different types of commons which can be seen as a federated Pluriverse of commons. Unlike capitalism (the economy) and liberal democracy (the political sphere), the Commonsverse integrates the economy with the political and social realms.

Communion is the process through which Commoners participate in interdependent relationships with the more-than-human world. Communion shifts a person's understanding of human/nature relations out of the economistic framework (e.g., "resource management," or the commodification and financialization of "nature's services") into one that respects the intrinsic value of the nonhuman world. This fundamental self-awareness leads to feelings of gratitude, respect, and reverence for the sacred dimensions of life in the ways that human Provisioning is organized.

Complex Adaptive Systems are self-organizing, self-healing, living systems such as the brain, cells, ant colonies, the biosphere, socio-ecological systems, and many commons. The term is used in complexity sciences, a heterodox scientific approach often used in evolutionary science, chemistry, biology, and physics. Insights from complexity sciences help move beyond a Newtonian worldview of cause and effect to one that is holistic, nonlinear, and interactive. The free interplay of agents following simple principles operating at the local level can — with no big-picture knowledge or end goals at the outset — self-organize in larger, more complex systems (or, as biologist Lynn Margulis put it, produce the mutual engendering of new living systems known as "symbiogenesis").[41]

Convivial Tools is a term inspired by Ivan Illich's *Tools for Conviviality* (1973). It refers to tools, technologies, and infrastructures that strengthen creativity and self-determination, such as everyday, general-purpose tools, the patterns for COMMONING we suggest in this book, or open source software-based tools such as OpenStreetMap.[42] Convivial tools are important because "we shape our tools and afterwards our tools shape us," as Marshall McLuhan reminds us.[43] A tool is convivial if people have access to the design and knowledge needed to create it; if it allows creative adaptation to one's own circumstances; and if it is appropriate in the specific local context. (Are suitable materials and skills available? Is it compatible with the local landscape and culture?) Convivial tools are fundamentally empowering because they help people discover and develop their own priorities, learning capacities, and skills. They emancipate us from proprietary closed tools that interfere with personal learning, sharing, modification, and re-use. However, the use of convivial tools can be impractical in some circumstances because of their time demands.

Cosmo-local Production is an internet-enabled provisioning system in which people share "light" knowledge and design via peer-to-peer learning and the internet, while building "heavy" physical things such as machinery, cars, housing, furniture, and electronics locally.[44] PRODUCING COSMO-LOCALLY lets one avoid the costs of proprietary design based on patents or trademarks. It also lets one reduce production costs through the use of less expensive locally sourceable materials and module designs that enable INTEROPERABILITY, which facilitates POOLING AND SHARING.

Crowdfunding is a practice of COLLABORATIVE FINANCING based on digital platforms. It refers to large numbers of people (the "crowd"), rather than just immediate group members, pooling small amounts of money to finance endeavors that will produce collective benefits. CROWDFUNDING does not necessarily help the COMMONS because some campaigns serve to provide free seed-capital for startup companies, with no shared equity or PEER GOVERNANCE. However, many CROWDFUNDING efforts, such as ones hosted by the Madrid-based Goteo platform, deliberately use this financing technique to advance COMMONING.

DIT means do-it-together. It is complementary to DIY, do-it-yourself, which in practice is often do-it-together. DIT helps name a form of DIY that is commons-based. Both seek to avoid relying on money and markets, and contribute to MONEY-LITE COMMONING.

Dividing Up, as distinct from SHARING, refers to the nonreciprocal allocation of objects — food, money, things, land, bicycles, tools — among members of groups (family, strangers, small groups, big networks) without calculating everyone's individual benefit in discrete units. DIVIDING UP sometimes happens in response to tacit or formal demands.

Emergence is the process by which the interaction among living agents unexpectedly produces entirely novel and more complex organization at larger scales. The new systemic properties are not contained within any individual element or aggregation of such elements, but emerge spontaneously without any obvious cause and effect. Countless local, individual interactions give rise to the complex structures of language and culture. So, too, the peer interactions of networked communities for open source software, scientific research, and COSMO-LOCAL PRODUCTION exhibit emergent behaviors.

Enclosure is the act of fencing land, forest, or pasture to convert shared wealth that commoners have depended upon for their needs into private property. Historically, enclosures were political initiatives by feudal lords and, later, by early capitalists and parliaments. Today enclosures are generally driven by investors and corporations, often in collusion with the nation-state, to privatize and commodify all sorts of shared wealth — land, water, digital information, creative works, genetic knowledge — dispossessing COMMONERS in the process. ENCLOSURES can be achieved through technical means such as digital rights management and paywalls; political means such as privatization, trade treaties, and financialization; and social means such as consumer culture, advertising, and the forced acculturation of people to Western capitalist culture. ENCLOSURE is the opposite of COMMONING in that it *separates* what commoning otherwise *connects*: people and land, you and me, present and future generations, technical infrastructures and their governance, rulers and the ruled, wilderness lands and the people who have stewarded them for generations. Enclosure is included here as a commons-friendly term (even though it is a hostile act!) because it enables us to name the private appropriation of shared wealth.

Enlivenment describes life and aliveness as fundamental categories for thinking about the world and world-making. This means that feelings, subjectivity, and meaning-making are empirical dimensions of living beings that science must reckon with as consequential forces in evolution. Enlivenment is a central idea in ecophilosophy (Andreas Weber), patterns philosophy (Christopher Alexander), and COMMONS. It is produced by UBUNTU RATIONALITY, CARE, and the use of CONVIVIAL TOOLS, among other activities.

Exonym refers to names or terms used by outsiders that mischaracterize phenomena that are experienced in very different ways by those on the inside. The discourse of economics, for example, typically uses terms that are ontologically incorrect in attempting to describe commoning. What economists regard as "resources" — fungible, utilitarian things — commoners regard as biowealth and care-wealth that have meaning for their community. Economic "rationality" presumes an ideal of humanity that commoners would not recognize. Political scientist and anthropologist James Scott first brought the term to our attention in his book *Against the Grain*.[45]

Faux commons is a term used to describe cooperative activities that resemble commoning but that are in fact hosted or governed by non-commoners such as businesses, state entities, or investment group. A prominent example is Facebook, a closed, proprietary network platform for sharing that exploits user data for private business purposes. Digital platforms like Airbnb and Uber purport to promote sharing, but in fact are transaction-based, capital-driven enterprises, not commons. Contractual partnerships that involve reciprocal benefits such as patent pools among drug makers are another instance of FAUX COMMONS. They are chiefly organized for specific market purposes, and not as long-term covenants among participants to share stewardship responsibilities and benefits over time. These distinctions matter because businesses enterprises are often eager to disguise their mercantile interests and claim democratic legitimacy by pretending to be about sharing, community, and the common good, i.e., to "commonswash."

Federation refers to a group of committed participants, teams, or organizations that elect to coordinate or collaborate with each other based on agreed upon objectives, ethical values, or shared history. Although the term *federation* is usually associated with nation-states or other state bodies coming together in some form — and therefore associated with the term *federal* — social collectives and organizations may also federate to pursue mutual protection, collaboration, and support. A FEDERATION is different from a network in that participants in a network may or may not share goals or deep commitments whereas participants in a FEDERATION are actively dedicated to a shared mission. Another difference: a (distributed) network is completely horizontal and a fully fledged P2P structure whereas a federation can be heterarchical. [See HETERARCHY]

Free/Libre and Open Source Software (FLOSS) is software with source code that is open to be SHARED *and* that has been licensed for anyone to use, copy, study, and change. These freedoms — authorized by a variety of licenses that reverse the normal workings of copyright law — encourage users to fix bugs and improve and develop the software. By contrast, proprietary software uses copyright law to prohibit users from seeing or modifying the source code and creates artificial SCARCITIES (access to code is restricted even though it can be shared for little or no cost). FLOSS increases the transparency of code, and as a result — as more people can scrutinize it — its security and stability. FLOSS also empowers people by enabling them to adapt code to their own purposes and to build more secure privacy protections into software. The GNU/Linux operating system, which powers millions of servers, desktops, and other devices, is perhaps the best-known FLOSS program.

Freedom-in-Connectedness is a notion of freedom that acknowledges that we are connected to nature, other people, communities, and institutions. It is how a human being unfolds, discovers their identity, and flourishes. It is a more realistic ideal than libertarian notions of freedom, which invariably focus on maximum individual choice and autonomy. In this sense, the idea of freedom as commonly used is an illusion because none of us can survive as Isolated-I's, let alone unfold our potential. The idea of the fully autonomous, self-made individual is actually ridiculous because no human being can survive without the psychological and social support of others. [See NESTED-I]

Generated Process is an exploratory, stepwise, and evolving process for generating an enlivening environment such as a COMMONS. It is a living, dynamic, adaptive process that is always becoming and incomplete. It stands in contrast to a fabrication process that builds something according to fixed, predetermined plans. A GENERATED PROCESS is the only way to bring about resilient structures and to deepen relationships because only living processes can beget living systems. Whatever has been generated creates a deeper resonance and feelings of wholeness and aliveness.[46] The collaborations that produced this book — not just between the co-authors but with their many colleagues and advisors — is an example of how something can be produced by a GENERATED PROCESS. Everyone involved, and the ideas themselves, grew and transformed over the course of *Free, Fair and Alive's* creation.

Gentle Reciprocity has a different character than strict reciprocity, in which trading partners try to calculate in precise terms who owes what to whom. In any tit-for-tat relationship, the goal is to achieve greater value than one spends, or at least a monetary equivalent. The reciprocity that exists in a COMMONS is generally a GENTLE RECIPROCITY in which people choose not to calculate in precise terms who owes whom a favor, time, money, or labor. In a commons, it is important to be neighborly, and not just behave as a "rational" market actor. Commons offer a hospitable context for turning GENTLE RECIPROCITY into a habit, which builds social trust and the capacity to work together in constructive ways.

Heterarchy is well-explained by the original Greek ετεραρχία: the term *heter* means "other, different," and *archy* means "rule." In a heterarchy, different types of rules and organizational structures are combined.

They may include, for example, top-down hierarchies and bottom-up participation (both of which are vertical), and peer-to-peer dynamics (which are horizontal). In a heterarchy, people can achieve socially mindful autonomy by combining *multiple types of governance* in the same system. For example, a hierarchy form may exist *within* a heterarchy. Heterarchies are not simply PEER-TO-PEER distributed ways of organizing, which are often hampered by a lack of structure. Nor is heterarchy the simple opposite of hierarchy. Rather, it is a hybrid that allows for greater openness, flexibility, democratic participation, and federation. When tasks are made modular, it becomes easier for heterarchical governance structures to flourish.

Interoperability means that different tools, computational systems, or technological products can interconnect and work seamlessly with each other, without needing a specific design to do so. INTEROPERABILITY by definition is enabled by specific data formats, protocols, and open standards. One example is ASCII (Abbreviated Standard Code for Information Interchange), a character-encoded standard for electronic communication. INTEROPERABILITY is key for processes to work well in a network environment, such as COSMO-LOCAL PRODUCTION. It is also critical in preventing one agent or market participant from securing a monopoly or controlling others through control of the design standards.

Intra-Action, a concept introduced by physicist and philosopher Karen Barad, describes how individual entities come together to create a new "entangled agency" that does not otherwise exist in preexisting individual agents. Think of crowd behavior and viral cultural phenomena. When two entities INTRA-ACT, their ability to act emerges *from within* the relationship itself, not as a function of the discrete individuals involved. The entangled agency constantly changes and adapts with the relationship itself. This concept helps us get beyond simplistic cause and effect explanations and suggests that responsibility for actions is spread among intra-acting entities, each of which may have different levels of intentionality and delayed manifestations. From the perspective of INTRA-ACTION, familiar ideas such as subject/object dualism, linear time, and individual agency are incomplete and misleading ways of understanding how events happen in the world. [See EMERGENCE]

Market/State. Although markets and states are often cast as adversaries — the public sector vs. the private sector — in fact they share many deep commitments and are highly interdependent. It makes sense to speak of them as partners in a shared vision. Both see market activity, economic growth, individualism, and technological innovation as the drivers of human progress. Each depends on the other in specific ways, too. Capital-driven markets look to the state for subsidies, legal privileges, research support, and mitigation of market externalities such as pollution and social inequality. And states, for their part, look to markets as sources of tax revenue, jobs, and geo-political influence.

Money-Lite Commoning is a style of COMMONING that seeks to reduce the need for money and markets. Commoning enables decommodified solutions to problems and therefore can avoid relying on markets and spending, both of which require that someone acquire more money. COMMONING itself is MONEY-LITE in that COMMONERS by definition rely on DIT, CO-USE, SHARING, DIVIDING UP, and MUTUALIZATION as much as possible. The point of money-lite commoning is to help people focus on their real needs, and to escape the endless cycle of buying and disempowerment that a consumerist culture generally entails.

Mutualizing means to contribute and belong to a group enterprise with a larger, enduring social purpose; this association in turn entitles participants to specific individual benefits. However, members do not necessarily receive equal value or the same benefits in return for what they give, as in a market transaction. They typically receive some stipulated benefit based on need or other criteria. The benefits of MUTUALIZATION are socially agreed upon, often based on differential shares and predetermined formulas. An insurance pool and social security fund are classic examples. However MUTUALIZATION is structured, it is critical that everyone with a stake in the MUTUALIZED pool have a say in the agreement. It is a peer-determined reciprocity, a specific form of practicing GENTLE RECIPROCITY.

Nested-I describes the existential interdependency of human beings on other humans and the larger world, which co-creates and supports our personal development. To use the term NESTED-I rather than "individual" is to recognize that one's identity, talents, and aspirations are ultimately rooted in relationships. With this self-awareness, the person who recognizes himself or herself as a NESTED-I realizes that self-interests and larger collective interests are not opposed to each other (INDIVIDUAL/COLLECTIVE), but can be aligned. The NESTED-I stands in contrast to the human ideal celebrated in modern, secular societies that everyone's life is defined by their individual achievements and pursuits, free from the associations of their communities, history, ethnicity, race, religion, sex, and so on. The "Isolated-I" is perfectly depicted by *Homo economicus*, the model of a human being used by economists: a person who is self-interested, rational, utility-maximizing, and absolutely autonomous. [See FREEDOM-IN-CONNECTEDNESS and UBUNTU RATIONALITY]

Non-Discriminatory Infrastructures are systems that foster mobility, communication, exchange, and energy flow in general ways open to all. The owner or steward of the infrastructure does not restrict access and use of the infrastructure based on specific criteria such as ethnicity, gender, social standing, nor charge one class of users more than another.

Ontology as a philosophical term is the study of a person's fundamental presuppositions about the nature of reality and how it is structured. ONTOLOGY is the "constitutional framework" of a person's belief-system — the window through which one sees the world, our way of seeing and registering reality. Is the world divided into humanity and nature, individuals and collectives? Is the world a static place or is it in a constant state of becoming? We perceive and describe the world, and often act, based on our assumptions about reality. Participants in modern politics typically pursue a different cosmovision than, for example, an Indigenous culture, which sees nature, humans, and past and future generations as an integrated whole. As this suggests, the OntoStories one believes, have far-reaching implications for the sorts of social, economic, and political order that seem plausible and attractive.

OntoShift refers to a shift in a person's fundamental presuppositions and perspectives about the nature of reality and how it is structured.

People's ontological viewpoints are reflected in their perceptions of how people and objects exist in the world, and, as a result, what general types of culture, political economy, and coordination structures they see as possible and desirable.

OntoStory is a shorthand term for an ontological narrative. [See ONTOLOGY]

Patterns are a way of understanding the nature of order in the world. They help us identify structural regularities and relationships among different types of phenomena (such as COMMONING) without relying on rigid abstractions or over-specified principles that tend to ignore context and history. A PATTERN of human interactions distills the essence of many successful solutions, as demonstrated by practitioners over time (such as COMMONERS), to problems that occur over and over again in similar contexts. Every COMMONS, for example, has the challenge of building trust, making decisions that reflect everybody's feelings, and using money in socially healthy ways, without its pernicious effects. PATTERNS are open and always interconnected; no PATTERN is complete unto itself. [See VOCABULARY]

Peers are people who have equal social and political power relative to other members of a group or network. PEERS have different talents and personalities, but they see each other as having the same rights and capabilities to contribute to a collaborative project and to decide how it shall proceed. [See NESTED-I, UBUNTU RATIONALITY]

Peer Governance is that part of COMMONING by which people make decisions, set boundaries, enforce rules, and deal with conflicts — both within COMMONS and among different commons. In a peer-governed world, individuals see each other as PEERS with the equal potential to participate in a collective process, not as adversaries competing to seize control of a central apparatus of power. Building on Elinor Ostrom's design principles, PEER GOVERNANCE is a central concept because there is no COMMONING and no COMMONSVERSE without PEER GOVERNANCE, which is distinct from governing *for* the people and from governing *with* the people (PARTICIPATION). It is governing *through* the people.

P2P (Peer-to-Peer) Networks are a powerful form of organization in which participants contribute to the production of Commons in nonhierarchical ways. The internet and digital technologies have given rise to significant P2P networks devoted to free and open source software, various wikis including Wikipedia, collaborative content creation websites and archives, and global design and production communities. As distributed networks that allow any node to connect directly with any other node, P2P networks unleash forms of collaborative creativity that are simply not possible in centralized networks, in which all nodes pass through a single hub, or decentralized networks, in which all nodes still pass through hubs of some sort.

Pluriverse names an understanding of the world in which countless groups of people create and re-create their own distinctive cultural realities, each of which constitutes a world. This term is necessary because many contemporary crises stem from the belief that there is a *One-World World*, a kind of single Euro-modern reality. To say that the world is a PLURIVERSE is to say that there is no single source of being (that is, to invoke a plural ontology) and that no knowledge system is inherently superior to others. A PLURIVERSE is "a world in which many worlds fit," as the Zapatistas say. This points to a conundrum: how can the different societies that constitute the human species accept that many worlds must coexist together on a single planet?

Pooling refers to a form of contributing to a common fund or provisions of any kind. The contributions are gathered together for agreed-upon purposes in sufficient quantities, and then allocated in agreed-upon ways for certain purposes.

Price Sovereignty means the capacity to reject the terms that markets offer, including prices. By achieving a certain independence from markets, COMMONERS acquire PRICE SOVEREIGNTY by transparently and collaboratively self-determining the terms of exchange among all interacting partners involved. As a result, they can choose to meet people's needs for free or at lower prices than charged on the market. This is a much-overlooked strategic power that gives people significant autonomy from market pressures and state coercion. Because commoners are *withdrawing* from markets and not seeking to dominate them, PRICE SOVEREIGNTY in this sense does not mean anticompetitive behavior prohibited by antitrust law.

Provisioning. Meeting people's needs through a COMMONS is called *provisioning*. The term is an alternative to the word "production," which is inextricably associated with the neglect of the nonmarket spheres of family, community, and Care, and a focus on market prices, efficiency, the externalization of costs, and so on. The purpose of PROVISIONING is to meet people's needs, whereas the purpose of production (whether capitalist or socialist) is to generate profits for those producing the goods and services, and by producing them. Provisioning through commons occurs everywhere, but they generate shared wealth using different ways of allocating and distributing it. A basic goal of provisioning is to reintegrate economic behaviors with the rest of one's life, including social well-being, ecological relationships, and ethical concerns.

Public/Commons Circuits of Finance is a strategy of COLLABORATIVE FINANCING that allows taxpayer funds administered by government to be used to support COMMONS — or even privilege commons-first strategies. However, unlike state subsidies to corporations, which primarily aim to spur economic growth and direct benefits to shareholders, PUBLIC/COMMONS FINANCING seeks to expand COMMONING and commons-based infrastructures. The goal is to help people re-order their lives so they can become more self-sustaining and less dependent on the MARKET/STATE and its imperatives.

Relational Ontology holds that the relations between entities are more fundamental than the entities themselves. It means that living systems develop and thrive through their interactions and INTRA-ACTIONS with each other. As a social system based on how people come together to collaborate and sustain themselves, a COMMONS is based on a RELATIONAL ONTOLOGY. This perspective stands in contrast to the vision of reality that undergirds market capitalism, which sees the world as based on isolated, self-made individuals with no primary relationships of history, religion, ethnicity, geography, gender, and so forth. Conceiving the nature of reality through relational ontology requires different relational categories such as NESTED-I and UBUNTU RATIONALITY.

Relationalized Property is about "other ways of having" that are aligned with COMMONING and go beyond the exclusion, extraction, and marketization associated with conventional property ownership. A society built around property ownership tends to produce haves and have-nots and abusive concentrations of capital and power. RELATIONALIZED PROPERTY is a novel class of socio-legal governance and provisioning that partially or completely neutralizes exclusive ownership rights over things regarded as property. People decide to adopt a RELATIONALIZED PROPERTY regime and manage shared wealth through PEER GOVERNANCE; the regime is not imposed on them. It enables forms of interrelated possession of property that is life-enhancing and strengthens relationships — with each other, the nonhuman world, past and future generations, and the common good.

Semi-Permeable Membranes are what the boundaries of a COMMONS should be. Like other living social organisms, COMMONS need to protect themselves from external forces that might harm them while remaining open to flows of nourishment and signals from the environment. Therefore, a commons functions best if it develops a SEMI-PERMEABLE MEMBRANE for itself rather than a tight, rigid boundary. This flexible skin, figuratively speaking, both assures its integrity by preventing ENCLOSURE and other harms while allowing it to develop nourishing, symbiotic relationships with other living organisms.

Sharing is a general, nonspecific term that points to forms of allocation that are nonreciprocal. Based on what is being shared, we differentiate it as SHARING, DIVIDING UP, and CO-USING. All of these forms are usually preceded by POOLING.

• SHARING is the voluntary, nonreciprocal transfer of knowledge, information, ideas, code, design, and other intangibles that are inexpensively copied. Free and open source software communities are classic practitioners of sharing.

- DIVIDING UP is the allocation of finite, depletable resources. It differs from SHARING because sharing generally increases the use-value of what is being shared; that effect does not apply for DIVIDING UP. (SHARING must also be distinguished from the "sharing economy," which is not really about sharing but about microrental markets.)
- Co-USING is a social arrangement for access and use of a shared resource or CARE-WEALTH.

Situated Knowing refers to the intuitive, embodied expertise and practical know-how that derives from living and working within a particular domain. When people grow up in a given environment from childhood, they are immersed in certain rhythms and techniques. They learn subtle cues about plants, wood, craft materials, game, the weather, and other elements of the local landscape. They develop a deep familiarity with their circumstances that cannot be obtained through book learning.

Stint is an access rule to prevent something from being overused or abused. In subsistence cultures, there are often highly specific rules for how and when a person may harvest wood from the forest or rushes from a wetland. A "STINTED COMMONS" is therefore one that is managed to protect the renewable capacities of a natural system. "Without STINTS there is no true COMMONS," writes commons scholar Lewis Hyde.[47] [See CAPPING]

Ubuntu Rationality describes a logic of human interaction that recognizes the deep connections between a person's interests and the well-being of others. It points to a dynamic where a person's unfolding requires the unfolding of others, and vice-versa. The term is a counterpoint to the conventional idea of economic rationality, which is defined as self-interested, calculative, acquisitive behavior which tends to be at the expense of others. When people can see themselves as NESTED-I's embedded in a PLURIVERSAL set of relationships, they begin to exhibit UBUNTU RATIONALITY. Ubuntu is a term in various Bantu languages in South Africa that denotes the deep interdependence of "me" and "other."

Value Sovereignty. Although most COMMONS exist within the MARKET/STATE system, making them vulnerable to ENCLOSURE, a COMMONS generally strives to protect its moral and cultural identity and to control the value it generates. In short, it seeks to secure its own VALUE SOVEREIGNTY.

Vernacular Law is a form of law that originates in informal, unofficial zones of society as an instrument of moral authority and social order. While VERNACULAR LAW may or may not be morally good in itself, it stands in contrast to State Law, which reflects the particular concerns of state power and jurisprudence. Custom functions as VERNACULAR LAW by expressing the practical judgments, ethical wisdom, and SITUATED KNOWLEDGE of people rooted in a particular place or circumstances.

Part II:

The Triad of Commoning

Introduction

O VER THE YEARS, there have been a number of attempts to conceptualize commons with greater clarity. But no one has yet imagined a framework that *at once* speaks to the mundane realities of self-organization, the inner transformations that commoning catalyzes, and how these might transform the political economy over time. That is the challenge that we take up in the next three chapters by offering a comprehensive framework for commons and commoning. We hope to get beyond the growing confusion and faux-populism associated with these terms, and provide a more rigorous conceptualization. If the notion of *commons* is used as a buzzword for everything in the world we would like to see shared, it loses its transformative power.

Frameworks are gateways. They subtly but deeply influence the ways that we perceive the world. They usher us into a specific interpretation of the world, much as opening a door takes us into one room and leaves others unexplored. Frameworks structure worldviews. They provide an analytical scaffold and a language for making sense of what we can observe. For these reasons, we provide in Chapters 4, 5, and 6 a scaffold and language for looking at the world of commons and commoning.

Our framework builds on the insights about the role of subjectivity, relationality, and language described in Part I of this book. Our *Triad of Commoning: Social Life, Peer Governance, and Provisioning* is based on the premise that commoning is primarily about creating and maintaining *relationships* — among people in small and big communities and networks, between humans and the nonhuman world, and between us and past and future generations. This *relational* understanding of the world will necessarily bring about new ways of thinking about *value*. It also helps us escape from standard economic and policy frameworks, and from overly economistic, resource-based understandings of the commons, both of which fail to express its social dynamics.

Two years before writing these lines, when we began to think about this book, we didn't aspire to propose a new framework. However, as we progressed, we felt increasingly uncomfortable with the ontological premises and languages used by most of the commons literature. They often did not come to terms with many of the things we had observed in the contemporary commons world. After a year of wrestling with this unease, we decided to start from scratch. In March 2017, we began to reflect more deeply and imagine a framework — one step at a time, slowly, iteratively — that could blend theory and practice. It was as if we were changing the point of departure for a journey. To explore the outskirts of Paris, for example, we could depart from either of the city's two most important train stations — Gare du Nord or Gare de l'Est, each only a stone's throw away from the other. Choosing Gare du Nord would take us towards Lille in northern France, or to St. Quentin in the Hauts-de-France region. But were we to instead enter Gare de l'Est, just five hundred steps away, a whole new set of destinations would be possible: Mulhouse in Alsace or Stuttgart in Germany, along with dozens of others. The distance between the gates is trivial, but the actual point of departure makes a huge difference in what kinds of worlds we can travel to. So it is with the frameworks we choose to interpret the world. The more a framing structure is true to our humanity and aligned with our aspirations and circumstances, the more likely that it will take us to destinations that are right for us.

Our framework aspires to articulate the deep correspondences among the bewildering diversity of the commons. Despite vivid differences among commons focused on natural resources, digital systems, and social mutuality, they all share structural and social similarities. Their affinities have just never been adequately identified and set forth in a coherent framework. Our idea was to make visible that which connects commons experiences in medieval times and today, in digital and analogue spheres, in cities and the countryside, in communities dedicated to water and to software code. Unraveling the tangled "genetic history" of commons to identify these connections can help explain why the commons is as old as mankind and as modern as the internet.

The structural commonalities that we identify are based on the recurring elements and relationships that we call patterns. Patterns help us see the common core of diverse world-making commons without ignoring their differences. A patterns approach recognizes that each commons develops and evolves in a different context, in different spaces and times. Each is shaped by different people, in different societies and environments. It is thus entirely logical that every commons will enact patterns according to its singular context. To fairly allocate water in the Swiss Alps in the sixteenth century requires a different set of rules than to fairly share bandwidth in the twenty-first. To govern a commons within a modern capitalist society is a different challenge than doing so within an Indigenous culture. What matters in each instance is for participants to produce a fair share for all.

When you have a closer look at how things are done in diverse commons, you begin to discover a world ordered by patterns. Using a patterns-based approach, we can grasp the idea that commons are enacted in myriad ways, without being merely arbitrary or accidental, and without ever being implemented exactly the same way twice. We can identify recurrent features of commons that are often not explicitly named. John C. Thomas has written that patterns "are one way to capture what is invariant while leaving the flexibility to deal with the specifics of geography, culture, language, goals, and technologies."[1] In this respect, patterns resemble DNA, a set of instructions that are underspecified so that they can be adapted to local circumstances. "Does the DNA contain a full description of the organism to which it will give rise?" asks Christopher Alexander in his book *The Nature of Order*. "The answer is no. The genome contains instead a program of instructions for making the organism — a generative program — in which cytoplasmic constituents of eggs and cells are essential players along with the genes like the DNA coding for the sequence of amino acids in a protein."[2]

Principles and Patterns

In describing the critical dimensions of a commons, what is the difference between a *principle* and a *pattern*? And why do we prefer to speak about patterns rather than principles of commoning? When patterns are expressed in a succinct form — as in "Ritualize Togetherness" and "Practice Gentle Reciprocity" — the phrase sounds like a principle. But patterns and principles are not the same. Each points to a different way of understanding the world and bringing about social change.

A principle points to an ethical or philosophical ideal that everyone should follow. It implies a universal, invariant truth. "Thou shalt not kill" and "the separation of church and state" are two familiar examples. Principles bring to mind scientific *axioms*, a term that comes from the Greek word *axíōma* which means "that which is thought worthy or fit" and "that which commends itself as evident."[3] Axioms are considered so self-evident that they don't need to be justified or explained. The same idea applies to principles, whose adherents regard their general claims about moral or political truth as beyond argument.

A pattern, by contrast, describes a kernel idea for solving problems that show up again and again in different contexts. The pattern will be the same, but *concrete solutions* will be different. For example, managing a cooperative in a German city will face similar problems as a co-op in an American city, but each will require approaches that take account of different legal, economic, and cultural realities. The idea of using patterns derives from the pioneering work of Christopher Alexander and colleagues in the 1970s in the field of architecture (see Chapter 1). A pattern isn't an ethical or philosophical ideal, but a concept that distills the essence of a variety of successful solutions that people implement because they work well and are life-enhancing.

Principles tend to make universal claims. This is problematic because it is virtually impossible to find the same institutional structures, cultural beliefs, and social norms in different places and contexts. By contrast, universal patterns of human interaction already exist. Take marriage: as a pattern it describes a universal social practice with countless variations in which people declare their commitment to each other (or have it declared for them).[4] A pattern does not over-specify the details of marriage, such as the sex of the people involved or the conditions under which it occurs. It is a kernel idea for working solutions derived from observing real-world situations. In this sense, patterns describe, they don't prescribe. They start with the need to deal with *tensions* that cause problems. And tensions are omnipresent in our lives. A formal pattern description frankly recognizes the positive and negative forces that affect a given situation and does not assume that these *forces* can be resolved by invoking principles.[5] The discourse of principles is less concerned with addressing these messy, complicated forces than in asserting a golden, inviolate ideal. In addition, a principle is usually presented as a standalone truth that need not take account of other principles with which it may conflict. For example, invoking freedom of expression does not address the tensions of that principle with the principle of respect for privacy and the dignity of others.

By contrast, patterns amount to design tools that help us address our practical challenges while speaking to our inner ethical, aesthetic, and spiritual needs. Patterns serve as a vessel for helping aliveness blossom. They are not a configuration of rules and metrics for how things can be controlled and regularized, nor abstract statements of principle with moral or normative meanings like "solidarity" or "sustainability." This is not to say that there is no underlying ethics; it's just that patterns recognize that ethical aspirations must take account of situational realities. This helps explain why no pattern is complete unto itself and necessarily relates to others.[6]

Our framework naturally draws on the robust scholarly literature exploring the commons — a body of work that has proliferated since Professor Elinor Ostrom won the Nobel Prize in Economic Science in 2009 for her pioneering studies of collective resource management. The International Association for the Study of the Commons (IASC) and its journal[7] continue this valuable work. Ostrom's famous eight design principles for enduring commons institutions — set forth in her 1990 book *Governing the Commons* and developed over the past generation with hundreds of colleagues — represent a major beachhead of understanding. But these principles do not say much about the inner life of commons or the complexities of what it means "to common." (They do speak strongly to issues of governance, which we take up in Chapter 5.)

Our Triad framework points to the idea that commoners are engaged in "world-making in a pluriverse" because that phrase captures the core purpose of commoning: the creation of peer-governed, context-specific systems for free, fair, and sustainable lives. At the heart of the Framework is what we call The Triad — the three interconnected spheres of Social Life, Peer Governance, and Provisioning. Or, in more conventional terms: the social, the institutional, and the economic spheres. We find it useful to structure our thinking around these realms, which doesn't mean that they are separate and distinct. Each sphere of the Triad simply provides a different perspective for looking at the same phenomena. Each is deeply interconnected with the others, as the accompanying image suggests.

Triad of Commoning

Cultivate Shared Purpose & Values
Ritualize Togetherness
Make & Use Together
Contribute Freely
Support Care &
Decommodified Work
Practice Gentle Reciprocity
Share the Risks of
Trust Situated Knowing
Provisioning
SOCIAL LIFE
Deepen Communion with
Nature
Contribute & Share
Pool, Cap & Divide Up
Preserve Relationships in
Addressing Conflicts
Pool, Cap & Mutualize
PROVISIONING
Reflect on Your Peer
Trade with Price
Governance
Sovereignty
Use Convivial Tools
Rely on Distributed
PEER
Bring Diversity into Shared
Purpose
Structures
GOVERNANCE
Create Semi-Permeable
Creatively Adapt & Renew
Membranes
Honor Transparency in a Sphere of Trust
Share Knowledge Generously
Assure Consent in Decisionmaking
Rely on Heterarchy
Peer Monitor & Apply Graduated Sanctions
Relationalize Property
Keep Commons & Commerce Distinct
Finance Commons Provisioning

It is reasonable to ask, how we can possibly generalize about the commons, knowing that there is no such thing as cultural universals? Is a coherent, general understanding of the phenomenon really possible? We believe it is — *if* such an understanding acknowledges the immensely varied on-the-ground realities and distills their essential regularities! That's what patterns do. They avoid the trap of reductionism, don't oversimplify messy realities, and help to avoid a totalizing way of understanding the world. Patterns provide a way to generate insights while relying on situated knowing — people's experiences, know-how, and intuition. And, most importantly, they help us create an *open* framework that is adaptable by design, and certainly not the last word. We therefore offer a flexible template, not a blueprint, and a commons vocabulary, not a classical, prescriptive taxonomy.

A Word on Methodology

By learning to see through a patterns lens, we began a process of what is called "pattern mining." It was fairly straight-forward. We asked: What problems show up in the commons again and again? Decision making? Money? Concerns for overexploitation of resources? And so on. There is an endless list of problems to be addressed if the commons narrative is going to be true to life.

We then looked for successful solutions that actual commons have implemented. We looked everywhere — in all realms of life, in the academic literature, and in working projects. We reflected on our own commoning experiences and we conducted many long interviews with commoners around the world while documenting their activities and answers. We looked at the solutions people had devised. Do they really work? Do they work but only in the short term? And do they resist the seductions and ruthless appropriations of capitalism? We compared what approaches people really applied with tentative theoretical insights or claims about the commons. Then we dared to coin abstractions — the patterns — that constitute our framework. We tested each one out with fellow commoners and scholars. We asked them if our insights resonated with their research and experiences, which then led to a long series of corrections, deletions, and adaptations.

The result is our Triad framework, which organizes and distills the patterns we identified. Together, they constitute the beginning of a commons language — a commons pattern language, as some would call it. We do not presume that our framework wholly captures the commons, which is, ultimately experiential — a phenomenon of life beyond representation. It is more like a map that provides structure, terminologies, and pathways for making sense of the topic. We certainly don't want our map to be confused with the territory. It's just a map. And like any map, ours is inflected with our own parochial biases. If we think of the world as a pluriverse — a fractal federation of countless unique and yet connected worlds — then we must emphasize that our framework unavoidably reflects some of our own cultural perspectives despite our best attempts to take a cosmopolitan perspective.

4

The Social Life of Commoning

THE BRITISH SOCIOLOGIST RAYMOND WILLIAMS ONCE WROTE, "Culture is ordinary." We could say much the same about commoning. It is terribly ordinary. Commoning is what common people decide for themselves in their specific circumstances if they want to get along with each other *and* produce as much wealth for everyone as possible. If commoning can be considered a way of life or a type of culture, then it provides what any culture must — "meaning both in a formal and in a deeply existential sense," as art sociologist Pascal Gielen writes.[1] Modern societies have largely forgotten about commoning. Therefore, showcasing its elemental dailyness opens the door for seeing how the commons can provide a platform for effective alternatives to capitalism.

We start our explorations with the Social Life of commoning because its motifs constitute the core of any commons while also manifesting in the two other spheres, Provisioning and Peer Governance. Over the course of more than fifteen years, we have visited dozens of commons, talked with hundreds of people, and read about scores of commons in the scholarly literature. We have come to see that commoning is not like an on/off switch, something that exists or it doesn't. It is more a matter of intensity like a dimmer switch on a light; the intensity of various patterns of commoning may be weak or strong, according to what people really do, but its degree of illumination and continuity lead us to the threshold of conscious self-organization. This means that we have the capacity to affect the process — to intensify commoning — at any given moment.

People may or may not be self-aware about these patterns of Social Life. In Indigenous cultures, tradition and habit can make commoning seem utterly normal, rendering it invisible. In Western industrialized societies, commoning is invisible as well, but for a different reason: it has been culturally marginalized. That is why we have embarked upon our "archeological excavations" of commons around the world — to bring the little-discussed realities of commoning into the bright light of day.

It is important that people experiment with these patterns so that they can understand commoning better and develop new ways of living, provisioning, and governing themselves. The capacity to make change lies right before us, and is at once cultural, organizational, generative, and political, if we keep in mind the three spheres of the Triad. It can transform our economy and our political systems, our institutions and ourselves. As J.K. Gibson-Graham have written, "If to change ourselves is to change our worlds, and the relation is reciprocal, then the project of history making is never a distant one but always right here, on the borders of our sensing, thinking, feeling, moving bodies."[2] Politics ultimately originates in our subjectivity, say Gibson-Graham, and in "the sensational and gravitational experience of embodiment."

Pascal Gielen refers to culture as "a stealth laboratory for new forms of life, an omnipresent incubator, hardly noticed precisely because it is everywhere."[3] The commons is such a laboratory. In modern times, market capitalism and its categories of thought have more or less mandated how we will behave, invest, organize institutions, and so forth, by presuming that human beings are basically selfish, materialistic, utility-maximizing individuals. No wonder commoning, with its different insights about human beings, is so often seen as strange. It has been eclipsed by the shiny cultural mindscape of modernity.

And yet, the way commoning catalyzes change is clear: the more you align yourself with a commons worldview and the more you practice commoning, the more you learn how to *become* a commoner. This, in turn, has sweeping ramifications for economics, politics, and culture. The patterns that comprise the Social Life of Commoning are specific forms of cooperation, sharing, and ways that people relate to each other. One could say that a commons arises when the patterns of Social Life reach a sufficient density of practice, threshold of self-organization, and continuity to express themselves as a coherent social institution.

The Social Life of Commoning

Cultivate Shared Purpose and Values
Ritualize Togetherness
Contribute Freely
Practice Gentle Reciprocity
Trust Situated Knowing
Deepen Communion with Nature
Preserve Relationships in Addressing Conflicts
Reflect on Your Peer Governance

Cultivate Shared Purpose and Values

Shared purpose and values are the lifeblood of any commons. Without them, a commons loses its coherence and vitality. But shared purpose and values can only arise when people contribute from their own passion and commitment, connect with each other, and share certain experiences. A commons does not necessarily *start* with shared purpose and values. These outcomes must be *earned* by commoners over time as they struggle to bring their diverse perspectives into greater alignment. This is important because the sense of shared purpose in a commons can't be formally imposed or declared. It must arise organically through meaningful commoning over time. A rooted culture cannot be built overnight.

Cultivate Shared Purpose and Values.

Just declaring shared purpose and values is like planting a tree and not watering it. Shared purpose and values need to be *cultivated* through collective reflection, traditions, celebrations, and participation in all kinds of activities. All this can help strengthen mutual commitments. To be sure, the formal design of organizations and infrastructures can help, but there is no substitute for commoning to align and deepen people's concerns and values. This takes time.

At Next Barn Over — the CSA farm described in Chapter 1 — the commitment to fresh, organic local food is cultivated by hosting family dinners, inviting people to volunteer, suggesting recipes using seasonal vegetables, and reaching out to help needy neighborhoods. The best way to bring people together is to be authentic. Ideally, everyone should be able to contribute something they really enjoy doing. The most helpful question is not, what do we need? It is, what do we have? What is possible with what is available here and now? This is reflected in the poems that Next Barn Over occasionally sends to members, which included this one by Wendell Berry:

> **What We Need is Here**
> *Geese appear high over us,*
> *pass, and the sky closes. Abandon,*
> *as in love or sleep, holds*
> *them to their way, clear*
> *in the ancient faith: what we need*
> *is here. And we pray, not*
> *for new earth or heaven, but to be*
> *quiet in heart, and in eye,*
> *clear. What we need is here.*

Ritualize Togetherness

One of the most important ways to strengthen shared purpose and values is by ritualizing togetherness — meeting regularly, sharing deeply, cooking together, celebrating successes, candidly assessing failures. This is essential to building a culture of commoning and a shared identity.

The rituals of togetherness can be as simple as regular meetings or as complicated as the specialized practices of an agroecology commons.

Ritualize Togetherness.

A fair amount of community fun and frolic is also required. The many farmers of Mexico, New Mexico, and Colorado who participate in *acequia* irrigation commons have learned over centuries to ritualize togetherness. Everyone is, of course, concerned about his or her own allotment of water, but everyone also works together to maintain the water ditches and track the ecological limits of water usage. Software hackers are renowned for their creative rituals such as hackathons to figure out how to solve software problems and invent jargon that is understood only by them. The Quechua overseeing the Potato Park in Peru are bound together through their spiritual values and practices, much as the religious practices of Indonesian *subak* rice farmers help them coordinate when to plant seeds and irrigate their fields without depleting finite waters.

Rituals tend to work best when they are woven into ordinary daily life, and are not treated as something separate and unusual. At Enspiral, a networked guild of several hundred participants, participants ritualize their group life through regular, in-person retreats. In many countries such as Greece, Italy, France, and Finland, regional festivals are a way that people have celebrated the ethic and accomplishments of commoning. What better way to RITUALIZE TOGETHERNESS than a party or festival, especially among strangers? Indeed, some commoners make a party out of everything. At the many open workshops of Konglomerat, in Dresden, Germany, when it's time to clean shared rooms, workshops, machinery, and toilets, members put a "Putzival" on the group's agenda. The term sounds cute, clean, and fun at once, because "putzig" (the adjective) means "cute" and "putzen" (the verb) means "to clean," making it kind of a cute Cleanup Festival. People get the music on and have fun getting rid of dust and dirt.

Contribute Freely

Contribute freely means giving without expecting to receive anything of equivalent value, at least not here and now. It also means that when people do receive something, it is without feeling the need to reciprocate in direct ways. Wherever we contribute freely, the use of *quid pro quos* is minimized and the potential for sharing and dividing up is enhanced. Such acts occur when community gardeners break ground in the spring, or when people submit editorial content to Wikipedia with no expectation of return or even formal credit. They just do it, for a variety of reasons — to learn a skill, join a community, earn respect, build job credentials, or simply to be part of something. By contributing freely, people also get back something they really enjoy, like the flowers from a community garden or the food grown there. People contribute freely when they give money to crowdfunding campaigns, volunteer their physical labor to maintain hiking trails, or organize neighborhood events. The giving is its own reward.

It is important not to make overly broad claims about how to contribute freely in a commons because so much is situational. As long as

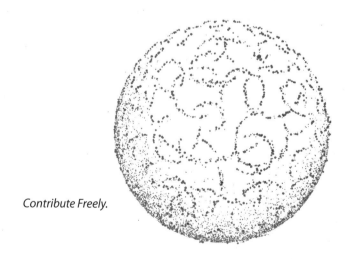

Contribute Freely.

a person's contribution is not coerced, everything is fine. There cannot be an even-steven calculation or strict reciprocity at work, even though that is always a temptation. And yet, it is intriguing that a freely given contribution often comes back to the giver, somehow, somewhere. In his classic book *The Gift*, Lewis Hyde explores the spiritual and emotional significance of gift exchange as revealed in diverse cultures, anthropology, and literature. Explaining the difference between "circular giving" and reciprocal giving, Hyde writes:

> When I give to someone from whom I do not receive (and yet I do receive elsewhere), it is as if the gift goes around a corner before it comes back. I have to give blindly. And I will feel a sort of blind gratitude as well ... When the gift moves in a circle its motion is beyond the control of the personal ego, and so each bearer must be a part of the group and each donation is an act of social faith.[4]

The idea to CONTRIBUTE FREELY is not a matter of unconditional, perpetual giving, however. Nor is it not necessarily circular. But if the goal is to contribute to a resilient commons, gift-givers need to make sure that their contributions are voluntary and commonly agreed upon, and not induced by pressure or sanctions from the outside. A commons won't survive without freely given contributions. The specific ways of contributing to the common pool — where? when? how? in what quantities? — depend first and foremost on what people *can* really give. This in turn reflects their socioeconomic situation, customary rules, the level of people's commitment, how they feel about a certain process, trust in decision-making processes, levels of participation, and so on. Of course, giving can also be simply an expression of goodwill or joy, or support for a cause.

To CONTRIBUTE FREELY helps build a healthy commons because it affirms the ethical norm of sharing, dividing up, and freely cooperating. A strict accounting of who gives what to whom may be helpful, but it is not always needed. While an accounting may work in larger and less personal contexts, a sharp focus on precise contributions and entitlements can undermine what makes a commons special: it's a space where money doesn't rule everything.

Practice Gentle Reciprocity

While commons surely need people to CONTRIBUTE FREELY, they are not a fairy tale land of self-sacrificing volunteers. There is also social exchange based on some form of reciprocity between persons. But the reciprocity in a commons is of a different character than that of trade in markets. Markets are based on individuals bargaining to extract as much as possible for themselves when making exchanges of equivalent monetary value (price).

Practice Gentle
Reciprocity.

What matters is the feeling of fairness, which is not necessarily the same as providing absolutely equal shares or equivalent money-value exchange to everyone. Fairness is about ensuring that all needs have been seen and met. A self-confident, gracious commons is thus one that is content with social equals enjoying a roughly balanced (but not absolutely equal) exchange over time. Choosing to not calculate in precise terms who owes whom is the practice of gentle reciprocity. It is often a matter of social wisdom and tolerance. Practicing strict, direct reciprocity by identifying people as debtors or creditors in the first place can create invidious social distinctions and fan divisive jealousies. Yet allowing free riders to shirk their fair contribution to a group's efforts can generate resentments and deplete the group's shared wealth and goodwill. "No one wants to be a sucker, keeping a promise that everyone else is breaking," as Professor Elinor Ostrom once wrote[5] So a commons must ensure a rough equivalence of contribution and entitlement among its participants without insisting upon fully audited reciprocity and without coercing contributions.

Trust Situated Knowing

People who are able to ride a bicycle, play the piano, or run a marathon often cannot explain how they do it. They don't consciously know what they know. That's because much of our knowledge is tacit or embodied, and not necessarily conscious and cognitive. "We can know more than we can tell," as Michael Polanyi puts it in his books on this subject.[6] Our bodies often know different things than our conscious minds. We feel the arrival of spring, sense when something is amiss in a social setting, and relax when we visit beloved bodies of water. It is fair to say that commoning begins with these deep reservoirs of embodied and situated knowing and perception.

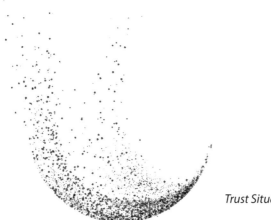

Trust Situated Knowing.

Political scientist Frank Fischer has documented the habit of professional experts and bureaucracies to "ignore local knowledge that can help relate technical facts and social values."[7] A number of movements and organizations are actively trying to change this by calling attention to the deep wisdom of situated knowing. Permaculture designers insist on the necessity to "observe and interact" and to "creatively use and respond to change," for example.[8] People in the Transition Town movement take pride in co-creating a post-fossil world through "mind, heart and hand."

Embodied experience opens up a very different way of under-standing how to govern people and shared resources, going well beyond cognitive, behavioralist approaches. It points to other ways of knowing — intuition, feelings, subconscious knowledge, historical experience. Just as the physical human body somehow gives rise to consciousness, so the coming together of an *I* and *we* yields a new sphere of group consciousness that is best known through experience, not language. Anthropologist James Suzman described how he puzzled over the meaning of the term *n!ow* as used by the Ju/'hoansi Bushmen in southern Africa. The term seems to refer to a fundamental property of people and meat animals that manifests itself in the weather when-ever such animals are killed or when a human is born or dies. But after failing to entirely grasp the elusive idea expressed by *n!ow*, Suzman con-cluded that some experiential and embodied knowledge simply cannot be expressed through language, let alone be translated into another language: "To know *n!ow* and understand it, you have to have been a product of this land, to have been shaped by its seasonal rhythms, and to have experienced the bonds that formed between hunters and their prey."[9]

Our feelings are exquisitely sensitive to changes in the living natural world and our social relationships. In her book *Tending the Wild*, M. Kat Anderson shows how Native Americans in the area now known as California developed an astonishingly subtle knowledge of their local ecosystems and the lives of specific plant and animal species: "Several important insights were revealed to me as I walked with Native American elders and accompanied them on plant gathering walks. The first of these was that one gains respect for nature by *using* it judi-ciously. By using a plant or an animal, interacting with it where it lives, and tying your well-being to its existence, you can be intimate with it and understand it."[10]

Situated knowing is obviously not confined to traditional peoples. Such forms of knowing and know-how are found among mountain-eers assessing the safety of ice sheets, athletes sensing where and how rapidly the ball is traveling, and politicians sensing the public mood. Situated knowing is especially important in commons, where people often have subtle insights about their care-wealth. Indeed, this is what makes so many commons so vital and robust. Situated knowing, then, is not just "knowledge." It is an outgrowth of doing and experience — including, often, deeper communion with nature and affective labor in stewarding it. Philosopher Donna Haraway has famously described situated knowledge as a "feminist empiricism" in the course of challenging the ideas of scientific "objectivity."[11]

Despite the overwhelming power of scientific rationalism, often leveraged by bureaucratic administration, it remains possible to honor situated knowledge and apply it. It is, in any case, within us and omnipresent around us, but not readily recognized and trusted.

Deepen Communion with Nature

The great appeal of many commons is their invitation — often, in fact, a necessity — to bring people into closer communion with nature. In commons that revolve around natural biowealth — water, farmland, forests, fisheries, wild game — people quickly realize that there are natural limits. People involved in agroecology, permaculture, community forests, and traditional irrigation become closely attuned to the rhythms of natural systems and the subtle indicators of their health or endangerment.

Deepen Communion with Nature.

In commons, people are not focused on the exchange value or financialization of so-called natural capital. The more they engage directly with nature, the more commoners develop intimate relationships of respect and understanding for the Earth as an elegant, sacred, living system. Commons give people practical vehicles for deepening their engagement with nature. When M. Kat Anderson asked native elders in California why some plants and animals were disappearing, they blamed "the absence of human interaction with a plant or an animal." They suggested that people need an active relationship with plants because "not only do plants benefit from human use, but some may actually *depend* on humans using them. The conservation of endangered species and the restoration of historic ecosystems might require the reintroduction of careful human stewardship rather than simple hands-off preservation."[12] Indigenous wisdom suggests that human beings must interact with nature as consciously helpful users, protectors, and stewards. This idea is finding its way into some state policies. In Guatemala, the government had long attempted to stop cattle ranchers, farmers, illegal loggers, and drug traffickers from destroying lands in the Maya Biosphere Reserve. After concluding that it could not stop such behaviors, the government realized that "the most effective way to protect forests is to give control of them to the communities who already live there."[13]

The same thing happened in Nepal, where community participation in the management of forests greatly improved ecological stewardship. Following the reintroduction of a multiparty system in Nepal in 1990, new policies and funding mechanisms were created to support grass-roots-based, self-governing groups. In all, some 16,000 community forest user groups are now managing 1.2 million hectares of land, or about one fourth of Nepal's forested areas.[14]

The point is not simply to develop economic or government policies that are more "sustainable." The point is for people to have opportunities to deepen their relationships to natural systems, and in so doing, come to know them, love them, and protect them. This is the seed from which grows the structured situated knowing of permaculture and ecomimicry in design,[15] among many other eco-friendly innovations. It is the "spell of the sensuous," in David Abrams's phrase, that pulls us toward a deeper understanding of the nature and ourselves.[16] Ecophilosopher Andreas Weber argues our connections to nature are so deep and existential that our inner lives and feelings bear the imprint of the outer world. Living organisms experience themselves as physical matter via their emotions, which is part of a larger drama of biopoetic relationships among living creatures. "We are of the same stuff" as the world, writes Weber, which is why a walk through a meadow or the arrival of spring causes such delight.[17] Deepening our communion with nature is an indispensable path toward responsible care of the teeming, living world that lies beyond humanity.

Preserve Relationships in Addressing Conflicts

Any cooperative endeavor will face serious challenges, many of them stemming from personal behaviors or power relations. The question is not if, but how the inevitable conflicts that arise will be dealt with. Ignoring them is not an option. What we mean by "preserving relationships" in addressing conflicts might be best explained by drawing on Elinor Ostrom's insights.

Preserve Relationships in Addressing Conflicts.

Like any institution, a commons must have rules and norms that apply to everyone. But what also matters a great deal is *how* those rules and norms are upheld. There must be an honest, transparent reckoning of conflict or violation, but also a spirit of respect and concern for all the people involved. In some contexts people are not able to leave, which makes it a priority to try to preserve relationships while addressing conflicts. Hence the use of graduated sanctions, one of the eight design principles for commons identified by Elinor Ostrom. (See Appendix D.) It is important to recognize and rectify the harm, but also to honor the dignity of the person involved and their relationships with fellow commoners. Relationships can also be preserved when group complicity or systemic problems are acknowledged. The idea is not to secure consensus through threats of punishment, but to prevent misaligned relationships in the first place. When transgressions do occur, it is important to mete out sanctions in gradually increasing severity, all in a context of trust, candor, and honesty. A frequent technique is to sit in a circle and discuss a problematic situation or behavior. (We have seen effective deliberations in circles with more than one hundred people.) The art is to give everyone the right to be heard, bear witness, and suggest changes while sharing the observed problem and its implications transparently.

When one of us observed a large circle of members of the Venezuelan federation of cooperatives, Cecosesola, she was perplexed at how complaints against people were often commingled with affection, with meetings concluding by people hugging the "accused." After what seemed to be a more than challenging session involving deep emotions and interpersonal conflicts, the expression of respect and conspicuous displays of hugs signaled that deep, honest criticism is linked to enduring respect and care. Other commons may use mediation or other forms of group deliberation. Many software commons have a choice that may or may not preserve relationships while addressing a dispute — the practice of "forking the code," which in effect splits the project into separate endeavors. One or several participants to leave but still work on the same base of software code and take it in different creative directions. Of course, not all conflicts can be bridged. At some point, forking a project or excluding a person may be the only practical option. What always matters, though, is striving to maintain collective morale while being unflinchingly honest. Denial and self-deception don't help anyone.

Reflect on Your Peer Governance

In many commons people are not fully aware of their own practices. The underlying values and social dynamics — both the constructive ones and the less helpful ones — may be only dimly perceived. This makes a commons vulnerable. Even engaged people may forget how to maintain themselves as a commons in the face of daily operational challenges, the necessity (and seductions) of making money, the enticements of wielding power, new ideas about organizational governance, and countless other factors. It is therefore vital that commoners reflect on their peer governance. That is the only way that they can protect the integrity of the commons against enclosure, cooptation, or the entropy that can sap institutions of their energy.

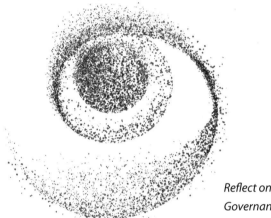

Reflect on Your Peer Governance.

We include this pattern, REFLECT ON YOUR PEER GOVERNANCE, as part of the Social Life of Commoning and not as an issue of Peer Governance, because we regard it as a foundational necessity. German economist and commons scholar Johannes Euler has pointed out that just as there is no commons without commoning, so there is no commoning without peer governance. If you want your commons to survive decades or even centuries, governance behaviors must be made explicit and honestly discussed. Unself-conscious forms of commoning risk losing their way. Unless a group has centuries of tradition, culture, and ritual to act as stabilizing forces, its members must consciously reflect upon the processes that make a commons work or that could make it better.

*   *   *

In the end, commoning is not just a state of enhanced awareness and being, like Zen practice or mindfulness. It is an enactment of peer provisioning and peer governance. It is the condition and means by which those occur. We might add that it is the cultural form of a new kind of politics. At its most ambitious, commoning begins a process of re-imagining the terms of modern human civilization at a time when its idealized notion of human aspiration, *homo economicus*, is revealing itself to be profoundly antisocial, indifferent to democratic norms, and ecologically irresponsible.

This is why a vital aspect of the Social Life of Commoning is the idea of strengthening the Nested-I. This is not a pattern as such, because it represents what happens more generally when other patterns of commoning are enacted: our individual and collective interests converge and align! We enter into a symbiosis among individual beings and our larger context. Participants in the WikiHouse network enact the Nested-I as they share and make shareable their design innovations with each other. The use of open standards and modularity encourages anyone to contribute freely in building something bigger than themselves, while reaping individual benefits in the process. The idea of the Nested-I also animates federated wikis, which vest individuals with the autonomy to create personal wikis to suit their own tastes and points of view, while inscribing such wikis within larger federations (known as "neighborhoods") to allow the easy sharing of wiki pages (see pp. 246–252).

The reality of the Nested-I is arguably that of the human species even if conventional economics continues to believe in the isolated-I as a sovereign, rational agent. What economics fails to comprehend is the biophysical absurdity of this foundational premise. Living beings are deeply and dynamically interconnected. Even Western medicine's fixation on single-agent pathogens that supposedly have a cause/effect relationship with our bodies, is giving way to a more complicated story. Increasingly scientists are discovering that individual living systems are *nested within* larger living systems while at the same time being *comprised* of smaller living elements. It's holism all the way up and down! The Human Microbiome Project has identified about 100 trillion nonhuman life forms — bacteria, fungi, etc. — that live within our bodies, especially in our digestive tract, taking up between two and five pounds of our body weight. It turns out that these organisms are essential to our health and well-being as "individuals." One might say that our individual bodies don't even have definitive boundaries; we are immersed in all sorts of symbiotic relationships to the food we eat, the bacteria around and within us, and the local landscape. In short, the

Nested-I has a more than human dimension. We literally blur into a network of other living organisms and systems.[18]

This is what the idea of the Nested-I and its Ubuntu Rationality expresses: an individual's actions not only serve his or her own interests, they are part of a larger, more intricate symphony of negotiation and change with other living beings in a living Earth. It bears noting that while this impulse to work with our fellow commoners may have elements of conscious choice, it is a fundamentally nonrational, embodied instinct as well. Strengthening the Nested-I means developing the space to express affection, respect, laughter, playfulness, passion, and love in the mundane chores of teamwork and ritualized togetherness that any commons must honor.[19]

It is also worth noting that a commons can get the mix of collective control and individualism wrong. A group may exert a suffocating presence on the individual, or on certain types of individuals. Patriarchy is a problem in many subsistence and digital commons despite women's significant role in commoning. A coercive conformism can quickly turn a community into a cult. Charismatic leaders may get things done by consolidating power, but at the cost of a weaker, less robust culture. Nourishing the Nested-I requires an artful, respectful balance between the needs of the individual and the imperatives of the group.

5

Peer Governance Through Commoning

C OMMONING MAY BE ROOTED in a variety of social outlooks and behaviors, as we saw in Chapter Four. But can it govern? Can it do so better than existing governments? Can it coordinate more effectively and better than the market? These are large questions that we will address at greater length in Part III. For now, we wish to examine how peer governance works *within* a commons. Property rights scholar Robert Ellickson has described how cattle ranchers in the Shasta Valley of California dealt with the problem of cattle escaping from their fields and trespassing on other people's land. Ranchers on their own came up with informal rules and social norms — what Ellickson calls "order without law."[1] Neighboring ranchers, for example, often follow the tradition of splitting fifty/fifty the cost of building and maintaining a shared fence. Or they agree that one rancher will provide the materials and the other the labor for building it. Or if one rancher has a greater average density of livestock on one side of the fence, custom holds that there should be a rough norm of proportionality for allocating the costs of fencing. If a careless rancher violates the social norm of promptly retrieving stray cattle, the rancher community often intentionally uses gossip to sanction and shame them.

The dynamics of peer governance at the cellular level of everyday practices matter because they provide regularity and stability to a commons. They also help us learn how to devise larger structures such as federated commons, commons-friendly law and policy, infrastructures, and commons-public partnerships, as we will see in later chapters. Here, we explore ten dynamics of Peer Governance that tend to be present in effective commons. The first seven revolve around interpersonal and social relationships. The final three involve commons-based methods for dealing with property, money, and markets.

Peer Governance
Bring Diversity into Shared Purpose
Create Semi-Permeable Membranes
Honor Transparency in a Sphere of Trust
Share Knowledge Generously
Assure Consent in Decision Making
Rely on Heterarchy
Peer Monitor & Apply Graduated Sanctions

Relationalize Property
Keep Commons & Commerce Distinct
Finance Commons Provisioning

A Few Words About Governance

In conventional parlance, governance generally means the rule of some over the many through *government*. Government exercises authority and control over people through laws passed by legislatures, rulings handed down by courts, and policies adopted by various officials and politicians. At the end of the day, most people regard government as something distant and often indifferent to their concerns. It is something that a group of people vested with power does *to* and *for* another group of people, perhaps with their participation and consent, perhaps not. But *government* and *governance* are different things. One could say, there is governance in the commons, but no government.

As we thought about how coordination works in a commons, we hesitated to use the term "governance" because it is so closely associated with the idea of collective interests overriding individual freedom. This perceived antagonism runs so deep that it is hard to imagine any serious resolution of the tension. But there is a resolution — to realize individual needs by addressing collective needs. The supposed dualism between the collective and individual is largely overcome by sharing authority among everyone directly affected by decisions. Authority, power, *and* responsibility for implementation are diffused among identifiable people, each of whom has opportunities to deliberate and make decisions with others.

That is why we like to refer to peer governance rather than just governance. It points to an ongoing process of dialogue, coordination, and self-organization. By recognizing individuals as active peers in a collective process rather than positioning them as adversaries competing to control a large, remote third party, *government*, a more trusted type of governance can emerge. Citizens in a nation-state may nominally be sovereign ("We the People ..."), but that sovereignty is delegated with only crude oversight and accountability to representative legislatures and rigid, formalistic bureaucracies. No wonder the state is seen as alien or hostile! In a commons, governance is more likely to take account of on-the-ground needs and realities.

Peer Governance amounts to an artful political dialectic between *culture* and *structure*. The shared motivations and visions that commoners wish to enact must have sufficient structure in law, formal organization, and finance to be protected and nurtured. But there must also be sufficient open space for individual creativity, deliberation, and action to flourish, which in turn recursively improves the structures of law, organization, and finance that guide a commons forward. For a commons to be coherent and durable, it needs some clear organizational forms and regularities. For it to be resilient and alive, it requires welcoming space for free play, flexibility, and creative novelty. One might say that the informal and the creative must be stabilized through friendly structural support and constraints, without being controlled by them. Commoners must figure out a Goldilocks zone in which the interplay between structure and culture is "just right."[2]

Getting the interplay right is the high art of commons governance. To illuminate it, we present in this chapter the generic patterns of Peer Governance that help a commons work well. How does self-organization occur in the first place and ripen into a stable, creative social organism? Is there a general developmental process that needs to occur? We don't believe there is, but there are patterns we can become aware of that will help us understand how a commons can maintain itself. It would be a mistake to offer prescriptive formulas for Peer Governance because they won't work in complex systems. You cannot fabricate a commons simply by assembling a certain number of people, adopting certain values, and applying certain operational rules and enforcement strategies. Following the eight design principles famously put forward by Elinor Ostrom is helpful,[3] but ultimately not enough. The principles do not provide sufficient guidance for people to respond flexibly to feedback in dynamic systems. Our analysis of Peer Governance therefore moves beyond Ostrom's landmark design principles in several ways. First, we look at all sorts of contemporary commons — social, digital, and urban, among others — not just at natural resource-based commons. We also attempt to go beyond resource management and allocation as primarily economic matters, and instead emphasize commoning as a social system. Any assessment of governance in commons must deal squarely with the systemic threats posed by markets and state power, so we look to Peer Governance as a form of moral and political sovereignty that works in counterpoint to the market/state.

Enacting Peer Governance needs to be a living, developmental process in itself. Therefore, instead of offering a full set of *prescriptive formulas*, our patterns amount to *procedural guidelines* that enable a stepwise, adaptable path for developing a commons. Enacting a commons through Peer Governance resembles the way in which DNA provides general guidance, but not strict instructions, for the autonomous development and differentiation of an embryo.

So, the bad news is that there is no blueprint, no panacea. Peer Governance is not a prescriptive, rule-driven program for fabricating commons or managing resources. But the good news is that Peer Governance is a *generative process*. It is a reliable means by which commoners can build authentic, living relationships among themselves, and in so doing, develop a coherent, stable commons.

This idea is consistent with Christopher Alexander's ideas about how to create enlivening environments that last. Alexander has written that a process that generates life must itself be a living process. It is *"the ONLY way, I believe — that it is possible to generate buildings or communities that have life. Living structure ... cannot* be created by brute force from designs. It *can only* come from a generative program — *hence from a generative process existing in the production* process of society — so that ... *its conception, plan, design,* detailed layout, structural *design,* and material detail are *all unfolded,* step by step in TIME."[4] (emphasis in original)

Formal structures are obviously needed, but living processes, which have their own regularities, lie at the heart of a commons. Commoning is the exploratory process by which people identify their needs and devise situation-specific systems for provisioning and governance. People are empowered to draw upon their own knowledge in assessing their problems. They must live with ambiguities and uncertainties, and show the creative agency to develop solutions that seem fair and effective to them.

Peer Governance is open ended. Its properties and implementation cannot be fully known or specified in advance. This idea obviously flies in the face of modern sensibilities, which generally try to design comprehensive, advance blueprints for implementation. The primary goals in modern systems are uniformity and simplicity, for the sake of controllability and political credibility. James Scott, in his book *Seeing Like a State*, provides a brilliant analysis of how this plays out in the exercise of state power. As a precondition for efficient control, modern systems look to previously defined indices, development metrics, and expert knowledge. Formal categories of thought and official policies tend to take on a life of their own, becoming more real than on-the-ground realities.

An example is the European Union's requirement that its member states keep their budget deficits below three percent of gross domestic product, ostensibly to assure that governments are prudently managing their economies. It turns out that this magical budget number had been invented by two French civil servants in 1981.[5] French President François Mitterrand, looking for ways to keep his government's budget deficits under control, had asked his budget department to come up with a simple but economically credible rule to help rein in government spending. Mitterand reportedly had asked the staffers to propose "a kind of rule, something simple [that exudes] competence in economics." Two staffers came up with the idea of budget deficits at or below three percent of GDP as a rough metric of fiscal responsibility. One of the two explained, "At the time, we were headed to a 100-billion-franc deficit. That corresponded to about 2.6 percent of GDP. So we said to ourselves: 1 percent deficit would be too tough and would be unattainable. Two percent would have put too much pressure on the government. So we said three percent."

In other words, the budget deficit criterion was purely circumstantial, with no basis in theory or substance. Indeed, former Bundesbank president Hans Tietmeyer has confirmed that the three percent benchmark is "not easy to justify … in economic terms." However, after its success in reining in French deficits over a few years, the EU decided to adopt it as well. Despite having no theoretical basis, the three percent benchmark has ripened into a hard-and-fast symbol of fiscal rectitude over the past thirty years. The number was enshrined in the Treaty of Maastricht that formed the European Union in 1992, and is routinely cited by conservative politicians and economists in countless pronouncements. But only three member states have actually met this standard between 1999 and 2015,[6] suggesting how easily official (and, in this case, fabricated) indicators can override people's situated knowledge and capacity to respond.

Commons and Peer Governance must be grown over time *and* deal with countless uncertainties that cannot be fully predicted in advance. This requires time for a culture of trust and transparency to emerge and yield a network of relationships. Rituals must be invented, and habits must ripen into traditions. It is therefore critical for commoners to *consciously decide* how to craft their governance systems.

This process is neither random nor precise. And yet, it has certain regularities. It is more akin to the method for making an outdoor fire: there is no single, universally correct way of doing it, but certain developmental steps must be followed, and in a certain order. One must first collect flammable materials of various sizes — logs, kindling, tinder — and arrange them so that the easily ignited tinder is on the bottom, which in turn will help ignite the larger pieces. A spark must be produced through a match, flame, or other means. There must be a bounded container for the fire (a fireplace, a ring of rocks, a hibachi), and sufficient oxygen flow and venting. The specifics of building a fire vary in a northern forest, where wood is plentiful, compared to a desert, where flammable fuel is scarce. And of course, the results — a roaring bonfire, a fire suitable for cooking, slow-burning embers — will vary, too. The point is that despite the many ways in which fires can be made, and the different outcomes, the basic patterns remain the same.

So, too, with the process of establishing Peer Governance: there are some reliable general patterns, but many idiosyncratic ways of doing it. Commons usually start with motivations or aspirations shared by participants — the need of farmers to irrigate their crops, the desire of software programmers to have an easy-to-use, shareable mapping program, the need of fishers to ensure fair access to a fishery.

Whatever the specific problem, a would-be commons must offer a credible vision for addressing it among people who often have different perspectives. Even though there may be no actual strategies or solutions in hand, a commons in its early stage must provide a spark and updraft that feeds interest and motivation. If people feel that the process resonates with their needs and context, they will be eager to engage. However, there must be an attractor that pulls them to self-organize and align their intentions and actions.[7] This could be the need to survive, the desire to reconnect with local ecosystems, an attractive alternative to extractive markets, the appeal of fair-minded cooperation, or any other number of factors.

Patterns of Peer Governance

In our analytical wanderings through the wealth of commons, we've identified ten patterns of Peer Governance. They not only help establish more trusted, transparent systems of deliberation and coordination. They explain the functional effectiveness of commons as governance systems, especially in contrast to the market and nation-state. When a commons works well, it is generally because people are able to diffuse authority and responsibility and prevent abusive concentrations of power. Peer Governance encourages open, frequent sharing of knowledge so that the best ideas and collective wisdom can surface. Defined systems of monitoring, sanctions, and enforcement are needed to protect the commons against free riders, vandals, and systematic enclosures.

Most importantly, commoners must find ways to prevent individual property rights and the quest for money from ruining group dynamics. That is why it is necessary for commoners to develop ways to relationalize property — a topic that we will explore in Chapter 8. A similar set of governance challenges arise in dealings with markets and capital. No commons can survive if commercial norms are allowed to colonize the commons, so Peer Governance strives to KEEP COMMONS & COMMERCE DISTINCT.

Let's explore each pattern more deeply.

Bring Diversity into Shared Purpose

A commons is not simply a group of like-minded people who somehow discover each other, or a cohort of well-intentioned people willing to be educated. It is a social system that can only be developed through many acts of relationship-building and deliberation over time. People almost always have all sorts of different ideas and motivations, if only because personalities and backgrounds vary. Peer Governance, artfully carried out, brings diverse viewpoints together. There is no substitute for this process because, without it, people may casually commit to some imagined, abstract idea about the future that may not reflect their actual feelings, needs, and feasible possibilities.

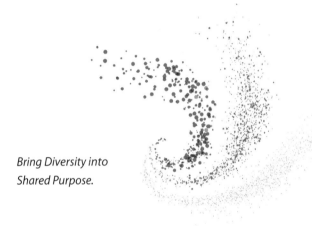

Bring Diversity into Shared Purpose.

This is a core insight among the Indigenous and non-Indigenous organizations that established Unitierra — Universidad de la Tierra en Oaxaca — in Oaxaca, Mexico. It is a "de-institutionalized university" founded by commoners for commoners that rejects formal roles and hierarchy.[8] Unitierra's founders regard the idea of shared purpose and objectives as unhelpful; what matters is shared action. In a real commons, says Gustavo Esteva, intellectual father and elder of Uniterra, people often have shared reasons to act and to act together, but initially they may not have a shared purpose. At Unitierra, people avoid trying to "pull from the future"[9] by declaring in advance an imagined idea of where they want to go. Instead they try to "push from the base and from the past," by drawing upon everyone's experiences and motivations.

Through commoning, a shared purpose eventually emerges. It is not necessarily self-evident or knowable in advance. An intentional community may have shared purpose and values from the very start, but in most cases a motley group of people find each other and teach themselves how to walk, run, and then dance. The process may be easier if people live in a shared space or depend upon the same river or forest. Sharing the same aspirations — to boost crop yields, to improve local exchange and mutualization, to keep information shareable — can also quicken a spirit of cooperation and solidarity. In any case shared purpose is not a given in a commons. But we believe that it must be identified and clarified if effective action is to follow.

Henry David Thoreau, the American essayist and poet, described this process nicely: "If you have built your castles in the air, your work need not be lost; that is where they should be. Now put the foundations under them." While this is often taken as fanciful idealism, it is actually an apt description of how a vision is set forth and then made real by the hard work of bringing different people into general agreement. The core task is to respect the individuality of diverse members while forging an ethic of solidarity. This insight is critical because a commons, like any ecosystem, needs a requisite variety for it to function well.

On the Origins of Peer Governance

Peer Governance in a commons can develop in any number of ways, but there are three paths that are frequently taken — spontaneous attraction, tradition, and conscious design.

Spontaneous Attraction. As described earlier, a small group of friends in the Kumpula neighborhood of Helsinki met to discuss how they might make an impact on climate change. As if guided by some collective muse, they enthusiastically decided to start a "credit exchange" to exchange services with each other. The idea quickly became popular and by 2014, some 3,000 people had joined a network now called Helsinki Timebank.[10] This may be the most common way that a commons arises and maintains itself — someone identifies a problem and comes up with a constructive solution, only to find it speaks to many people in similar circumstances.

Many legendary projects in digital contexts were started by creative iconoclasts who wanted to do something different, and then invited others to join in. In 1991, Linus Torvalds, a 21-year-old Finnish computer science student, decided to build his own shareable version of Unix, a complex operating system. Within a few months, hundreds of hackers — including those supporting the GNU free software project started by Richard Stallman — had joined together to build Linux. Within a few years, thousands of programmers had joined the effort to build a world-class operating system that now rivals Microsoft's Windows and other proprietary systems. A similar story can be told about how Jimmy Wales developed the initial idea for Wikipedia, which soon attracted tens of thousands of others to join the worldwide project to write an encyclopedia through free contributions by anyone, without monetary incentives. There are now 299 versions of Wikipedia in languages from Albanian to Tarantino (an Italian dialect) to Waray (the fifth-most-spoken regional language of the Philippines).

Tradition. Shared purpose and values also become well-established through decades or centuries of customary practices. In Valais, Switzerland, farmers in the fifteenth century built a network of canals in the mountains to bring irrigation water from the mountains to their fields.[11] Similar irrigation systems — known variously as *waale, acequias, faladji, quanats, johad* — exist all over the world. They all depend upon traditional forms of cooperation in managing water, such as setting rules for a fair allocation of water to farmers. On the South Korean island of Jeju, a community of women divers from age seventeen to more than seventy practice a traditional art of harvesting shellfish from as deep as twenty meters underwater using only a knife or simple iron hook. The women, known as *haenyeo*, stay underwater as long as three or four minutes without any oxygen device, using breathing techniques similar to whales and seals. The *haenyeo* not only dive together (for safety reasons), they conscientiously pass down their traditional knowledge to the younger generations as a culturally meaningful, eco-friendly way to feed their families.[12] The great power of traditional commons is their use of cultural practices that respect the singular features of a given forest, fishery, river, or pasture.

Conscious Design. When strangers come together to collaborate, a deliberately designed system can help shared purpose and values to emerge. One helpful tool is a social charter that explicitly names the group's fundamental ideas and working practices, and in so doing, helps the group self-constitute itself. (More about charters in Chapter 10.) Other communities find that digital platforms can bring together a commons. A notable pioneer in this area is Enspiral, a New Zealand-based network of social entrepreneurs that developed Loomio, a deliberation and decision making platform. Loomio provides a series of staged choices by which a group can propose new ideas, debate them, add modifications, and accept or reject proposed actions. Enspiral has also developed CoBudget, a collaborative software system for helping people keep track of a shared budget and allocate funds to proposals made by members.[13]

Designing a tech platform to facilitate governance is a tricky challenge. Libertarians, for one, seem to think that they can embed their values and norms into the design of a tech platform and thereby avoid the messy disagreements that human beings inevitably have in governing themselves. For example, the designers of some digital currencies like Bitcoin mistakenly believe that governance is largely unnecessary and oppressive, and that secure authentication for a digital currency is enough to let libertarian freedom blossom.[14] The fierce squabbles within Bitcoin circles over the future of the blockchain's design show otherwise. Real-life governance, social practices, and culture play inescapable, ongoing roles in any system, notwithstanding the significant structural influence of software designs.

Create Semi-Permeable Membranes

Commons need protection, as we love to say. Scholars have confirmed from extensive field research the need for what they call boundaries. The first of Ostrom's famous eight design principles for successful commons is "clearly defined boundaries," which are needed to delineate the boundaries of the resource system and the membership of the commons. While agreeing with this general idea that boundaries are essential to stewardship, we believe that a better term is "semi-permeable membrane." After all, the point is not to establish a hermetically closed system that can exclude everyone else and hoard resources for members only — the goal of property law and "club goods" (as economists would put it). The point is to exclude influences that undermine Ubuntu Rationality in a commons while remaining open to the flows of energy and life that create value in a commons and sustain it.

Create Semi-permeable Membranes.

So commoners must somehow learn to deal with a paradox — to protect against capitalist threats to enclose common wealth while at the same time taking nourishment from the rich diversity of life. Commoners achieve this deft trick by creating semi-permeable membranes around themselves, much as any living organisms does. Unlike strict boundaries, semi-permeable membranes *selectively allow* what may or may not enter a commons, much as we choose the food and relationships that nourish us. A commons must remain open to all the external nutrients that might deepen the whole.

This is central to the ability of commons to generate a new system of value that it can safeguard and grow. If capitalism is based upon accumulating and centralizing wealth, commons rely on their semi-permeable membranes to be able to interact safely with the larger world. They capture and store flows of energy in "catchment areas," to use the language of permaculture. Joline Blais, a media scholar and permaculture designer, writes:

> Catchment is a system for accumulating a critical mass of a needed resource, like water or soil or minerals, in order to trigger self-organizing systems, i.e., life forms, that then spread over the landscape. Some natural examples of catchment include the sun, plants, carbohydrates, bodies of water, geothermal energy, and plate tectonics.[15]

Life arises when there are sufficient flows of energy. That is what commons attempt to do — create catchment areas for the self-organization of life. So instead of conceiving of commons as closed systems of common property managed by a "club," it is more productive to see them as social organisms who, thanks to their semi-permeable membranes, can interact with larger forces of life — communities, ecosystems, other commons.

This resembles the functioning of the blood-brain barrier as it separates the blood circulating in our bodies from brain fluid in the central nervous system. The blood-brain barrier allows the passage of water, some gases, and lipid-soluble molecules, and the selective transport of molecules such as glucose and amino acids that are crucial to neural function. But — and this is critical — it prevents the passage of potential neurotoxins into the brain.

Any commons requires a similarly effective membrane to allow the passage of beneficial substances while screening out "neurotoxins" that could harm its healthy functioning. The social impact of money in a community — who benefits from it, the purposes for which it is used, the distortion of relationships it may engender — is perhaps the most potentially troubling force in a commons. (See KEEP COMMONS AND COMMERCE DISTINCT, pp. 151–155.) Living in a capitalist society, it is often impossible to simply withdraw from the power of money and market relationships. A semi-permeable membrane can help a commons prevent markets from colonizing and destroying it. It helps commoners protect their living wealth (not commodified wealth) in efficient ways.

Honor Transparency in a Sphere of Trust

You might say that there are two kinds of transparency — the *legal* kind that liberal democracies require to ensure official accountability, and the *real* transparency that can happen only when people know and trust each other. Real transparency is not just about official accountability based on formal authority and protocols — "covering your ass" in a bureaucratic sense. It's about personal disclosure and sharing one's authentic feelings. When a difficult decision must be made in combat, for example, or if a top general gives an order that subordinates regard as problematic, whom should they obey — their official superior in the chain of command or their close colleagues whom they know and trust? In politics and bureaucracies, transparency is often more of a formal charade than a candid sharing of knowledge because anything disclosed can and will be used against you. Minimally acceptable disclosure is therefore the norm.

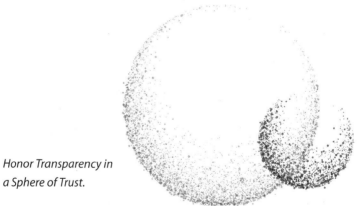

*Honor Transparency in
a Sphere of Trust.*

Real transparency is more meaningful precisely because it penetrates the veneer of formal roles and rules. And it is one of the reasons why commoning is not only challenging, but also transformative in a very deep, personal way. Stefan Brunnhuber, a prominent economist and clinical therapist, argues that cultural transformations cannot be properly understood or achieved through conventional rational-dis-cursive approaches alone. Brunnhuber notes that "trying to reduce complexity through, say, more transparency [information disclosures alone] or the simplification of procedures, will be of little use." What is required is "a different psychosocial practice."[16]

Commoning is such a practice. It allows us to deal with the fact that transparency cannot just be organized, it has to be *felt*. It won't suffice to rely on organizational forms or disclosures to address matters of the heart and culture. Or, as Brunnhuber puts it, "We have to deal with complexity emotionally."[17] This is also true for the complexity of commoning. This insight helps us see once again the ongoing dialogue that must occur between organizational structure and culture. In the end, we cannot depend upon structures to do the work of culture. Transparency is not just about legal arrangements and procedures, but about social practices that build trust.[18]

The Cecosesola network of cooperatives in Venezuela cultivates a culture of such deep trust that people are willing to express and receive sharp criticisms while showing great respect and affection for one another (see page 185–187). This sort of TRANSPARENCY IN A SPHERE OF TRUST is essential. It is the only way that reliable information can be elicited — some of it embarrassing — while sustaining solid personal relation-ships. A commons needs truly honest judgments and wisdom, not just formal professionalism.

Of course, in most groups and networks there is also misbehavior and social cliques that can make it difficult or impossible to create serious trust, let along be open and transparent. Also small group size by itself is not a guarantee of trust or transparency. But in combination with other patterns of Peer Governance — such as SHARE KNOWLEDGE GENEROUSLY and RELY ON HETERARCHY — commoning can succeed more consistently. Commoning can be consistently success.

Share Knowledge Generously

The sharing of knowledge (or its objectified cousin, information) seen in all commons is not just a nice thing to do. It is a crucial instrument by which people generate a social order of their own. That's how online communities, for example, develop free and open source software. Christopher Kelty, a cultural historian of this demimonde, argues that we must go beyond the simple-minded claim that "sharing is a natural condition of human life." The story is far more interesting, he notes: "Sharing *produces* its own kind of moral and technical order, that is, 'information makes people want freedom' and how they want it is related to how that information is created and circulated."[19] (our emphasis)

Share Knowledge
Generously.

Early projects to develop shared bodies of code — such as the UNIX operating system that eventually became Linux — show how sharing of knowledge is generative in its own right. Complex social systems gradually emerge as information is shared. Kelty writes: "The fact that geeks are wont to speak of 'the UNIX philosophy' means that UNIX is not just an operating system but a way of organizing the complex relations of life and work through technical means …"[20] UNIX and Linux are artifacts of a generative relational economy.

The specific circuits by which knowledge is shared define the character of a commons. The diversity of contributors, their know-how and ways of knowing, the criteria for validating these, the methods by which people absorb and use explicit and tacit knowledge — these things matter. Different commons do it differently, of course. The most familiar form of knowledge sharing is surely the meeting, or in larger groups, the general assembly. We have seen how Cecosesola reinvented meetings as loosely structured get-togethers that are occasions for both social bonding and knowledge-sharing. However meetings are structured, the point is to share insights with the group easily and widely so that wise collective choices can be identified and adopted. This includes choices about how to stint resource use and allocate benefits.

In settings where people cannot know each other (group size matters) many commoners gather and share information through a process known as "stigmergy," a kind of situated information sharing that provides "both the stimulus and instruction for further work."[21] The Greek roots of the word "stigmergy" mean "to incite to work"; the idea is a key concept used by complexity science to describe how simple rules in distributed systems can yield a formidable collective intelligence. Think of ants as they go searching for food. They mark their paths with pheromones — that is, they leave a trace, an informational signal — so that their fellow ants can follow the pheromone-marked paths to find food. Stigmergy provides a way for various discoveries to be shared widely and quickly, stimulating prompt follow-on responses and distributed self-organization, with no need for centralized direction. Termites use stigmergic learning and coordination to build their complex nests without any designer or supervisor. Coordination occurs horizontally, asynchronously, and irregularly as individual termites share information and immediately adapt their behaviors.

Stigmergy is a way to diffuse information, decisions, and responsibility to a larger, diverse pool of people, which then enhances effective sense making, learning, and action, even though everyone is spatially separated. For contributors to Wikipedia, the famous red links you find in many Wikipedia entries — the ones you click on only to find out that there is nothing yet written about the topic — signal that more information is needed. They are an invitation to supply it. A simple signal encourages stigmergic coordination on a massive scale, resulting in a complex body of writings — the Wikipedia pluriverse.

Or consider the peer coordination of volunteers for the Humanitarian OpenStreetMap Team. After a natural disaster strikes, such as the Haiti earthquake in 2014, tech volunteers scramble to create detailed online maps to help first responders locate sources of water, food, and medical care.[22] One person's nugget of information or clever map improvement is shared with others, which starts a cascade of follow-on enhancements. People of many different talents living in different spots around the world soon produce a digital map that is often more accurate and more rapidly produced than maps produced by teams of professionals.

The challenge for Peer Governance is to ensure that information and knowledge can flow widely and often — and with minimal resistance. This creates social circuits of communication and coordination that, over time, propel the emergence of a commons-based order.

Assure Consent in Decision Making

It is fundamental that commoners have a meaningful say in developing the rules by which they shall be governed. The ways people directly participate vary greatly, of course, but at the very least, commoners must be able to register their views about Peer Governance and consent to the decisions made. This pattern resembles Ostrom's third design principle: "Most individuals affected by the operational rules can participate in modifying the operational rules."[23]

Assure Consent in Decision Making.

In small groups, discussion and conversation in a circle are the customary practices for making decisions. This approach is used in the *panchayat*, or village councils, of India, which manage community forests or farmland. Some commons may be largely directed by governing committees or coordinating staff, and thus have less direct participation. Examples include the boards of open-access scholarly journals such as the Public Library of Science, the management of timebanks, some community supported agriculture (CSA) farms, and the foundations directly associated with open source software projects. Yet even commons with some form of central management are generally mindful of the need to consult with those affected by decisions.

One way by which commoners assent to rules is by upholding traditions. Customary practices amount to a kind of "blanket consent." This might not always be progressive, but it has the capacity to build the rules of Peer Governance into the very culture. Farmers who irrigate their fields in Bali, for example, have addressed the complexities of pest outbreaks and water shortages by observing religious rituals on specific dates. Under *subak*[24] irrigation practices (*subak* means "irrigation community"), peasants coordinate their rice farming by observing certain rituals. They plant rice at *different* times to avert too much demand on water and thus shortages, but they harvest rice at the *same* time, minimizing pest proliferation. The syncing of social and religious practices with ecological timing functions as a kind of collective consent-and-coordination system.[25] Priests at water temples oversee water management practices, interpreting the Tri Hita Karana philosophy that integrates the relationships among people, the Earth, and the divine. What strikes the Western mind as religious conservatism or odd cultural traditions produces an exquisitely coordinated solution to ecological problems. Interestingly, decisions are not really being "taken" — they are the result of a customary process.

But in many contexts, an explicit decision-taking process is needed. And in these contexts, what matters as much as the process are the *criteria* by which decisions are finally justified. While it is often assumed that consensus is the ideal way to go in the commons, or that everybody has to agree to everything, this type of harmony doesn't necessarily exist. In fact, this notion of consensus is something of a caricature. Disagreement is a reality of human existence. And even when consensus can be achieved, it is not the same as unanimity. Small groups can strive for unanimity, or they can apply a "unanimity minus one" or "unanimity minus two" rule (meaning, a decision to act despite one or two dissents). But it bears noting that these procedures of decision making are not limited to small groups. In large commons, it can be complicated to make decisions about indivisible resources with sharply divided majority/minority factions. However, the Sociocracy methodology (see box on p. 140–141) has proven very useful in surfacing tacit objections and concerns, and moving discussion to a more substantive level in an orderly, fair way.

What enhances the chances of success in any commons, small or big, is to reject at the outset the winners and losers scheme — the big structural flaw of majority rule, otherwise known as democratic voting. Majority rule generally requires support from more than fifty percent of those eligible to vote. If 49.99 percent disagree, too bad; 50.01 percent is good enough to prevail. No wonder representative democracies based on this assumption have trouble healing deep divides or securing cooperation from the losing minority. No wonder ideologies arise to sharpen the differences among parties rather than find common ground. Relying on competitive voting framed by a win/lose choice cannot help but yield this outcome. Decisions by plurality, where the largest bloc in a group prevails even if it falls short of a majority, has the same basic deficiency.[26]

But how then to avoid the winners and losers scheme? How to make sure that all those who have a stake agree to go along with a certain course of action, without feeling coerced or manipulated? And more subtly, how to design decision making in such a way that it doesn't end up creating, and then suppressing, frustrations — which are so often channeled into all sorts of secondary aggression?

As mentioned above, it is crucial that any decision-making process encourage open discussion and actively elicit people's deeper, often unstated concerns. The process-designs can be diverse, but they must all allow for collaborative proposal building so that people can refine ideas and action proposals. A number of models have been developed along these lines, including the Quaker-based model and the hand signals famously used by Occupy protesters in their group negotiations.[27] Now that the internet is everywhere and software has become quite sophisticated, it is possible, for the first time in history, for strangers on a global scale to enter into such collaborative decision making. Digital platforms offer a great deal of versatility in structuring how people can interact. They can have asynchronous communication and use tiered procedures for moderation, deliberation, voting, and so forth. One of the major infrastructures for facilitating such a process is Loomio.

The designers of Loomio, the Enspiral cooperative based in New Zealand, purposely avoided a hierarchical decision-making format. They wanted a process that allows people to deliberate and come to agreement, with decisions emerging from the bottom up. However, because collective processes are sometimes dominated by vocal factions who marginalize other people and perspectives, Loomio was designed to give people plenty of opportunities to express alternative and dissenting opinions. As Richard Bartlett put it:

> The added value of Loomio is that the deliberation and the conclusion are displayed side by side [on the computer screen]. The disagreement is visualized through a pie chart, in a way that you must pay attention to it, so that the concerns can be resolved. This is the difference with polls and other voting mechanisms: you can change your mind as you discuss the proposal. So it becomes almost like a game, participants have to work through the concerns and get them to change.[28]

Loomio does not allow a group to entertain multiple proposals at once because the idea is to force the group, at a certain point of an ongoing discussion, to give its undivided attention to a single pending proposal and come to a final decision. This might be regarded as a design limitation because at a certain point the platform shuts off simultaneous consideration of other proposals. On the other hand, Loomio's minimalist yet adaptable design lets a group make its own choices about how to deliberate and decide — including with majority rule — while documenting the arguments that people present.

It is certainly true that there is no single best way of decision making. What is critical is choosing the right process, criteria, and tools (or combinations of them) for each specific context. Two basic distinctions are important in shaping policies to Assure Consent in Decision Making. The first is the distinction between *consensus* and *consent*. The second is the distinction between *common criteria* and *voting*.

To give my consent to a proposal does not necessarily mean that the proposal is my first choice. I might simply wish to cooperate with the group and not stand in the way. I might not have a better proposal or I may hope that others won't insist on their personal preferences next time as I didn't this time. Sometimes commoners choose to use a relaxed threshold. They frame the vote with a question like this: "Is this proposal something you can live with?" Such an approach can help to achieve full consent, which again does not mean that everyone is in full agreement.

Consent — as opposed to agreement — is defined by the absence of reasonable objections. The basic assumption is that people tend to have good reasons for disagreeing with something and that there has to be a place and space for airing these reasons. In other words, "Consent deliberately seeks objections, which reveals wisdom that can be used to improve proposals and agreements."[29] Consent is reached by choosing the proposal with the least objections. The lowest level of objection — resistance — results in the highest acceptance. James Priest, cofounder of the Sociocracy 3.0 practice, writes: "Consensus is seeking to find the best decision for the purpose. Consent decision making is seeking to find a good enough decision that can then be tried out, tested, and improved over time."[30]

Sociocracy and Consent-Based Decision Making

Some people loathe the idea of Peer Governance because discussions can be so difficult and time consuming. Sometimes a know-it-all dominates discussions while other important points of view go unheard. Sociocracy addresses these problems by convening formal circles of people with specified responsibilities. It is a formal process that relies on consent rather than majority rule. James Priest, cofounder of the Sociocracy 3.0 practice method, explains: "Consensus is seeking to find the best decision for the purpose. Consent decision making is seeking to find a good enough decision that can then be tried out, tested, and improved over time." "The default process in Sociocracy is to talk in rounds," explain Jerry Koch-Gonzalez and Ted J. Rau of Sociocracy for All. "Everyone gets a chance to speak, one by one. That means you can be sure you'll get to speak. No one can be ignored. That saves time in the long run!"[31] When objections arise, as they inevitably do, everyone is invited to improve the proposal with continuous feedback.

Sociocracy has been used extensively in schools, cohousing groups, cooperatives, and many other settings around the world. But it need not be confined to small, face-to-face groups. Small teams using Sociocracy can be nested within a larger "parent circle" that has broad oversight and decision making responsibilities. This helps

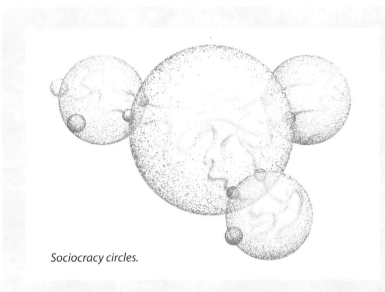

Sociocracy circles.

assure that power is distributed as much as possible to the lowest possible levels ("subsidiarity") while coordinating the work of the whole enterprise. This is achieved by making each circle "double-linked," which means that two circle members serve as full members of both the smaller team and the parent circle at the same time. This ensures that each team can focus on what's important to them while assuring that important information is shared with everyone and acted upon.

Sociocracy is a commons-based governance method because it relies on heterarchy (or as Rau and Koch-Gonzalez call it, "circular hierarchy"). It helps groups achieve maximum transparency, opportunities for participation, and effective outcomes based on collective wisdom.[32] Some groups and consultants dedicated to Sociocratic methods have unfortunately chosen to present their systems as proprietary, which is why we favor commons-friendly approaches such as Sociocracy for All that use Creative Commons licenses.

One method that relies on "good enough" decisions is called Systemic Consensing, which could well be considered one of the backbones of Peer Governance. Systemic Consensing was created in 2005 by Austrian physician and mathematician Erich Visotschnig. The system invites participants to rate multiple proposals on a scale from 0 to 10, with 0 (no resistance at all) meaning, "I have no objection, I support this proposal strongly," and 10 (maximum resistance) meaning, "I have huge objections. I utterly reject this proposal." The in-between values of 2 to 9 are chosen based on the subjective judgment of each individual. A context-specific "zero option" is usually included to signify "keep everything as it is" or "let's decide next time." This option can be considered as the "limit of reasonability." No proposal can be accepted by the group if it is ranked lower than this zero option.

Whoever uses the Systemic Consensus Principle will appreciate that each proposal is not only taken into account, but stays in the game until the very end of the process. Anyone can express objections to any of the proposals throughout the entire process.[33] Digital platforms such as Systemic Konsensing (Consensus) (http://konsensieren.eu/en) allow large numbers of people around the globe to systematically consent to proposals, without spending too much time discussing them face-to-face or feeling disconnected from the center of decision making, because such a center doesn't exist.

Beyond the distinction between consensus and consent, a second helpful distinction for guiding decision making in the commons is that of *common criteria* versus *voting*. Common criteria are, for instance, general standards of ethics and practice that people can agree upon to guide their decision making. They are an attractive alternative to voting because people may prefer to spend their time getting the work done rather than debating complex proposals and voting on them.

In the federation of Cecosesola cooperatives (See pp. 185–187.), there is no representational system or voting to make decisions, but instead open get-togethers and circles that allow everyone's voice to be heard and everyday needs to be discussed. Hundreds of operational decisions are taken every day, many of them requiring sound judgment, such as how to deal with the lack of medications in the hospital or whether to suspend normal procedures because producers arrived with big loads of vegetables six hours earlier than expected. And yet, they never vote because they don't want to split into a majority and a minority. People's decisions are guided by the common criteria that Cecosesola participants have developed for all sorts of everyday situations. "In the end, the decision itself can be made by one, two, or three people. One of the common criteria is that whoever makes a decision in the end is also responsible for the decision and for communicating it."[34] Noel Vale Valera explained: "We never expect to make decisions together in our assemblies. We just talk a lot about how a decision *can* come about and according to which criteria." His colleague Lizeth adds: "It has been working for decades. Of course, it isn't easy. After all, we're a group of 1,300 people. But we don't have to discuss everything together," adding that members are confident that others will make appropriate choices reflecting group sentiment.

Agreeing to common criteria of decision making — instead of making common decisions through voting — requires, and brings about, a culture of trust and solidarity. Such trust-based, routine delegations of individual decision making based on common criteria open up flexible, reliable ways of assuring commoners' consent while empowering individuals with the freedom to make their own judgments in a given situation. It is not a one hundred percent rational process, but rather one driven by people's feelings and intuitive sense that group members can be trusted to do the right thing in most cases.

Rely on Heterarchy

Unlike centralized and hierarchical structures, commons tend to function as *heterarchies*. A hierarchy assigns people to clearly defined formal roles in a pyramid-shaped organizational chart and divides groups into progressively smaller categories and subcategories. It is a more rigid, rank driven order,[35] in which power is consolidated and formally structured.

Rely on Heterarchy.

Heterarchy brings together top-down and bottom-up (both hierarchical), and peer-to-peer dynamics. One can think of it as reconciling distributed networks and hierarchies.[36] It has the potential to bring into alignment responsible individual autonomy and the need for multilevel governance (hence some sort of hierarchy). A heterarchy allows people to make their own choices in how they will interact, making the system more flexible and adaptable than conventional hierarchies.[37] It tends to have unranked horizontal relationships of power and authority among participants, which enables the role of individual agents within the system to be reconfigured in multiple ways. While there are hierarchical elements in a heterarchy (the two systems of organization are not polar opposites), a heterarchy allows the same group of elements to be conjoined or divided in any number of ways. A hierarchy is a pyramid of rigidly prescribed power relations; a heterarchy allows power to flow dynamically through multiple and changing nodes in a social network.

Heterarchy Concept.

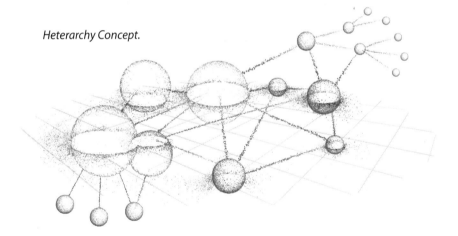

As we saw in Cecosesola, participants operating in a culture of trust and responsibility do not necessarily need formal, advance permission to do something. The open source software ethic encourages this attitude in countless fields: if you see a bug, if you have a great idea, if an urgent problem needs attention, you are authorized in advance to take action. There may be subsequent reviews and second-guessing, and even reversals of such decisions. But experience has shown that individual initiative, when linked up with larger swarms of such actions, is amazingly reliable and effective in achieving results. One need not rely on formal representation or delegation to tackle complex, sophisticated tasks. Transparency in a Sphere of Trust, knowledge sharing, and networked relationships are far more adaptive.

Mainstream observers usually regard governance in a heterarchy with astonished disbelief. When Occupy Wall Street protesters organized their community in Zuccotti Park in Manhattan, *New York Times* columnist Nicholas Kristof wrote: "The protesters are dazzling in their Internet skills, and impressive in their organization. The square is divided into a reception area, a media zone, a medical clinic, a library, and a cafeteria. The protesters' website includes links allowing supporters anywhere in the world to go online and order pizzas (vegan preferred) from a local pizzeria that delivers them to the square."[38] Yet there was no central executive directing this improvised social order. Drawing upon knowledge of previous forms of peer organization, it emerged on-the-fly as participants identified what needed to be done, and then coordinated their initiatives with others'.

We all recognize the desire to collaborate on shared endeavors and take them to larger, more versatile levels; that is arguably the history of the human species. We also know that spontaneous, peer-to-peer forms of organization often don't endure. The challenge for our time — when the market/state has captured and controlled so many forms of cooperation — is to devise new structures that can protect and extend the cooperative impulse. We believe the patterns of the Triad of Commoning can assist and enact these structures within a protected commons. Peer Governance can not only achieve things quickly and effectively; it minimizes social castes, bureaucratic administration, and inequality. A rough equality is more achievable in a heterarchy because, as the Wikipedia entry on heterarchy notes, the structure enables "the flexibility of formal relationships inside an organization. Domination and subordination links can be reversed and privileges can be redistributed in each situation." It continues:

> [H]eterarchies divide and unite groups variously, according to multiple concerns that emerge or recede from view according to perspective. Crucially, no one way of dividing

a heterarchical system can ever be a totalizing or all-en-
compassing view of the system; each division is clearly
partial, and in many cases, a partial division leads us, as
perceivers, to a feeling of contradiction that invites a new
way of dividing things.[39]

What may seem counterintuitive to twentieth-century organizations
is — in the age of ubiquitous digital networks and frequent bottom-up
emergence — a perfectly functional structure of Peer Governance.

Peer Monitor & Apply Graduated Sanctions

No commons can survive long if it does not ensure that its members
adhere to the rules that they have agreed to. In the jargon of social science, if anyone can simply free ride on a commons' work or unilaterally
defect from agreements, then the shared wealth will soon be depleted
and the community will disintegrate. Sanctions are an important way
of deterring such anti-social behaviors, and therefore must be part of
any robust Peer Governance scheme.

*Peer Monitor & Apply
Graduated Sanctions.*

But what should the sanctions be, and how should they be applied?
There is a vast literature exploring this topic, sometimes in the Ostrom
school of scholarship, sometimes in the economic subdiscipline of
prisoner's dilemma experiments and game theory. Various experiments
and theories have been put forward that attempt to explain how and

why people defect from agreements, and what responses might induce greater cooperation.

Ostrom herself found out that long-enduring commons tend to have a series of graduated sanctions. "Graduated" refers to the fact that penalties start out small — a warning, a call to do better — and, if necessary, become more severe. Sanctions are needed to help persuade everyone else to stick to the rules because, as she points out, "enforcement increases the confidence of individuals that they are not suckers."[40] She calls this "quasi-voluntary compliance," citing Margaret Levi, noting that cooperation is contingent on people seeing that others are also following the rules. Like paying one's taxes, people are willing to do something they would prefer to avoid, but only when others comply as well. In most cases, some threat of coercion is essential to achieve cooperation. But it makes a huge difference if this threat of coercion comes from within and with consent — as in a Peer Governance process — or as an imperative from outside.

What is interesting is that the mere existence of possible sanctions is often effective in itself, even if actual penalties are rare. If there is already a great deal of solidarity in a commons, the social consequences of breaking the rules can be severe. Breaches are therefore quite rare. The mere existence of monitoring may not be as important as who is actually doing the monitoring — i.e., a friend or neighbor whom you do not wish to alienate. Sanctions generally play a less significant role in commons because, as Michael Cox et al. have noted in the case of a water management system in Zimbabwe, "people prefer to spend more time negotiating consensus than establishing and imposing sanctions."[41] In the English Lake District described by James Rebanks, it is considered a shocking breach of social honor if someone misleads another shepherd or sells a sheep for an inflated price. The *zanjera* irrigation communities of the Philippines reduce the burdens of enforcement by prescreening prospective members, and by suspending or even expelling anyone caught violating the rules.[42] For socially cohesive commons, it seems, sanctions may be important tools but ones that are seldom used. For commons based on casual, informal relationships where full trust cannot be developed — digital communities come to mind — sanctions may play a more necessary role.

------ **Peer Governance and The Cash Nexus** -------

We cluster the next three patterns of Peer Governance together because they have a special focus — protecting the commons from the risks posed by money, property, finance, and market activity and the calculative rationality associated with them. These patterns attempt to safeguard the Nested-I, Ubuntu Rationality, and other dimensions of commoning while allowing necessary interactions with the cash nexus.

Relationalize Property

As they come and go from their houses every day, many Germans are reminded that their relationships with property are ambiguous. Craftsmen in the early Middle Ages often inscribed a bit of traditional wisdom on the facades of countless homes: "This is mine but is not mine. Nor does it belong to the one who had it before me. It's not his, nor mine. He went out, I came in. And after me, it will be the same thing." The conundrum of property is that all sorts of things may be "owned" as a matter of law, but what really matters are their possession and use — and both of those rights are grounded in social relations.

Relationalize Property.

The Relationalize Property pattern is all about recognizing this reality. It means that the care-wealth of a commons does not belong exclusively to one person, nor even to a well-defined group. It has origins that precede us and will likely survive beyond our lives. But much as *homo economicus* is a caricature of what human beings really are, so property law has been designed to sanctify only certain types of human relationships with resources. Property is seen as an inert, separate thing with which we can do whatever we wish.

To Relationalize Property is to open up a new conception of property that recognizes the social relationships that are inextricably blended into any landscape, creative work, building, or sacred space. As French anthropologist of law Étienne Le Roy has rightly pointed out, what truly matters in a legal and political sense is the interpretation of the term "belong." To whom does a piece of land or knowledge or earthly life belong, and why? And how should the law recognize and operationalize such relationships? These are questions that property law as it now stands mostly avoids, or, at least, regards as choices that individuals should make unilaterally, usually in selfish ways.[43]

But people can and do nonetheless Relationalize Property, which is truly what human beings have always done and will always do. They have shared relationships with public parks and monuments, artworks, gravesites, and places of worship. They have shared memories and experiences with certain buildings, bodies of water, mountains, and forests. In a commons, these relations are recognized and respected — a challenge that is often mischaracterized as a choice between individual rights and collective interests. But as our earlier discussion about the Nested-I suggests, it is entirely possible for the two to be blended into a new paradigm entirely, a kind of "Ubuntu property."

Monasteries have done this for centuries. Monasteries are meant to be supportive environments for collective practices, and yet even here, care is taken in most religious orders to ensure that individuals have sufficient private space. Monks may live in simple personal cells or dwellings, but they are built around a cloister open to all. In the famous Florence Charterhouse, in Galluzzo, Italy, monks' dwellings even include a courtyard for individuals and a small corridor that lets them be alone outside when rain falls. This Carthusian cloister is designed in such a way that individual spaces are generously protected and no one except the monk living there has access to it. The dwellings are organized so that the door of each cell comes off a large corridor used by all. It is no coincidence that medieval commons, too, assured individuals their private space, called curtilage, while managing shared fields as collective enterprises.[44] Curtilage has survived into modern jurisprudence as the area around a person's house that, in the words of the US Supreme Court, harbors the "intimate activity associated with the sanctity of a man's home and the privacies of life.'"[45]

The land use practices of the Brazilian Landless Rural Worker Movement (Movimento Sem Terra, MST) revolve around this blending of individual and collective interests. Everyone together acts as stewards of occupied lands that no individual or collective can own absolutely. On MST lands, farmers can work on their own individual plots of land and use them for whatever purposes they want, but no one can excise their discrete piece of land from the land collectively occupied by the movement and sell it individually. Their use of the land is wrapped up with their belonging to the movement. In other words, the destiny of both individuals and the collective are deeply conjoined. Hundreds of thousands of Brazilian families[46] live or have lived in MST's land-occupation settlements in an effort to redistribute land to rural workers for small-scale farming. Much of MST's approach and practice are inspired by Catholic social doctrine, which regards the dignity of the human being, the common good, subsidiarity, and solidarity as fundamental principles. Interestingly, similar philosophical strains can be seen in the *Grundgesetz* — the constitution of the Federal Republic of Germany — which states that private property is not just for individual purposes, but must also serve a social function.[47] This is why so many communities authorize people to use land so long as they cultivate it — a "use it or lose it" rule that honors need over absolute ownership.

The essence of relationalized property is the blending of individual and collective interests into a new paradigm. In Chapter Eight, we elaborate on this theme and explore it through five specific examples of "other ways of having." In each case, the relationalized property helps commoners avoid the domineering or dependent social roles that conventional property rights generally entail. As explained in Chapter Eight, the Park Slope Food Coop uses unpaid, decommodified labor as a way to Pool & Share the benefits of a supermarket among its members. The Open Source Seed Initiative has pioneered ways to let farmers legally save, replant, and share seed, and breed new varieties. A large federation of German co-housing projects, Mietshäuser Syndikat, has taken a vast amount of housing off the market, enabled residents' stewardship of the buildings, and prevented the sale or liquidation of the housing.

All of these vanguard projects embody the idea of existential co-possession and use over the idea of absolute dominion that property generally fosters. The purpose of Relationalized Property is to enable us to nourish relationships with each other, the nonhuman world, and past and future generations by design.

Keep Commons & Commerce Distinct

You might wonder why cooperatives are often cited as examples of the commons when in fact many of them seem to produce for and sustain themselves entirely from the market. Why do we have tens of thousands of cooperatives bringing together "over one billion people around the world" according to the International Co-operative Alliance, with sales of $2.2 trillion among the largest three hundred cooperatives worldwide[48] — and yet the dominant economic model remains firmly in the saddle? The reason is that many cooperatives have not found cultural means to KEEP COMMONS & COMMERCE DISTINCT. And the law doesn't help. It almost always encourages, if not privileges, market-based activity over nonmarket, and commons-based options.

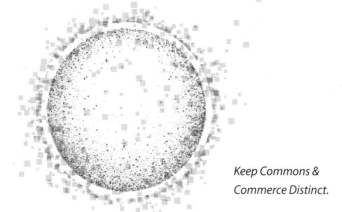

Keep Commons & Commerce Distinct.

One of the top priorities of any commons, therefore, is to preserve its integrity in the face of an often-predatory market order. A commons must take special pains to protect itself from enclosure.

Enclosures as a Threat to Commons

Enclosure is the opposite of commoning in that it *separates* what commoning otherwise *connects* — people and land, you and me, present and future generations, technical infrastructures and their governance, conservation areas and the people who have stewarded them for generations. The process of enclosure is generally driven by investors and corporations, often in collusion with the nation-state, to commodify shared land, water, forests, genes, creative works, and much else. The motivation is usually to monetize whatever can be controlled as private property and sold.

Enclosure is thus a profound act of dispossession and cultural disruption that forces people into both market dependency and market frames of thought. They must buy access to the essentials of life. They must bow to the conditions and prices set by investor-owners. They need permission to use resources they once stewarded for themselves.

Commons are also jeopardized by people who have trouble imagining social alternatives to the market ("co-optation from within"). Examples include coop housing members who seek to cash out when market prices rise, or medical researchers who attempt to patent drugs developed through community collaboration. Enclosures overturn a comprehensive culture of Social Life, Provisioning, and Peer Governance — a way of acting, knowing, and being in the world. They usher in a culture of calculative rationality and short-term, impersonal relationships that undermine commoning.

In a society where so much importance is placed on money, it is impossible to avoid the collision between commons and commerce. To protect commoning, affirmative steps to keep commerce at arm's length are essential. This is a lesson illustrated by free software. Many programmers find "their development environment radically changed, sometimes for the worse, by the entrance of paid labor into their communities," according to the free software programmer and academic Benjamin Mako Hill.[49] Once money is introduced into a commons for free software development, he notes, "it brings with it a new style of working and a new type of inter-developer relationships." Commoners lose their motivation to CONTRIBUTE FREELY (see p. 106–107), not because they can't necessarily afford to, but because they feel unjustly treated if others are getting paid. When money is part of the picture, people often begin to reorient their aspirations and focus on the norms that markets regard as important. Slowly and subtly, the gravitational pull of money tends to undermine the integrity of commoning — its social relations, independent values, and long-term goals.

Hill cites empirical evidence that paid labor in socially driven endeavors tends to crowd out volunteers, who see their work as less indispensable and meaningful, inducing them to contribute less or even quit.[50] Once money is introduced, it also creates a problem of how to spend it, and who makes those decisions. "It's easier for a successful volunteer free software project to get money than it is to decide how to spend it," Hill once pointed out. This is not an insuperable problem, of course, and many needs can only be fulfilled through markets. Yet if purchases of goods and services, or paid labor, *substitute* for what can be performed through commoning, it will begin to erode intrinsic motivations.

To be sure, commoners generally need money too, at least in some modest ways. In medieval times, commons were a way to meet everyday needs with only a minimal need for cash for occasional purchases. Commoning provided what we would now call a basic income — access to resources that ensure one's basic survival. While contemporary commons can hardly avoid the use of money, they can (and must) strive for as much *structural independence* as possible. This is a gradual process that requires the ability to flip the script and ask the right questions. Instead of asking how I can earn more money, it is more appropriate to ask, how can I organize my life in such a way that I become less dependent on money? How do I decommodify daily life? Similar questions should be asked at the level of a project, initiative, infrastructure, or platform.

Those accustomed to buying services generally act as consumers, an ethic that tends to work at cross-purposes to commoning. In a way, whenever something is designed as a bidding process or requires a set of deliverables or presents itself as a buy and sell transaction, or warns that if you don't participate, others will, a calculative rationality and money are being used to supersede Peer Governance. It is not just the promise or exchange of money that can override commoning, however. This can result from the presumption that "this is the only way to get things done."

And yet, there are ways for a commons to interact with the market economy while preventing the logic of strict reciprocity (equivalent exchange) and highest bidders and cheapest rates to prevail. When a French city council offered to pay EnCommuns, a commons-based network of database programmers, to do some work, it suddenly introduced external performance pressures, trumping the project's original goals and its self-determined work rhythms. As one participant reported, "A gap opened up between those who deliver a lot and get the money and those who [can only] deliver from time to time and do so without payment." A subtle, almost imperceptible shift in the inner dynamics of the commoning resulted. Instead of contributing to the project for intrinsic reasons (fun, networking, learning from others, social impact), people became focused on "meeting the contract." Soon the priorities of an outside contractor were seen as more important than the desires of other commoners. The logic of competition and efficiency surged to the fore, eclipsing the goal of voluntary cooperation. "Instead of helping people to change the behavioral patterns triggered by a flawed economic system," the participant noted, "it reinforced these patterns."

In response, EnCommuns created a semi-permeable membrane, an ingenious way to preserve the spirit of its commoning while engaging with commercial actors. First of all, EnCommuns demanded that any commercial enterprise pay for work produced by the commons. The point was to generate money to support the (nonmarket) activities of the commons. But rather than treating it as a conventional market transaction — payment for specific services — it required that any contracting company make a financial contribution to the commons for work that commoners would perform in any case. In other words, the business would not be "paying for a special service or product," it would be making a donation. In addition, all contributions are publicly disclosed. EnCommuns's goal is to make sure that it doesn't come to depend mainly on revenue from selling something, whether its people's labor or products. Why? Because a commons based on such a design will quickly prioritize market success over commoners' needs, which is likely to begin to unravel its social fabric. By treating payments as donations, EnCommuns decouples acts of giving to and taking from the commons, remaining sovereign in how it makes use of money *within* its commons. EnCommuns explains, "Our idea is to help commercial organizations gain confidence in the commons approach while helping the commons to be funded when they are used for business purposes."[51] This same approach has been used by the P2P Foundation in its Peer Production License (p. 402 #16), which grants free use to anyone to use work from the commons except for commercial users, who must pay.

The transnational Guerrilla Media Collective — a socially minded group of translators, designers, and media workers — has developed a governance system that integrates commoning and paid work. Their Commons-Oriented Open Cooperative Governance and Economic Model, version 2.0, lets people pursue mission-oriented work and paid work while explicitly requiring people to care for the health of the collective and individual members.[52] Group decision making and responsibilities are based on different levels of engagement — casual, unpaid involvement; a formal process of "dating" that is partly paid; and committed, paid membership with specified responsibilities. A credit system tracks people's pro bono projects and paid work, while care work is explicitly visualized and weighed against productive work. The purpose is to keep commoning as the core priority.

To Keep COMMONS AND COMMERCE DISTINCT, the stewards of many community forests allow the cutting of trees for personal use only, not for market sale. Fisheries commons often stipulate the amount of fish that any individual fisher may sell on the open market. University administrations tend to serve as intermediaries between funding sources and scientists so that researchers can have open, honest debates and share their findings without the taint of corporate influence.

Finance Commons Provisioning

In a world in which capitalist finance and money are ubiquitous and the default tools for getting things done, a question arises: how can provisioning in commons be financed without the harmful influences of money and debt? We have found that three general approaches can be effective in helping people escape dependency on capitalist finance while enhancing their security and freedom. These are *money-lite commoning* to reduce the need for money and markets; *collaborative financing* that lets commoners create and circulate money or credit for themselves, wholly from within their commons; and *new public-commons circuits of finance,* which allow taxpayer funds administered by government to be used to support commons.

Finance Commons
Provisioning.

Before exploring these three approaches, some general observations must be made. As we have seen, the health of any commons depends upon preventing money from dominating its social dynamics. If debt or capital compromise people's independence or sow social divisions, a commons will likely fall apart. It is therefore helpful for commoners (or anybody) to become less dependent on money and markets. Peer-driven approaches enable commoners to recirculate the value that they create for mutual benefit, rather than letting creditors or outside equity holders siphon value away in the form of interest or dividend payments.

A basic question that must be addressed in a commons, French commons thinker Philippe Aigrain once said, is, "What type of relations do we want to exist between the monetary economy and the commons?" We must also ask, What type of money culture do commoners want to develop for themselves? These questions should be answered in such a way that, at a minimum, capital or money does not metastasize and convert cooperative activities into capitalism. The pursuit of money and market success, usually seen as a necessary path to community well-being, too often ends up subordinating it to outside markets and capital. Therefore, it is imperative to KEEP COMMONS & COMMERCE DISTINCT (p. 151). Another way to minimize the harmful influence of money is to PRACTICE GENTLE RECIPROCITY (p. 108) so that the calculative rationality of market relationships does not become the cultural norm, crowding out solidarity and the generative creativity of commoning.

Tech entrepreneur Frank Karlitschek discovered this lesson the hard way. In 2010, he started an open source file hosting community, ownCloud, to compete with the likes of Dropbox, Google Drive, and Microsoft OneDrive. These platforms allow web users to synchronize the use of data and documents among diverse digital devices and to store that information in the cloud on someone else's servers. This software architecture enables multiple parties to reliably access and use large collections of files in authorized, secure ways.

To expand development of the ownCloud platform, Karlitschek in 2011 secured millions of dollars in venture capital financing to start a company, ownCloud, Inc., at which he became chief technology officer. But by 2016 he learned how profoundly outside money influences an organization's strategies and practices. Even though hundreds of programmers were contributing to ownCloud as an open source project, company executives did not properly acknowledge the contributions of the community or share internal corporate deliberations with it, according to Karlitschek. Quite abruptly, he decided to resign, concerned that investors had "thrown the project under the bus." In his resignation letter, Karlitschek wrote: "Without sharing too much, there are some moral questions popping up for me. Who owns the community? Who owns ownCloud itself? And what matters more, short-term money or long-term responsibility and growth? Is ownCloud just another company or do we also have to answer to the hundreds of volunteers who contribute and make it what it is today? These questions brought me to the very tough decisions: I have decided to leave my own company today."[53]

Weeks later, Karlitschek announced that he would fork the code and reconstitute the community of contributors under a new project called NextCloud. It would not have external investors, but be driven by the talents and commitment of a large community of volunteer programmers, in a more authentic open source manner. In addition,

NextCloud, with its modular structure, would offer a variety of new functionalities, such as an address book, photo galleries, music and video playback, task manager, feed reader, email program, word processing, mindmaps, administrative tools, and more. Within two years, the Nextcloud project had 1,800 unpaid programmers and millions of users around the globe, including many large corporations such as Siemens and ARD. It continues to build out its shared vision — *without* the artificial limitations imposed by investors. At the Bits & Bäume (Bits & Trees) conference in Berlin in 2018 — a first-ever gathering of environmentalists and free software hackers (the "critical technology movement") — Karlitschek reflected that his ownCloud experience taught him to focus on ensuring independence when financing an endeavor. A critical lesson for commoners as well.

Commoners have a variety of strategies for minimizing the pernicious influences of money, which we will now explore, but whichever one is chosen, the tail must not wag the dog by allowing money to drive our aspirations and practices.

Money-lite commoning. Commoning means relying on sharing, dividing up, and mutualization to meet needs as much as possible, and on collaborative financing. This lets people minimize their reliance on money and markets. We call this "money-lite" — the ethic and social practice of reducing one's need for money as much as possible through sharing, co-using, DIT (do-it-together), and other practices that minimize reliance on market exchange. This is fundamental to all commons. Commoners can improve their long-term independence by withdrawing as much as possible from dealings with the market/state system.

Money-lite commoning is how hackers helped neutralize Microsoft's proprietary abuses of its monopolies over Windows and Office in the early 2000s (see pp. 128 and 167–168). They developed GNU/Linux, Open Office, and scores of other high-quality open source programs as practical, low-cost or no-cost alternatives to the standard programs offered by the market giants. Through shareable, peer-produced programs, people can create digital commons of their own and escape draconian licensing agreements and abusive technical designs. Users can rest easy that their code is compatible with other systems and legally modifiable. They can't be extorted into paying for expensive, unnecessary upgrades.

In nondigital spaces, there are many proven systems for reducing one's individual costs or eliminating the need for market activity. Community land trusts, by decommodifying the land under buildings, can reduce the cost of housing and small enterprises. Co-housing and peer-to-peer car-sharing and tool-sharing projects are forms of money-lite commoning. Cosmo-local production (see pp. 195–197) sheds the costs of proprietary design (based on patents, trademarks, etc.) and enables less expensive modular, local production.

The point of money-lite commoning is to help people focus on their real needs and escape the endless cycle of disempowerment that a consumerist culture generally promotes. The capitalist economy spends extraordinary energy and money trying to get people to individually consume even though much of this is wholly unnecessary. David Fleming calls the resulting infrastructures of dependency "regrettable necessities" — which then spawn a whole layer of products like cars and smart phones that are soon considered essential. Commoners can escape many of these "necessities" by developing their own systems, infrastructure, spaces, and resource-pools for sharing.

Collaborative financing consists of pooling money from individuals, the community, and the wider public to finance common wealth. This strategy not only strengthens a commons here and now, it gives structural support for commoning in the future. Historically, collaborative financing has included such models as mutual credit societies and insurance pools, cooperative finance, community-controlled microfinance, and local currencies. In recent times, crowdfunding has been taken these capacities to new levels in both small and very big projects. Goteo, a crowdfunding platform for the commons that started in Spain, is a preeminent force of collaborative finance. From its founding in 2012 through 2017, it has raised more than 7.3 million euros, funded more than 900 commons projects throughout Europe and Latin America, and provided online assistance to 2,500 additional projects.[54] Goteo differs from conventional crowdfunding websites by requiring that projects actually advance the principles of commons.

At a larger scale, the Wikimedia movement in 2016-17 received 6.1 million donations totaling US$91 million, with an average gift of $14.79. This pooling of money, distributed among sixteen wiki projects, means that anyone can have noncommercial access to an online dictionary, quotation database, collections of digital books and learning materials, databases of plant and animal species, repositories of photographs and images, and travel guides. By shifting these materials out of the commercial market, where sellers are constantly trying to capture people's personal data and advertise to them, the many wiki projects let people escape all that.

Terre de Liens, a French organization, pools money to buy land for aspiring contemporary "peasant-farmers." The goal is to decommodify land in perpetuity — i.e., remove land from the market and hold it in trust forever, in the manner of a community land trust. One portion of funding is dedicated to "solidarity savings," which is used exclusively to help acquire new farmland. In Germany, a federation of housing commons, Mietshäuser Syndikat, does something similar. It offers collaborative financing to help groups of residents buy co-housing projects, in effect decommodifying them. Then, to continue that process of what it calls "solidarity transfers," it collects one-tenth of a euro per square meter of living space from every resident in its more than 160 co-housing projects. (For more on Mietshäuser Syndikat, see Chapter Eight.)

Artabana, a federation for community-based healthcare funding with thousands of affiliates in Switzerland, Germany, and Austria, uses a similar strategy. Artabana is organized in small groups whose members provide social insurance to each other. There are no restrictions regarding people's choices of physician, treatment option, drug, or remedy. The groups jointly determine, in a sphere of trust, the mutual assistance and the appropriation of solidarity fund resources each group contributes to at a group level. Additionally, a portion of the local pools of money goes into a so-called emergency fund run by Artabana International. Usually, a group can cover the healthcare expenses for its members simply through pooling and dividing up money. However, if someone in a local group faces unexpectedly high medical expenses — for instance, in case of chronic diseases or complicated operations — the federation's emergency fund can provide additional support. It functions as a kind of reinsurance within the community-based insurance system.

When "Jane" in Australia found that she needed surgery for a severe heart condition, she and her husband planned to use their home mortgage to finance the anticipated cost of AUS $35,000. But it turned out that her local Artabana group had contacted Artabana Germany, and their emergency fund was able to pay for her surgery. "We were humbled and surprised that Artabana Germany's emergency fund would support me without knowing me ... Within a week the money was in our account at Artabana Hobart. It was initially hard to accept the gesture from strangers. We felt self-conscious about the generosity." All of the Artabana projects function as federated pools of funding to cover larger magnitudes of risk and future needs.

A dynamic worldwide movement is attempting to minimize the pernicious influences of money by inventing their own community-created and -controlled currencies. This often takes the form of a local currency to serve specific needs within a limited geographic area or among registered users. For example, in extremely poor neighborhoods in Kenya, the Bangla Pesa and Lida Pesa are neighborhood-owned and -controlled currencies, part of the larger Sarafu Credit system. The currencies enable members to capture and recirculate value created within the community while preventing the outside economy from siphoning it away. Such systems are complementary to conventional (fiat) money and serve as building blocks for a commons-based economy. Researcher Grzegorz Sobiecki estimates there are more than 6,000 alternative currencies worldwide.[55]

Each of these platforms and federations — Goteo, Terre de Liens, Mietshäuser Syndikat, Artabana, local currencies — requires some sort of collective return. Goteo, for example, requires that works are released under Creative Commons or other free licenses. This ensures that future creators will be able to copy, share, and/or modify those works. The basic principle is that anyone who takes from the commons must give something back to it. Also, they do not just seek to amass financial contributions, but to pay forward specific benefits so that others may enjoy them or so future commons can be created.

Creating new public-commons circuits of finance. The state provides plenty of support to market capitalism such as subsidies, legal privileges, and state-approved monopolies. There is no reason why it should not recognize and support the value of commoning as well, through state investment, cofunding of commons, and creative financial tools and systems. This could take many forms.

The most obvious approach would be for the state to provide generous direct financial support to commons-based projects. The state already uses taxpayer money for all sorts of important national purposes; certainly commoning creates immense value of its own that should be similarly supported. However, state funding tends to rely on restrictive bureaucratic procedures and strict sets of deliverables, while any commons requires the space and time for experimentation and creative evolution. In engaging with any state program that purports to support commoning, commoners must be wary of the procedural burdens of state funding and the risks of depending on such support. State funding can easily distort the integrity of a project, open the door to outside political influence, and risk the abrupt termination of support when the political winds shift.

Some of the problems of direct state funding might be avoided by instituting regimes for statutory resource-pooling, for example, similar to a government-mandated flat fee on recorded music, performances, and other types of creative content. The mandatory fee would recognize the actual role that nonmarket creative communities play in helping commercial entertainment: they help companies identify and recruit promising new commercial talent, and keep various musical traditions alive. Why shouldn't commercial players indirectly repay the debt they have to collaborative creative communities? The finance mechanism of mandatory flat fees would be predictable and easily scalable, and could help large groups of creative people.[56]

Just as government agencies often assist businesses by providing loan guarantees or actual loan funds, the state could create state funding programs to finance commons-managed housing, Fab Labs, cosmo-local production, telecommunications, and other activities. The state could require that a percentage of tax revenues from fisheries or timber harvesting be put into a pool of funds managed by multistakeholder organizations acting as community-based trusts to manage coastal lands, forests, or natural reserves. Perhaps the most ambitious state–commons financing scheme would be an unconditional basic income. At present, this idea takes many forms, but the one that would most empower commoners would be to authorize communities to decide how to use and share their time and talents.

6

Provisioning Through Commons

THERE IS A SAYING IN SILICON VALLEY: eat your own dog food —
meaning people at the company must actually use the software
they make, in real-world circumstances.[1] "Dogfooding" is considered
the best way to ensure that something truly works well. It is revealing
that the software industry has such a term to describe the internal
testing of its products. It points to a hidden weakness of the conventional economy — the treatment of production and consumption as
separate activities, and the ultra-specialization of production in ways
that segregate design, documentation, and manufacturing as separate
professional silos. This bureaucratization means that each employee
depends on the work product of others without really understanding
the complexities involved. It also makes it easier for any department to
cut corners on quality and safety, knowing that unwitting consumers
may or may not be able to do anything about it.

Some companies realize that integrating the lessons of real-world
consumption into the design and production process is indispensable. As the primary creator of TeX Typesetting software, Donald E.
Knuth, once confessed: "I came to the conclusion that the designer
of a new system must not only be the implementer and the first
large-scale user; the designer should also write the first user manual.
The separation of any of these four components would have hurt
TeX significantly. If I had not participated fully in all these activities, literally hundreds of improvements would never have been
made, because I would never have thought of them or perceived
why they were important."[2] Users have firsthand knowledge that is
invaluable in design and production, even if economists regard the
separation of production and consumption as an inexorable fact of
modern life.

Trained to see the dismemberment of complex production processes as efficient and natural, and its segregation from consumption as a core premise of "the economy," economists tend to overlook a more elegant, practical approach to provisioning — commoning. Commoning is at heart an act of social self-organization and constant learning whose central purpose is to help people meet needs by producing things or services together. (We prefer to use the word "provisioning" as a nonmarket version of "production.") Meeting needs has long been a standard definition of what an economy is all about, so commoning should properly be seen as part of "the economy," too, even though economics textbooks generally ignore this fact. Commons let people produce food and clothing, shelter and means of transportation, machinery and microscopes, software and hardware, drugs, healthcare, and even prosthetics.[3] It is breathtaking how much people can provide for themselves by aligning interests, motivations, and agency toward a common goal. Commoning provides a way to leverage social trust within new organizational forms to coordinate people's actions.

Through commons, people can blend their social and economic needs, providing the basis for re-integrating production and consumption. This practice is especially prevalent in the digital realm, where users and producers tend to be the same people ("prosumers"). In conventional economic terms, a commons helps reduce the need for administration, lawyering, "human resource" management, and marketing by instead relying on a community of trust and individual commitment. Who needs advertising when the goal is to meet needs, not promote consumption?

So why put the interests and needs of producers in one box and those of consumers in another box, and blindly assume that the marketplace will somehow reconcile them? Why not re-imagine the whole process as an enterprise where production and consumption are integrated as one organic process of planning, design, documentation, and provisioning along with use, reuse, and waste management? Production need not consist of a series of complex, interlocking *markets* for labor, commodity sourcing, manufacturing, distribution, retail, advertising, etc. It can occur through commons that let people decide to co-make and co-use what they need, often with a division of labor but without that strict provision of roles, organized through hierarchies. The most significant difference with corporate bureaucracy is that the output is made available to others and the benefits are retained and shared. Different skills, talents, and knowledge can all be orchestrated to contribute to production. Knowledge can be readily shared, designs can focus on quality, and provisioning methods can be adjusted to improve results — all without catering to the harsh quarterly profit demands of investors. Tasks can be rotated so that people do not need to organize their work according to narrow roles defined by objectified, artificial value (price, wages) and fixed job categories. Freed of market imperatives, greater flexibility and adaptability are possible.

Besides reintegrating production and consumption, as well as fragmented steps of production, commons can re-incorporate care into our conceptualization of the economy (see pp. 169–173). With the rise of capitalism, caring, childrearing, and education have been seen as activities external to the working of the economy. Except for public education, they are something for individuals to take care of on their own time, and at their own expense. A commons does not externalize care, and so is more able to take account of a person's fuller life, not just their need to earn money.

*   *   *

In this chapter, we describe the character of "production in common," or, more precisely, "provisioning through commoning," by examining ten key patterns. These are the structured regularities that tend to be needed for commons provisioning. These patterns manifest each time in distinctive ways, much as a flower will grow differently in forest shade, direct sun, or moist riverbanks. Whatever the circumstances, provisioning remains a practical enterprise that aims to get things done.

The critical difference between commoning and the capital-centric economy is that the latter regards its work results almost exclusively as marketable products. They are fungible artifacts whose value is mostly defined by their price. Since commons blur (or even eliminate!) the roles of "producers" and "consumers," so too the very character of the "products" changes. The things produced are not designed to be sold, or sold in high volumes at the highest prices, or to pander to our consumer fantasies and then fall apart through planned obsolescence so that the cycle can be repeated. Provisioning through Commons means producing useful, durable things that will have ongoing social importance to their makers and users, and so the end results are not "goods" or "commodities," as the classical economist would call them. Commoners instead cultivate affective ties to their care-wealth — forests, farmland, water, urban spaces — which often become part of their culture, social lives, and identities. The goal of Provisioning through Commons is not maximum efficiency, profit, or higher Gross Domestic Product. It aims simply to meet needs and provide a stable, fair, satisfying, and ecologically minded way of life. There is no economic growth imperative built into provisioning except its motive to increasingly displace, and substitute for, exploitative or expensive market practices.

Most of the concerns that the dominant economy obsesses about — growth, market share, competition, copyright, patents, advertising, branding, opening new markets — play hardly any role in the commons. This is because the commons economy invites people to reorient their perspectives and aspire to a different set of outcomes than those of market capitalism — the satisfaction of real, not contrived, needs. Security. A sense of belonging and connection. A meaningful life. Implicit in many commons, too, is a vision of advancing greater freedom, fairness, and sustainability for all.

The biggest shift that the commons economy brings is a move from the economy as an autonomous, globalized supermachine to an economy that nurtures life on its own terms, at appropriate scales. In the course of Provisioning through Commons a *tapestry of relationships* is woven, which confirms the wisdom of ecophilosopher Thomas Berry: "The universe is primarily a communion of subjects, not a collection of objects."[4] The basic difference between the commons and capital-driven markets could not be stated more succinctly.

The difficult challenge, however, is how to devise structures and encourage social dynamics for commons provisioning. We have identified ten recurrent, hardy patterns that can build out a more robust commons economy:

Provisioning Through Commons

Make & Use Together
Support Care & Decommodified Work
Share the Risks of Provisioning

Four Modes of Contribution and Allocation
Contribute & Share
Pool, Cap & Divide Up
Pool, Cap & Mutualize
Trade with Price Sovereignty

Use Convivial Tools
Rely on Distributed Structures
Creatively Adapt & Renew

Make & Use Together

Make & Use Together is a time-honored way for people to meet shared needs. To reduce costs and affirm commonality, people often decide to co-create and share access to pools of information, knowledge, money, working spaces, tools, and infrastructures. To make and use something together is as old as the human species and as new as the internet.

Make & Use Together.

As in other patterns we introduce in these chapters, the "&" matters. The pattern is Make *and* Use Together, not simply "Use Together." If you think like a commoner, you think about the thing produced *and* the entire generative process as something to be used by yourself, shared, and potentially used by others. The process is not primarily about making and producing for your own or other people's consumption. It's about meeting shared needs. When making new creative works, a person forfeits his or her proprietary control under copyright (using Creative Commons licenses) to ensure that certain use rights such as copying and sharing are available. Commoners don't want to restrict others from co-producing the same thing; they want as many people as possible to join in the enterprise. Encouraging more commoning in online contexts is highly attractive, because, as Linus Torvalds discovered in those early days of the World Wide Web, the more the merrier. On open digital platforms, where it is virtually costless to reproduce things (but for the energy-intensive infrastructure), *more value* can be generated as more people have the capacity to participate.

The making that goes on in a commons should not really be regarded as DIY (do it yourself) but as DIT — "do it together," to meet one's own needs and potentially the needs of others. This explains why CSA farms, for example, have no interest in preventing other CSAs from forming and flourishing in their region. You hardly ever read or hear about a CSA competing with another CSA. It is pretty much the opposite. As a member, you want to encourage other CSAs to form, at least until everyone has easy access to a nearby CSA farm.

This pattern has endless variations. It is the standard process in the *makerspaces, open workshops* and *Fab Labs* around the world that bring together hackers, professional technologists, digital artists, and amateurs to tinker, experiment, and fabricate things together. According to a Study by Cedifa (Center for Digital Fabrication), a Fab Lab (fabrication laboratory) can be opened within seven days and a basic investment of only US$5,000 if it relies on commons-oriented approaches, including the use of open source software.[5] *Open design and manufacturing communities* build furniture, electronics, farm equipment, and open source motor vehicles in this manner.

In some commons, the focus is on shared use, in others it is on shared making. The popularity of both approaches can be seen in the 260 open workshops in German-speaking countries where hobbyists, master craftspeople, and others work with wood, 3D printers, metal, and electronics. Most anything that normally comes from a factory can be DIT-produced — bokashi buckets for urban composting, cargo bikes and solar-powered cars, lamps, microscopes, and motherboards, cloth, toilets and replacement parts, wooden furniture, and visors. Worldwide, volunteers in more than 1,300 repair cafes are fixing broken appliances and household items, bringing to life an idea introduced in 2009 in the Netherlands by journalist and blogger Martine Postma.[6] The open workshops and repair cafes are places for community building, collective thinking, and learning. They CREATIVELY ADAPT & RENEW (see below) countless objects that are considered waste, giving them a second life cycle.

Support Care and Decommodified Work

Work in a commons is not a purchased unit of commodified work, aka "labor." It is an activity that draws upon people's deep passions and values — their whole selves. Geographer Neera Singh calls this sort of commitment "affective labor"[7] because people show love, devotion, and care — or simply awareness for what needs to be done — when stewarding a forest, caring for elderly parents, designing and curating a web archive, teaching a craft or tending a community garden. Care and commitment in a shared endeavor is central for commoning. It is the elemental glue that holds people together. It occurs, for example, when parents cook, clean, and provide personal support to their children, relatives, and parents — the household as the core focus of the economy, as in the original Greek sense of the term *oikos*. In a commons this household is bigger than in a Greek polis; it comprises the space and all the people and elements involved in meeting needs.[8]

Support Care and Decommodified Work.

Care occurs when people bring their full humanity to a task instead of having impersonal, money-mediated relationships with market resources. Affective labor in effect converts a mere commodity into something that is cared for. One might more accurately call it *care-wealth*. Unlike a market resource whose value is defined by its price, care-wealth has value because there is a nimbus of memories, meanings, and special feelings associated with it, the result of people dedicating their time and care. The social energy that hovers around care-wealth resembles the halo of electrical energy that pulsates around a magnet. It is no surprise that many communities have special feelings for sacred places or the focal points of people's care — a public square, a riverfront, an ancient tree. Certain theaters of commoning — a food cooperative, a local forest, a land trust, a collaborative website — acquire special meaning and emotional resonance as people commit their heart and soul to them (and, indeed, *only* if they do so).

The personal and social energies of care accomplish a lot of meaningful work without which a society could not hold together. As we describe in this chapter, countless commons rely on care that is contributed freely, shared, divided up, or developed through gentle reciprocity. Caring is not the result of commoning, but clearly a core force of commoning that also takes place everywhere, even in markets. The difference is that the market economy — while welcoming what care and intrinsic motivation can accomplish — is incapable of summoning and supporting care. Cash inducements (wages, fees, bribes, subsidies) may or may not elicit genuine care because market incentives are mostly concerned with "productive labor" — outcomes that have measurable, tangible economic benefits. Caring and commoning, by contrast, attempt to speak directly to our inner selves, as Nested-I's, with integrity and sensitivity. This helps explain why commons are better hosting spaces for enabling care and decommodified work to flourish.

To be sure, the conventional economy has commodified all sorts of care into "care work," including childcare and healthcare. Care is often structured into units of labor organized by the logics of productivity and measurability. But it is impossible to squeeze human relationships and care into a regime of schedules, forms, and productivity metrics. When subjected to a calculative rationality, care is no longer care. It is a form of robotics performed by human automatons.

However, as we saw with Buurtzorg Nederland, the neighborhood home care described in Chapter One, genuine care can be provided to large numbers of people without market incentives degrading its essential human quality. What's key is retaining the appropriate scale. "People are not bicycles who can be organized according to an organizational chart," as the Buurtzorg founder put it. Providing care through commons, in defiance of market principles, does not mean that quality of care suffers. It *improves care* because people have the freedom and time to provide personalized, situationally appropriate attention to people.

While some care activities have been commodified, most care still takes place outside of the formal economy. Economists have externalized it, which is their way of simply ignoring this area of life. This indifference towards care and meeting basic human needs means that caring for countless societal problems — family life, intergenerational support in extended families, local culture, informal social pursuits — is made invisible. The care jobs created by markets are not only badly paid, but usually relegated primarily to women, immigrants, and non-white minorities.

The irony is that care and decommodified work are utterly indispensable to the functioning of the economy, including "productive labor." No civilization could function without care activities. Where would the next generation of employees come from if families did not raise, educate, and socialize them? How could a community exist without people helping each other as neighbors and socializing young people to be good citizens? Once you enumerate all of the uncommodified work that is needed to keep a society functioning — subsistence provisioning, householding, civic life, voluntarism, etc. — it becomes obvious that money and markets are only the tip of the iceberg of the economy. "Unpaid work is worth billions," as a German journalist has put it, using the only language many seem to understand.[9]

To SUPPORT CARE & DECOMMODIFIED WORK is to rescue this neglected care sector from oblivion and put it at the center of economic thinking. It is to validate a different logic for organizing the economy. Commoning invites us to *forgo* self-advantage rather than maximize personal gain. By providing care, we make ourselves vulnerable and dependent on others. We sacrifice our time, energy, and

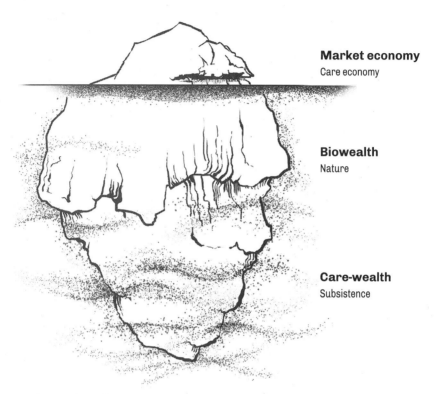

Iceberg with market economy.

awareness in order to develop healthy relationships — toward ourselves and our bodies, toward others, and toward nature. Instead of striving to be super-efficient with our time and money, we prioritize human presence and connection. In this respect, the commons challenges the very heart of market economics by asserting different standards of valuation. When economic traditionalists carp that care models cannot scale, they miss the point: real care *is supposed to occur* in small, intimate contexts where authentic relationships can develop. There is obviously a role for larger systems, but care is not just about units of service delivery. It is about another way of understanding the economy as an "oikonomy" or "ecommony" where "economy is care," as Ina Prätorius of Care Revolution, an advocacy network in Switzerland, Germany, and Austria, puts it.

Two generations of feminist economists,[10] many of them associated with the International Association for Feminist Economics, and researchers like Diane Elson, Julie Nelson, Alicia Girón González, Brigitte Young, Adelheid Biesecker, and Friederike Haberman, have pioneered incisive critiques about the deficiencies of mainstream economics when it comes to care. This literature shares a great deal of ground with commoning because both are generally ignored or dismissed as externalities. Both discourses attempt to leapfrog over the flawed premises of standard economics (e.g., *homo economicus*; value as equivalent to price) by asserting a different epistemological framework.

Studies show that people who can escape market regimes of valuation (i.e., money, prices) often show *greater* care, motivation, and concern for quality.[11] This occurs because the use of wages, bonuses, bribes, and other cash incentives often sends a signal that induces people to behave as competitive and even cynical market players. By contrast, commoning tends to encourage people to give the best of themselves and nourish deeper relationships and social trust. By providing care and decommodified work, they become a Nested-I. The classic example of this (not necessarily conscious) dynamic is the gift economy of blood donation. British researcher Richard Titmuss in the 1960s found that volunteers who give blood are more likely to have safer, healthier blood than the people who are paid money for their blood — because the latter often have substance abuse problems or illnesses.[12]

Share the Risks of Provisioning

In the capitalist economy, companies are said to shoulder the risks of creating and marketing a product, even though their research and development budget is often subsidized by taxpayers and even though they often displace risks and expenses on to consumers, the environment, and future generations. This is their rationale for reaping the profits after production. In a planned economy, some risks are assumed by the state or simply ignored. In a commons, however, where the distinction between consumer and producer gets blurred, *everybody* who is actively involved accepts co-responsibility for the sharing of risks before and during production. These risks may include the uncertainty of the crop yields from a CSA farm, the complications of maintaining a community-based Wi-Fi infrastructure such as Guifi.net, or the uncertainties associated with the open source process needed to design an affordable, nonproprietary tractor such as the Life-Trac of Open Source Ecology.[13]

Share the Risks of Provisioning.

The ways of sharing risks take many different forms. In crowd-funding campaigns, donors essentially give a gift to project leaders to develop a new software app, invention, or social service. When contributions are pooled for a collective investment, the risks are fairly small for any individual while the potential benefits for everyone are large. In many German CSAs, there is a process known as a "bidding round" (*Bieterrunde*) in which the CSA farm informs members at the beginning of the planting season how much money will be needed to grow the year's crops. Members then gather in a circle, reflect together on the group's overall need, and decide individually what each person can afford to give. Then members submit anonymous pledges of money into the common pot. If not enough funds are raised in the first bidding round, the size of the shortfall is announced and a second round of contributions starts. Usually the needed sum is raised in only two rounds. This is the way that risks for growing the season's crops are shared without requiring people of unequal capacities to contribute equal shares toward dividing up the harvest equally.

When risks are shared, everything changes: the power relationships, the decision-making processes about what to produce and how, the cash flow, and obviously, the sharing of the wealth. For these reasons, sharing the risks of provisioning provides an important step in transcending a market-driven economy. This brings us to the next four patterns of Provisioning through Commons, each of which addresses how to allocate wealth that is generated. Before looking at each pattern, it helps to make some conceptual clarifications and to review the basic choices that commoners face.

Contribute & Share

Pooling means contributing to a stock of resources to reach a common goal or solve a specific problem, spontaneously or by voluntary agreement. Then the pool is shared. You can pool virtually everything – knowledge, physical resources, one's time, energy, food, tools, ideas, or money. Pooling is not just about putting things into a collective pot, it's also about contributing one's talents, energy, imagination, and services to create a commons that can benefit everyone. When people Contribute & Share, whatever is needed is freely contributed (sometimes with a gentle nudge) by all participants. And then it is shared without calculating everyone's individual benefit. Participants reduce their individual costs of provisioning, increase the likelihood of meeting everybody's needs better, and develop a sense of co-responsibility and solidarity. As in Pool & Divide, everybody can participate regardless of their financial means or social status.

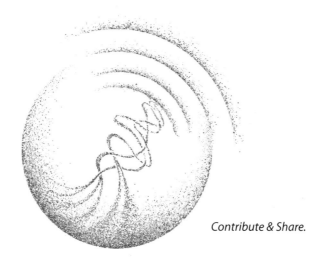

Contribute & Share.

Contribute & Share works in all realms of commoning, but it is particularly powerful on open networks, where the usefulness of information, ideas, knowledge, code, and design grows the more that they are shared and adapted. However, what matters most here as well is the "&." Pooling without sharing in the commons is like shopping without money in capitalism: it won't work. You can only share what you pool, contribute, or co-produce in the first place.

Contributing software code has been likened to throwing vegetables into a common cooking pot into which everyone contributes what they have, and everyone can take what they wish.[14] Indeed, Pool & Share is a routine practice among programmers and designers who contribute to a shared body of code and designs. It is also a routine practice among global communities of open hardware designers who create shareable blueprints for farm equipment (Open Source Ecology, Atelier Paysan), furniture (Open Desk), houses (WikiHouse), motor vehicles (Wikispeed), and prosthetics (Open Prosthetics Project). Institutions may Contribute & Share, too. A classic instance is the Europeana Initiative of nearly 400 museums, archives, and cultural institutions, which are collaborating on a public process to label and preserve public-domain art works.

Varieties of Allocation in a Commons

After pooling wealth or talents, things start to get more interesting. Sharing is only one option among many for allocating what gets produced. A resource can be divided up among people in some negotiated or equitable fashion, taking account of individual needs, but *not* in equal units. Or maybe the resource is mutualized according to some formula agreed upon in advance among participants, perhaps correlated with how much an individual has contributed ... or perhaps not. There is yet another choice — to trade the outputs from the commons for cash. This should be a conscious, careful decision (see "Keep Commons & Commerce Distinct," p. 151–155) because it could abruptly take the group out of the paradigm of commoning and into the world of conventional markets and its pitfalls.

Each of the possible approaches for allocating and distributing common wealth elevates a particular rationality that shapes the group's identity. Each engenders different expectations and feelings among participants. Some of these approaches differ merely in nuance; others have implications for the core mission of the group and its constitutive principles. Let's explore two elementary distinctions that must be made.

The first has to do with the characteristics of a given resource. A key question is: Is the resource something at risk of being used up ("rivalrous," in economic lingo) or something that can't get used up ("nonrivalrous")? If something is rivalrous, it means that if one person uses it, there will be less or none for another person. There may not be enough to go around to everyone, or the resource could be overused.

Think about water or food. If I eat an apple, you can't eat it, too. Only so many farmers can use river water for irrigation before it ruins the river. By contrast, certain types of resources — creative works, knowledge, ideas, information, software code, traditions — don't get used up. They are not rivalrous. In fact, for these things, as mentioned earlier, the participation of lots of people can *greatly increase* the value generated and the collective benefits, especially if this is happening on digital networks. That's one reason that Linux and open design have grown in value. For those things that can't get used up, the problem is not free riders who might deplete them; the challenge is curating the intangible code, information, or music; preventing vandals and trolls from disrupting cooperation; and ensuring adequate financing of the commons.

The second basic distinction involves the social terms of exchange and circulation. Shall it be *reciprocal* or *nonreciprocal*? Sharing & Dividing Up a resource are nonreciprocal, meaning the giver doesn't necessarily get or expect anything in return. This pattern expresses a relationship that lies between giving and taking. If the allocation of a resource is reciprocal, there are two options — mutualization and trade. In each, the giver, contributor, or seller is assured that he or she will get something in return. Reciprocal exchanges, whether via mutualization or trading, are a very different social beast than nonreciprocal sharing or dividing up.

With these two distinctions in mind, let us have a closer look at the different ways people interact.

Nonreciprocal Interactions

Sharing. We use this term only when we refer to the sharing of things that do not get depleted as they are used. Sharing is a way to allocate such resources in informal, flexible, and even improvisational ways. This definition of sharing is in stark contrast to the overly broad and confusing way the term is often used today, in which the commercial activity of Uber and Airbnb is characterized as the "sharing economy" rather than what it is: the microrental economy.

Dividing Up. We speak of *dividing up* when something at risk of being used up is being shared. Dividing Up is a nonreciprocal allocation of objects — food, money, land, bicycles, tools — among family and strangers, smaller groups and bigger networks, without calculating everyone's individual contributions or benefits in discrete units. When we divide something up, one person can get more than someone else, based on individual needs and the context. Dividing up sometimes happens in response to tacit or formal demands.

We believe it is helpful to use different words to distinguish the sharing of intangibles and information (what we will call "sharing") from the sharing of things ("dividing up"). This distinction was brought to our attention by psychologist Michael Tomasello, who makes the point that the effects of having to share something that gets used up are different from sharing something that doesn't get used up. Rather than use the same word to describe both ("sharing"), we use the verb "divide up" to describe the particular challenge of fairly allocating a resource that can be used up.

Reciprocal Interactions

Mutualizing. To mutualize means to contribute and belong to a group enterprise with a larger, enduring social purpose, and then to receive a specific individual benefit. However, members do not necessarily receive equal value in return for what they give, as in a market transaction. They typically receive some stipulated benefit based on need or other criteria. An insurance pool and social security fund are classic examples of mutualization.

Mutualization is clearly a reciprocal process, but the benefits are not *equal* to what is contributed. Instead they are *socially chosen benefits* that members agree to in founding the group and in ongoing governance decisions. Everyone's share in benefits is usually calculated in precise individual units, but often in differential shares and according to predetermined formulas or agreements. However mutualization is structured, it is critical that everyone with a stake in the resource system have a say in the agreement. It is a peer-determined reciprocity.

Mutualization bears some resemblances to a commercial transaction. What makes it different is that participants generally have an interest in each other and goals that are not just monetary. (This condition does not hold in national, state-administered mutualization systems, of course, whose populations have scant relationship to each other except citizenship.) In mutualization regimes, there are likely to be shared social purposes, a common history, or strong traditions.

Trading. Trading is a reciprocal process as well. It is based on the idea of equivalent exchange, with a price signaling that the two things exchanged are thought to be of equivalent value, as expressed in monetary terms. This is the essence of a market: a transaction-based encounter (exchanging money for a commodity) rather than an enduring social relationship. Someone who trades in the market generally cares only about the transaction itself; any social relationships or commitments are secondary or absent entirely. That's why the phrase "it's just business" is often invoked to justify a good business deal in the face of adverse personal or social consequences. In short, mutualization is socially driven reciprocity; trading is a market-based reciprocity.

Capping Resource Use

Capping means setting an absolute limit on how much of a resource may be used in a certain time, usually to prevent harmful overuse. Such limit-setting is often necessary for finite, depletable resources such as land, agricultural harvests, and irrigation water, which would otherwise be used up if everyone could take as much as they wanted. Capping is the classic mechanism used in medieval English commons to preserve a collective resource. As Lewis Hyde has written, "The commons were not open; they were *stinted*. If, for example, you were a seventeenth-century English common farmer, you might have the right to cut rushes on the common, but only between Christmas and Candlemas (February 2). Or you might have the right to cut the branches of trees, but only up to a certain height and only after the tenth of November. Or you might have the right to cut the thorny evergreen shrubs called furze, but only so much as could be carried on your back, and only to heat your own house." Hyde notes that "stints, the constraints placed on use in the name of longevity," are present in all enduring commons. "Without these there is no true commons."[15]

Caps are used in all kinds of contexts — rural, urban, ecological, digital. In arid regions of Latin America where irrigation water is precious, commoners managing *acequias* establish caps on the usage of water so that everybody's needs can be met. Mindful of privacy concerns, data commons that consolidate data from many sources place limits on how data may be collected and used. Cooperatively managed apartment buildings have a finite number of living units that can be rented or sold — a simple physical limit.

The need for caps is often elastic because there may be ways to accommodate one more participant-user, but at a certain point groups generally realize that there is not enough income, physical space, or organizational infrastructure to support everyone. At the Cologne cooperative SSM, the customary way of dealing with people who want to make too many purchases is to identify discretionary cuts. It starts by identifying what discretionary cuts — "This new TV simply won't be bought" — followed by "going deeper to ask what people really need," said Rainer Kippe, cofounder of SSM.[16] The cooperative does not lay off people as a matter of principle nor ask the state for additional public assistance money.

Capping is a classic governance principle that today is often linked to trading, such as the familiar "cap-and-trade" regime used to deal with CO_2 pollution. Under cap-and-trade systems, corporations are given or buy rights to emit specific amounts of pollutants. If businesses choose to reduce their emissions, they may not need their "pollution rights" and so they may choose to sell them to other businesses that find it cheaper to buy the rights than to abate their emissions.

While capping is often indispensable, creating a right to pollute as a saleable commodity can undermine the very goal of capping. It can, for example, result in sophisticated evasions of the caps and corrupt gaming of the system. Larger players may use their disproportionate market power to manipulate prices. Cap-and-trade also elevates market valuations over the inherent value of ecosystems, affected communities, and their cultures. In effect, the price system falsely purports to represent ecological value. For the same reason, cap-and-trade systems end up ignoring the actual carrying capacities of ecosystems because the caps tend to reflect political compromises, not ecological realities.

Thus we prefer Cap & Divide Up (better known as Cap & Share) and Cap & Mutualize to the cap-and-trade approach. Sharing or mutualizing a "capped" natural resource has the advantage of enlisting the affected people to apply their own situated knowledge, creative ideas, and peer enforcement skills to the challenge of curbing usage. Money is less effective in mobilizing those energies.

Pool, Cap & Divide Up

In cases in which a common resource is finite and can be used up, Pool, Cap & Divide Up is a variant of Pool & Share. A cap on usage, set through a peer governance process, can address a threat of overuse or insufficient supplies that might occur if everyone takes what she wants. To Pool, Cap & Divide Up speaks to timeless experience and necessity. Hunters manage to kill only so much game but there are many people who need to eat … gatherers acquire only a limited store of nuts and fruit … guests at potluck dinners bring only so much food, which somehow must be made to serve everyone.

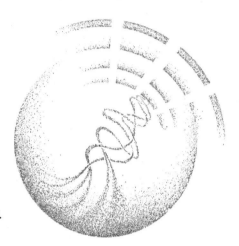

Pool, Cap & Divide Up.

Farmers or pastoralists who use the same land for agriculture or grazing animals often create rules specifying how much and in which months an individual may harvest. It is typical in a commons to limit individual usage so that the land is not overexploited. Dividing Up the available water, fish, fruits, and harvest can be done in any number of imaginative ways.

POOL, CAP & DIVIDE UP is arguably the most prevalent pattern of cooperation in the world today. It always has been. Its prevalence and practicality are often ignored because they don't conform to the standard economic narrative, which insists upon seeing human beings as selfish, materialistic, rational individuals unable to negotiate a fair division of benefits. "In the conventional economy, they [economists] cannot see any more what really works," said Rainer Kippe of SSM. "What we are doing seems impossible to a typical economist who has studied mainstream textbooks. According to classical theory, what we do can't work. But in fact … we do it everyday."[17] They Pool, Cap & Divide Up. Indeed, beyond the ken of standard economics, as many as 2.5 billion people around the world manage about eight billion hectares of land through community-based ownership systems, according to the International Land Coalition.[18] For things like land, water, forests, and wild game, POOL, CAP & DIVIDE UP is arguably the fairest, most practical strategy.

Pool, Cap & Mutualize

POOL, CAP & MUTUALIZE is useful for dealing with limited resources that you wish to use and steward in common, but don't necessarily want to divide up. Everyone does not necessarily get an absolutely equal share. The point is for a distinct group of cooperators to collectively meet their needs in a roughly equivalent way and, in so doing, express a basic social solidarity. Cap & Mutualize is a familiar modern principle used in social security systems and healthcare, for example. It can also be seen in the Artabana community health insurance system, described earlier.

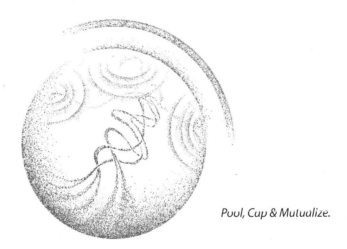

Pool, Cap & Mutualize.

There is a reciprocity at play, in that everyone helps oversee the proper, respectful use of the common grazing lands while enjoying benefits from it. But the reciprocity is not a transactional, market-like trade because the commoning has the character of neighborly support and flexibility in fulfilling a shared agreement. This is far different from a cap-and-trade scheme in that users are deciding what an acceptable cap on usage is, based on their own experiences and careful observations. Another benefit of Cap & Mutualize is that it preserves a shared intentionality among the user group, whereas trading encourages individual exploitation of the resource to maximum legal limits (and beyond), otherwise known as the tragedy of the market.

Trade with Price Sovereignty

One of the great powers of a commons is its ability to emancipate itself from markets — and the prices they dictate. Somebody who participates in a commons to support some facet of her life does not need to submit to the omnipotence of many markets. A commons enables people to go their own path. If they need to engage with the market, they can choose their own terms.

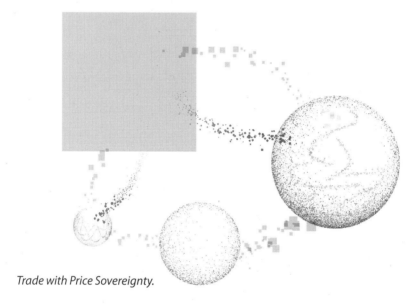

Trade with Price Sovereignty.

In the United States, civil rights activist Fannie Lou Hamer came up with a shrewd strategy in the 1960s for dealing with community disempowerment, which in her case was caused by exploitative white-owned businesses. With support from singer Harry Belafonte and a Wisconsin charity, Measure for Measure, she founded an interracial farming cooperative in 1969 on a few dozen acres of Delta land. The goal was to empower poor blacks to grow their own food. "When you've got 400 quarts of greens and gumbo soup for the winter, nobody can push you around or tell you what to say or do," Hamer noted.[19] Imagine what might happen if commoners emulated this strategy in dozens of realms. It would begin to put serious pressure on the market! That can already be seen in northwest Venezuela, thanks to the commons-based provisioning of Cecosesola.

Cecosesola, or How to Ignore the Market

Cecosesola is a robust, mature "omni-commons" that connects many smaller entities in a federation of around 30 cooperatives and the same number of grassroots organizations, which taken together have around 20,000 members.[20] The urban and rural cooperatives, scattered around the state of Lara, Venezuela, in the pre-Andes region, have survived the most challenging economic and political circumstances imaginable to provide food, care, transportation, and even communal burial services for more than five decades. Cecosesola's top priority is hosting a process of creating spaces of togetherness. But it has also been deeply rooted in the local economy since its very beginnings in the late 1960s.

Cecosesola has succeeded by adopting a bold strategy: ignoring the market. It establishes it own prices and its own trading spaces — four huge markets, one in each section of the state capital, Barquisimeto, a 1.25 million metropolis in the northwest of the country. At Cecosesola community markets, the federation sells some 700 tons of fresh produce at a single price per kilo, which is significantly lower than the prices charged by conventional grocers. The impact is such that Cecosesola commons have driven down market prices in the region. About 700,000 people enjoy both lower prices and half of their diet through this system.

How could this possibly work, you might wonder. Cecosesola asks a simple question to its farmers and service providers, all of them members of the federation: what do you need to produce the harvest that you do? (It is exactly the same question some CSA members ask the CSA farmer so that they can share the risk of provisioning.) The rural cooperative members working in the fields, and Cecosesola members who coordinate the federation or sell at markets in Barquisimeto, gather in the shadow of a tree. While sitting on simple wooden benches, their casual chat slowly turns to the serious work of estimating what is needed for production: So many days of work, this much seed, that much fuel, enough irrigation pipes, and so forth. The more experienced members remind the less experienced ones that things may fall apart and need to be repurchased, or that more mule fodder may need to be bought because the last 800 meters up steep hills will increase transportation costs. Bit by bit, members bring their situated knowing to bear. Together, they identify the very concrete costs for production in their specific conditions of life and farming. Producers and distributors (people from Cecosesola's central office in the city; traders or middlemen in the conventional economy) coordinate together.

This is price-making, right in front of everybody's eyes. Each cooperative within the Cecosesola system does the same. At the end, the federation sums up the results of all the meetings, adds in some additional sums for extras and losses (yes, tomatoes get spoiled on their way to the capital and some get stolen at the market). Then Cecosesola takes a radical, counterintuitive step: "We decouple the price of vegetables from the time and effort we put into them," as coop member Noel Vale Valera explains. "We add up the number of kilograms produced across the entire produce range, on the one hand, and we add up the costs on the other hand. Then we divide one by the other to figure out our average price per kilogram. Our yardstick is simply the production costs including what the producers need to live …What matters for us is that we earn what we need." Cecosesola members don't think of producers, traders, and consumers as separate, each having *separate* interests. They think of everyone as a *whole* in which everyone has to meet their needs along with the entire enterprise.

Vale's colleague Jorge Rath insists, "This system saves people quite a lot of money … Our price per kilogram reduces red tape, we don't work with middlemen, and seasonal fluctuations don't make a difference, either."[21] The single per-kilo price for all produce emerges from open discussion among all those who produce and the many others who collaborate with them. In the end, it is no surprise that costs and therefore prices are significantly lower than those of conventional markets. There are no hidden costs, thanks to the trust and transparency within Cecosesola. There are no costs for marketing and advertisements. There are no intermediaries charging inflated prices to act as a wholesaler or distributor. Cecosesola is able to show money efficiency and price sovereignty.

The really stunning fact is the remarkable strength of Cecosesola as a provisioning system in times of political and economic crisis. It is

basically due to the federation's capacity to react quickly to dramatically changing circumstances. As we completed this book, the people
of Venezuela were reeling from hyperinflation estimated at one million percent in 2018. And yet, amazingly, Cecosesola has been able to
survive the country's economic downturn and political upheavals by,
once again, adapting its operational systems. In late 2016, Cecosesola
began to identify new sources of agricultural production in the rural
part of the state of Lara. This brought more people and producers into
contact with the federation's approach, not to establish a common
seller-buyer relationship (which doesn't make sense in a hyperinfla-
tionary context in any case), but to forge a "Do-It-Together" partnership
that could adapt to the incredibly fast-changing circumstances of the
economy. It is *because* the federation revolves around a culture of
horizontal participation and trust that it has won the support of both
commoners and consumers. With lower debt and overhead costs and
a culture of solidarity, Cecosesola and its people have somehow hung
on. But nobody really knows if or how they will survive if Venezuela's
deep crisis continues to drag on.

By creating a quasi-independent provisioning system that operates
independently of conventional markets, commoners acquire some
freedom from market demands, including price. They can declare their
own terms. The ability to assert price sovereignty is a significant source
of power, for example. It includes the option to provide people with
goods and services for free, or at lower prices than the conventional
market does. This is a much-overlooked strategic power. By decommodifying production and rooting it in social practices and trust,
commoners can pursue their own agenda in the face of the formidable
powers wielded by capital and corporations.

The price-making exercises conducted by Cecosesola (and other commons) means that they are less vulnerable to the highly irregular forces
of supply and demand. They have partially withdrawn from conventional markets and so are less dependent on its expenses and volatility.
(Of course, peasants still have to buy seeds and other inputs for production from markets.) But the group's relative price sovereignty is not

anticompetitive in the ways prohibited by antitrust law. Price sovereignty is about counting provisioning costs accurately and transparently in the first place, based on actual need and context. Prices as set by conventional markets, on the other hand, tend to reflect the extra expenses of working within a bloated system: advertising, employee recruitment and retention, complicated value chains of suppliers and middlemen, lawyers, market research, packaging, brand identities, government lobbying, campaign contributions to buy better regulation, etc. All of these expenses are opaque and invisibly folded into prices. By comparison, commoning has a much lower cost structure for which it offers a straight-up reckoning.

One might say that there are *two* forms of price sovereignty — the ability of a community-governed system to determine prices through its own internal processes, and the ability to assert price sovereignty when trading with the outside market world. The goal in either case is to strive for as much autonomy as possible to insulate the commons from market pressures. By having a commons support a significant part of their subsistence, and by gaining price sovereignty, commoners can selectively trade with markets knowing that such interactions will not jeopardize the integrity of the commons itself. Commoners who, for example, participate in a commons of shareable research or databases, or reap the harvest from a cooperative farm, or live on an urban parcel or acreage held by a land trust, are insulated from the often harsh demands of debt and high prices.

The Linux operating system is another example of a commons asserting price sovereignty in its dealings with the market. Because it is available to anyone at no cost, commercial distributors of branded version of Linux are constrained in what they can charge. Similarly, open access scholarly journals such as the Public Library of Science (PLoS) bypass the market entirely, making high-quality, peer-reviewed scientific research available for free. To be sure, PLoS journals rely on public funding to pay their costs as open access periodicals, but the point is that they have the price sovereignty to charge whatever price they want, including no price. This has put pressure on commercial journal publishers to offer their own open access journals (which, however, often charge excessive upfront author's fees to publish works). Open access journals can succeed by out-cooperating commercial journals.

*   *   *

Once commoners pool their resources, should they Share, Divide Up, or Mutualize them? Each has different implications, but in general, any of these approaches is likely to reduce individual costs. Each is also more likely to meet people's needs while developing a sense of co-responsibility for the entire provisioning process and its impacts. To summarize this discussion, here is a chart showing the different ways of allocating resources in a commons.

General Types of Allocation in a Commons

Type of transaction	Character of Shared Wealth	
	Can Be Used Up (Rivalrous)	Cannot be Used Up (Nonrivalrous)
Reciprocal	Mutualize or Trade with Price Sovereignty	Reciprocal exchange of nonrivalrous resources makes no sense
Nonreciprocal	Divide Up	Share

General Types of Allocation in a Capitalist Market Economy

Type of Exchange	Character of Shared Wealth	
	Rivalrous	Nonrivalrous
Reciprocal	Trade according to market price	Propertize and privatize, then trade according to market price
Nonreciprocal	This is a blind spot in standard economics because, by definition, caring, helping, sharing, and dividing up are not considered to be part of the economy.	

*   *   *

Use Convivial Tools

The term "convivial tools" was introduced by the social critic and philosopher Ivan Illich in his 1973 book *Tools for Conviviality*, which described a vision of a world in which a community of users develop and maintain their own tools. Using convivial tools — a term that we extend to technologies, infrastructures, and processes for provisioning — is about enhancing our individual freedom while enriching our relationships and interdependence — the essence of a commons.

Use Convivial Tools.

Many contemporary tools and technologies are closed systems that lock us into their particular way of performing a task. Think of a factory assembly line, genetically modified crops, or an encrypted DVD. Such systems structure how we are allowed to work and relate to others, while making us dependent on control-minded corporations or state bureaucracies. By contrast, convivial tools are open-ended systems that anyone can use and adapt for their own purposes, in their own ways. As Illich explains:

> Tools foster conviviality to the extent that they can be easily used, by anybody, as often or as seldom as desired, for the accomplishment of a purpose chosen by the user. The use of such tools by one person does not restrain another from using them equally. They do not require previous certification of the user. Their existence does not impose any obligation to use them. They allow the user to express his meaning in action.[22]

Techniques for stable, eco-responsible agriculture such as permaculture and agroecology are convivial tools because anyone can use and share them, and contribute to their improvement. GMO seeds that have been genetically engineered and patented, by contrast, can only be used as mandated by the corporate owner. A free or open source computer operating system such as GNU/Linux can be used, shared, and modified however a person wishes, whereas Microsoft Windows® and Apple's iOS® prohibit users from even looking at the source code of the program without permission. Convivial tools invite creative adaptations in a myriad of contexts. They deepen connections among people and with the Earth. They help bring about small, incremental, and socially appropriate solutions to problems. People can use them to escape institutional systems that inhibit our humanity and create dependencies.

The social character of our tools and technologies matter because, as Illich wrote, "Any individual relates himself in action to his society through the use of tools that he actively masters or by which he is passively acted upon. To the degree that he masters his tools, he can invest the world with his meaning; to the degree that he is mastered by his tools, the shape of the tool determines his own self-image." Ultimately, the tools we use shape the kind of society that is possible. "The result of much economic development," writes Illich, "is very often not human flourishing but 'modernized poverty,' dependency, and an out-of-control system in which the humans become worn-out mechanical parts."[23] This dynamic is reaching alarming new extremes as a new surge of artificial intelligence technologies reach into our family life, households, personal health, and consciousness.

In our times, open source tools and technologies are convivial tools with great potential for Provisioning through Commons because users can determine how they will be used. They are open, accessible, modifiable, and shareable based on user wants and needs.[24] Convivial tools allow for many applications, some very different from the originally intended use.

Rely on Distributed Structures

There is no inherent reason that commons cannot work at larger scales, as we have seen with countless networked communities that rely on internet platforms. Making a commons grow, however, requires not only political support, but also discrimination-free structures and infrastructures that make commoning easier. People must have fairly simple means to participate and give their consent, and systems must be devised to engender social trust, shared purpose, and coherence. Such (infra) structures need to be available for distributed use, when possible — e.g., peer-to-peer (open source software), team-to-team (Buurtzorg neighborhood home care), or node-to node structures (FairCoop). This means that the (infra)structures should enable peers, teams, and local nodes to interconnect and form semi-autonomous spheres of self-provisioning and -governance. Each part of the whole can then operate semi-autonomously, according to its own distinct rules and situational needs, while also coordinating with their other semi-autonomous peers.

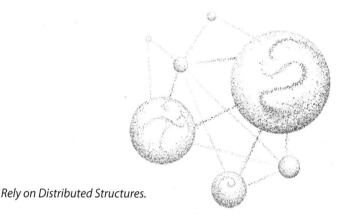

Rely on Distributed Structures.

Distributed structures differ from *decentralized* structures in that the latter are connected to central hubs whereas the former are interconnected peers (or teams, groups, nodes, or local commons) that relate directly to each other through a network or a federation, without a central hub.[25] Distributed structures tend to behave more autonomously and enjoy greater self-determination. This helps prevent the consolidation of political power and render coercive, command-and-control authority systems unnecessary, but it does require initiative, creativity, and self-responsibility. Decentralized structures usually relate to a more authoritarian central body (municipality to states to a national government; franchisees to the corporate headquarters) and thus cede some of their autonomy, imagination, and potential to it.

Centralized, decentralized, and distributed relationships.

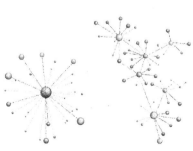 

CENTRALIZED   DECENTRALIZED   DISTRIBUTED

In modern times, many institutional infrastructures and tools — law, bureaucracy, the internet — have been used to enlarge the size of stable, functional groups. While this has enabled the creation of modern institutions, it has also facilitated the centralization of power at the expense of individual participants and local knowledge. The challenge, then, is to transform and adapt modern institutions so that they can support human empowerment and conviviality.

Can the commons coordinate large numbers of people across large geographies while retaining a convivial human scale? The answer is yes, but this generally requires some infrastructure to enable participants to reap the advantages of both distributed self-determination *and* larger-scale cooperation. This is essentially how many transnational projects are now operating. Examples include the Wikimedia Foundation's funding and coordination of more than a dozen quasi-autonomous wiki projects with commoners dispersed around the world; major open source software communities whose foundations and shared platforms enable small armies of programmers to show bottom-up initiative; and citizen-led movements such as the Transition Towns, and open design and manufacturing, which function at local scales yet coordinate across political jurisdictions.

The goal in each case is not to consolidate management through a central body, but to enter into a process of Emulate & Then Federate using digital networks. Power and creativity can then be dispersed locally or regionally while retaining important elements of large-scale coordination.

Creatively Adapt & Renew

Creatively Adapt & Renew.

Modern industrial culture has placed such a premium on "innovation" — fueled in large part by an endless quest for competitive advantage — that innovation is often seen as an absolute good in itself. In such a world, its general goal is to help businesses prevail against competitors in the marketplace, improve return on investment, and entice consumers to buy an endless stream of "new and improved" products. By contrast, the commons as a system of provisioning is often considered backward, premodern, or tribal — ways of producing things that are seen as static, stodgy, and not innovative.

This is a gross caricature if not untruth because many commoners are extremely capable of adapting to changing needs, including the need to reduce one's ecological footprint. In a commons, there is no imperative to constantly expand production and profit, and so creativity can be focused on what really matters — ameliorating quality, durability, resilience, and holistic stability. Innovation need not be linked to boosting market sales and ignoring planetary health. Countless commons exhibit the pattern of CREATIVELY ADAPT & RENEW as part of their everyday activity.

As Eric von Hippel shows in his book *Democratizing Innovation*, all sorts of practitioner-communities — bicyclists, hang-gliders, skiers, extreme sports buffs — have developed breakthrough ideas that were later commercialized by conventional businesses.[26] Indigenous peoples, too — long considered fixed and traditional in their ways — have shown immense creativity over the centuries in co-creating robust ecosystems through seed-breeding and animal domestication. The fertile soil in the Amazon region known as *terra preta do indio* — "dark earth of the Indians" — writes political economist James Boyce, "is not a random anomaly, but rather a deliberate creation of Indigenous farmers who long ago practiced 'slash-and-char' agroforestry in the region. A noteworthy feature of *terra preta* is its remarkable capacity for self-regeneration, which scientists attribute to soil microorganisms."[27] Such practices can also be seen in the creation of gravity-fed *acequia* irrigation in the upper Rio Grande valley, which transformed the semi-arid region into a rich landscape of wetlands, cultivated fields, and riparian corridors that allowed many animal species to flourish. The ETC Group, an organization that studies technological innovation, has called such creativity "Indigenous innovation" and "cooperative innovation"[28] because Indigenous peoples have made countless ethnobotanical and ecological discoveries that transnational corporations have later sought to appropriate for free and privatize ("biopiracy").

Commoners survive through creative adaptation and renewal. It is in their blood. They habitually have to make do with what is available and improvise. Among peasants and poor people in India, there is a word for such innovation — *jugaad* — the Indian practice of slapdash innovation from whatever is at hand.[29] Creative adaptation, in truth, is a part of the human condition. Struggle and need *induce* creativity as a matter of survival.

*   *   *

The patterns of Provisioning that we have described here are dynamic and alive — which means that new configurations of commoning often emerge. One of the most salient in recent times is the rise of what many call cosmo-local production. People share "light" knowledge and design via peer-to-peer learning and the internet, but build "heavy" physical things such as machinery, cars, housing, furniture, and electronics locally. In the peer production community there is a saying, "If it's light, share it globally — if it's heavy, produce it locally."

This phenomenon is taking many forms. Imagine a Cuban farmer working with peers from India and Peru to figure out ways to improve rice yields, a routine practice among farmers associated with SRI, the System of Rice Intensification. Or imagine designers in Amsterdam working with engineers and architects in Australia and the US to design low-cost, modular housing that anyone can build with local supplies. This is now a working norm among participants in the global Wikihouse network. There is a long tradition of cosmo-local cooperation in agriculture, as seen in such networks as Campesino a Campesino. This is an international mutual aid project that peasant farmers started in Guatemala in the early 1970s as a self-help alternative to multinational development interventions.[30] Or consider Masipag, a nonprofit partnership between resource-poor farmers and scientists at research institutions around the world, devoted to breeding and cultivating locally adapted seeds.[31]

HETERARCHICAL STRUCTURE

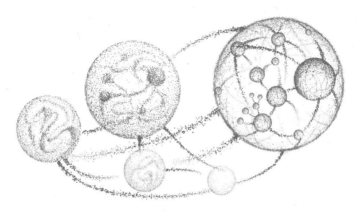

FEDERATED STRUCTURE

Heterarchical and federated structures.

In recent years, digital technologies have greatly empowered global collaborations that have local outputs. Global communities of designers, engineers, and programmers are collaborating online to develop design prototypes for everything from farm equipment (tractors, wind turbines, rototillers and soil pulverizers, compressed earth block presses for brickmaking)[32] to high-end scientific microscopes (OpenSPIM)[33] to sailing robots to detect ocean pollution (Scoutbots).[34] All of these machines are licensed to be shareable, open source style. This means that any farmer, scientific researcher, or curious amateur can take advantage of world-class innovation by building their own tools less expensively using modular, adaptable, locally sourceable materials.

Open Source Ecology is one such project that designs diverse non-proprietary types of farm equipment and machinery that can be locally produced. The project started in 2003 in the USA and now has local hubs in Germany, Guatemala, and other locations around the world. An array of architects, engineers, and designers with the WikiHouse project have developed an "open source construction kit" that is akin to "a big IKEA kit for your home that is easy to assemble and affordable." In a similar vein, the Open Building Institute, an offshoot of Open Source Ecology, builds low-cost, modular houses that are ecological and energy-efficient using techniques that are open source, convivial, and distributed. These remarkable forms of "cosmo-politan localism," as Wolfgang Sachs puts it,[35] could not work without convivial tools.

The same dynamics of cosmo-local provisioning can be seen in the Wikispeed project, which is building a next-generation mail delivery vehicle and taxi cab, among other vehicles, using open source principles at a global scale. Also notable is Arduino, a global open source community that designs easy-to-use hardware and software systems for 3D printing, education, wearable computing, and Internet of Things applications, among other tasks.

Michel Bauwens, founder of the P2P Foundation and a leading theorist of peer production, divides cosmo-local production into three distinct stages: input, process, and output. The *input* (resources, talent, creativity) comes from voluntary contributors who do not have to ask permission to participate. They can use "open and free raw material that is free of restrictive copyright so that it can be freely improved and modified," writes Bauwens.[36] The *process* is an open, peer-production system that is designed to be inclusive. There are "low thresholds for participation, freely available modular tasks rather than functional jobs, and communal validation of the quality and excellence of the alternatives," Bauwens explains.

Finally, the *output* is licensed to ensure that the value generated by the commons will be available to all — again, without permission. Commonly used licenses include the General Public License for software, Creative Commons licenses for various forms of content, and the Peer Production License. The commons that the peer community creates is used, in turn, to create a new layer of open and free material that can be used for a next iteration. In general, open global design combined with local manufacturing has profound implications for potentially reducing the material throughput in the production process and especially the energy required for transportation. The authors of a 2017 report argue that "mutualization and relocalization" are "answers to the problem of nonrenewable materials."[37]

Part III:

Growing the Commonsverse

Introduction

W E HAVE COME A LONG WAY. Part I explained the importance of an OntoShift for understanding the insurgent power of the commons, and how language is an indispensable tool in helping us shed archaic understandings and cultivate commons-friendly perspectives. Then, in Part II, we introduced the Triad of Commoning as a way to explain how people can enact commons by emulating existing patterns of social life, peer governance, and provisioning. These first six chapters give us a fairly solid grasp of the dynamics of commoning. They explain how — *within* a commons — people can produce a world that is free, fair, and alive.

But as capitalism teeters under the weight of its own contradictions, leading to such existential crises as climate breakdown, economic inequality, and violent nationalism, an obvious question on the lips of most people is, how can the Commonsverse grow larger and transform the political economy and culture? How can we achieve changes in state power, law, and policy based on a commons approach? These questions are the focus of Part III.

It turns out that patterns of commoning, especially of peer governance, are crucial not only *within* a commons, but equally in handling relationships *among* commons. At both levels, it is important to BRING DIVERSITY INTO SHARED PURPOSE, ASSURE CONSENT IN DECISION MAKING, and SHARE KNOWLEDGE GENEROUSLY, among other patterns identified in the Triad of Commoning. However, as commons grow and spawn a varied ecosystem of players, a new set of complications arises. Each separate commons must learn to connect and coordinate with others based on the commons ethic described in Part II. This requires new forms of cooperation not just *within* commons (the "micro" level) but in the spaces *among* individual commons (the "meso" level) and in complicated struggles and negotiations at the societal level (the "macro" level). This tripartite division of levels is too tidy

201

a description because the dynamics at each level are all intertwined. It is nonetheless a useful way of conceptualizing how commons fit into a larger societal context.

Four strategies are particularly important. First, commoners must learn how to *Beat the Bounds* of their commons to prevent enclosure and/or reclaim privatized wealth. This is a basic survival imperative. Beating the bounds, you may recall, is the practice used by many English villages of walking the perimeter of their land to identify any fences or hedges that had encroached upon their shared wealth. In our times, beating the bounds may initially involve direct action resistance and civil disobedience against enclosures, and attempts to "de-enclose" them. The point of beating the bounds is to restore some measure of commoning with respect to land, water, seeds, code, creative work, and culture, and to restore the integrity of the community. Such tactics may be followed by longer-term strategies such as enacting laws, developing technological safeguards, or adopting protective social traditions. Institutional stability and legal security are fundamental.

But this is only a start. As the number of commons in a given field of endeavor increases, it is important for commoners to *Emulate & Federate* to build more integrated, collaborative networks and shared infrastructures. That is the approach used by La Via Campesina, the decentralized grassroots movement of millions of peasants, small farmers, landless people, rural women and youth, Indigenous peoples, and migrants and agricultural workers. The movement amounts to a large, loosely connected transnational federation. Similarly, community-supported agriculture farms in Germany (known by the German acronym SoLaWi) have federated as the Netzwerk Solidarische Landwirtschaft, following the growth of CSA farms in Germany from three in 2003 to thirty-nine in 2013 to about two hundred in early 2019. The purpose of the federation is to allow individual farms to trade insights, jointly sponsor research, develop new initiatives, connect commoners and farmers, and write shareable free software specifically designed to meet CSA needs. In digital spaces, there are many collaborations among commons involving free and open source software, Creative Commons licenses, open access scholarly publishing, the open educational resources movement, and open data initiatives, among other free culture projects. Participants in one community of practice keep loose track of advances in other communities, — such as new user interfaces, security protocols, or sharing behaviors — and adapt them within their own context.

These federations, whether organized or casual, do not function as representative bodies in any formal sense. They are shared spaces for forging mutual commitments. They are evolving heterarchies of mutual aid, consensus building, and joint action among commoners. The goal of federations is to fortify the many individual commons while building collaborative ventures such as shared infrastructure, finance, and political advocacy.

Beyond the activities of Emulate & Federate, it is important for commons projects and networks to pursue strategies of *intercommoning*. This is the process of active collaboration and mutual support to assist and inspire individual projects, make sense of unfolding events, and develop proactive strategies. All that's needed is an open space in which people who would not otherwise meet can come together to work freely on self-determined agendas: hackers with farmers, for example, or low-income people with makerspaces, or open educational resources advocates with co-housing residents. The process of intercommoning also builds a shared culture, particularly as a new language of the commons takes root.

Why is all this needed? Because the harsh realities of the market/state system otherwise impede the development of commoning. State power is real and dominant, and generally privileges capitalist modes of production and culture as normative. It elevates legal frameworks that honor private property, capitalist-driven market transactions, and contracts among individuals. So if anyone wishes to advance an OntoShift, they must find ingenious ways to deal with some deeply rooted biases of the capitalist economy that are reflected in various structures of state power, law, policy, and socially embedded markets.

This is a formidable challenge, indeed! However, the hardy survival of many commons over the centuries suggests that they are not without their own remarkable powers of creative self-protection and expansion. It's just that commoners generally do not have the support of conventional law, finance, technology, and state power that players in the market economy take for granted.

The next chapters therefore embark upon a bold quest. We try to imagine how state power and law might begin to support commons in both operational and structural ways. However, unlike many pro-posals that focus on enacting new laws, regulations, or state programs to change existing market or state structures — a setup for disap-pointing results — we propose a Grand Strategy that draws its energy and strength from the ontological shift and the patterns of commoning introduced earlier. In other words, politics, state law, and policy will not be the primary drivers of change. Commoning will. A great deal can be achieved *right now* without having to become embroiled in the compromises, betrayals, co-optation, and legal paralysis of conven-tional politics and government. This is not to say that politics and state powers can be ignored or utterly avoided; it is simply to declare that commoning must lie at the heart of any strategies for change. Politics must remain a means to an end, and not an end in itself. The best way to avoid the seductions of politics and state power, which have often co-opted leaders and derailed social movements, is to hew closely to patterns of commoning, even in macro-scale endeavors.

A fair question to ask is whether the powers of commoning can truly be transformational. How can we know if commoning can actually provide leverage points for a Great Transition away from state-sup-ported market fundamentalism to something better? Geographer Dina Hestad of the University of Oxford has studied what characteristics must be present for actions and strategies to be socially transformative. She has provisionally identified the following criteria:[1]

- Work towards a vision which reflects the need to live in balance with the carrying capacity of the earth
- Consider that change in a complex system cannot be controlled due to uncertainty
- Avoid displacing problems to other locations or times, which could prevent wider system change
- Tackle the root causes of acceleration and growth — the feedback loops that cause most of today's ecological and social crises
- Work towards systems that avoid unchecked imbalances of power and help avoid triggering humans' (destructive) ancient tribal circuits
- Promote understanding that humans are part of a much larger whole, and create possibilities for resonance and meaningful, affective rela-tionships between people and nature

- Develop healthy human agency at individual and collective levels for transforming and co-creating our future
- Open up new possibilities for acting rather than shrinking our opportunities to act
- Communicate a compelling and inspiring story of system change that names the problems and identifies commensurate leverage points and resonates with people from all walks of life and across ideologies
- Promote social cohesion and a sense of togetherness at different levels, which includes trust, a sense of belonging, and a willingness to participate and help
- Promote critical thinking, generosity of spirit, and openness to learn from diverse ideas and perspectives

Commoning has a rich potential to meet all of these criteria. Of course, implementation is critical! That is to say, strengthening and expanding commoning from within a market/state polity will be *really difficult*. But it is entirely feasible. The following four chapters of Part III offers some broad recommendations.

*   *   *

In proposing ways that state power can support commoning, we hasten to call attention to what we are *not* proposing. We are not trying to re-imagine the polity. We are not trying to reinvent the nation-state, much as that may be needed. We are not trying to smash capitalism in a traditional revolutionary sense, although of course any advance of the commons diminishes its power and represents an incremental triumph. The commons surely has a lot to say about these challenges, philosophically and politically. But one cannot simply propose a grandiose, long-term agenda and then try to educate others to agree and follow the prescribed insights. That approach ignores the deeper wisdom of the commons, which accepts the idea of distributed, local, and diverse acts of commoning whose very aliveness produces the creativity and commitment to develop solutions adapted to every context.

In this sense, the long-term agenda must be one of emergence through commoning. Our priority must be to grow the capacity to think like a commoner and to grow the Commonsverse as much as possible now, planting seeds of culture, social practice, and institutional power that can unfold in the fullness of time. It is this developmental unfolding of the ethics of commoning that makes it so hardy in the first place. It is this dynamic that we need to honor and develop rather than plunging prematurely or naively into frontal assaults on a highly fortified market/state system, a strategy doomed to fail.

The most natural opening for cooperation between state power and commoners is the local level. In smaller-scale political contexts, government tends to be less driven by ideology or party politics than by sheer practicality — what works? At the local level, politicians cannot so easily ignore needs nor hide behind ideology. Moreover, people at the local level can more easily make their political voices heard and pressure governments to innovate, as seen in the burgeoning "city as a commons" movement in Europe and dozens of urban commons initiatives documented by *Shareable* magazine.[2] It is no accident that the words "commons" and "municipality" share the same etymology with the root Latin word *munus*, which combines the meanings "gift" and "duty." Our challenge is to find ways to reinvent this ethic in the larger modern state structures in which we are inexorably entangled. Let's begin.

7
Rethinking Property

To visit downtown Florence these days is to walk amidst dozens of lovingly restored fourteenth- to eighteenth-century buildings and public squares, the Galleria dell'Accademia containing Michelangelo's statue of David, the priceless art of the Uffizi Museum, overpriced cafés and gaudy souvenir shops pandering to tourists. But look more closely, right behind the apse of the Carmine church, on the other side of the Arno River, where the Renaissance began, and you will discover the last part of the old town that has not yet been turned into a Disneyland of the Renaissance.

This neighborhood, the San Frediano parish, is only a few steps away from the world-famous Ponte Vecchio. Even though it is within an area of gentrification, a startled visitor who stumbles across the Nidiaci Community Garden will encounter, especially in the afternoons, a leafy oasis filled with energetic, noisy children and their parents. Rambunctious six-year-olds race around the grounds and play on swings while their older brothers take lessons with the city's only self-managed soccer school, "The Lebowskis." On certain days, a Portuguese musician who lives nearby teaches violin to children. On other days, a British writer teaches English in a studio space on the grounds. Families organize free swaps of outgrown children's clothes. Some residents tend to a small vegetable garden. Others have organized a project to monitor city pollution and traffic.

This space of togetherness, tucked away in a corner of the central city, is stewarded as a commons. Its use "depends on what people decide to put into it," as Miguel Martinez, an amateur historian of the Nidiaci garden put it. "It's hard to say what we are doing there, because everything depends on what new arrivals want to create." But in a neighborhood in which about forty percent of the children come from families born abroad, simply having a space to common is no small blessing.

How is it possible, you might ask, that this beautiful spot in the center of Florence — easily worth more than several million dollars on the real estate market — has not yet been sold to the highest bidder and turned into condos? How is it that a group of neighbors actually stewards this space? When we went looking for answers to these questions, we learned a great deal about how property law can be used for more than the buying and selling of real estate; it can be used to help people lead a more satisfying community life.

The land now occupied by the Nidiaci Community Garden has a long and complicated history of ownership. It was originally donated to the Carmelite church by a widow in 1273, nationalized by the Napoleonic mayor of Florence in the nineteenth century, and later sold to a private owner. What started out as a private donation to the church became public property before becoming private property again. At the beginning of the twentieth century, the land was again sold to two individuals, one of whom rented it to the municipality of Florence for use as an elementary school.

Then, something critical happened. Although the details are murky, the owner of the land in 1920, the head of the American Red Cross mission in Italy, Edward Otis Bartlett, donated it to a trust charged with using the land "for popular education, with special attention to children." Ownership of the property was now tied to a social mission, providing a play space for children. In 1954, after trusteeship of the land had passed to another generation, most of the land was donated to the municipality of Florence, becoming public property once again. But because legal documents declaring the intended social uses for the land were lost or never kept in the first place — and perhaps because the later generations of trustees had commercial intentions for the land — city authorities had allowed a building and part of the garden to fall into the hands of real estate investors, who then tried to build luxury apartments and a parking lot on the site.

Thanks to some dogged legal sleuthing by neighborhood residents in the 1990s, a document from the 1920s was found showing that the land was supposed to be managed for the benefit of children. Families of the San Frediano district mounted public protests in 2011 to try to restore the trust but failed. However, the city — eager to save money and stung by neighborhood protests — agreed to let residents manage the garden themselves, at their own risk, expense, and responsibility. A neighborhood association was formed to sign a legal convention with the city to keep the space available to people, without cost to the city administration. It resembles similar agreements for other neighborhood gardens in Florence in which residents were authorized to act as custodians of the gardens. But the city government retained the right to revoke access at any moment through an unappealable decision. Commoning at Nidiaci Gardens can continue, but it remains legally vulnerable — the fate of countless commons around the world.

*　　*　　*

There are thousands of such stories of people trying to find legal protection for their commoning. The stories are different, but tend to be similar in at least two respects. First, legal forms matter because they privilege certain uses of the things around us and certain social relations. And second, the social reality of commoning must precede any property forms. The recovery of the Nidiaci Garden happened in the first place only because neighborhood residents organized to press for appropriate legal and political solutions. Legal forms matter because, as we see in the Nidiaci Gardens history, a trust can be a better legal vehicle than state property for advancing the goals of the donor and neighborhood residents. Even though the Nidiaci commoners prevailed in one sense (commoning is now possible there), they came to understand that there was really no suitable form of property law to protect the social relations they wish to cultivate.

This is usually the case. Commoners routinely must rely on "alien" legal forms to protect their shared wealth and community culture. For example, software programmers who wanted to assure that their code could be shared and modified by anyone — free and open source software — discovered that they had to engineer a "legal hack" on copyright law, which is normally used to turn creative works into private property. (More on this on pp. 258–260.) When American entrepreneur Douglas Tompkins wanted to preserve more than two million acres of wilderness in Chile and Argentina, there was no legal instrument to manage it as a commons. He had to buy the land as private property and donate it to a private land trust, which later gave the land to the governments of those two nations to administer as public property. Sometimes a group of farmers may make a local diner their favorite hangout, or bikers and football fans in a given city will make a certain bar their favored place. But the owners of such private commercial establishments may have their own ideas about to manage these de facto social commons, perhaps leading to tensions between the property owners and the users.

As these examples suggest, property law and commoning are not generally made for each other. That's more or less the problem that Nidiaci commoners faced: they were not able to acquire clear title to the land or secure a legal vehicle that recognized their vernacular practices. But they got lucky — they were able to work out a deal that lets them use and peer-govern the space for children and families. They secured the municipal government's legal permission, and for the purposes of commoning, that was enough, at least in the short term. But it is certainly not a reliable legal solution over the long term. Faced with existing frameworks of property law, commoners who wish to legalize their Peer Governance may have little choice but to attempt to creatively modify the law or turn to political pressure, social organizing, or civil disobedience.[1]

This should not be surprising. Guardians of the dominant economic and social order naturally see property law as an instrument to advance their interests. When early capitalism enclosed the commons and overrode customary practices, writes historian E.P. Thompson, the "political economy aided and abetted the law."[2] Property law was an essential tool of dispossession. In our time, a similar dynamic is at work, as we see in copyright laws that lock research away from the scholars who produced it, patent laws that prohibit farmers from sharing seeds, and large corporations that ravage local landscapes to extract fossil fuels. As the great political scientist and philosopher C.B. Macpherson once wrote:

> For when the liberal property right is written into law as an individual right to the exclusive use and disposal of parcels of the resources provided by nature and of parcels

of capital created by past work on them, and when it is
combined with the liberal system of market incentives and
the rights of *free contract*, it leads to and supports a concentration of ownership and a *system* of power relations
[...] which negates the ethical goal of *free* and independent
individual development."[3] (emphasis in original)

In short, the combination of property law with capitalist markets
and state enforcement of contracts has created a powerful narrative of
freedom — but a freedom that is mostly reserved for owners. If we
really want to be free, and we wish *everyone* to enjoy that possibility, we
need to rethink property.

This is a very large and complicated topic, of course. It is not easy
to imagine how we might subordinate property rights to the needs
of our society and ecosystems, reversing the power of tradeable property to dictate terms for nearly everything. Chapters Seven and Eight
are devoted to this ambitious challenge. We start by rethinking some
fundamental dimensions of property that have long been neglected or
ignored, but which have great importance to commoning. Then, in
Chapter Eight, we explore the possibilities and ways of relationalizing
property. The point is not to abandon property law as such, but to situate the things we use (sometimes known to the law as "property") in a
rich, diverse, and meaning-making web of relationships — social, economic, ecological, temporal.[4] The legal concepts of possession, custom,
and inalienability are important in helping us rethink the meaning of
property.

In rethinking property, it is vital that we understand a basic idea —
property is relational and not just an object. This insight opens the door
to a richer, more realistic discussion of how property actually affects us
and the world. We also need to recognize that familiar forms of *collective property* — trusts, coops, partnerships, nonprofits — can achieve
a great deal, but they ultimately do not overcome the structural biases
embedded in property itself: the right to exclude, the over-reliance
on markets, the habit of equating value with price, and the power of
owners to dictate how nature and people will be treated.[5]

In this chapter, we will also clarify why the notion of possession is
so important to the commons. In an existential sense, we cannot *not*

possess. But something interesting happens as we possess. As firsthand users of water, land, wood, soil, landscapes, seeds, and much more, we develop knowledge and affection, a sense of responsibility, and situated knowledge about the resource — enough to convert it into care-wealth. Such attitudes are less likely to develop among owners primarily focused on the exchange value of their property.

By focusing on possession, we can begin to think about ways of having that may not be officially sanctioned by legality (as at Nidiaci Garden), but which are entirely functional and effective. Moreover, we can begin to think about how state law might recognize or facilitate these other modes of possessing, collaborating, sharing, and commoning. This mode of having and using is what we call Relationalized Property — a topic we will develop in Chapter Eight.

Finally, we explore why *inalienability* is critical to any vision of stewardship through commoning. Inalienability is the idea that it is ethically offensive to appropriate and sell certain cherished things. As creatures of the market, we moderns generally dismiss this idea as archaic. But the legal history of inalienability, especially during the Roman Empire, shows how a prohibition on alienation enables all sorts of vital relationships to flourish precisely because limits are set on market activity.

Me, My Freedom, and My Property

It's no exaggeration to say that our ideas about property express a vision of personhood — one that radiates into the deepest corners of society, affecting our social identities and relationships, commercial dealings, institutional behavior, and treatment of nature. "The premise underlying the personhood perspective," writes property law scholar Margaret Jane Radin, "is that to achieve proper self-development — to be a person — an individual needs some control over resources in the external environment. The necessary assurances of control take the form of property rights."[6] But property is not just a reflection of our sense of what a human being is; it is a legal enactment of our social relations. A vast market apparatus ratifies and reinforces a culture based on property norms every day. Thus the *juridical* way that we think about property largely determines the actual *social* relations that we can imagine and develop. Of course, this happens in other realms of life, too: how we think about "the economy" also determines how we relate to each other.

For the past 250 years, modern, liberal notions of property have been the defining feature of our general archetype of personhood. John Locke, Thomas Hobbes, and the other early theorists of the modern state and liberal property rights started with the assumption that the individual matters most, and that everyone is "proprietor of his person and capacities."[7] Most of Western culture has embraced the idea that freedom is "freedom from *dependence* on the wills of others, ... and freedom is a function of possession. Society becomes a lot of free and equal individuals related to each other as proprietors of their own capacities and of what they have acquired by their exercise. Society consists of exchange between proprietors."[8]

This modern catechism of freedom anchors the cherished cultural ideal of individual autonomy and individual property. The human being is conceived as an isolated-I with absolute freedom, expressed through ownership. It is a world in which we stand as selves ultimately disconnected from everything else — community, tradition, ethnicity, religion, nature. In such a world, property ownership constitutes an institutional bulwark for the freedom of the utterly autonomous individual. These three ideas — the individual, property rights, and freedom — have become the pillars of free-market ideology and Western civilization. The linkage among the three defines a world in which individual property rights are seen as determining people's "actual freedom and actual prospect of realizing their full potentialities."[9] Once this linkage was established as the dominant political theory — modern liberalism — it was *read back into the nature of the individual* as if it had always been there and was not culturally created. It was presented as a self-evident, universal *fact*.

By sanctifying this vision of humanity, modern property law functions as a massive system of social engineering. It elevates instrumental, commercial uses of nature. It encourages the treatment of human beings as commodified labor and the internalization of such norms as people learn to sell themselves on the labor market. It creates artificial scarcities through copyright and patent law to help create markets that wouldn't otherwise exist. Property law as it is today systemically privileges the individual versus the collective, self-serving control over relationships, and exchange value over intrinsic or use value. One might say that the very premises of property law dictate these outcomes. This makes it difficult to entertain legal schemes that might reflect a broader array of human values, practices, and social organization.

How then might we inaugurate an OntoShift (as discussed in Chapter Two) and new approaches toward value to achieve a more life-nurturing conceptualization of property?

Property is Relational

At the very moment we recognize our condition to be that of human beings in relatedness, it becomes clear that the default premise of property law — that everyone is absolutely autonomous and separate from each other and the Earth — is highly problematic if not silly. The three pillars of modern liberal society — 1) the lone individual and 2) property rights as the basis for 3) "contract freedom" — represent a fairly crude, narrow vision of human fulfillment and social order.

If we wish to recognize our actual interconnectedness and take it seriously, we must start to imagine new types of institutional and property arrangements that recognize this fact. If we acknowledge that the libertarian individual as a cultural ideal is a fantasy, then we need to begin to rethink the very concepts of "freedom" and "property" as now construed. We must reassess the idea that boundless individualism is truly liberating, that property rights are the best guarantor of freedom and social well-being, and that we can continue to pursue market growth in a world of ecological limits.

The prejudices in modern thinking about property go back a long way. In his famous 1753 treatise on property, the English jurist William Blackstone wrote, "There is nothing which so generally strikes the imagination, and engages the affections of mankind, as the right of property, that sole and despotic dominion which one man claims and exercises over the external things of the world, in total exclusion of the right of any other individual in the universe."[10] Blackstone's notion of an individual as an obsessive, self-regarding owner is something of a caricature, of course. Moreover, he talks as if property were only an object — an idea that has been commonplace in Euro-American contexts. The only relevant relationship raised by property seems to be between a person and a thing, as in, "This bicycle belongs to me. I am its owner." Because property law privileges the idea of the lone, discon-nected individual and property as an object, it has trouble grappling with the *relationships* that lie at the heart of commoning and, indeed, life itself.

Blackstone's quote is interesting for yet another reason. He bluntly notes that one is either an owner or a non-owner, which means that property rights create a social boundary in the first place. The statement, "This bicycle is mine. I am its owner," is more accurately understood as, "This bicycle is mine, *therefore* I can decide if *you* can use it or not." The legal connection between me and the bicycle priv-ileges my entitlements and denies yours. In other words, the *legal* relationship (property ownership) profoundly shapes and determines *social* relationships. Property law determines who may decide how the bicycle may be used — if it can be sold, destroyed, altered, co-used, or parked in a garage, and under what terms. Legal ownership determines everything, but particularly, the right to exclude. The way we construct and apply property rights actually reveals much more about us and our relationships to others than about our relationships to the actual thing owned.

There are, of course, some significant exceptions to the unlim-ited freedom of "sole and despotic" ownership. Owners of land, for example, are subject to zoning laws that restrict how land may be used. Nuisance laws prevent owners from making too much noise or burning leaves. Building codes protect health and safety. And so on. Despite such limitations, the presumption that property rights confer absolute dominion remains the default norm. This idea contains a built-in conundrum, however. In real life, *everyone's* property rights cannot be absolute, so there are inevitable conflicts about the scope of one's rights. These conflicts cannot be resolved through the law alone, but only through politics. What is allowed and forbidden to owners and everyone else is essentially a "policy determination, not a matter of neutral deductive reasoning" by courts, notes one legal commenator.[11] Law reflects the political and economic order.

The Federal Republic of Germany's Constitution, known as *Grundgesetz*, actually has a provision (in paragraph 14.2) that stipulates, "Property entails obligations. Its use shall also serve the public good."[12] The philosopher who provided the main arguments for contemporary

property law, John Locke, gives passing recognition to the social implications of individual ownership by stipulating that a property right is
legitimate "only if there is enough, and as good, left in common for
others."[13] This so-called "Lockean proviso" is an attempt to acknowledge that one person's property rights may directly affect other people's
lives, but in practice the proviso has been largely ignored.[14]

As this legal history suggests, highlighting the general idea that
property is relational is not that remarkable. It quickly becomes con-
troversial, however, when it comes time to hammer out specific
entitlements, their scope and term, and limitations. Then we get to the
heart of the matter. We see that property law is not about making a
general statement about normative relationships, it is all about *enacting*
those relationships with the enforcement powers of the nation-state.
We need to be clear that property law has no content in itself; it is the
outcome of politics — a struggle to determine what sort of enforceable
meanings "property" will have in law and what its legal disposition will
be. In this way law both reflects and profoundly shapes and determines
social relationships. Something significant happens when states affirm
certain types of social relationships through such property laws as the
right to own land, music, water, or images: It becomes difficult to question the moral justifications for ownership. After all, once a sovereign
state throws its authority behind certain classes of property, it in effect
forecloses any further discussion about the legitimacy of ownership.

This often leads to a disturbing gap between *legality* and *legitimacy*, a distinction used by French legal scholar Étienne Le Roy.[15]
Political and corporate elites embrace formal law, bureaucratic rules,
jurisprudence — "legality" — while the experiences and vernacular
norms and practices of ordinary people — "legitimacy" — go ignored.
Farmers around the world consider it entirely legitimate to save and
share seeds, and scholars and internet users generally want to share
their knowledge with each other. However, to the guardians of legality,
such activities are often regarded as criminal. Property rights must be
defended. Legality is thus used to eclipse the Vernacular Law of the
commons — the informal, unofficial norms, practices, and customs
used by peer communities to manage their affairs.[16] In this way, we
can see how property is given a higher legal standing than possession,
regardless of the legitimacy of the arguments for the latter. Because

law has endorsed a certain social order of property through ordained state processes (legislatures, bureaucracies, courts), customary practice, tradition, and possession can be shunted aside as illegal, or at least suspect. Property ownership is lawful, but possession is not accorded the same level of protection.

Wesley N. Hohfeld was an early twentieth century law scholar who popularized the idea that each right conferred by property law corresponds to a "non-right" that afflicts others. Each time the law recognizes a right or a privilege for one person, it denies a corresponding right or privilege to somebody else. Any legal power for one is related to a legal disability imposed on others.[17] Or as one property scholar put it: "Legal rights are not simply entitlements, but jural relations."[18] Because property is a complex set of legal relations that govern how people may interact "no person can enjoy complete freedom to use, possess, enjoy, or transfer assets regarded as theirs," writes Gregory Alexander. And this means that "[s]ome degree of social interference with one person's ownership interest not only does not negate ownership, it is *unavoidable*."[19] (emphasis in original)

This insight is more profound than it may seem. Property not only establishes a relationship between a bicycle owner and a bicycle, and between the bicycle owner and non-owners. It indirectly establishes a dense web of *multiple relationships* — with the people who mined the metal for the bicycle and produced the parts, with the manufacturer and retailer, with the person to whom you may have lent it, with people driving cars and bicycles on the road, and so on. An object designated as property is not just implicated in a complex web of social relations, but also in *myriad other relationships* such as with a local community, the ecosystem, nonhuman life, and future generations. Property law focuses on the rights of the owner and sometimes the direct effects on others; it is essentially a short-sighted, parochial viewpoint.

The serious limitations of property — the market individualism and societal order that it prioritizes — prompt us to ask: can we come up with different ways of having, that honor relationships of life outside of the market — ones that formal jural relations and property law don't fully recognize?

This is a difficult challenge because the capitalist economy, expressing a certain configuration of social relationships (competition, exclusivity, etc.), has its own propulsive logic and power that commodifies nature, labor, and money. Property law aggressively tracks and reinforces this very logic, creating a self-reinforcing, self-enclosed cycle. Law both reflects and fortifies the political and economic order. It's a vicious cycle that must somehow be broken and overcome.

Collective Property as a Counterpoint to Individual Property?

Could *collective property* serve as a vehicle for recognizing a larger set of relations? That is certainly what a broad spectrum of political progressives have sought to do through cooperatives, land trusts, public trusts, foundations, nonprofit organizations, and other legal forms. Within the market/state system and property law, this approach certainly has a logical appeal. It is a way that groups of people try to serve collective social needs over private business interests. This approach has fed the belief that collective property is quite different from individual property. But in truth, they are more alike than different. Individual property means that there is one owner.[20] Collective property has two or more owners, or even thousands of co-owners. But in either case, the character of property rights (the ability to exclude, transfer, etc.) is much the same. The chief difference is in the number of owners, not in the nature of the property rights.

What we are suggesting is that collective property is only modestly different from personal property. There is no difference in principle between the two. It helps to realize that the etymology of the word "private" traces back to the Latin word *privare*, meaning "to deprive." Individual and collective property rights both authorize the *right to deprive*, or exclude others from use of the property. But beware of binary thinking: when we point to the commonality between individual and collective property, we are not naively suggesting that all property should instead be open to anybody at any moment, without limitation.

We are suggesting a reconceptualization — that it *is possible to reimagine property in ways that limit use, honor social relations, and prevent domination.* These are, of course, some essential features of commons. Finding ways to rethink property could help us support commons and reverse engineer the totalizing dynamics of capital. We will return to this topic in Chapter Eight, but for now let's have a closer look at the supposed differences between private and collective property.

There are significant differences between the ways in which property rights are exercised by *one* owner as opposed to *several* owners. Collective property requires at least a common agreement among all co-owners, which itself can be quite complicated. And some forms of collective property such as co-ops, trusts, and nonprofits avoid the structural imperative to maximize profits, in the ways that corporations and businesses must. So some forms of collective property can achieve a great deal of social good despite using legal forms philosophically rooted in an individualist mindset.

Ultimately, however, the potential of collective property as a legal form has limits. It still divides the world into "mine" and "yours" or even "for our group alone" (a "club good," in economic terms). As a result, even collective property can be bought out by those with more money or sold out by co-owners abandoning their mutual commitments. The owners of a co-op, for example, upon seeing an appreciation in the market value of their assets, may decide to cash out. Or its leaders may decide to turn away from a mission of mutual support and become a market competitor that functions as a quasi-corporation. Or the trustees of a foundation or trust may decide unilaterally to liquidate the entity without regard for the designated beneficiaries.

If we wish to imagine a post-capitalist order that gets beyond the built-in presuppositions of property law and the host culture of capitalism, we will have to look elsewhere. We see two general approaches: a *Pre-Property Regime* that allows anyone to access and use resources without restriction; and *Relational Ways of Having* that recognize and support commoning. A Pre-Property Regime is in effect an open access regime or free-for-all. This approach is attractive for the use of knowledge, ideas, and digital code because it establishes open platforms and open exchange, escaping direct proprietary control. However, in the case of finite resources like land, a Pre-Property Regime amounts to a free-for-all that can result in overexploitation.

The following table illustrates the differences between personal property and collective property, and how they differ from a Pre-Property Regime.

	Private Property Regimes			Pre-Property Regime
	Personal property	Corporate property	Collective property	open to all as default (even if over-exploitation occurs)
Number of owners	1 person	1 legal person "owned" by many shareholders	1 + n persons	nobody

The differences between personal property and collective property are gradual. However, there is a qualitative difference between private property regimes (personal/corporate/collective) and a No-Property regime.
SOURCE: AUTHORS' ELABORATION ON G.G. STEVENSON'S CLASSIFICATIONS IN *COMMON PROPERTY ECONOMICS: A GENERAL THEORY AND LAND USE APPLICATIONS* (CAMBRIDGE UNIVERSITY PRESS, 1991), P. 58.

Relational Ways of Having is a way of using things that lets participants flexibly decide among themselves how shared wealth and social relations shall be managed. This regime moves beyond the presuppositions of conventional property law and its market norms. No single party or faction has absolute legal control over the wealth, and certainly no one has authority to sell it. It is protected from both internal capture and external alienation. This also means that the resource is protected from what we call Governing-through-Money, the capitalist practice of allowing those with greater money to out-govern and control others. This flaw is baked into property law. By presuming that value=money and that therefore more wealth=greater value, the principle of "money rules" is inescapable. It is not only a problem for commoners, but for capitalist enterprises forced to dance to the tune called by the owners of finance capital.

Relational Ways of Having help us realize that there are many ways to steward and deepen the multiple relationships affected by property. This conceptualization helps us see how individual use rights and collective property regimes are not mutually exclusive. Indeed, they need each other! Individual use rights are *a key condition* for a flourishing collective property regime. Individuals must always have spheres of personal discretion and privacy. To better understand how use rights and collective property can coexist, we need to see the distinction between Possession and Property.

Possession is Distinct From Property

In both common law and civil law systems, *possession* is what happens when you personally have control over something by (sometimes literally) "sitting on it." The Latin word *sedere*, from which the word "possession" derives, means "to sit." Think about the flat you've rented. From a property law point of view, you may possess it as a tenant, but you don't own it. You cannot give it away, bequeath it to your children, transfer or sell it, or, in legal terms, "alienate" it. You can sell only what you own, not what you possess.

Privileging ownership over possession has far-reaching consequences. It means that the state, in alliance with corporations and investors, becomes the champion of owners. It installs a hierarchy of subordination and capitalist social roles. This can be vividly seen in the history of states sweeping aside Indigenous rights and traditional use rights, installing in their place modern, liberal property rights and the market system.

In the late 1880s, for example, the US Government sought to eradicate Native American commoning of land by imposing a system of private ownership. The Dawes Severalty Act, which mandated this radical cultural dispossession, granted US citizenship only to those Native Americans who took up "residence separate and apart from any tribe" — i.e., to those who gave up their tribal identities and became private property holders. The prime author of the Dawes Severalty Act, Senator Henry Dawes of Massachusetts, explained that under common ownership "there is no enterprise to make your home any better than that of your neighbors. There is no selfishness, which is at the bottom of civilization."[21]

On countless other occasions, European and American imperialists have repeated this pattern. They have forced Indigenous cultures to surrender their stewardship of inalienable common lands and treat their land as "private property" and tribal members as individuals. Historian E.P. Thompson described how this model was imposed on Indigenous peoples in North America, India, and the South Pacific:

"Property in land required a landowner, improving the land required labor, and therefore subduing the earth required also subduing the laboring poor." Thompson cites a Lord Goderich, who explained in 1831: "Without some division of labor, without a class of persons willing to work for wages, how can society be prevented from falling into a state of almost primitive rudeness, and how are the comforts and refinements of civilized life to be procured?"[22]

Once again, *ownership* implies a different social order and set of relationships to the earth than *possession.* The two are similar in that both provide clear rights of access and use, and neither is "open to all and shareable without restriction." If you own a flat, you are entitled to sell it or give the key to the person who rents it. If you only possess a flat (because you rented it), you can still determine access rights (you have the key) but are not entitled to sell it.

As this difference suggests, possession is focused on concrete use and use value (which are critical to commoning) while property ownership is oriented toward exchange value. Custom, vernacular practices, ethical norms, sacred places, and historical things are generally subordinated to the rights of owners.[23] However, custom, or what we call Vernacular Law, has its own underestimated powers. It commands the respect of large numbers of people, and therefore has a moral authority and political power that the guardians of property law may be reluctant to acknowledge or confront. Vernacular Law also can provide participatory, localized solutions for problems that stymie bureaucracies and markets. We now turn to Vernacular Law as a potential counterforce to the overreaching claims of property rights.

Custom as Vernacular Law

In traditional commons, use rights were not enforced through formal, written law, but through social memory and lively traditions. Community life featured "an annual procession around the boundaries of the village and the lands belonging to it, and a communal drink after auditing the common box (the community funds)," as one property historian writes.

> Folk customs were combined with the common pasture.
> To the peasants, the bell that the village bull wore around

his neck on the pasture signaled, 'the reeve is coming, the reeve is coming!' (The reeve kept the community's breeding bull.) On New Year's Day, the herdsmen blew their horns, went from door to door and sang their song, asking the peasants to give them something — such as their best-smoked sausages. The gifts were considered an expression of the peasants' esteem for the community employees' careful handling of their livestock."[24]

In all cultures, largely outside the gaze of state law and monarchies, another legal tradition has successfully managed resources on its own terms. It is not driven by the formal logic of state jurisprudence, and some might not even regard it as law because it is unwritten. But certainly the everyday practices, rituals, and ethical norms of ordinary people *function* as a powerful form of law. Custom is one way that people have sustainably managed themselves and their care-wealth without the centralized, top-down apparatus of state power.

Examples are plentiful. Throughout the world, fishing communities stage rituals to express thanks for the return of the fish. Harvest festivals celebrate and enact the proper ways to bring in the crop. The *subak* rice farmers of Indonesia have developed elaborate religious rites to coordinate when to irrigate and harvest. Forest commoners agree on ways to monitor for poachers and theft. The scholars associated with the International Association for the Study of Commons have produced hundreds of case studies about similar commons.

Sometimes the state chooses to recognize custom for its own administrative convenience, in effect ratifying customary practices as a matter of law. This can be seen in the *ejidos* of Spain and Mexico, the *acequias* for water irrigation in New Mexico, the *obştea* of common land and forests in Romania,[25] the *iriaiken* for harvesting mushrooms and other natural resources in Japan, and their equivalent in Switzerland, the *OberAllmeindkorporation*.[26] All of these customary commons have existed longer than any state or nation-state in history. The *Allmeindkorporationen* actually date back to 1114!

Although these forms of peer governance are variously referred to as informal, Indigenous, common, or local, we prefer to use the more general term Vernacular Law. We are inspired by social critic

Ivan Illich, who used the term "vernacular" to refer to the living, social character of this mode of law. Vernacular Law thrives in "places and spaces where people are struggling to achieve regeneration and social restoration against the forces of economic globalization," as one commentator put it.[27] Custom as a form of law commands our attention because it can be an effective way for ordinary people to apply their moral sensibilities and practical wisdom to the management of their property, independent of the moral and political logic of the market/state. Precisely because custom defies Lockean notions of property (fixed, based on individual rights, market-oriented), it honors a richer set of relationships among people and the environment. By giving people a way to communicate their existential *and* affective relationships with rivers, forests, pastures, wild game, and fisheries that sustain them, custom expresses what is meaningful to people. Culture molds itself around natural rhythms. Custom thus can represent a more benign, relationship-based way of having than those sanctioned by modern property law and markets. People's cherished, tried-and-true practices can be given due respect as a legitimate force in law and governance. Custom can ripen into a functional form of law, and the state may see the wisdom of validating it. The tradition of common law jurisprudence has done this for centuries (while generally subordinating custom to property rights). American jurist Oliver Wendell Holmes, Jr. made the classic defense of customary practice in his famous 1881 essay "The Common Law": "The first requirement of a sound body of law is that it should correspond with the actual feelings and demands of the community, whether right or wrong."[28]

Vernacular Law is valuable because it emerges from the community itself, and can evolve and mutate as new conditions arise. It reflects the sentiments of ordinary people, not the priorities of their elected representatives, political elites, or jurisprudential thought. As Holmes put it: "The life of the law has not been logic; it has been experience."[29]

The modern world often denigrates custom as backward, superstitious, or inefficient. It sees bureaucratic systems — which purport to be based on scientific rationality, fair and uniform rules, and central administration — as the superior way to manage things. But custom, which mixes celebration and conviviality with the serious work of stewarding a living environment, has its own efficacy and moral authority. The annual beating of the bounds — the village procession around the perimeter of a commons described in the Introduction to Part III — was both a festive event with cakes and beer and a serious assertion of commoners' entitlements.

Custom can be needlessly inflexible, to be sure, but it generally distills the wisdom of years or even generations of everyday experience in a particular landscape. It reflects a rich legacy of experimentation about what works, what doesn't, and how people can achieve successful, long-term outcomes. In evolutionary terms, one might say that customs are adaptive because they take account of a multitude of subtle, dynamic relationships. That's another reason why custom can be effective: it embodies people's situated knowledge, ethical convictions, and emotional bonds to their land, forests, rivers, and mountains.[30]

Property law professor Carol Rose calls custom "a medium through which a seemingly 'unorganized' public may organize itself and act, and in a sense even 'speak' with the force of law."[31] This, indeed, is one reason why the state is often wary of custom: it embodies a moral authority and power that the state powers may regard as a threat. An American court in 1860 rejected the claims of traditional rights, saying that they are "forms of community unknown in this state."[32] Courts have generally declined to recognize custom as compelling because "if a community were going to make claims in a corporate capacity, then the residents would have to organize themselves in a way legally authorized by the state," explains Rose.[33] Despite the desire of politicians and state ministries to supersede and marginalize custom, an estimated half of the world's arable land is managed collectively by some 2.5 billion people, according to Land Rights Now.[34] A significant percentage of these people clearly look to custom as a force in Peer Governance.

Custom as a vehicle of moral authority and practical wisdom poses something of a conundrum for state power: how can it grant formal recognition and legitimacy to social practices that are so deeply informal? Yet the question can also be reversed: can state law enjoy legitimacy and support — and deliver effective results — *without* recognizing custom? Elinor Ostrom speaks to these concerns with her seventh and eighth design principles — that commoners must have the right of self-organization and that commons must be nested in multiple layers of governmental systems.[35]

Inalienability: A Crucial Concept for Commoning

While the social practices of Vernacular Law challenge the totalizing logic of property, history has shown the value of a legal doctrine to do the same. The concept of *inalienability* had its origins in Roman law, and is described in the original Latin texts as "things, the alienation of which is prohibited" and "things with which there is no trade." The basic idea of inalienability is a *prohibition of market exchange*. What is inalienable cannot be bought and sold on the market. An inalienable thing cannot be inherited, mortgaged, seized, indemnified, or taxed.

Today, of course, almost everything is subject to almost unrestricted property rights. Virtually everything can be owned. The modern mind has seen fit to make property out of genes, words, smells, and snippets of sound. When combined with the sacrosanct "freedom of contract," property rights facilitate the constant trading of nearly everything as a way to generate greater (monetized, private) wealth. The market/state enthusiastically encourages this dynamic because it promotes economic growth and tax revenues. In the process, however, trading relationships have an anti-social dimension: they constantly reenact the line between you and me and dissolve the bonds that connect the members of a society.

Surely one reason that inalienability has been such a hardy idea is that it originates as a social and ethical judgment — that it is wrong for some things to be appropriated. People would consider it a violation of community ethics or feelings of the sacred and profound if, for example, someone were to spray paint hateful graffiti in the town square or if religious shrines were used for commercial purposes. Most societies today regard the sale of babies, body organs, sex, legal rights, and votes as morally repugnant. There is a sufficiently strong social consensus that these things have such profound significance that the moral identity of the community itself would be compromised if they could be legally sold. Inappropriability is always a social judgment first, which legal systems later elevate into a legal prohibition. Roman law was endorsing the judgment that ancient places, theaters, roads, rivers, water conduits, and so on, should not be appropriable and tradable in the same way that bread and butter were.

It's worth pondering the implications of this idea for our time. What if society were to regard certain artifacts as inalienable to anybody in general? What if our property rights did not entail absolute dominion, which includes the right to sell, but were instead limited? What if we recognize that the power of the commons also depends on the fact that, as French legal scholars Dardot and Laval put it, "Commons define a norm of inappropriability."[36]

If this were the default legal position for certain realms of life, it would help reverse the damage associated with the alienation of so many things as tradeable property. As economic historian Karl Polanyi documented, the fledgling capitalists of the eighteenth and nineteenth centuries forcibly redefined land, money, and labor as tradeable commodities.[37] Polanyi called them "fictitious commodities" because none of them is actually *produced for sale*. Land is actually a gift of nature that teems with living creatures. Labor is human life itself. Money is merely a token of purchasing power — a means of trade — and not the object of trade, money itself as a commodity. Converting land, labor, and money into tradeable property was a precondition for creating market society.

It is therefore worth emphasizing: possession is not the problem. Tradeability, enacted through property rights, is. So what if we were to reconsider our treatment of land, labor, and money — and, we would add, knowledge — as commodities that can be owned? What if we began to treat them as something that should not be appropriated in the first place or be alienated for market use? What if we were to declare that digital code and knowledge, for example, could not be appropriated for individual use exclusively, but must be available to many individuals, separately and together, at the same time?

Creating protected spheres of inalienability in contemporary life may seem utopian. After all, modern society idolizes ownership. But it is neither far-fetched nor impractical to create zones of inalienability. When Dr. Jonas Salk, a co-creator of the polio vaccine, was asked in 1955 who owned the patent, he famously replied: "Well, the people I would say. There is no patent. Could you patent the sun?"[38] Salk found it morally repugnant that a life-saving vaccine might be used as a source of private profits and become unaffordable to people who needed it. He therefore entrusted the polio vaccine to the World Health Organization to help assure that its benefits would be made widely available. A different cultural ethic has taken root in subsequent decades, of course, as nation-states grant patents to all sorts of essential medicines, mathematical algorithms, business methods, and knowledge that should be available to everyone.

In New Zealand, an inalienability rule is used to protect the trout population in Lake Taupo. The fishery regulations not only declare a cap on how many fish can be taken — a daily bag limit of six trout — but also a rule making it "illegal to sell or purchase trout."[39] So even though Lake Taupo is full of trout, you can't eat any of them in local restaurants unless you fish them yourself, as allowed under the "daily bag catch." You can bring your fish to the restaurant and they will prepare it for you — just as some restaurants in the US without a liquor license allow you to bring your own bottle of wine.

Rediscovering the Power of *Res Nullius*

Any project to reinvigorate the idea of inalienability would do well to study the history of an important doctrine of Roman law, *res nullius*. It is revealing that contemporary scholarship has all but forgotten this legal category and its judgments about shared culture. How did this happen? And could something similar to *res nullius* serve today as an effective legal element for responsible stewardship?

Res nullius had its roots in the early sixth century, when Emperor Justinian ordered a systematic synthesis of all existing imperial laws drawing upon the most important works in jurisprudence. The result, the Justinian Code — or, more formally, Corpus Iuris Civilis which means "Body of Civil Law" — issued between 534 and 528 B.C.E., greatly influenced modern law. The Code partitioned into separate classes the great mass of things that could be subject to property ownership, with different access and use rights for each class of property. (See table below.) Today, while we assume that property ownership falls into two basic categories, *public* and *private*, the ancient Romans remind us that there are more. They had a legal classification for personal property rights — *res privatae*. The state acted as a protector and trustee of *res publicae* — lands, civil buildings, and infrastructures — and recognized common property regimes, the so-called *res communis*, for air and water.[40] It also declared that certain things known as *res nullius* cannot be owned.

	Legal owner/steward	Object of ownership or stewardship
res publicae	the state holds and manages on behalf of citizens	national parks, public gardens, infrastructure
res privatae	an individual	house, household possessions
res communis	a community/ a bounded group of people	parcels of land
res nullius	no one	atmosphere, oceans, fish, and other fugitive wildlife as well as all that was considered sacred

Table based on definitions in the Institutes of Justinian.

A question that ought to concern we moderns is *why* the idea of unownability has virtually disappeared over the centuries. This is hard to say with any certainty, and diving into details and differing interpretations is beyond the scope of this book. But history tells us that when scholars were creating the new Justinian Code, they reinterpreted the original Latin terms used by prior legal scholars.

We can get an idea of how that happened by looking at one legal source, a text by Gaius, the celebrated Roman jurist of the second century. Gaius recognized five categories of property — the sacred, religious, and holy, (yes, three distinct realms!) as well as public and private — which the Justinian Code collapsed into four (see chart above). Why and how exactly this was done is hard to say with any certainty, but the point that is important to us is that new legal categories were invented, and old ones reinterpreted, as the Justinian Code was devised. and the very premises of law were reinvented. In that process, some pivotal shifts in the idea of ownability occurred, especially in distinctions that property law had previously made between things governed by divine law (*ius divinum*) and human-made law (*ius humanum*).[41] While the latter body of law is clearly based on a social agreement, divine law (also sacred law) refers to any law that was believed to have come directly from the will of the gods (or in other societies, God or the Creator). And what was sacred, part of divine law, could not be appropriated and sold.

But to make matters more confusing, some pre-Justinian legal sources referred to so-called *patrimonial* things, such as objects of cultural heritage, that could not be sold. These were the opposite of *extrapatrimonial* things that could become commercial objects. The core of the matter is that things that belonged to the patrimonial sphere, or to divine law (depending on the text you look at), were considered inalienable *by definition*, and thus illegal to sell.

When the legal scholars assembled the Code of Justinian from such very diverse sources, they had to grapple with two sets of basic classification that existed in parallel — *ius divinum/ius humanum* in some sources, and *patrimonial/extrapatrimonial* in others. This obviously posed a problem. The classifications were not only overlapping, they were incompatible with each other. If the scholars were going to construct a single coherent restatement of law, they would either have to abandon one basic set of legal categories or generate a new classification system entirely. It's as if designers were trying to meld the design logic of one interlocking, modular set of blocks — say, Lego — with a different set such as Playmobil. Within either system, everything fits together perfectly, but the two systems do not work together. This partly explains why the idea of unownability sank into oblivion: the framers of the new code of law could not accommodate the idea of sacredness, which had been attached to the idea of inalienability. The latter therefore lost its previous standing in law.

The process for synthesizing the new Justinian Code took another turn that affects us today. The ancient Romans, smart as they were, had wrapped the idea of inalienability in a "double cover" of protection. Legal historian Yan Thomas calls it a "double modus of being public and sacred," by which he meant that inalienability pointed to the sacred character of public things. In other words, the Roman concept of "public" reflected a veneration for eternity and the sacred while also signifying something usable by all and publicly controlled in perpetuity.

Over the centuries, this latter idea of the *patrimonial* has been more explicitly preserved in law than the idea of "the sacredness of the public." In fact, the idea of the patrimonial was given fresh life in 1982 when the Law of the Sea Convention (also known as UNCLOS III) was ratified. It declared that resources in waters beyond national jurisdiction, such as deep sea minerals, would be regarded as the "Common Heritage of Mankind." However, it would be a mistake to presume that things considered part of the Common Heritage of Mankind are treated as inalienable and protected. Nation-states make conflicting claims to common heritage resources, and in fact, most negotiations revolve around how they should be exploited, by whom, and how profits will be distributed. Inalienability and protection of our heritage are not salient parts of the conversation.

The Oceans as the "Common Heritage of Mankind"

In the Law of the Sea Convention, UNCLOS III Article 136 declares the resources in the waters beyond national jurisdiction to be the "Common Heritage of Mankind." This has meant that minerals on the ocean floor, such as manganese nodules, cannot be claimed, appropriated, or owned by any state or person. Such rights belong to humankind as a whole, with the International Seabed Authority acting on its behalf (Article 137). Despite the ambitious pretensions of a legal concept known as the Common Heritage of Mankind, its actual impact has been disappointing. A close reading of the treaty text makes it clear that ocean "resources" are "only a small part of the international commons," notes international law scholar Prue Taylor, and that the "freedom of the high seas," the legal doctrine that allows the freedom to navigate the seas in extraterritorial waters, has not been replaced. The Common Heritage of Mankind idea has sparked neither a legal revolution nor strong United Nations' support. Even diplomat Arvid Pardo, the driving force behind the Law of the Sea Convention, sardonically noted that the application of the doctrine had been reduced to protecting "ugly little rocks lying in the darkest depths of all creation." But even this is largely incorrect because even the ugly little rocks on the ocean floor are being exploited. The idea of the Common Heritage of Mankind is a concept we should cherish; it was revolutionary enough that the United States of America refused to adhere to UNCLOS III. But it must be linked to the idea of inalienability and given legal teeth if it is going to actually protect our common heritage.

The UNESCO World Heritage Convention is a treaty whose primary purpose is to protect the patrimonial, which includes "superlative natural phenomena or areas of exceptional natural beauty and aesthetic importance" as well as "masterpiece[s] of human creative genius and cultural significance." Examples include the Serengeti National Park, the historic heart of Cairo, Egypt, and the ancient sanctuary of Machu Picchu in Peru.[42]

You, dear reader, might wonder why all this ancient legal history matters to us today. How do Roman legal categories help us to rethink property? First of all, they allow us to identify and move beyond legal principles that destroy the commons (such as the idea of property as "sole and despotic dominion"). Equally important, this history helps us recover forgotten legal categories such as *possession* and *usufruct* that privilege use over ownership.[43] These terms help us more easily name moral and social concerns — heritage, inalienability, sacredness, *res nullius* — that ought to have greater legal standing. To be sure, the idea of the Common Heritage of Mankind has had a disappointing fate in international law. Still, it remains one of the few instances in which *res nullius* has been invoked by representatives of nation-states to authorize collective stewardship of shared wealth. An intriguing question is whether *res nullius* from the Justinian Code might be a versatile legal concept useful for declaring certain things inalienable, thereby empowering commoning.

Property and the Objectification of Social Relations

Here is a basic problem we encountered — much as the Common Heritage of Mankind as a legal concept has been marginalized, so the concept of *public* also appears to have lost its association with the sacred. It appears as if *all* legal categories to express inalienability or bans on unconditional appropriability have been abandoned. There are surely many reasons for this neglect, most significantly the rise of capitalist markets and culture. Western industrial societies eager to boost economic growth love to alienate as much as they can — they consider it progress.

There is another tendency that we must directly confront: the propensity to treat formal law itself as a reliable map of social and ecological reality, when in fact, both of those worlds are dynamic and changing. In his amusing book *Slide Mountain: Or, the Folly of Owning Nature*, Theodore Steinberg explores the silly pretensions of property law to control nature.[44] Can farmers have a legal claim against a company that purports to make rain and fails to do so? How can property rights be claimed in land next to a river bend that is constantly eroding and forming elsewhere? Similar questions might be posed about law that asserts fixed social norms and applies formal logic. The problem is, people and societies are pulsating and alive. Values and norms change, such as social support for transgender rights and same-sex marriage.

The dynamic of using law to objectify social relationships seems to be a pattern in the history of modern law. Let us call attention to ways in which the notion of *res nullius* has transformed over time. The term *res nullius* is generally used to refer to unoccupied land or natural wealth that is free to be appropriated under the law.[45] *Res nullius* has thus provided an important legal justification for the violent seizures of "unowned" lands through colonization. But there is another category: *res nullius in bonis*. This term points to realms that it would be legally and ethically wrong to taking appropriate. "Divine law" (*ius divinis*) made similar prohibitions on taking sacred things. *Res nullius in bonis* simply indicates that something is truly inappropriable and thus inalienable, now and forever. Why, we wondered, did only the first version of *res nullius* survive — meaning "things that have not *yet* been taken" and which therefore *may be taken*?

It is unclear why and how the legal meaning of *res nullius in bonis* disappeared over the centuries. Perhaps it has something to do with a cultural reinterpretation of the term *res* itself. Reading the studies of respected Roman legal historian Yan Thomas, we came to realize that in our times, *res* is usually translated as "thing." Before the Justinian Code, however, it was *not* understood simply as an object or a thing,[46] but as an *issue to be dealt with* or *legal matter*. The term *res* always referred to a thing *in the context of a legal procedure*, and therefore referred more to an *affair* than to just an object.[47] While this may seem to be a subtle difference, it isn't. This more accurate understanding of *res* obliges us to take account of particular social and legal realities. In other words, *res* was not just a matter of "property." Remember that one of the basic qualitative distinctions before the Justinian Code was between *patrimonial* versus *extrapatrimonial*. If the *res* in question was considered patrimonial (heritage), it could never be treated as property and made tradeable. It would remain unowned and protected, and the legal proceedings could only discuss appropriate use rights. By contrast, something that qualified as *extrapatrimonial* (commercial) could be taken, occupied, and owned. *Res*, one could say, was always treated as "something in context." It did not refer to a fixed, essential attribute of "the thing," the property itself. It referred to the contested piece of property, but at the same time to its proper social and legal status. This is not a trivial detail. It helps us see that long before modern law began to dominate our minds, *the web of relations in which a particular* res *was embedded was a primary legal concern. Res* was not reified, one could say, but referred to a legal affair.

Understanding *res* or anything subject to property rights in relational terms means that there is no such thing as the natural character of the thing itself that determines the appropriate property rights. This approach is nonetheless still in vogue today. Economists routinely declare that certain classes of what they call goods can be managed only as public property or as private property.[48] This mentality can be seen in a classic economics chart that declares the existence of four types of goods — private, public, club goods, and common goods — based on supposedly intrinsic traits of the goods themselves.[49]

This matrix of four types of property and corresponding governance regimes is profoundly misleading. It quietly suggests that what is actually a social choice inheres in the goods themselves. In other words, the chart reflects a serious ontological confusion — one that is taught to economics students around the world. Standard economics ascribes characteristics to physical resources that are in fact entirely open to social choice and governance. It is neither necessary nor most efficient for a lighthouse to be managed as a public good, for example. Civil infrastructure can often be successfully managed as a common good, as we have seen with Wi-Fi systems (Guifi.net). Digital code need not be treated as a private good or even as a club good; it too can be practically managed as a commons. And so on. The neoclassical monoculture for economic theory has simply chosen to ignore the sociopolitical choices that affect the creation of property rights, preferring to attribute those rights to something inherent in the resource itself.[50] It has superimposed its objectivist worldview onto the field of goods, much as the legal profession transmuted a social matter, *res*, into an object. Despite the efforts of modern capitalism to objectify social relations into property, different notions of property expressing different ways of being in the world persist. Each authorizes or constrains how we may live in the world.

*   *   *

As we have seen so far, modern property law performs a great deal of social engineering in the guise of "natural, universal" principles. It privileges a distinct repertoire of capitalist/liberal relationships and it precludes, complicates, or even criminalizes other relationships such as sharing. Property law normalizes a worldview that sees human freedom and fulfillment deriving from individual ownership and market exchange. But more convivial, eco-responsible forms of law, and even "relationalized property," are possible, as we explore in Chapter 9.

8

Relationalize Property

A S WE SAW IN CHAPTER SEVEN, our thinking about property and the legal categories for property shape the kind of human beings we become. They also shape the kinds of society we allow ourselves to build. We are encouraged to work hard, become owners, and become rich. This may not be especially meaningful or enlivening, but it is certainly a sensible and functional approach in a world that celebrates the competitive, acquisitive, self-serving mindset.

To be sure, a rich spectrum of noncapitalist behaviors — sharing, cooperating, assuming co-responsibility, practicing social solidarity — do not disappear. But neither do they flourish on their own terms. Such behaviors are often patronized as idealistic, innocent, and somehow unworldly. Unless they can be conscripted to serve the interests of property, markets, and capital (even corporate systems require cooperation), they are left to atrophy on the outskirts of the formal economy. It is no surprise that the idea of the commons has been nearly forgotten in the resulting capitalist thunderdome, where Governing-through-Money is the default.

It is beyond our capacity to propose a transformation in property law itself. We have a more modest ambition — to show the feasibility of alternative pathways that Relationalize Property, as we call it. We use this term to point to sociolegal systems that elevate concrete use rights and social relationships over absolute property ownership. As the following five fascinating examples show, it is possible to facilitate other ways of having without falling into the domineering or dependent social roles that ownership generally entails. Our examples explain some of the ingenious ways by which commoners have decommodified access and use rights, which in turn opens up an enlivening range of relationships that are otherwise marginalized or impossible. As we will see, regimes of Relationalized Property make it easier to use things to meet real needs as opposed to maximizing investment returns or asserting power over others.

Decommodifying a Supermarket

To visit the Park Slope Food Coop in Brooklyn, New York, is to experience a supermarket that has been transformed to live, breathe, and function instead as a social community. The Coop is a busy, well-organized, and fully staffed operation like most any other supermarket. But this place, in the heart of New York City's commercial culture (Manhattan is two miles away), feels very different. The Coop isn't a business that seeks to pander, cajole, and flatter its customers to buy, buy, buy. There is no promotional signage or splashy displays designed to spur impulse purchases. The Coop has a rather simple goal, skillfully enacted: to let people obtain high-quality food inexpensively by "buying from themselves."

It takes a moment to realize that none of the cashiers ringing up groceries at the check-out counters are employees. Everyone who works there is a coop member themselves — perhaps even a friend or neighbor. More than 17,000 members take care of everything from unloading trucks and stocking shelves to serving up delicatessen meats and cleaning up — without pay. Upon arriving at the Coop, our guide, member Paula Segal, took us upstairs to the welcome desk to get a badge that let us to enter the store. (To prevent free riders, only members can enter and shop at the store, but anyone can join.)

The Park Slope Food Coop is at once a physical building, social institution, and distribution infrastructure. It also serves as a community center, meeting place, and ongoing host of bottom-up democracy for decision-making (without overcoming the limitations of representation or majority rule, however). Since its founding in 1973, the Coop has become a stalwart, beloved community institution in Brooklyn, not just because its groceries are cheaper than those of typical supermarkets. It is a vibrant institution because cooperativists don't just *own* the Coop. They *enact* their ownership directly and have developed a social commitment to its success.

Much of this spirit of Peer Governance and Provisioning at Park Slope Food Coop stems from its organization as a *labor cooperative*, which is different from a consumer or producer cooperative (often con-flated with commons). Each member is required to contribute exactly two hours and forty-five minutes of unpaid work every four weeks.[1] This is a key element of the Coop's success — a pool of more than 17,000 member-owners who reliably show up to work their scheduled shifts each month. The arrangement allows the Coop to slash the single largest expense for a normal grocery store, its payroll, and thereby keep costs to a minimum. Approximately seventy-five percent of the work at the Coop is performed by its members (the rest, around sixty people, are paid staff members). This work does not give members direct cash benefits for time expended (e.g., lower grocery bills for unpaid work), but on average the work performed by members translates into savings of twenty to forty percent off the retail price of groceries. For a family that might otherwise spend $500 a month on food, that is a saving of $100 to $200.

The scheduled workslots are part of a bold strategy to decommodify work at the Coop and cultivate a community ethic. The enterprise is not simply a bundle of market transactions for products, labor, physical infrastructure, and so forth. The Coop is not just servicing members with lower prices. Like Cecosesola in Venezuela (see pp. 185–187), whose below-market prices express its value sovereignty, the Coop is a serious force in taking "some control away from corporations" in the retail grocery market.[2] With annual revenues of more than $49 million, the Park Slope Food Coop is in fact one of the biggest food or labor coops in the United States.

The strategy to decommodify labor has been well planned. Near the welcome desk, there is a child care space where members take care of other members' children while the parents shop, run errands — or, often, while members work their mandatory monthly workslot. Most members fulfill their work commitments as members of "squads" that meet at the same time and place once every four weeks to do the work that needs to be done: packaging spices, bagging olives, cutting and wrapping cheese, answering phones, assisting members, doing admin-istrative tasks in the membership office, receiving deliveries, keeping the shelves and coolers stocked, totaling groceries bills at checkout, bagging groceries, cleaning, and much else. Squad leaders, also unpaid members, take on the extra responsibility of running the squad.

Working on these tasks via squads helps members get to know each other on a regular basis and develop a kinship with the Coop community. Everyone ends up having to make a personal commitment to the Coop's mission. No member can simply send a surrogate to do their workslot or pay someone, like a nanny or teenager, to do the work. This decision was taken by members at a general meeting, where important decisions are usually taken. The purpose was to "prevent members from paying their way out of a shift and losing the connection to the Coop as working members."[3] If you miss your shift, you can't shop there again until you work two additional shifts. Members who don't work or shop at the Coop for a year can obtain an "amnesty" and make a fresh start — but the amnesty privilege can be invoked only once in a lifetime.

Following a visit to the coop, a question that stuck with us was this: why aren't there more labor coops? Why has this kind of labor cooperative model not spread around the world in the way that "normal" cooperatives have? There are many reasons, but one important answer is that most coops ignore the power of decommodifying work as a built-in feature of their property regimes — as a form, that is, of relationalizing property. Let's explain: people at PSFC are member-owners, which means that the two roles are deeply and inseparably connected to each other. Whoever joins the Coop cannot be just a member or just an owner; they must assume both roles together. As the Coop's membership manual puts it: "Membership is defined by a person's participation in the so-called workslot system, while ownership is defined by your financial contribution. This contribution is officially called a member-equity investment." It costs $25 to join the Coop — a one-time fee. A $100 financial investment is required as well, refundable upon leaving the Coop.

The real novelty of the Park Slope Food Coop is thus its redefinition of property ownership as a set of entitlements intrinsically bound up with decommodified work for shared purposes. This concept is a simple but ingenious way to POOL & SHARE (see Chapter Six) in the improbable context of a supermarket. The essential point is that you cannot share in the benefits — inexpensive, high-quality, local food products, free child care while you go shopping, community support and solidarity, and the satisfaction of co-shaping your environment and living conditions — if you don't pool two hours and forty-five minutes of unpaid work a month. This arrangement is both economically effective in reducing costs and legally clever — it uses cooperative bylaws to define special terms of ownership.

Decommodifying work also changes the terms of institutional life by creating the conditions for people to develop shared emotional ties and community spirit. Property ownership is turned into a social vehicle for meaning-making and building a commons culture. "We studied why other co-ops failed, and in most cases, it's because they were too dependent on super committed members who eventually burnt out," Joe Holtz, a cofounder of the Coop, once explained.[4] "One of our theories was to try and emulate what retailers do: stay at our place and have deliveries come to us …We decided that if we were to last, we'd have to operate as a real store, with set hours." In one stroke, the work requirement helps solve the problems of altruistic burnout, high labor costs, and weak community culture.

Why Relationalize Property?

What exactly do we mean by "relationalizing property"? Before moving on to our next examples, let's pause a moment to elaborate on the suffocating and repressive social implications of conventional property arrangements — to see how relationalizing property can help us slip the shackles of property law to open up enlivening new possibilities.

Property law as we know it has created a social order resembling a puppeteer and puppets. The property owner holds the strings that control the arms, legs, and head of the puppet — i.e., the non-owner. The property owner can jerk the puppets this way or that based on what he believes will be profitable or attractive to him. No wonder we all want to be puppeteers rather than puppets! As we are split up into haves and have-nots, property owners accrue great accumulations of capital and power, and acquire the motive, means, and opportunity to abuse non-owners and the natural world. When property rights are allied with markets, they radically disempower large segments of the world socially and economically.

To relationalize property means to arrange the enactment of use rights in ways that nourish our relationships to each other, the nonhuman world, and past and future generations. People are required and encouraged by design to take responsibility for these relationships and for the common good. Such cultural norms simply can't take root and flourish within systems of conventional property grounded in the old ontology of Isolated-I's, dominion, and exclusion. With Relationalized Property, they can.

"Relation" derives from Latin *relatus* (past participle of *referre*), which means "bring back" or "bear back." To relationalize thus implies the idea of bringing something back — something that might have existed before an act of appropriation or market alienation. It essentially means to recognize and honor a wide range of relationships that preexist the ones that modern property law and markets generally impose. Instead, we must design systems that can strengthen a richer, more open variety of relationships through new ways of having.

This bring us back to the idea of *affordances*. Our ways of having must be able to support a larger spectrum of relationships, behaviors, and culture than is generally permissible through normal property rights and market exchange. Property must be able to support social cooperation, ecological stewardship, and nonreciprocal gifting. Once puppeteers/owners can escape their role in manipulating the puppets/nonowners, a new, more collaborative social dynamic can emerge.

Relationalized Property regimes help us escape the trap of helpless subordination to the wills of others. They recognize our interdependence, which is quite different from the subordination associated with modern property rights. Relationalized Property should not be confused with coercive collectivism, however. If property arrangements in a twenty-first century commons feel like an imposition or a trap, then something has gone utterly wrong. Everyone at the Park Slope Food Coop *chooses* to become a member-owner and, in so doing, to assume certain shared burdens and commitments. This is of utmost importance, because there is a big difference between voluntarily entering into relations with others and being tied to others. In the case of the Park Slope Food Coop, people join on a fully voluntary basis — and the legal arrangements then nurture these relations. In fact, they are enacted again and again *through* the specific property regimes. This can hardly be compared to situations where the relationships are formed by necessity or coercion from the very outset. Relationalized Property is about enhancing our range of individual options and enriching our humanity — while minimizing the hierarchical subordination to (or dominance over) others and the associated feelings of distrust and fear.

Individuals continue to enjoy individual use rights, as we have seen in the Brazilian Landless Rural Worker Movement (MST) case in Chapter Five. But those individual entitlements are brought back to and embedded in their very specific circumstances. They are not decontextualized, abstract rights disconnected from obligations towards others holding similar rights. Nor can individuals shirk their co-responsibilities for what is co-owned, co-used, and stewarded. One could call this arrangement a Nested-I approach to property.

The great virtue of Relationalized Property is its ability to open up all sorts of robust relationships that are otherwise stifled or commodified under conventional property regimes. Instead of placing the owner/object (puppeteer/puppet) relationship at the center, which triggers a cascade of harms, Relationalized Property makes it possible for human, social, and ecological relationships to live and breathe more naturally. People can escape the instrumentalist, money-making logic usually associated with property-rights regimes.

Relationalized Property helps align and empower at least six relationships that private property does not. The first relationships are (1) with ourselves, in helping us see more clearly the meaning of property in our lives; and (2) with our peers, in fostering mutually acceptable rights and responsibilities. At least four additional relationships are enhanced — our relationships with (3) lived experiences (memories, traditions, feelings) connected with places and property, which inspire our stewardship of what we love; (4) with other generations, as we honor previous generations and pay forward benefits and respect to future generations; (5) between commons and other societal institutions such as the state and markets; and (6) with the mysteries of the human condition as we search for ultimate meanings. To Relationalize Property means to respect, protect, and deepen these relationships through our use of property — which itself can only be achieved through commoning that negotiates consensual access and use rights.

Six Key Relationships that Relationalized Property (RP) Fosters[5]

	Relationship of concern	Guiding question	Convivial Tool
1	Relationship to oneself	Are my needs being met?	Self-reflection about the meaning of property in one's life[6]
2	Relationships among peers	Do peers enjoy equal decision-making rights and negotiate mutually acceptable use rights and responsibilities (even if differentiated among participants)?	Park Slope Food Coop's workslot system within the member-ownership concept
3	Relationships between humans and the more-than-human world	Do the rules and rights deriving from RP respect and nurture shared, affective relationships that people have with, for example, parks, artworks, gravesites, places of worship, bodies of water, mountains, and forests?	Taboos, rituals, and celebrations; *res nullius in bonis;* Common Heritage of Mankind (cultural and natural)
4	Relationships between past, present and future generations	Do the use rights and responsibilities reflect a "long now" perspective,[7] especially the principle of intergenerational justice?	Pay-it-forward mechanisms (see pp. 254, 313); gift-provisioning in traditional practices
5	Inter-institutional relationships among commons, and between commons and the market/state	Does the RP regime recognize a semi-permeable membrane around a commons that prevents it from being exploited from the outside? Does the RP regime allow commoners to enjoy entitlements that are not available via market exchange?	Licenses that protect open content or commons such as the General Public License (pp. 258–259) or Open Source Seeds (pp. 263–266)
6	Relationships between a specific property arrangement and people's quest for ultimate meanings	Does the RP arrangement create a sense of belonging and does it contribute to a free, fair, and sustainable world?	

In a scheme of Relationalized Property, the familiar bond established by property — between the owner and the owned thing, as if it were only a subject/object relationship — continues to exist. But this relationship, while certainly important, is no longer considered the essence of property. Relationalizing Property is about restoring the legal space for myriad nonmarket relationships to flourish — affective care and customs, the aliveness of land and other natural systems, intergenerational respect. Through a different sociolegal framework for property, we can bring back all sorts of relationships that the modern, liberal understanding of property (dominion, monetized exchange value) has either banished or marginalized.

It is worth repeating, as noted in Chapter Five, that we are *not* suggesting a novel scheme that exists on a spectrum of property rights, situated somewhere between individual property and collective property. The goal is not to make individual property and collective property coexist in greater harmony as separate, independent realms. It means to say farewell to the argument that one or the other is superior. It means to open our minds to new configurations of use rights and new ways of having that enhance both individual and collective benefits *at the same time*. Rather than simply "balance" the benefits from individual versus collective property rights, the goal is to *integrate the two by design* so that both are more organically aligned, minimizing potential conflict. And still, conflicts will arise. Tensions do not automatically disappear through relationalized property. This is why the many patterns of commoning identified in Chapters Four, Five, and Six are so useful: they provide a means or methodology for addressing conflicts in relationship-preserving ways.

When this occurs, care-wealth emerges. Relationships animated by a person's deep convictions, traditions, and love change how we perceive and experience property. We ascribe certain meanings and significance to the objects of our attention and love. These could be landscapes, sacred objects, heirlooms, or something otherwise regarded as "property." Artisanal works bear the signs of careful, personal attention that mass-produced goods do not have. The Park Slope Food Coop feels very different from a supermarket, precisely because everyone who works there cares about the place in ways that go beyond the relationships people have as consumers or employees.

In sum, the concept of Relationalized Property reminds us that property relations are not just bilateral relations between the owner and owned thing. They always entail *multiple* relations — economic, ecological, social, intergenerational, psychic, spiritual, and so on. It is important to recognize this fundamental insight, that all property, all ways of having, and all societies ultimately depend on a living Earth and its dense web of relationships. Recall Thomas Berry's wisdom that — the universe is "not a collection of objects, but a communion of subjects."[8]

A Platform Designed for Collaboration: Federated Wiki

The most important design choice for commons may be to recognize ourselves as Nested-I's with Ubuntu Rationality. This imperative is especially germane in the design of the next generation of wiki software, the Federated Wiki platform, which is based on the technology that Wikipedia helped popularize. Federated Wiki is a stunning server program that allows individual works of creativity to seamlessly combine into collectively available content without the administrative hassles and editorial disputes of a traditional wiki.

Since its founding in 2001, Wikipedia has proved to be a remarkably robust and flexible way to assemble authoritative, up-to-date knowledge on countless topics, with plentiful space for dissenting and diverse points of view. However, as a wiki designed to let multiple individuals ("clients") interact with a single wiki platform (the "host"), Wikipedia requires that a moderator or editor make choices about what shall be posted. This can result in editors choosing the least-objectionable content and in disagreements among contributors and even flame wars. In a Federated Wiki, however, every individual user has his or her own wiki site, which can freely draw upon content from countless other Fedwiki sites. This means that all voices can be heard in their rich, authentic diversity. Participants in a Federated Wiki can decide to interconnect their wiki pages into a neutral, shared neighborhood of content, through which a consensus of viewpoints becomes visible.

This shift from the standard wiki to a form of writing based on "one person, one wiki, in a federated environment," may sound like a step backward from the Wikipedia style of open collaboration.[9] But in fact the effect is quite the opposite: giving online platforms to individual voices while bringing them together into a shared neighborhood of wikis results in a richer, more robust commons. We talk from experience: we used Federated Wiki in the course of researching and writing this book.

What does it mean to have and own something in a Fedwiki world? What does it feel like? How does it resemble and differ from conventional ownership? Imagine a huge continent of diverse residences.[10] Some have only a few rooms. Others exist within skyscrapers and provide space for hundreds of rental homes with multiple rooms. Some are clustered together as neighborhoods. Others are smaller and more isolated from other flats and houses. These residences are dispersed all over the continent, but there are irregular corridors, pathways, and roads that can potentially interconnect them all. This roughly describes what having a site in the Fedwiki ecosystem is like. Everyone has a flat or a home of their own, but everyone can also be connected to anyone else. I might enjoy and value having visitors at my place, but when they leave it is still my personal space, my protected comfort zone. But unlike my actual home, visitors to my Fedwiki world can decide for themselves when and for how long they want to stay. Because a site is not a physical space but rather a virtual space, anyone can freely draw from the content that I've put in my "rooms" and copy it into theirs (the software keeps a record of where the content came from and who gets credit for it). As the developer of Fedwiki software, Ward Cunningham, explains, "I value visitors because I gain from their presence. My gain is not their loss."

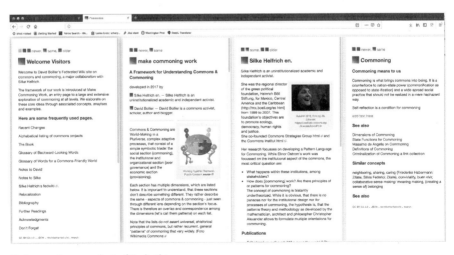

Enhanced screenshot of Fedwiki page.

It takes only a few clicks to make a flat your own in the Federated Wiki ecosystem. You login and register with your online identity as if you were using the key to a flat you've rented. "You login to a site as if you were unlocking the front door of your home," explains Cunningham. "To possess that key is what confers power over what is within." This means that on these sites — within your "rooms" — the software is designed to allow only you to add text, images, videos. Only you can write, delete, and edit. However, others can easily draw from and integrate any elements from your site simply by dragging and dropping the desired wiki pages to their own wikis. You, in turn, can draw from their sites — or anyone else's!

In other words, the Fedwiki software creates protected individual spaces for content generation while facilitating diverse permutations of collaborative authoring on a massive scale. It opens countless paths for individuals to organize their own knowledge while easily sharing it with others, and, what's more, enabling a commons of knowledge to arise, without the intervention of an editor. To use another metaphor: people using Fedwiki sites are like gardeners or farmers. They can plant as many fields or gardens as they want, and reap the harvest from their own Fedwiki, but anyone else can also use someone's harvest to

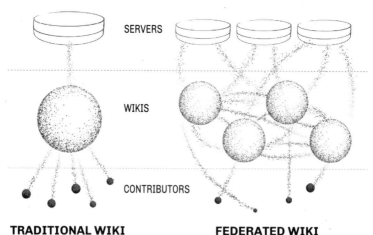

TRADITIONAL WIKI   **FEDERATED WIKI**

In a conventional wiki, multiple individual users contribute to a single wiki on a single server, as shown in the figure at left. But in a Federated Wiki, the contents of multiple individual wikis hosted on multiple servers can be selectively compiled on a single person's wiki, as shown in the figure at right.

enhance their own fields and gardens. Instead of toiling under a regime of private, competitive exclusion, the system encourages cooperative gains through commoning.

Whether you work on your own Fedwiki space or join a neighborhood of sites, you keep the control over what is happening on your site. But meanwhile, sharing among sites through federating remains incredibly easy, by dragging and dropping content or forking it into new sites. This is how Federated Wiki sets up a protected space of individual control while nurturing the knowledge commons through a self-directed process of federation.

Consider how this technology design helps us achieve an OntoShift. The Fedwiki platform blurs the supposed duality of the individual and the collective. By design, these two realms in Fedwiki world are integrated in a mutually enlivening way. Having my personal wiki does not contradict or interfere with my contributing to the commons — quite the opposite. This is Ubuntu Rationality at work and a vibrant example of the Nested-I! The default position is that an idea becomes more powerful as it is shared, without the interventions (or interference!) of corporate algorithms (e.g., Facebook), editors (Wikipedia), crowd ratings (Yelp), or other hosts. Federated Wiki creates a digital environment in which whoever contributes enriches others without requiring anyone to give up control over his or her own site. It is like saying: "Come into my home, the door is open. Use what you wish, and don't worry, you can't mess up my space." The Federated Wiki software prevents people from altering your content while still allowing them to "take" it.

But taking someone else's content does have *some* strings attached. "We insist that the takers credit our home as the source," writes Cunningham. Obviously, this is not meant in a literal sense. You won't discuss or argue, nor send emails, letters, or threats of legal proceedings to others. Within the Federated Wiki environment, the software does it for you: it references any drag and drop or fork back to the source, basically by attaching a colorful little flag in a special shade associated with you. "A home," muses Cunningham, "defines us while making room for others."

The mutually nourishing relationship between one's personal Fedwiki and the Fedwiki Commons is just one remarkable feature of the way ownership is reinvented in this cosmos. If a user decides to

connect to the federation, claims to exclusive private control are sur-
rendered and the fruits of collaboration are automatically shareable.
(Of course, the user can also choose to retain exclusive control over his
or her Fedwiki by not connecting online to the Fedwiki network.) This
represents a dramatic re-imagining of the very idea of ownership of
content. Instead of making sharing an individual, case-by-case choice
(the strategy used by Creative Commons licenses, for example), the
Fedwiki platform boldly uses technological design to make content
sharing the default. Once a user chooses to use the Fedwiki software,
deviations from this default norm, such as absolute private control or
stipulated licensing conditions, are not an option.

All content posted on Fedwiki sites is automatically licensed under
a Creative Commons Attribution-ShareAlike 4.0 license upon publication — meaning that it is "born shareable" the moment someone
publishes it, making it available to the federation of sites. The Fedwiki
recordkeeping "journal" tracks who has posted what, so authorship can
be chronicled even if people make mashups of someone else's content.[11]

In the physical world, property law often establishes different ownership regimes for underground minerals, oil, or gas than for surface rights
(conventional land ownership). It is common for infrastructure to be
treated under one legal regime while the fruits produced via that infrastructure are treated under another one. Ownership rights for a building
can be separated from ownership of land, for example, and ownership of
website content is considered separate from ownership of the Wi-Fi network and telephone lines upon which the content flows. How layers of
property rights interconnect can have significant implications. In most
Latin American countries, national constitutions declare that underground minerals belong *de jure* to the nation-state.[12] This legal power
allows governments to exploit the resources via state-owned companies
or to grant mining concessions to private entities, usually transnational
companies. Clearly this property arrangement does *not* prevent the
overexploitation of minerals or guarantee responsible stewardship of
the landscape; indeed, it seems to promote highly destructive, neoco-
lonial extractivism. In any case, the idea of regulating surface rights
in one way and subsurface rights in another points to the fact that
any arrangement of property rights is not self-evident or "natural." To
put it bluntly: there is no logical or compelling reason that those who

extract oil or minerals should necessarily have the right to own it. That right is simply a political construct that has been sanctified by law.

Similarly, at one time landowners not only owned their plots of land but also the air rights reaching up to the sky, which legally meant that airplanes were violating private property rights.[13] The principle followed the Roman legal maxim known as *cuius est solum eius est usque ad coelum et ad infernos* — "whoever owns the soil, it is theirs all the way to Heaven and all the way to Hell"[14] — a principle that Blackstone reaffirmed centuries later, declaring that property ownership extends to "an indefinite extent, upwards as well as downwards."[15] Over the centuries, however, this idea has been radically curtailed, usually to augment the power of states and corporations. In other words, the *interconnections* among legal regimes are a potential zone of political struggle.

That is more or less what the Federated Wiki platform has overcome via an organic interconnection among legal regimes while relying on distributed structures. It has cleverly rearranged layers of property rights — indeed, transcended them, in a fashion — as a way to promote commoning. "We distinguish owning and operating a server[16] from owning and operating a site," explains Ward Cunningham, noting that content is strewn across many web servers. Digital content is widely distributed and therefore largely beyond the control of any single server owner. In addition, as mentioned, the platform software privileges and empowers the sharing of content as a built-in feature. This, along with the required use of Creative Commons licenses, also helps move content beyond the reach of private property.[17] The Fedwiki platform creates a space of creativity and culture in which the messy tangle of copyright law is functionally moot. Fedwiki empowers users to preempt outside legal challenges for control and to assert greater sovereignty themselves, on their own terms.

The Fedwiki commons does have one vulnerability to outside control that it has not, as yet, been able to evade: the authentication of digital identity. Because of the complexities of providing a commons-friendly alternative, Cunningham and his colleagues have relied on the identity systems developed by Google and Facebook that function as a default for many sites on the internet. This choice is understandable. It is technically complicated and expensive to create digital systems that can reliably authenticate that a self-identified person really is that person and not an impersonator or criminal. For the time being, this makes Federated Wiki vulnerable to the commercial power of the two tech giants, but this deficiency may be remedied in the future.

Nonetheless, we have seen how Fedwiki represents a new type of network platform that sidesteps the domination/subordination dynamics of conventional property. In this sense, it is a lodestar that holds lessons and inspiration for future commons-based innovation. It is possible to devise distributed, commons-based alternatives to the highly centralized and capitalized platforms that foster social polarization, user manipulation, privacy invasions, and concentrated political power. The presumption that private property (copyright, patents) is the only way to order online behavior and spur innovation is simply false. Interestingly, the core idea enshrined in the design of Federated Wiki is similar to the design of many monasteries, as discussed in Chapter Five, in providing supportive environments for collective life while also protecting personal choice.

Using law to balance personal rights with community needs and the common good is possible not only on digital platforms, but in our analog physical environment as well, as we now see in the case of the Mietshäuser Syndikat in Germany.

Neutralizing Capital in the Housing Market: The Mietshäuser Syndikat Story

In cutthroat real estate markets dominated by ruthless investment banking, speculation, landlords, and apartment management firms, it may sound unlikely that we could carve out successful commons for housing. Yet that is precisely what Mietshäuser Syndikat has pioneered in Freiburg, Germany, a lovely scenic town at the southern edge of the Black Forest, before expanding throughout Germany and adjacent countries. Mietshäuser Syndikat is a federation of housing commons that has been operating since 1987. Its name, which translates roughly as "syndicate of rental apartment buildings," conveys its basic mission — to help develop a commons federation of residential real estate peer-managed by residents. People own the buildings but at the same time individually pay rent to themselves and to the federation to keep the whole system going.

In societies where virtually all real estate is considered private property to be used for capital investment and profitmaking, the achievements of Mietshäuser Syndikat are remarkable. "Actually, we should not even exist [according to standard economics]," declare the syndicalists,[18] "because our basic approach violates the rules of the market." This is why the experience is so refreshing: dozens of Mietshäuser Syndikat projects are thriving and people enjoy living in them, yet no one fears that the market will force them to sell their apartments or that the syndicate will sell the buildings and evict people (it can't). Over the past thirty years, Mietshäuser Syndikat has removed more than 130 rental buildings from the real estate market. This has made permanently affordable, collectively owned housing available to more than 2,900 ordinary people. Between 2013 and 2015, the syndicate nearly doubled in size, from fifty affiliated housing projects to ninety-five. By the end of 2018, 136 projects were associated with Mietshäuser Syndikat and another 17 were interested in joining it.

To newcomers, the housing syndicate appears like a hodgepodge of very different rental housing projects. Its holdings scattered across Germany — and now, beyond the nation's borders, in Austria and the Netherlands — include a project for senior women, commercial buildings, a large apartment building for single parents, and a converted former military barracks that now houses more than two hundred people. However different in shape, location, and size, each project represents an attempt to decommodify the land, buildings, and individual apartments that people need.

"The idea of organizing buildings and real estate as commons is nothing new," writes Stefan Rost, an organizer of the Freiburg project, citing the historic role played by large cooperatives and housing associations.[19] What makes the syndicate so unusual is its distinctive sociolegal structure for decommodifying housing and keeping it off the market indefinitely. This structure has made it possible for renters to escape the often exploitative, speculative housing market, and to acquire nice places to live with reasonable "rents" and stable futures. (Monthly payments are not really rents because they do not reflect market prices or pressures, but rather normal building maintenance costs and pay-it-forward contributions to the solidarity fund.)

This is not easy to achieve over long periods, let alone generations. As mortgages are paid off and real estate prices rise over the years, even cooperatives and co-housing residents are often tempted to cash out. The idealistic sacrifices made by an earlier generation that started a housing cooperative, for example, may be liquidated when a later generation of residents decides that it wants to monetize decades of social equity for itself — and market interests once again prevail. This familiar dynamic poses a conundrum: how can a peer-governed commons be prevented from alienating the permanent assets upon which everyone depends? "One cannot simply supervise oneself," as syndicate member Jochen Schmidt put it, because that does not always work.[20] Commoners cannot seek (and don't wish to seek) external supervision without triggering a risk to their sovereignty. And to whom would it surrender its authority in any case? Stefan Rost described the challenge well: "Rules and forms must be found — from *within* the Syndikat — that assure the longevity of the project and prevent its re-privatization and subservience to the capital market."[21]

Mietshäuser Syndikat met this challenge by coming up with an ingenious legal mechanism that seems counterintuitive.[22] It vests the ownership title for each real estate property not in the residents' association alone but in a GmbH — Gesellschaft mit beschränkter Haftung — which is the equivalent of a limited liability company (Ltd. in the UK, and LLC in the US). The LLC has two and only two owners: the residents' association for each housing complex and Mietshäuser Syndikat. The point of this arrangement is to give Mietshäuser Syndikat the authority to act as a watchdog body. It is given very limited voting rights over fundamental issues involving the real estate, such as the right to sell the property or convert it into condominiums, and to changes in a housing association's governance rules. Otherwise, the residents' association retains full powers of self-determination. This structure means that any fundamental changes regarding real estate holdings require agreement by *both* the residents' association and Mietshäuser Syndikat. Each therefore has functional veto power. The syndicate can act as a check on any residents' group that wishes to sell their property. And no single residents' group can change the governance of the limited liability company itself, because it cannot be unilaterally altered or liquidated by one voting member acting alone. Thanks to this mutual veto mechanism, the syndicate is able to achieve what it calls "capital neutralization," a term coined by Matthias Neuling.[23] This mechanism can prevent assets held by housing commons from falling back into the market.

For the 136-plus projects associated with Mietshäuser Syndikat at the time we wrote this, each manages their own social and economic affairs as a peer-governed entity. Each is legally independent and functions as a typical housing cooperative. A members' assembly makes democratic decisions about policies and practices for renting and managing the building, undertaking renovations, financing, and so forth.

The legal scheme for the group helps solve another challenge — how to federate so many different housing commons. If all housing projects are peer governed and legally independent (and should remain so), but all participating projects share a larger purpose (to decommodify real estate), how can this latter goal be assured when there might be disagreements among the dozens of projects? Mietshäuser Syndikat provides an effective vehicle for knitting together diverse types of housing commons. It is a so-called *nicht eingetragener Verein* (n.e.V., a German legal term that roughly translates into "unregistered association"). The n.e.V.

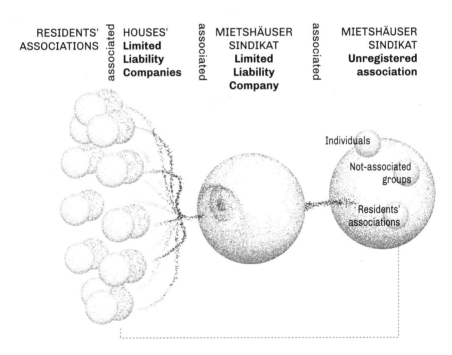

Mietshäuser Syndikat organizational structure. Credit: Mietshäuser Syndikat 2017: Das Mietshäuser Syndikat und die Hausprojekte, Die Häuser denen, die drin wohnen, p.9. https://www.syndikat.org/wp-content/uploads/2017/02/broschuere_nr7.pdf

legally owns Mietshäuser Syndikat GmbH. It is comprised of three types of members: individuals interested in decommodifying land and housing, groups that are not associated housing projects, and the residents' associations for each housing project.

By creatively using the law in such an unusual way, syndicalists have been able to redefine the sense of ownership in housing. In conventional property terms, the residents are collective "owners" of the building who also, as "tenants" of individual units, pay a "rent." But these terms imply the existence of a housing market and price mechanism, which is simply irrelevant here. The residents of a building self-determine how much they will pay to live in their units based on what they need to finance the purchase and renovation of their buildings and support the larger mission of Mietshäuser Syndikat. They are asserting a price sovereignty similar to what we saw at Cecosesola, the Venezuelan social-solidarity cooperative.

During one of our conversations, one resident proudly explained this specific way of having: "Of course I own my house *and* we own ours."[24] By this, the resident means that his family has effective ownership — i.e., permanent use rights of his residence (without the right to sell it outright), but everyone in the complex also has a sense of collective ownership in the building; they are not subservient to banks or outside financial interests. The circle of collective ownership is actually even larger because all of the real estate in all 136 housing projects *also* belongs to *all* of the members of Mietshäuser Syndikat. The levels of use rights are so entangled that "mine" always means "ours" and vice-versa. Remarkably, all work in running the Syndikat is performed by volunteers except for a paid contractor who does twenty hours a week of accounting, membership management, and basic administrative tasks.

The syndicate has succeeded in relationalizing a vast amount of property. For over thirty years, with one exception, no one has been able to liquidate the collective assets used by these housing commons for private cash-outs.[25] This has resulted in attitudes toward property that are more about existential co-possession than absolute dominion. By taking real estate out of the market and sharing responsibility for its stewardship, residents have not only developed an allegiance to their own housing commons, they are committed to scores of other housing projects associated with the syndicate.

This is not just an ethical or social posture. Surplus syndicate revenues are used for so-called solidarity transfers to those projects that need capital to invest in their own housing commons.[26] Existing projects contribute to a common pot, the Solidarity Fund, which is then used to support the launch of new housing projects — a clear instance of POOL, CAP & DIVIDE UP. The financial transfers from older to newer projects help the federation grow. In a typical condominium, there are highup-front capital costs for investors and high profits later when they sell. In contrast, the housing commons collaboratively finance their projects (often combined with loans from banks), but the point is never to generate profit, but to make decommodified and peer-governed housing more widely available. The pay-it-forward ethic of the solidarity transfers underscores how intercommoning support is an integral part of the whole system.

In recent times, Mietshäuser Syndikat's success and size have prompted some to suggest that perhaps the syndicate should begin its own mitosis, the biological term for a cell dividing itself. "The bigger we grow, the greater the complexity and the more work that has to be done by the watchdog organization," said Jochen Schmidt. For some, this could imply the need for a cap on the number of projects that can affiliate with Mietshäuser Syndikat. But whether that would be wise or not, a cap could be a healthy recognition that continuing to develop housing commons will need *multiple* versions of Mietshäuser Syndikat, not just one of them. Syndicate members are discussing possible regionalization of the federation, perhaps reflecting the insight that the Mietshäuser Syndikat idea is best spread through a process of EMULATE & THEN FEDERATE.

Hacking Property to Help Build Commons

In the three cases we have examined so far, we have seen how commoners have used ingenious means to relationalize property. In the case of Park Slope Food Coop, commoners used their co-op bylaws to define member-ownership not just as a financial stake, but as an entitlement that can only be secured through unpaid workslots every four weeks. The Federated Wiki platform created a clever software architecture that elevates sharing content as the default. Mietshäuser Syndikat's creative legal structure and social norms have enabled it to decommodify residential buildings, prevent their being sold, and facilitate commoning.

Each of these examples amount to hacks on property. The concept of hacking goes back to the Tech Model Railroad Club at the Massachusetts Institute of Technology in the 1960s. These hobbyists were always searching for creative technical solutions for problems with their model trains — a practice that they began to call "hacking." The term was later picked up by amateur computer programmers who assembled their own personal computers with pieces of hardware and software code that they had scavenged, purchased, or improvised in some way. In his seminal 1984 book, *Hackers: Heroes of the Computer Revolution*, journalist Steven Levy wrote, "Hackers believe that essential lessons can be learned about systems—about the world—from taking things apart, seeing how they work and using this knowledge to create new and interesting things." Hackers revel in overcoming difficult, complex problems with brilliant, elegant solutions. They also care deeply about their peers and the public good. As Eric Raymond put it in his *Hacker Dictionary*, hackers believe they have "an ethical duty … to share their expertise by … facilitating access to information and to computing resources wherever possible."[27] (Hackers distinguish their practices from the malevolent, illegal activities of "crackers."[28]) The same practice and ethic of hacking has moved into a number of legal circles. It is especially important to commoners, who frequently find that they must attempt a hack on legal forms in order to decriminalize or advance commoning. To perform a "legal hack" essentially means to use and recombine *existing* legal tools to change the purpose for which they were originally designed. Lawyers and activists who dream up legal hacks have similar ethical ambitions: to subvert conventional legal forms with ingenious legal workarounds that can support commoning. Legal hacks take myriad forms, some more audacious than others, but they generally require some measure of courage, creativity, and legal literacy.

Two famous ones have had far-reaching consequences: the General Public License (GPL) for software and the Creative Commons licenses. The GPL was developed by the legendary free software hacker Richard Stallman in the 1980s in response to the growing commercialization and private control of software. As software for personal computers became proprietary, the copyright holders — usually businesses — could prevent programmers from re-using, modifying, or sharing the code. This was immensely frustrating for coders like Stallman who wished to share code and collaborate to make it better. So Stallman, with the help of attorneys like Eben Moglen, devised a license based on copyright ownership of a program. It authorizes anyone to copy, share, and modify someone else's code, in whatever way they want, without permission or payment. The only requirement is that any derivative versions must also be available on the same terms. The General Public License, or GPL, legally enabled the rise of free and open source software and spawned countless programs that have transformed computing, the internet, and commerce.[29] Just as Mietshäuser Syndikat buildings cannot fall back into the market, GPL-protected code cannot be privately re-appropriated.

The Creative Commons licenses, inspired by the GPL's success, is another important legal innovation that has facilitated commoning. CC licenses, as they are called, let copyright holders authorize in advance that their works can be freely shared, copied, and modified — something that copyright law makes no provisions for. They are free, standardized, publicly available licenses that any copyright holder can use to signal in advance that their works are shareable. Like Stallman, the primary creator of the CC licenses, Harvard law professor Lawrence Lessig, wanted to find a way to use copyright law to make the sharing and remixing of works legal. After extensive deliberations with law scholars and the creative world, the nonprofit group Creative Commons issued a series of licenses that allow works to be re-used under certain conditions, such as only for noncommercial purposes (the NonCommercial license); only if no changes are made to the original work (No Derivatives license); or only if any derivative work is also licensed under the same license (ShareAlike license). The CC licenses have served as an indispensable legal infrastructure for legal sharing in countless contexts — scholarly publishing, scientific research, music, photography, video, writing, and much else. More than 175 legal jurisdictions around the world have adopted the licenses, and more than one billion digital documents are estimated to be available under CC licenses. Not surprisingly, many programmers with a hacker ethic contribute to software architectures that directly enable commoning. To date, legal hacking has been one of the few effective strategies that commoners can pursue to normalize their commons in a market/state system that has very different goals. Wikipedia and thousands of open-access scholarly journals would not be around if they were not protected by Creative Commons licenses.

In the early 2000s, Lessig famously wrote, "code is law." By that, he meant that the design of software code so profoundly shapes what users can do on their computers and online that it has the effect of law. Code becomes the foundation for new forms of Vernacular Law. That is in essence what the design of the Federated Wiki platform is all about. It goes beyond the affordances of the conventional wiki by providing a more flexible, community-friendly design for codeveloping knowledge. Similar software designs are being developed by the platform cooperative movement, which is building new web platforms and mobile apps that will enable cooperative alternatives to Uber, Airbnb, and dozens of other proprietary, capital-driven platforms.

Platform Cooperatives

Digital networks have immense capacity to enable sharing and cooperation. Unfortunately, tech companies have captured much of these social energies for their own purposes, namely, to carry out the usual work of capitalism on powerful platforms. They call the result the "sharing economy" and "gig economy," but in fact it is simply a new species of markets designed for microrentals, piecemeal labor, data mining, and consumerism.

Platforms like TaskRabbit and Mechanical Turk have re-introduced piecework on a massive scale by offering pennies for a variety of microtasks that computers can't perform, such as image tagging, transcription, and data cleaning. Other platforms entice us into converting our cars, apartments, and private time into rentable assets to compensate for our plunging incomes. As sophisticated computer algorithms constantly ratchet down wages for "independent contractors," it is eroding the very possibility of stable jobs with benefits.

To counter these trends, the platform cooperatives movement arose in 2015 as a field of experimentation. Its goal is to try to develop more socially constructive websites and mobile apps. If people can own and manage their own platforms as cooperatives, argues Trebor Scholz, one of the catalysts of the movement, they will be able to reap greater long-term benefits and control in the face of well-capitalized tech giants like Uber and Airbnb. "What if we owned our own version of Facebook, Spotify, or Netflix?" writes Scholz. "What if the photographers at Shutterstock.com could own the platform where their photos are being sold?"[30] A number of efforts are underway to do just that. The idea is to help producers and users co-own member-driven websites for distributing stock photography, streaming music, and other artworks.

Another type of platform cooperative is apps codeveloped by city governments and local users. Seoul, South Korea, for example, has been developing a Munibnb platform to enable apartment rentals on better terms than Airbnb, with revenues earmarked for public services. The app is also intended to prevent the conversion of stable rental properties into "ghost neighborhoods" used mostly by tourists, a problem afflicting many major world cities like Amsterdam, London, and Barcelona.

While still an emerging strategy, platform coops hold great promise for preventing monopoly, exploitation, and data surveillance in digital spaces. They can also help democratize ownership and control over platforms, and assure greater self-determination for working conditions.

Hacks on the law remain a rich field of experimentation making artful twists on conventional state law. The Indigenous Quechua people in Peru developed the Indigenous Biocultural Heritage Area to protect lands with great agroecological and cultural significance, especially for the biodiversity of native potatoes. In India, the Traditional Knowledge Digital Library serves as a huge repository to document traditional knowledge, which can then be used to block patent applications that seek to privatize biomedical knowledge, plants, and therapeutic practices.[31] The Community Environmental Legal Defense Fund, an advocacy group based in Pennsylvania, USA, has been prolific in developing town ordinances and charters to protect against unwanted corporate investments and ecological damage such as fracking.[32] These initiatives are creative attempts to use conventional law to protect community autonomy in a state system that otherwise restricts it. The Legal Defense Fund has also worked to develop model statutes for states and localities to adopt to protect the rights of nature from industrial abuses — again, using legal hacks to try to establish principles that go beyond what law formally recognizes, or indeed, beyond what legislators originally intended. Since property is so foundational to how resources may be used, we are especially interested in legal hacks that can relationalize property. We turn now to impressive efforts to re-conceive ownership rights in seeds, because it is hard to imagine a physical object more deeply immersed in the web of life yet at the same time strictly controlled as private property to produce profits.

Open Source Seeds

For millennia, people have treated seeds as a mystical, sacred source of fertility and nourishment. Out of nothing, it would appear, life begets life. From its inception ten thousand years ago, agriculture entered into an intricate dance with living, natural forces — soil, water, animals, and the entire ecosystem — as a way to grow a rich bounty of food. That web of aliveness is under siege as large multinational corporations try to own and control seeds as much as possible. Since the early 1980s, companies have agitated for far-reaching intellectual property rights over plant genetic resources, giving them new powers to control plant breeding and production. As private ownership of seeds has consolidated into fewer and fewer hands — globally more than sixty percent of commercial seeds is now controlled by four agrochemical/seed companies[33] — it has reduced the biodiversity of germplasm (living tissue from which new plants can be grown), making agriculture more vulnerable to pests, diseases, and climate change. The big industry players are intent upon controlling the basic inputs for food production — seeds, fertilizer, Big Data — to serve the interests of large-scale industrial agriculture, commodification, and profit extraction.[34] This approach is eroding the independent production, stewardship, and biodiversity of seeds.

The concentrated ownership of seeds has radically disempowered farmers. Companies like Dupont and Monsanto use their oligopoly power to impose use restrictions — essentially, legal "fences" such as plant patents, utility patents, Material Transfer Agreements (MTAs), licenses, and use agreements — that restrict what farmers can do with their seeds. A "limited license to use" for example, turns out to mean: no saving the seed, no replanting the seed, no breeding of seeds, no research on the seed, and one-time use solely for planting. The licenses may also authorize the seed company to access the farmer's land and online crop records to determine which seeds are used where. The seed corporations are not *selling* seed. They are *renting* seed for one-time use! Being the legal owner of the seed lies at the heart of this business model. On top of such restrictions, the seed industry legally treats the industrial farmer in the US reliant on 250-horsepower farm equipment in the same way as the campesino in Guatemala with his donkey. Each can use seeds only as specified by corporate licenses, much as software users are constrained by the software industry's one-sided "shrinkwrap" licenses.[35]

Extensive privatization of seed has resulted in an institutionalized market failure. The global seed market has been captured by an oligopoly of large companies that have thwarted competition, promoted crop monocultures, failed to develop innovations to deal with climate change, and undermined organic local farming.[36] "Corporations have used IPRs [intellectual property rights] over genetic materials not just to accrue monopoly rents, but to actively undermine the independence of farmers and the integrity and capacity of plant science," writes Jack Kloppenburg, a leading seed activist and professor at the University of Wisconsin-Madison.

The appropriation of seeds raises a profound challenge to farmers and, really, everyone, because we all have to eat. How can we steward the natural gifts of life that seeds provide and overcome the genetic engineering that has made them sterile or nonshareable under patent law, contract law, regulation, and/or court rulings? How can we restore the ethic of seed sharing and popular sovereignty over seeds that has been appropriated by large corporations through market power and the law?

Over the past thirty years, a movement comprised of farmers, agronomists, public institutions, lawyers, and sustainable food system advocates has tackled this question in a number of ways. Most seek to liberate seeds from the artificial constraints of property law. This fight is often blended with fights over land tenure, water rights, gender equality, and other concerns. These issues are important, for example, to two leading organizations in the Global South, La Via Campesina, a network of peasant-farmer and Indigenous groups, and Navdanya, an Indian advocacy group for seed freedom founded by Vandana Shiva.

Despite their different styles and emphases, most of the various seed-freedom players wish to establish a protected commons for seed sharing compatible with the imperatives of living ecosystems. Jack Kloppenburg notes that there is general agreement about the need for four universal rights: to save and replant seed; to share seed; to use seed to breed new varieties; and to participate in shaping policies for seed.[37] The big seed companies generally oppose these rights by invoking legal tools that privilege private ownership of seed biowealth. The political and legal obstacles to seed sharing have led many seed advocates to look to a self-help option: building their own legally protected seed commons. Inspired by the success of the GPL and free and open source software over the past thirty years, some leading players in the seed movement decided to align behind the banner of "open source seed." With two friendly but separate arms of the movement based in Europe and the US, respectively, the open source seed movement has adopted two general approaches to restoring user sovereignty over seeds: new types of licenses similar to the GPL, and campaigns to create strong community cultures of seed sharing. Both approaches seek to facilitate plant breeding and seed sharing as protected commons.

Just at the time when the huge ag-chemical and biotech companies Bayer and Monsanto merged, OpenSourceSeeds, a nonprofit project of AGRECOL e.V., the Association for AgriCulture and Ecology,[38] based in Germany, launched its own legal response: an open source license that prohibits users from patenting any derivative plants grown from licensed seeds.[39] It also prohibits the use of proprietary protections for plant varieties licensed under open source licenses, and applies these same rights and obligations to any future users of the seed. The Open Source Seed license does not grant exclusive rights in the way that most conventional licenses do; it confers the right to share the seed and any developments or enhancements conditional on fulfilling a duty of making it available for public use. Any follow-on users must then accept the same conditions. The license implicitly applies as well to the genetic information contained within seeds.

Open Source Seed Initiative (OSSI)[40] decided against using legal contracts and enforcement, for reasons of both practicality and principle. OSSI believed that it would be hard to print dense, complex legal licenses on a packet of seeds, and that legal language that might be honored by courts would probably not be understood by most farmers. Moreover, many people in Indigenous and Global South contexts objected to the very idea of legal contracts that define seeds as property. They preferred to base sharing on a peer-enforced social ethic. Finally, many farmers and plant breeders are wary of licenses because, while eager to share seed, they want to retain the right to receive payment for any breeding innovations that they do.[41]

Because of such diverse motivations among growers, the Open Source Seed Initiative decided to promote a vernacular seed law in the form of a pledge: "You have the freedom to use these OSSI seeds in any way you choose. In return, you pledge not to restrict others' use of these seeds or their derivatives by patents or other means, and to include this pledge with any transfer of these seeds or their derivatives." The pledge does not have the force of state law and enforcement behind it, but instead looks to the ethical and social norms of plant breeders to model behavior and shame transgressors. Drawing upon the ideas of the GPL for free software, the pledge means that users will treat seeds as openly available to all, and will not assert any private control over them. In other words, it is a pledge not to restrict access or use. Nourishing this ethos is at least as important as complex legal agreements that may or may not be understood by farmers and that may not be practically enforceable in any case. Can a peasant farmer realistically hope to prevail in litigation against Bayer-Monsanto? As of mid-2018, said Kloppenburg, "We have 400-plus varieties, fifty-one species, thirty-eight breeders, more than sixty companies [who have signed the Pledge]. We are there, we are real, we are doing it. And I didn't think these breeders — public breeders — existed in the USA. Guess what: they do. They are real. They are there, they are surviving. We didn't create them. We are building on a pre-existing network. This is why OSSI works … because we created connections to what already existed."[42] Kloppenburg's comment points to the reality that relationalized property often exists already and doesn't necessarily need to be created; it needs to be protected, whether through law, social sanction, or norms.

Despite the philosophical and tactical differences between the two open source seed projects, both share a concern with treating seeds as a commons — i.e., as something that does not belong exclusively to any individual owner, but whose value arises precisely because it can circulate freely and be shared. The open source seed movement seeks to affirm seeds as something that has deep, symbiotic relationships with other aspects of the ecosystem and human life as well as to past and future generations. The movement wants to restore the dynamic agency of seeds in living ecosystems, rescuing them from their status as sterile, controlled units of intellectual property. This insight is important not just as a moral claim made by commoners (who are responsible for breeding improvements) and by public institutions (which often finance agricultural research). It is a necessity for our planetary ecosystem and agriculture, especially as climate change intensifies.

Commoning Mushrooms: The *Iriaiken* Philosophy

Once a community escapes the conventional ideas of property (or never embraces them in the first place), it acquires the capacity to nourish new types of relationships, both within a commons and beyond its immediate boundaries. Stewarding seeds as biowealth deepens the interdependencies between human and nonhuman life. One inspiring example is the traditional Japanese right to common known as *iriaiken*. Its root, *iriai*, literally means "to enter collectively." *Iriaiken* is "the right to enter collectively." *Iriaiken* usually refers to the collective ownership of nonarable areas such as mountains, forests, marshes, bamboo groves, riverbeds, and offshore fisheries. From the 1600s through 1868, villagers in Japan allowed people to collect wood, edible plants, medical herbs, mushrooms, and more, but only if they followed rigid, peer-enforced regulations for usage.

In practice, *iriaiken* translates into many different, context-specific forms of collective ownership. There was *sòyù* (joint rights) and *gòyù* (joint ownership), for example. The most common type of the latter was called *mura-mura-iriai*, meaning "collective ownership of an area by the inhabitants of several neighboring villages." This is intriguing because unlike most European commons that dealt with a specific human settlement and piece of land, the rights of an *iriaiken* extended to several villages, not just one. They were regarded as integral to the region and could not be divided up among villages. Thus the rights to common were not executed by the villagers of a village but by a federation of villages!

In the Meiji period of the late nineteenth century, when a new legal code was adopted and modern legal principles were introduced, the right of villagers to common was not abolished, but acknowledged as a rule of custom. So in modern Japanese law *iriaiken* is still recognized. It is defined as having the nature of joint ownership. Not surprisingly, the two conceptions of law — modern law and the law of the commons (Vernacular Law) — have come into conflict, especially on matters of property rights. The more that full private ownership of land and exclusive land titles were recognized, the faster the decline of *iriaiken*-style property regimes. But even today we can find *iriaiken*-based property arrangements in Japan. One of the most intriguing examples can be seen in the stewardship practices of matsutake mushroom gatherers in Japanese villages.

Matsutake are delicious wild mushrooms that grow in forests and cannot be artificially cultivated. This is partly why they are very expensive. Some Japanese varieties regularly sell for more than US$1,000 a kilo, with especially rare ones going for $2,000 a kilo. Annual harvests of matsutake peaked in the 1950s and have declined steadily since then,[43] mainly due to two factors: the decline of their habitats (especially from a disease afflicting Japanese red pines, with which matsutake is associated) and the decline of traditional harvesting practices such as collective harvesting, undergrowth clearance, the thinning of forests, and the gathering of leaf litter as fuel or fertilizer, which once helped improve growing conditions for the mushrooms. Interestingly, forests that are hospitable to matsutake mushrooms tend to be disrupted, scarred landscapes with young trees. They are often full of human traffic, especially for gathering matsutake, explains anthropologist Anna Lowenhaupt Tsing in her acclaimed book, *The Mushroom at the End of the World*. The presence of human visitors "keeps the forests open, and thus welcoming to pine; it keeps the humus thin and the soils poor, thus allowing matsutake to do its good work of enriching trees," she writes.[44]

Kyoto Prefecture in Japan has been famous for its matsutake production. It is there that a unique traditional auctioning system for matsutake gathering developed in the seventeenth century, at Kamigamo shrine in 1665 in the first instance, before being adopted by almost all villages in the prefecture. Two centuries later, in response to the privatization and dividing up of communal forests during the Meiji Period, villages adopted holistic bidding systems, reinterpreting the *iriaiken* spirit in modern times.[45]

The core of the holistic bidding system is difficult for the modern mind to grasp because harvesting rights do not correspond to property ownership. As the anthropologist Anna Lowenhaupt Tsing explains, "[E]ven if a villager owns a *matsutake-yama* (a forest or mountain where matsutake grows), he must bid for the right to harvest the matsutake growing on that land ... and those who do hold the exclusive rights to the gathering and selling of matsutake ... change from year to year through the bidding process."[46] This means that the owner of a plot of land is not allowed to harvest mushrooms that grow on that plot of land. Yet at the same time, neither is the owner absolutely *forbidden* from harvesting mushrooms because he or she may win that right through the community's bidding process.

How is that possible, and what does that mean? The answer lies in the *iriai* philosophy and more concretely in the way villagers conceive the interconnectedness of the whole system. They see deep interconnections among the mostly invisible matsutake rhizomes in the soil with the mushrooms that grow on the land, and the relationships among the villagers and owners of different plots of land, among other relationships.

We can see one way in which the bidding process plays out in the village of Oka in Kyoto prefecture, where the *iriai* philosophy has always been strong. The basic challenge faced by villagers is how to aggregate and share mushrooms that are distributed unevenly across many different plots of privately owned land. The mushrooms are regarded as shared wealth because they arise naturally, without anyone's active cultivation, and because the mushroom roots are a vast underground system that sprawls across the entire village, without regard to property boundaries on the surface. So the problem is how to allocate biowealth that is seen as both collectively owned (in the subsoil) and privately owned (on the surface) in a fair and equitable manner.

The villagers' solution is an auction. That name is a bit of a misnomer because the bidding system is not used to raise money to grow the mushrooms in the first place, as members of a CSA farm might do for the upcoming crop. Rather, the auction helps assure that everyone gets some benefit from the mushrooms, either through direct harvesting, allocations of mushrooms reserved for collective use, or through community income.

The first step is to divide the whole terrain into five parcels without regard to anyone's formal land ownership rights. Then, as in other villages, Oka auctions off gathering rights for three of the five parcels. The two remaining parcels are reserved for weekly Sunday expeditions by members of cooperatives established for managing the matsutake. "All participants climb up to the forest at the same time and gather matsutake together. In 2003, the highest daily amount harvested jointly was twenty-eight kilograms (about sixty-two pounds). Afterwards, the harvested matsutake are assembled and distributed to all participants in equal amounts, except when they are reserved for a joint feast..."[47] A nice example of POOL, CAP & DIVIDE UP. To make things fairer (and more complicated), the two types of parcels reserved for community use rotate every year. Thus a parcel that is bid out one year may be reserved for joint harvest the next year. Only cooperative members are allowed to participate in the bidding meeting and in joint harvesting activities.

Any villagers can participate in the bidding process, through which the community assigns harvesting rights to the highest bidder. The winner then holds exclusive rights until November 15, when the game hunting season starts. "During this time ... no one, not even the land owners, can walk in their own forest even if it is not *matsutake-yama*, without permission," write Saito and Mitsumata. "If they try to even get near the forest area without permission, they may be suspected of being a matsutake thief."[48]

The purpose of the bidding is to get the mushrooms on private lands into a common pot that can be reallocated for community benefit. In essence, it's a scheme to monetize three-fifths of the annual mushroom crop from sales to villagers only, and to apply all income from the bidding on activities and tools that improve the matsutake habitat. The bidding process is thus not like a normal auction. Because villagers agree that the mushrooms cannot belong to anybody exclusively, the auction provides a way to redistribute the anticipated income from selling matsutake to benefit all villagers. The partial monetization of the annual crop lasts for only one season, and it is used to benefit the village and mushroom ecosystem over the long term.

Communal income from matsutake harvesting in Oka fluctuates from years to year. But in a 2004 study, the village collected ¥329,000 in 2003, or about US$9,087.[49] This income is not divided up among members,[50] but is used to pay part of the cost of a group tour/celebration each year. In other communities it has been used for improving the infrastructures or education in the communities. In Oka, since 1962, all members practice what is called *deyaku*, compulsory work days, very similar to the famous *minga* system in Andean countries or irrigation ditch maintenance in *acequias* in New Mexico. Villagers can choose a preferred day from two designated days for *deyaku*. If a member doesn't participate, a ¥7,000 penalty is levied, but the coop rarely needs to sanction anyone. The joint harvest activities and *denyaku* work to RITUALIZE TOGETHERNESS and forge a sense of community. When in 2004 researchers participated in the compulsory work sessions, "the work that day was easy and a sociable atmosphere prevailed — the female participants especially enjoyed talking to each other, and a break was held every thirty minutes."[51]

The core idea of the holistic bidding system — that the owner of a specific plot of land is not entitled to harvest the matsutake that grow on that land by dint of ownership — is similar to laws that govern many individual forest owners in Europe who cannot simply decide on their own to cut a tree on their property. Villagers obviously have a particular understanding of who owns what — a multilayered tableau of protocols, as it were, for treating the world. Landowners consent to this arrangement because it is a traditional community arrangement; they see themselves as co-designers and co-decision makers of this process as part of the community. Community-regulated access is not seen as a prohibition, but rather as a sensible consensual agreement — obviously, a cultural shift from the Western, proprietary mentality. According to the researchers, "at a subconscious level," the land belongs to the whole village.

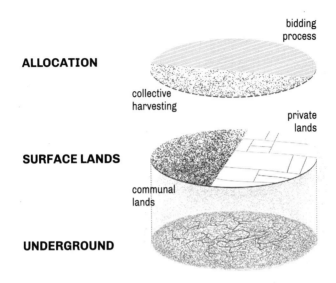

Common land coexists with private rights. In harvesting matsutake mushrooms, Oka villagers regard the underground soil in which the mushroom fungi grows as commonly held land that cannot be alienated or privately owned. On the surface of the land, peer governance determines how people may access the mushrooms.

This understanding illustrates a larger point about property itself — that "private assets most always grow out of unacknowledged commons," as Tsing writes. "The point is [that] privatization is never complete; it needs shared spaces to create any value. That is the secret of property's continuing theft … The thrill of private ownership is the fruit of an underground common."[52]

One must wonder why this ethic should not also apply to the extraction of coal, gas, and oil from deep underground. There is obviously a difference between the value of that which exists in the ground, untouched and prior to any human activity, and the costs of exploring, mining, drilling, and refining — that is, the costs of making it available to human use. This is a serious difference. But consider what our economy might look like if the full value of oil could not be privately appropriated by corporations or by the nation-state simply because they drill it. The only economic return would be on the work invested to extract oil and refine it into useable fuel. The rationale for such a property scheme is simple: oil and minerals were formed over millions of years without any human contribution, so why should any private party be able to own them?[53] This is the exact logic that Oka's matsutake commoners have put into practice — a fair, ecologically minded way to steward the wealth generated via their shared underground wealth.[54]

In recent years, the *iriai* system has come under siege, particularly by younger people who don't work in the villages and, not surprisingly, by those who own *matsutake-yama* where the mushrooms grow. In the villages of Kanegawachi and Takatsu, the classical Lockean arguments have been made, that "every landowner has the right to the fruits of his or her land on the one hand, and ought to pay a fixed asset [property] tax on the other." It has been argued that these customs don't guarantee "enough rights to *matsutake-yama* owners," and that they have therefore created "a disincentive to landowners to carry out the habitat improvements needed to enhance matsutake production."[55]

These assertions are groundless, however. No evidence to support them has been brought forward. In fact, the evidence points in the other direction: the most serious habitat improvement projects in the Kyoto region have been sponsored by the Association for Promotion of Matsutake Production of Kyoto, with help from government subsidies. Seven years later, a survey on improvement activities noted efforts "on 405 sites totaling 310 hectares in 15 districts, and in almost all cases the sites were communal forests as opposed to privately held lands."[56] This makes perfect sense because habitat improvement requires specific knowledge, regular activity, and patience. Most individual land owners, in contrast, discontinued their improvement efforts after a year or two. As the evidence suggests, there are not only philosophical but very practical reasons for treating the *matsutake-yama* as wealth to be owned and managed by the whole village.

According to the research, the decline of the *iriaiken* land use system has had negative effects on both village finances and matsutake productivity. Villages that chose other systems than Oka — e.g., allowing owners to harvest on parcels of their choice by paying sixty or seventy percent of the bidding income — have now had to introduce membership fees or other taxes to boost village revenues and maintain village infrastructures. Kanegawachi is such a case. Since the holistic bidding system was turned into a piecemeal bidding system in 1999, "bidding income has declined by more than 75% — from 250,000 Yen in the early 1990 to 60,000 Yen in 2004."[57] At the same time, the willingness of *matsutake-yama* owners to work to improve matsutake habitat has declined and a vicious circle of individual exploitation has arisen. This stands in stark contrast to the virtuous circle of the Oka villagers who common matsutake.

The Oka story tells us a great deal about how property, typically seen as a right of absolute dominion over a bounded object, can be re-imagined in socially minded yet practical ways. But this is not just a matter of enacting a state law or regulation; it requires a cultural ethic that can only be cultivated through social practice and agency. There must be a commitment to the shared ecosystem and infrastructure upon which everyone depends while also providing space to nourish social relations and human/nonhuman relationships. Notably, this does not preclude individual usage rights or even the right to sell a renewable resource. Perishable mushrooms, for example, can be treated as usufruct, which is the right to use something that belongs to someone else so long as the underlying resource itself is not diminished.

In a larger sense, the matsutake story demonstrates the virtues and practicality of relationalizing property. It is entirely feasible to use property to strengthen social and ecological relationships rather than rend them asunder through ownership and capitalism. Just as the peculiar history of the Nidiaci Garden (pp. 207–209) showed us how a single plot of urban land can be treated as both private property and public property, each with different outcomes, we can see in the matsutake story that managing land as a commons allows for *qualitatively different kinds of value* to emerge. That value is at once personal, social, and ecological, as well as economic. Things can belong to us as individuals and as part of a collective at the same time. Property arrangements can be designed to respect our *freedom-in-relatedness* to use things, *fairness* in providing wider access and use of them, and *vibrant living communities* as effective forms of Peer Governance.

Building Stronger Commons Through Relationalized Property

The idea of Relationalized Property is perhaps incomprehensible if seen through the lens of conventional property relations. People immersed in the dominant worldview doggedly refuse to concede that there might be other ways of experiencing and representing the world. We have tried to show through five vivid examples how people's conceptions of property can escape the traditional forms, all of which entail some significant measure of exclusivity and separation. Instead, Relationalized Property opens up spaces that allow for developing different sorts of relationships that do not revolve around ownership or market exchange. These relationships take many forms — with other commoners, with the more-than-human world, with past and future generations, with external institutions, and with the cosmos.

It is worth emphasizing that practices for relationalizing property can be emulated, but they cannot be copied. Each instantiation is unique. There is no one-size-fits-all legal tool or model. Rather, the design of legal regimes for relationalized ways of having in the commons must be guided by this question: what do we (the respective community) need to protect our commons as a commons?

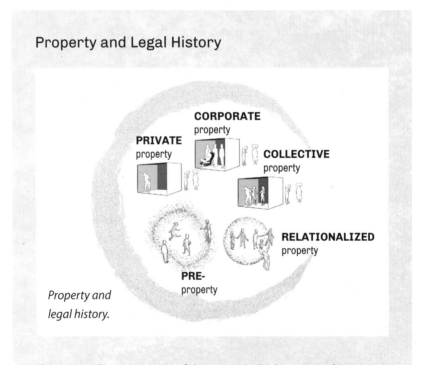

Property and Legal History

Property and
legal history.

This image illustrates some of the ways in which property law engenders specific types of social order. It empowers owners (the occupants of the squares in each drawing) and marginalizes and disenfranchises nonowners. The circle — a Buddhist ensō, which is often used to symbolize absolute enlightenment and the universe — encircles familiar property regimes.

Private property and corporate property are two familiar ways in which owners assert dominion over things that other people need or want. The market/state system as a polity and a legal system privileges these forms over all others. Even *collective property* enacts this dynamic, perhaps in less severe forms, because it also rewards owners and excludes non-owners.

Pre-property — social relations before any formal property rules are established — may appear more benign, but the resulting social order may or may not be cooperative, egalitarian, and fair. Hobbes argued that a "state of nature" allegedly preceding the rise of states was a barbaric war of all against all; anarchists and communitarians tend to have a more benign view. In any case, there is a void of larger political authority. We mentioned how the legal doctrine of *res nullius in bonis* once served to protect the land and other biowealth that everyone and future generations need. But we are not naive enough to think that this will be enough in today's world — hence the need for legal innovations to secure the commons.

Relationalized Property is an attempt to steward resources for the benefit of commoners (or anyone else) through Peer Governance structures while respecting the inherent limits of the biowealth. Note that the line around the commons is not a strict boundary of ownership and separation; instead, the dotted line symbolizes a semi-permeable membrane that allows selective interaction with the larger world.

We encircle the various property regimes with an *ensō*, a hand-drawn image that Zen Buddhists use to symbolize "absolute enlightenment, strength, elegance, the universe, and *mu* (the void)." (Wikipedia) We wish to use this symbol to suggest that in reality we partake of the larger, integrated, whole in which everything is connected. A living cosmos encircles *all* property regimes. Only Relationalized Property formally recognizes this reality, however.

Our descriptions of relational ways of having in this chapter may sound a bit complicated and convoluted. This is partly because the very idea is so unfamiliar. Moreover, describing something new can be much more difficult than experiencing it, just as describing how to ride a bicycle is much more difficult than doing it. Nor do we yet have a default set of legal forms for relationalizing property. We therefore wish to conclude by providing some conceptual definition to the idea of Relationalized Property so that it can be recognized as a distinct species of "beyond property" stewarded by a commons.

We have seen that not one example of Relationalized Property is exactly like another. Each represents a unique layering and overlapping of different forms of property, ingeniously interconnected. Each is based on a commons ethic and birthed through living social practices. A key purpose of such property forms is to open a protected space for commoning to take place. A way must be found to neutralize the usual power relationships associated with property, especially the inequality among owners and nonowners, and the domination associated with Governing-through-Money. Property rights — which today are so often allied with capital and calculative rationality — cannot be allowed to preemptively dictate the terms of social order. Within the context of capitalism and liberal democracies, Relationalized Property can create a kind of modern *res nullius in bonis* that makes shared wealth — an apartment building, a software platform, a supermarket, seeds, underground fungi — quasi-inalienable.

Let us try to describe some basic patterns of Relationalized Property and thereby make some generalizations about how to secure the special affordances that they make possible:

Redefine the line that separates owners and nonowners. Instead of strict boundaries of control, the boundary around the commons is treated as a semi-permeable membrane. This makes it easier to take account of and integrate the needs of all.

Blend individual use rights with collective possession as the default norm. Excessive conflict is symptomatic of a design problem. When individual use rights are created in conjunction with a collective way of having (which is always a relative achievement), a virtuous cycle of cooperation and trust emerges. It can eventually supplant the beggar-thy-neighbor ethic of individual competition that capitalism requires of everyone. For example, a Federated Wiki sidesteps the flame wars that plague so many conventional wikis. Mietshäuser Syndikat enables people to escape the cutthroat speculation, rising prices, and insecurity of housing markets based on individual or corporate ownership. Blending individual use rights with collective possession helps to generate more stable, fair outcomes, which itself is an affordance for minimizing conflict.

Avoid Governance-through-Money and control by stakeholders with investment interests. This is a central flaw with conventional property because it privileges those with money to override the ability of the many to govern themselves and protect their interests. Governance-through-Money is a problem even in nonprofits and cooperatives because wealthy board members and funding sources tend to have a disproportionate say and even veto power in governance.

Bypass conventional categories of property and the market/state social order they imply. Instead of a system that pits private property against collective interests, and owners against nonowners, Relationalized Property opens up a new safe space for more commoning. It also insulates people from being evicted or separated from the biowealth around them.

Give clearer legal standing to existential possession and use that satisfies needs rather than enhance dominion. Instead of a production venture revolving around an asset (a factory, a product, a brand name) and the choices of the owner(s), commoners relying on Relationalized Property are free to devise a governance system of their own making. They can build a culture committed to collective stewardship, Peer Governance, and mindful interaction with the more-than-human realm. The Park Slope Food Coop functions as non-property in the sense that no one can privately appropriate the co-op assets or sell them. The same holds for open source seeds: everyone can use them, and no one can monetize them at the expense of others. It is critical to note that in each instance social practice and culture must keep the system alive. Formal legal charters or bylaws are not enough.

Recognize the value of peer-negotiated use rights. Pre-existing formal property arrangements such as customary law or vernacular practice can evolve into Relationalized Property regimes. This is important, because moral legitimacy and effectiveness stem from commoning, not only from state law. Relationalized Property can work well because it draws upon so many of the patterns of commoning described in Chapters Four through Six, such as POOL & SHARE, POOL, CAP & DIVIDE UP, TRUST SITUATED KNOWING, the desire to SHARE KNOWLEDGE GENEROUSLY, RITUALIZE TOGETHERNESS and DEEPEN COMMUNION WITH NATURE. All of this enhances a person's security and freedom. Commoning precedes and enhances the possibility of Relationalizing Property. Needless to say, if there is no commoning, there can be no Relationalized Property.

Weave property into the web of life. Property that is deeply rooted in living, interconnected systems has less need to sustain itself via markets or state support. Remember how Mietshäuser Syndikat lets each of its affiliates maintain a high degree of liberty and autonomy? When commoners can determine their own access and use rights at the local level, the resulting system will be distributed, diversified, and stable. This makes it easier for it to self-replicate, self-heal, and develop at appropriate scales. These capacities reduce the risks of system failure and the need for external supervision. They also prevent concentrated power and monoculture, and reduce dependence on the market/state apparatus — a big step toward enhancing resilience.

Keep conflicts over use-rights in the local arena as much as possible. This enables dispute resolution that is lower-cost and more accessible to ordinary people. Formal systems of state law may assert noble, universal rights for all. But the actual costs and complications of vindicating those rights are often enormous (imagine a peasant farmer challenging a large corporation), which makes state jurisprudence a charade of justice and equality. By contrast, Peer Governance in commons tends to provide accessible systems for addressing problems.

Recognize the need for future forking and emulation to avoid "bigness-problems." At some point in the growth of any commons, complexity becomes so great and Peer Governance so thin that some form of forking, or bifurcation of energies, is needed. The Park Slope Food Coop works because it has deep roots in its local community, Brooklyn. It is huge, but it has no need to become bigger and bigger, just as the Mietshäuser Syndikat has no imperative to add more housing projects. In the commons there is no internal compulsion or systemic mechanism that requires constant growth, as businesses need to do in the capitalist market economy. Both Park Slope Food Coop and Mietshäuser Syndikat would welcome others to emulate their experience. In the Commonsverse, it is most logical to keep property regimes at a manageable scale to keep systems simpler, more modular, and functional, and with lower overhead costs — otherwise known as elegance.

Re-Introducing Meaning Making into Modern Law

The ramifications of Relationalized Property extend well beyond property law; they reflect the larger impact that commoning can have on law in general. As a form of world making, commoning enables people to play a genuine, formative role in making law. It provides a way to fight the pervasive alienation of modern times. This is what really is at stake in debates about commoning and property — and law in general.

Historically, law was embedded in the community. This enabled the relations and norms of the people as a whole to find expression through law itself. In countless subsistence communities around the world, even today, commoners are able to see that the pasture is being overgrazed or the fishery overharvested. They can then come up with their own appropriate solutions. While this is often a difficult process, it is one that necessarily builds the sinews of social connection and mission. It connects people to their landscapes and previous generations, and in this way becomes a vehicle of meaning making.

However, with the ascendance of the modern state and bureaucracy, the forms and procedures of law tend to become ends in themselves, supplanting law as a vehicle for expressing a society's sense of purpose and identity. What matters most in modern law today is its self-referential logic and process, not really the suitability of outcomes. If your (expensive) lawyer makes a procedural mistake, or if some arcane technicality crafted through a political compromise decades ago is not satisfied, you lose! The point is not "justice," as a famous professor of civil procedure once told one of us, as a first-year law student. It is whether there is "sufficient evidence and procedural integrity for the administration of justice." Or as French novelist Anatole France put it more tartly: "The law, in its majestic equality, forbids the rich and poor alike to sleep under bridges, to beg in the streets, and to steal loaves of bread."[58]

In a strange sense, modern law is radically disconnected from social reality and real people. It is an abstract system of rules that presents itself as a neutral, impersonal process — "justice is blind" — but whose practitioners strive for this goal only by recognizing the world through the categories of law itself. As a creature of the state and its priorities, law has increasingly lost touch with the lives of people, especially their inner lives, perhaps because it is administered through cumbersome and often-corrupt processes. Even if prevailing legal forms offer modest scope for people to use the law for their own purposes (contract law, business governance, etc.), law is not really a robust source of meaning making any more. There is a simple reason for this fact: few people can realistically participate in or affect the character of law today. It is held forth as an expression of state power that must be complied with.

This is partly why so many people feel alienated toward the modern nation-state and its bodies of law. To be sure, the separation of legal forms from meaning-making activities has overcome many oppressive communal imperatives and enhanced our freedom, at least in a narrow, individualistic sense. Modern, liberal law has dispelled many stifling, unjust forms of domination and control — feudal, patriarchal, authoritarian. But such liberation has often entailed disconnecting people — sometimes forcibly and in the name of freedom — from the worlds they cherish. Countless Indigenous peoples throughout history have learned that the freedom to be treated as an individual, shorn of one's collective identity, landscape, traditions, and cultural heritage, is an act of radical dispossession. So today, even among we moderns: state law often imprisons ordinary people within abstract formal categories that do not adequately take account of the full context of our lives and inner needs. Law may be able to assure the civil liberties of the homeless and mentally ill to live on the streets without harassment, and even to mandate basic housing for them. But it cannot provide meaningful relationships, purpose, and dignity.

In our time, law's connection to people's inner aspirations and desire for meaning is irregular at best. At worst, it is grandly indifferent, triggering displaced frustrations about law's inability to speak to meaning and identity. This should be no surprise when law is a servant of the market/state polity and its priorities; when it is controlled by a remote priesthood of lawyers and legislators; and when it asserts universal legal categories that don't take account of changing realities and desires.

When law fails to meet needs effectively and cannot change to reflect new circumstances and ideas of justice, law loses its legitimacy. The "imagined community" that the nation-state purports to represent, and which law seeks to constitute, begins to fall apart.[59]

Commoning and Relationalized Property rights are antidotes to these contemporary trends. They can help us re-imagine the very nature of law as a vehicle for meaning making. Instead of ceding this task to a distant national state and legislatures unresponsive to ordinary people, commoning re-integrates democracy and law-making into people's everyday lives in substantive ways. It can be a vehicle for recovering and building relationships that are otherwise quiescent or suppressed in modern life — relationships among people, with the more-than-human-world, with our ancestors, and with posterity. It can help build new bridges between modern law and older, vernacular legal forms. The guardians of state law can learn to recognize the dynamic, situational nature of Vernacular Law — think how social norms rapidly evolve and mutate in online communities and social networks. And commons, for their part, can attempt to hack state law to open up new, protected spaces for exploratory commoning. They could humanize the impossibly remote and capital-oriented law of the modern nation-state.

This brings us to an inescapable dilemma: How to advance the commons with the help of the alien apparatus and laws of the state? How might commoning flourish within systems of state power closely allied with capital and markets — systems that are determined to assert their own power-enhancing ways of organizing the world? We turn to these questions in Chapters Nine and Ten.

9
State Power and Commoning

W E HAVE SEEN HOW INGENIOUS SOCIOLEGAL FORMS and ancient legal doctrines have the potential of neutralizing conventional property claims, thereby limiting the power of the modern market/ state. But what might be achieved if state power were used to *support* Relationalized Property and commoning? How might states support commons-based governance and provisioning? Could state law establish a more muscular doctrine of inalienability for shared wealth? Could we develop legal regimes, infrastructures, and programs to empower commoning? There are no easy answers to these questions, yet there is no way around actively engaging with state power. How to do so, however, is a tricky challenge.

Most of the politicians, autocrats, and legislatures of the world's 195 states agree that economic growth is their top priority. They believe that the only way to meet people's needs is through relentless capital accumulation — and so they are always eager to expand markets, extract more natural resources, promote consumption, and contrive new needs. All of this keeps the capitalist machine humming and tax revenues rolling in. The market/state system is understandably interested in challenging or co-opting systemic threats such as the commons, by marginalizing them through the usual mystifications ("socially responsible business," the "green economy") or trying to make us ignore them.

This suggests that we need to be utterly realistic about the nature of state power and its alliance with capital and markets. At best, those in power and making decisions in modern state institutions are highly ambivalent about upholding the inalienability of shared wealth. They typically want to boost investment and market activity at every opportunity. As we saw in Chapter Seven, the international community adopted the legal doctrine of the Common Heritage of Mankind in a 1979 United Nations agreement governing the moon "and other celestial bodies," and in a 1980 international treaty to protect the oceans. The idea was that certain significant planetary elements — deep-sea minerals, Antarctica, the atmosphere, the moon — should be treated as common goods, now and in the future. But few states, least of all the United States, have shown enthusiasm for respecting or extending this principle. This stems from the claim that something regarded as the Common Heritage of Mankind cannot be exclusively owned by any individual nation-state or other actor. It means that no state is allowed to claim national sovereignty over a resource, or try to use it solely for military or commercial purposes.[1] They must share the benefits. In fact, the principle of "access and benefit sharing"[2] has become a key line of argument in the debates about the Common Heritage of Mankind. This idea sounds helpful in principle and seems to prevent a system of first come, first served. But it isn't quite that simple. To put it bluntly, the pragmatic political discussion about the Common Heritage of Mankind is mostly about economic interests. The premise of the discussion is that if we exploit the few areas of the Earth that are not fully commercialized, for example, through deep-sea mining, then the benefits should be distributed in a fairer way. And the only things considered "benefits" are those things that people can use and express in numbers and money — a framing that naturally favors commercial exploitation. After decades of debate about the Common Heritage of Mankind, the idea of inalienability of what is common has been completely lost.

This is true of outer space as well as the ocean floor. Today, all sorts of privately funded space exploration projects threaten to override the principles of the Outer Space Treaty, which was ratified in 1967. In 2018, President Trump's commerce secretary, Wilbur Ross, proposed "turning the moon into a kind of gas station for outer space." He noted that the dark surfaces on the moon are actually hundreds of feet of solid ice, "so the plan is to break the ice down into hydrogen and oxygen, [and] use those as the fuel propellant."[3] The Trump administration is also exploring the feasibility of "the large-scale economic development of space," including "private lunar landers staking out de facto 'property rights' for Americans on the Moon, by 2020," as well as the right to mine asteroids for precious metals.[4]

The dismaying history of the past forty years (at least) reveals how noble-sounding declarations such as the Common Heritage of Mankind doctrine are more symbolic than serious. There is a very simple explanation: the market/state system is *structurally biased* against protecting shared wealth as commons. It tends to interfere with private investment and market returns.[5]

The grab for celestial wealth merely extends the commercial exploitation of the Earth that has been going on for centuries. And it enacts a basic logic: contemporary markets and states co-constitute each other and are deeply interdependent on each other, even while each retains a sphere of relative autonomy. Market players need the political legitimacy and predictable rule of law that states provide, and states, in turn, need the tax revenues, geopolitical influence, and infrastructures that flow from an economy committed to relentless growth. Within such constraints, both market players and political decision makers have a loosely defined field of authority within which discretionary power can be exercised.

So constituted, the market/state system generates strategic dilemmas for political decision makers. At the end of the day, they cannot help but be ambivalent about anything that might impede investors and corporations from monetizing the Earth's wealth (and beyond!). It's no wonder that the governments of the world's leading industrialized states have failed to take serious action against carbon emissions over the past thirty years despite growing evidence of a climate breakdown. When an actual attempt was made to keep the oil in the soil — as the Government of Ecuador proposed in a plan to sequester twenty percent of its oil deposits, with financial help from the Global North — the international political community simply ignored it.[6]

So, in trying to legalize the commons, we should have no illusions about the meliorative intentions of state power. The way that states are constituted today, it is not only difficult for the guardians of state power to support the commons. They can barely comprehend the *idea!* State power is committed to a static, individualist worldview, at least in liberal democracies allied with market capitalism. The polities of liberal capitalist democracies elevate individual rights and economic liberty over everything else — except perhaps the idea of sovereign state power itself.

If we wish to take the commons idea seriously, then, we have to fundamentally rethink our ideas about how state power might be used strategically to advance the interests of commoners. Needless to say, that is a daunting task we can only begin to tackle in this book. But one thing is clear: the prevailing forms of state power as a governance system — the nation-state — will surely have to change.

"The State" and "The People"

Before going any further, we must make two important conceptual clarifications about what we mean when talking about "the state." First, the state is not really a subject or entity as popular usage of the term implies. The concept of the state is *relational.* Just as the notion of "I" cannot exist without "you" — both are defined by and exist in relationship to each other — so the state is a relational notion (as is the commons). Seen in this way, the state must be understood as a counterpoint to what it is *not.* "The state," explains political theorist Bob Jessop, "is constituted as a division between itself and its *other.*"[7] This means that the state only exists by distinguishing itself from and in relation to the market, civil society, religion and family even though no state is conceivable *without* these social systems. That's because the state *relates* to these social systems.

So the state is more accurately seen as the power that shapes these relationships. Therefore, we prefer to talk about *state power* — or, more accurately, state *powers* — because it helps us see that the state as such does not really exist. It is not a monolith but a configuration of power relations that are constantly being (re)produced. So the state as such never acts; only specific groups with specific interests and positions of power act, relying on various instruments such as law, police, bureaucracies, etc.

And yet, the state is real in the sense that it functions as an ensemble of institutions — bureaucracies, an organized military, courts, etc. — that directly affect people's lives. These institutions have their own way of fostering individuation — namely, by granting credentials (drivers' licenses, occupational licenses) and defining us as "citizens," which confers certain responsibilities and entitlements. To be a commoner is to understand the individual — and his/her responsibilities and entitlements — in another sense entirely. The notion of a commoner is at once locally rooted but also transcultural, universal, and beyond any state form. It is not simply an identity that lies somewhere in between the citizen and the individual. To be a commoner is to understand social reality in a different way. One sees that the *I* as an individual is always connected to others, and in a pre-political sense. The unresolved question is how to modify state powers to recognize and support commons-friendly modes of individuation — that is, to bolster the commoner in all of us.

To understand state power, we need to recognize how the term "nation-state" is misleading. It conflates the idea of belonging to a people (an anthropological concept) with a system of power, the state (a concept from political science and theory of the state). The term "nation," from the Latin *natio*, is derived from *nasci*, "being born." The term *natio* simply means "people, kin, type of people" and denotes a community of people of the same background and sharing a common language and customs. Even today, "nation" is often considered synonymous with "people." The people of a nation are thought of as ethnically homogeneous — often for political reasons — which makes the term loaded. The term *nation* emerged in France in the sixteenth century, where people used it to designate themselves as a people with political/state unity; it was used more broadly in the rest of Europe only after the French Revolution. Today, two centuries later, "nation" is very familiar to us as the designation of the people of a state; so familiar that we forget that the citizens of a state are not necessarily a people in the anthropological sense.

The conflation of peoplehood and state is so familiar and deeply rooted in our minds and language that the difference described here may seem like splitting hairs. But pause for a moment to consider that almost no territorial nation-state is based on a single shared past and a single people (in the original meaning of *natio*) — not in Iraq, Mexico, India, or Bolivia, and not in other modern territorial nation-states, either. They are all composed of diverse ethnicities, distinct social traditions, and cultures. Bolivia is the only state in the world that officially recognized this diversity in its 2009 constitution, where it is defined as a unitary *plurinational* state.

States and many political players today routinely nourish a sense of national identity and patriotism. It is not unusual for modern state power to be founded upon and supported by it. Following years of debate, in 2018 Israel elevated the conflation of state power and national identity to quasi-constitutional status.[8] In the text of the law, which is generally known as the Nation-State Law, Israel is defined as the "Nation State of the Jewish People."[9]

The blending of nation and state is an endless source of strife and political trauma because it rides roughshod over the lived realities of ethnic identity and culture. In the end, it fuels racist, nationalistic, and fascist social movements, as can currently be seen in Brazil. As philosopher Hannah Arendt concluded in 1963: "The inability of precisely this state form to survive in the modern world was proven long ago, and the longer it is maintained, the more viciously and ruthlessly the perversions not only of the national state, but also of nationalism, will prevail."[10]

We take pains to parse the nation from the state because it is second nature for citizens, as well as those exercising state power, to adhere to a narrative of the shared identity of a single people. Commoning offers a way out of this trap by acknowledging the actual diversity of social, ethnic, cultural, and religious identity. Identity-building processes emerge autonomously through commoning, with no imperative to integrate into one single political configuration, such as citizenship of a nation-state. In this sense, commoning serves as something of a staging area to co-create transnational, post-state identities that can get beyond the abuses of patriotism and nationalism.

Equal Under Law, Unequal in Reality

Even though modern states may constitute all citizens as legal equals, in practice the exercise of civil liberties and rights often depends upon one's wealth, reputation, political connections, and so forth. Societal discrimination plays a role as well. For example, discrimination may be so deeply embedded in our thinking, language, and institutions that people do not even see different points of view or they consider them irrelevant. Then, no individual person appears directly responsible for discrimination. It's "nobody's fault." But in the end, it is people from Africa who clean offices at night and women (often Eastern European) who perform low-status care work.

Equality before the law can even provide a clever way to give certain groups of actors preferential treatment. In other words, equality before the law can serve as a brilliant disguise for privileging certain players in backdoor ways. Policies and regulations may purport to be neutral, for example, but in fact favor a certain class of large businesses over others. Finance, automobile manufacturers, and agricultural sectors have become too big to fail and too relevant for Gross Domestic Product to actually be held responsible for antisocial behaviors. This leads to privileged economic players more or less dictating the terms of law at the expense of unorganized individuals and the common good. Or as an unknown author wrote about English land enclosures ratified by the Parliament in the seventeenth century:

> The law locks up the man or woman
> Who steals the goose from off the common
> But leaves the greater villain loose
> Who steals the common from off the goose.

In our two concluding chapters, we have two ambitions — to imagine how commoning can help catalyze an OntoShift and thus use and potentially alter state power in significant ways (this chapter); and to suggest new legal forms and policies that commoners might use to transform specific state actions and in so doing support commoning (Chapter Ten). If we apply the worldview outlined in Chapter Two to our understanding of the way state power works, we can see no such thing as *the* state. This reorientation helps us envision new strategic opportunities for dealing with state institutions. It helps us to focus on specific institutional designs and bureaucratic processes that privilege certain groups over others, notwithstanding formal equality before the law.

A relational approach to state power helps us envision all sorts of piecemeal ways of advancing the commons. All can contribute to a more consequential, transformative agenda that will reconfigure power relations 1) within the state institutions; and 2) between them and commoners. If we can focus on the different agents and layers of state power instead of the fictional monolith known as "the state," we can imagine other ways of involving the public in the day-to-day business of governing. We can get a glimpse of the possibilities in open platforms that invite citizens to help city councils in urban planning, government websites that encourage citizen feedback about public services, participatory budgeting programs that let citizens make spending decisions, and government support for co-housing and volunteer networks for the elderly. A fruitful collaboration between a commons and the state can arise because commoners can provide services that neither commercial enterprises nor government agencies can or want to provide.

The Barcelona internet provider Guifi.net, which we introduced in Chapter One, has developed a constructive relationship with the municipal government because it provides an infrastructure solution for a problem that politicians have trouble addressing — how to provide high-quality connectivity in the countryside and other remote, low-density areas. Guifi.net started by "connecting a pig farm to a cow farm," and in a few years the network, functioning as a commons, was serving tens of thousands of people.[11] "What if government trusted the people to share the job of governing?" asked Geoff Mulgan in a major report published by the UK think tank Nesta in 2012.[12] A richer government-citizen dialogue in the exercise of state power would certainly help enhance the trust and legitimacy of states.

In more general terms, it is fair to ask what a strategic relational approach to state power in liberal democracies might look like in practice. Would it really lead to a situation in which, as British Labour MP Tessa Jovells writes, state agents "prioritize the giving of power to individuals and communities [...] by allowing local residents to commission their own services, by giving communities the opportunity to identify the priorities for local spending, or by putting people in touch with local residents with skills and time to give." This is certainly possible, but only "if politicians are prepared to trust staff and local people to make decisions."[13]

It is all about trust! This insight is basic and challenging at once. State agents generally seek to assert control, and to use numbers, standard units, and bureaucratic systems to do so — even though all of us live in particular landscapes with unique histories, personalities, and webs of social allegiances.

There is a structural mismatch between state power and living systems. To be effective and trusted, state power cannot just impose bureaucratic master plans; it must learn how to foster relationships among real people who have their own creative agency. This requires that we get away from the idea of human beings as units of need to which "service providers" must minister — a mentality that has produced the dehumanizing, disempowering institutionalization so trenchantly critiqued by Ivan Illich.[14] Focused on administering services, state agencies and service professionals tend to dismiss people's own creative talents, desire to contribute, and capacities for commoning. In short, they neither recognize people's actual human agency nor strengthen that power. For their part, most people have internalized this image of themselves as passive consumers of professional and government services, and fail to regard themselves as potential participants in Peer Governance or the state polity.

Thus, the central challenge we face is to *re-imagine* state power in ways that support commoning. We must find ways for state powers to provide time, space, assistance, legal authority, and organizational systems for people to devise their own solutions to problems.[15]

Some Working Notes on State Power

Many people presume that humanity has made a linear progression from hunting and gathering to nomadic tribes and clans, followed by small agricultural settlements and early states, monarchies, and feudal societies, finally culminating in the civilizational peak that we now enjoy, the modern nation-state. The narrative is a self-congratulatory exercise that celebrates liberal democracies organized as states as the best, most civilized form of governance in human history. Conversely, anyone who criticizes this point of view or wishes to avoid the governance of states is regarded as ignorant, primitive, and backward, or even prehistoric.

But what if the modern state in its intimate alliance with capital represents an evolutionary dead end? Has this centralized, hierarchical system of power become too brittle and inefficient to govern the riotous complexity of local realities and human diversity, notwithstanding its adaptations to the realities of networked society and hybrid governance institutions? Has it become too alienated from the more-than-human world and oblivious to its imperatives? Some critics note that civilization is not just facing the challenges of Peak Oil — the declining availability of inexpensive fossil fuels — but also of Peak Hierarchy, the declining effectiveness of centralized, hierarchical structures of administration. Michel Bauwens writes that "horizontality [in social and economic relations] is starting to trump verticality; it is becoming more competitive to be distributed, than to be (de)centralized. The two combined forces of Peak Oil and Peak Hierarchy are going to dramatically change the world we will live in."[16]

Given these fierce pressures on the traditional lineaments of state power, we believe it is time to think about new possibilities that reflect a constructive, wholesome relationship with commoning. The theorist who has probably done the most to develop a coherent historical theory of the state from a commoner's perspective is Yale anthropologist James C. Scott. Scott argues that countless populations have historically sought to avoid state power because of its military aggression, taxation, autocratic mandates, and propensity to enslave people. They also sought to avoid being drawn into living and working conditions that brought about disease and even pandemics.[17] While the Leviathan[18] purports to guarantee many rights and liberties for its citizens, the rise of the market/state is at least as important as a force for *controlling* people. The Great Wall of China was built as much to keep Chinese citizens *in* as it was to keep "barbarian" invaders *out*. In our time, nations like India, China, and the United States are deploying pervasive digital technologies to enable panoptical, constant forms of surveillance of their citizens and foreigners.[19]

State power too often regularizes the governance of life and consolidates power through centralized, bureaucratic systems, as Scott explains in his book *Seeing Like a State*:

> [T]he modern state, through its officials, attempts with varying success to create a terrain and a population with precisely those standardized characteristics that will be easiest to monitor, count, assess and manage. The utopian, immanent and continually frustrated goal of the modern state is to reduce the chaotic, disorderly, constantly changing social reality beneath it to something more closely resembling the administrative grid of its observation.[20]

The state's many attempts to impose a universal order are not without value. There are gains for a society when a state issues its own money; identifies everyone in order to collect taxes and control territorial borders; establishes weights and measures to make land and agricultural output legible; and so on. However, a state's obsession with standardizing its means of control and ability to coerce compliance can be highly repressive, too. State power often relies on positive law and police action to insist upon state-friendly behaviors and norms. Bureaucracies are especially useful in this task because their centrally managed systems can override the many natural differences among people. Over time, states prod their citizens to internalize values and goals, to bring about a unified, regimented order from what they regard as the chaos and barbarism of the pre-state. Thus, while modern, liberal states may manage to enlarge the scope of freedom that ordinary people have, such gains come at a price: special privileges for the political authority of the state and the market power of capital.

The drama of the modern liberal nation-state, however, is precisely its *inability* to truly control everything within its territorial borders. It cannot really control countless ethnic subcultures and social activity; cross-border flows of information, software code, and drugs; the quasi-independent credit systems that capitalists and organized crime have created; and the stability of ecosystems, among many other things.

The state, which presents itself as a stable, durable institution reliably exercising authority and power, cannot escape the reality that it is immersed in a churning ebb and flow of relationships. A state consists of a menagerie of bureaucracies, each directed by officials enmeshed in different political and professional networks and committed to different political and technical agendas. Even though modern states seek to standardize life, each does so in different ways. One might say there are variations among states — a left-wing variation that focuses on fairness and material equality, for example, and a right-wing variation that accents economic freedom, the terms of legal contracts, and other commercial concerns. In other words, social outcomes may vary from one country to another, but the essential political functions remain much the same.

This means that states are handicapped when it comes to honoring diverse forms of self-determination or delegations of power. As Marc Stears puts it:

> States work best when a problem has a technical, mechanical solution which can be employed everywhere within a shared geographic space. They are at their worst when they need to respond flexibly to local particularities, when they need to act nimbly or with nuance, and — most importantly of all — when they delve into problems of the nation's spirit or of the human heart. Anything which requires difference, contingency and essential unpredictability is not going to be a skill of the state.[21]

Indeed, you might say that states are afflicted with *methodological nationalism* for good or ill, whether to spread "civilization and democracy," or to seek colonial or imperialist conquest. Fetishizing the sovereignty of the state blinds us to the pluriversal, self-governed worlds that everyone lives in, day in and day out. It is no surprise that the world making and Peer Governance that commoners routinely engage in are generally invisible to state bureaucracies. That is why viewing the world through the lens of the commons is useful: it brings into focus a plethora of solutions and widens our opportunities to act.

Once we choose to see the state not as an omnipotent monolith but as a configuration of power that varies a great deal and is even parochial and vulnerable in certain respects, we can begin to imagine ways to alter state power in piecemeal ways, as opportunities arise. We can see how social practices and relations can help us transform state power, at least at some incremental level. While modalities of governance and state authority vary immensely, people in more intimate local contexts experience politics as more accessible, adaptable, and accountable.

This is one reason why cities and towns are likely to play an outsized role in transforming state power. Their smaller scale offers more opportunities for change. Political scientist Benjamin Barber saw mayors as vital figures in the transformation of societies in the future[22] and theorist Murray Bookchin argued that "libertarian municipalism" offered the best opportunities for social change by empowering democratic assemblies and confederations of free municipalities.[23] It should not be surprising that one of the most robust forces for change in Europe is a "new municipalism" movement that is trying to decentralize the power of the state and remake state power from the bottom up.[24]

In the standard understanding of the economy and politics, local action is often patronized as too small-scale to be significant. But in today's world, everything is in fact SLOC — small and local, but open and connected[25] — which means that even discrete, particular actions can catalyze important change. An obscure Occupy Wall Street protest in Manhattan's Zuccotti Park in 2011 sparked scores of Occupy protests around the world and made wealth inequality an urgent public issue. The Global Covenant for Mayors for Climate and Energy, similarly, has been highly influential in bringing valuable initiatives to the attention of international policymakers.[26] When São Paolo activists fight for affordable housing as something that helps reduce carbon emissions, or when Barcelona activists turn Airbnb apartments into social housing, the reverberations are felt across the globe in many other cities, state legislatures, and international fora. "What some people deride as 'localism' is actually the very foundation of transformative change," argues the Symbiosis Research Collective.[27]

This is entirely plausible, not just because local political arenas are smaller and more accessible, but because localism allows for new types of grassroots, networked political organization that goes beyond political parties. We see this in Spain, for example, where the 15-M movement is influencing municipal power. It has helped the idea that "the personal is political" become visible and easy to grasp. This concept means that individual, concrete experience — instead of theoretical or strategic considerations — is taken seriously and employed as the starting point for policy. It is fundamentally different from "conceiving politics as 'technically correct' management of 'unavoidable' necessities of global capitalism," in the words of journalist and writer Amador Fernández-Savater.[28]

When activists gain radical democratic experience — simple things such as the "procedural forms of 15-M, assemblies with direct democracy, facilitation methods, working groups, shows of hands, or consensus-oriented decision-making,"[29] — they are able to contribute at the municipal level. Radical municipal activism, when federated with similar actors elsewhere, can help carve out protected spaces for commoning ultimately to flourish and expand, with formal legal authority and administrative support.

Beyond Reform or Revolution

The primary goal of commoning is *not* to seize state power through revolution or elections. It is to develop stable independent spaces that have relative freedom to establish their own systems of Peer Governance and Provisioning. History has shown that even when leftists win state power through democratic means, it has dubious results in achieving system change. Since 2015, the Greek political coalition led by Syriza discovered that its stunning electoral victory, nominally giving it control of a sovereign state, was not enough. The Greek state was in fact still subordinated to the power of international capital and the geopolitical interests of other states. The rise of Indigenous politician Evo Morales to the presidency of Bolivia revealed a similar lesson: even smart, well-intentioned electoral movements have trouble transcending the deep imperatives of state power because the state remains tightly yoked to an international system of capitalist finance and resource extraction. Pablo Solón Romero, a long-time Bolivian activist and the former Ambassador of the Plurinational State of Bolivia to the United Nations (2009-2011), told a cautionary tale:

> Fifteen years ago [in the early 2000s], we had a lot of commoning in Bolivia — for forests, water, justice, etc. To preserve this, when our enemy was the state and privatizing everything, we decided we would take the state. And we succeeded! And we were able to do good things. Now we have a plurinational state. That's positive. *But* ... ten years later, are our communities stronger or weaker? They are weaker! We can't do everything that we wanted to do via the state. The state and its structures have their own logic. We were naïve. We didn't realize that those structures were going to change *us*.[30]

What this suggests is that while electoral politics can achieve some important things, it has clear structural limitations as well. The

guardians of state power constantly strive to constitute and extend the
very culture that sustains it: a patriotic and civic mythos, infrastructure and institutions, money and commerce, and, of course, vigilance
against potential challenges and subversion. *Reformers* are quite happy
to seek gradual transformations through the apparatus of state power
itself. *Revolutionaries* might appear to want the polar opposite — to
abruptly overthrow state power entirely. And yet, "the substance of
modern revolutionary theories is unfortunately thin," write German
political theorists Sutterlütti and Meretz.[31] Revolutionaries focus on
the old structures and have to situate themselves *within* them, and
then seek to overthrow or abolish them. But they usually don't have
much to say about what the new order should look like. Nor do they
speak to the inner transformations needed to bring about a new polity
and culture. Sutterlütti and Meretz conclude: "Reform and revolution
turn out to be children of traditional Marxism: They can imagine how
to seize political power and redesign the state, but not how to enact a
free society."[32]

We need to go beyond the "reform or revolution" narrative! Perhaps
towards something that German political scientist Joachim Hirsch
calls "radical reformism." Radical reformism need not be fixated on the
state. The term refers to the role of cultural and societal changes, the
importance of which cannot be overstated. First, there was the revolt
of 1968, then the changes in the law — not the other way around,
But the idea of radical reformism still remains "reformism" because,
in Hirsch's words, "it is not about seizing power through revolution"
and it is "radical" because its target is "the societal relationships that
bring forth the dominant relations of power and domination."[33] The
idea is also radical because it encompasses how people can change
themselves. That, in turn, Hirsch claims, is possible only "if people
succeed in creating forms of political-social self-organization beyond
and independent of the existing governing apparatuses, the state, and
the political parties, and in putting a concept of politics into practice
that takes up the 'political' aspects of the 'private.'"[34]

This brings us to our contemporary impasse. Can we imagine a
transformation of the world that avoids the pitfalls of both reform and
revolution? Can we envision a world that is not utopian — in the sense
of being "nowhere" (the literal meaning of utopia) — but built on

successful experiences, inhabited and run by real people? That is what we attempted to do in Chapters Four through Six — to sketch the *actual dynamics* of social life, governance, and provisioning in the new order. There must be practical pathways for the vision to be achieved, and for no one to be left behind. As Murray Bookchin wrote, "Perhaps the greatest single failing of movements for social reconstruction — I refer particularly to the Left, to radical ecology groups, and to organizations that profess to speak for the oppressed — is their lack of a politics that will carry people beyond the limits established by the status quo."[35]

So our questions are: Can commoning as we've described it potentially enact a more humane social order at scale, notwithstanding state power? Can commoning generate new ways of governing and provisioning that advance freedom, fairness, and eco-responsibility for everyone? Can this occur in ways that make us feel alive, rather than like puppets at the command of a totalistic megamachine?[36] Can commoning help us regain sovereignty that the systemic power of the megamachine has eclipsed? We immodestly think the answer is yes. Yes, it is indeed possible! That is the power of commoning. We are convinced that it starts with learning how to *be* the revolution rather than only *doing* it — often known as "prefigurative politics." That means trying things out. Living with them for a while. Reflecting on them. Making corrections and adjustments. Our focus need not be on state policies as such, even if they cannot be completely avoided. The focus must be on building a new social order.

There is a simple reason for this approach: a truly free and fair society cannot be generated out of a political or state-driven process which is based and dependent on "the way things work." This won't change the cultural foundations of society or its inner mindscape. Real transformation must draw upon the foundations we sketched out in the first chapters of this book. It must develop its own vision and be actualized through its own structures. It must enact *a social process that can constitute an alternative order over time* at all levels — individual, collective, societal — for independently fulfilling people's aspirations for transformation. To recall J.K. Gibson-Graham's advice again: "If to change ourselves is to change our worlds, and the relation is reciprocal, then the project of history making is never a distant one but always right here, on the borders of our sensing, thinking, feeling, moving bodies."[37] Dealing with state power poses a formidable challenge. But perhaps the most powerful, durable way to meet this challenge is to reorient ourselves and build protectable commons. *This* approach offers a path for moving ahead *despite* state power because it transforms us *as well as* external political and institutional structures. The two must proceed together, with the details emerging and not truly predictable.

The importance of state power is undeniable, but the ambition to take over state power is almost certain to result in disillusionment. The capitalist state is simply too deeply committed to property, individualism, and a culture of commodification. And those political leaders who may wish to explore post-capitalist possibilities will find themselves locked into a global system of states that themselves are locked into a world market. This is why, at the end of the day, the strongest argument that *any* politician in the world can make for a policy is, "It will create jobs." In other words, everyone must constantly recommit to the prevailing economic model and simply accept the collateral damages. Various social movements have proposed other ways forward — other ways of living that are less dependent on the market/state megamachine — but this path is largely blocked because state leaders in alliance with the corporate sector can usually co-opt or subvert any perceived threats to the system.

The Power of Commoning

Where does that leave us? How might commoners grow the Commonsverse while living within a market/state system that is otherwise poised to ignore or fight it? Any answers must deal with a paradox: state power is too formidable and coercive to ignore, yet conventional attempts to transform it are likely to be unsatisfactory. Somehow the very terms of politics, governance, and law must be re-imagined and changed. Bold manifestos or rhetorical postures will not be enough. Only actual social practice and living culture can make headway. If this may sound a bit fanciful to some people, remember Hannah Arendt's concept of power as something that "springs up between men when they act together and vanishes the moment they disperse," as she wrote in *The Human Condition*.[38] If power arises whenever people come together, it is always capable of being created. It does not inhere in state institutions themselves; it is not a fixed, inherent capacity that can be stored. Such power is not necessarily power *over* something or somebody; it can empower people to take their lives into their own hands, rather than making them powerless vis-à-vis the omnipotence of those in power — if it is created through enabling structures, dialogue, and responsibility.

Seen from this perspective, commoning is a vehicle for creating power. Perhaps, in time, it can also become a means to incrementally challenge state and market omnipotence by withdrawing its fuel and depriving the megamachine of its sustenance — us. Our participation fuels the market/state. Of course, there are reasons for this. Viewed individually, it is functional, if not essential, to play along with the game being played. Otherwise, we will lose income and status, forms of security that we are accustomed to, or even our jobs. That's why so many of the familiar strategies for pursuing long-term social transformation are, structurally speaking, dead ends.

The most powerful feature of commoning may be its ability to redirect people's energies and stop feeding the power engines of modern markets and nation-states. It does this by providing alternative ways of meeting needs and by building quasi-autonomous modes of power. The modern state retains many enormous advantages, of course — its alliance with capital, its commitment to economic growth, its consolidated control of power. These capacities seemingly insulate it from the *need* to negotiate with citizens about transformational change. This is a darkly hilarious conceit because in this time of climate breakdown, ecosystem collapse, desertification, etc., even state power cannot defy planetary systems that are becoming political agents in their own right, as Bruno Latour has noted.[39] The sheer amount of energy and material throughput needed to sustain economic growth is reaching physical limits, exhausting everyone and the planet. Growth is subverting the very social emancipation and progress that is the alleged justification for growth. And this is occurring even *before* the governments can contemplate fairer redistributions of wealth — a possibility that itself is shrinking as the wealthy use their money to undermine liberal democracy.[40]

While most commoners have no aspirations to frontally seize state power or compete in markets, their activities nonetheless have important long-term ramifications. They help reallocate power. Commoning creates new vessels of non-state power *simply by bringing people together to collaborate*. We can see this effect in the ways that GNU/Linux, and other open source programs profoundly, albeit indirectly, transformed software markets and a massive industry. Today it would be silly to produce an encyclopedia the old way, through a top-down assemblage of experts producing an expensive commodity, when the bottom-up, cooperative alternative, Wikipedia — with its flexible, decentralized structures, multiple languages, diversity, and topicality — has so many advantages. We can see how local organic farming and allied food movements, by building an alternative universe of wholesome agri-culture, have induced industrial agriculture to grow organic produce and reduce processing in food products. The more food commons that arise to "crowd-feed the world"[41] and the more CSA farms that provide fresh, local, affordable food, the less people will have to depend on industrial agriculture or charity handouts. The bottom-up activities of feminist movements worldwide, too, have changed how state power is exercised on all sorts of reproductive, gender, and workplace issues, as the #MeToo movement has shown.

Such histories persuade us that social movements are more likely to be transformative if they develop parallel economies with *structural independence* from the conventional market/state. This means also that commons are more likely to survive and retain their independence if they are *less* entangled with the conventional economy and state power, and if they can rely on internal systems (Peer Governance, knowl edge-sharing, federated support from other commoners) for resilience. At the same time, it is imperative to engage with state power through elections and traditional advocacy, if only because that field of action can change the conditions for widening spaces of commonality. It is too consequential to be ignored.

So commoners need a two-track mindset in dealing with state power: a primary focus on building the new — keeping the conceptual insights above in mind — while also attempting to neutralize the old.

Revamping State Power to Support Commoning

We have outlined a general stance towards the state in moving forward, but we have not burrowed into the deeper questions: In what specific ways can state power *itself* be altered to support commoning? What openings in law and bureaucratic behavior, or in politics and local action, might be exploited to secure stable beachheads for commoning?

The first priority is to convince state institutions to back off. Recall Elinor Ostrom's wisdom in her seventh design principle for successful commons. She asserted that state authorities must recognize the right of commoners to govern themselves.[42] External governmental authorities must not challenge the right of the users of common resources (or "appropriators," in Ostrom's language) to devise their own rules and governance regimes. This is our starting point and a minimal requirement. We could derive a principle of noninterference from it. The state must get out of the way so that commoners can engage in the value-generating activities that only they can do.

Given the realities, however, commons may find that they need legal recognition to grow and flourish. In instances where state institutions regard sharing as a crime — e.g., seed sharing, software collaborations, information sharing — commoning must be decriminalized. This is part of normalizing commons and acknowledging that the moral and political legitimacy of commoning exists prior to and independent of modern states.[43]

Consider how state power has been used to let investors form corporations and limit their liability, ostensibly because such organizational forms serve the public good. Monarchs and, later, legislatures saw corporations as a way to encourage activities that the state itself could not or did not want to undertake. Early ventures such as the investor-owned British East India Company, for example, developed colonial trade regimes, extracted natural resources, exploited cheap labor, and built railroads and waterways. Why shouldn't state power also recognize the immense value generated by commoners by granting their institutions legal standing?

Such recognition will not come easily, of course. Political leaders and bureaucrats who bow down before the standard economic narrative have trouble seeing other modes of value. Moreover, some state institutions themselves are designed to depend on market revenues. For example, the European Patent Office — an interstate governance body that grants patents under the European Patent Convention — is designed to finance most of its one billion euro budget by collecting fees from patent applicants. Since the more patents it grants, the more money it collects, the Patent Office has a strong incentive to make more scientific and technical knowledge proprietary. While it is understandable to charge patent holders for services provided — and not, say, the general taxpayer — this mechanism is a disincentive to support a world in which we SHARE KNOWLEDGE GENEROUSLY. Such a societal ideal tends to be regarded as aberrant, if not faintly ridiculous. So are any ambitions to achieve social harmony and intergenerational continuity and protect cultural heritage. As for the potential contributions that subsistence communities and nomadic tribes make to eco-sensitive choices, many moderns continue to depict them as primitive, uncivilized, and hopelessly backward.[44]

Thus, we are imprisoned within a progress narrative validated and reproduced by state institutions. We are told the economy must grow (to fulfill targets contrived by corporations) so that we can compete successfully on the global market. World leaders urge us not to fall behind. Being outpaced in technological innovation is considered by the business and political communities to be the worst fate of all. One innovation after another — driverless cars, synthetic biology, nanotechnology — is pushed through regulatory procedures, at times with too little time to consider the full societal costs and benefits. All this makes it difficult for people to embrace a shift to the commons. Moreover, guardians of state power understandably think: why should the state cede *any* authority to nonmarket, decentralized activities or provide funding support to things that have no market value? It would only enrage elites and disrupt internal political arrangements. In addition, letting people withdraw from the circuitry of the market/state system will only embolden the yearning for self-determination, goes the thinking … and that could be dangerous. It would only encourage unregulated activity, amateur experimentation, and perhaps demands for greater autonomy. The guardians of state power may understandably fear that if people decommodify their everyday lives and wean themselves away from dependencies on market/state systems, it will reduce the state's moral standing, political authority, and tax revenues.

Thus the challenge: if the commons is going to evolve as an alternative matrix of governance and provisioning, it must somehow overcome a deep-seated skepticism about commoning among many bureaucrats, politicians, and governments. This does not mean that no workarounds are possible. As stated earlier, the state is not a monolithic institution. State decision makers, despite their zeal in defending their authority, could find it advantageous to authorize and support commoning under the right circumstances. At the local level, this means: allocating land for community gardens and co-housing; facilitating the formation of community land banks and trusts; encouraging local agriculture and food systems; using open source software in public administration; providing free community Wi-Fi everywhere; using open educational resources (OER) in classrooms; providing space and support for timebanks, repair cafés, hackerspaces, and much more.

This is not a quixotic agenda. Those who wield state power are mindful of the need for public support and legitimacy. Many politicians, feeling the heat from fierce social protests against extractivism and the international trade regime, are looking for credible ways to escape the iron cage of neoliberal capitalism. Some political leaders are willing to concede the failures of the market/progress narrative to address climate breakdown, inequality, poverty, and hunger; but on the other hand, they are also fearful of breaking from dogmas about free markets and national identity.

Around the world, many authoritarians have seized upon the many failures of the market/state system to promote various forms of nationalism. Although a complicated and varied process, much of this political trend is fueled by a search for meaning, purpose, and belonging that the market/state is incapable of fulfilling. The political left and center, meanwhile, cling to conventional vehicles for change: new laws, policies, programs, and procedural reform. While sometimes significant, these approaches generally are carried out in distant state venues (courts, legislatures, government agencies) and fail to engage people personally. In the end, many liberals and social democrats remain tethered to the dominant narrative of progress and show little interest in bottom-up empowerment or social transformation. The cultural dimensions of commons-based initiatives such as agroecology, community land trusts, platform cooperatives, and cosmo-local production, are generally ignored or seen as too small and inconsequential to be taken seriously. Businesses, for their part, generally see them as threats to their market share and profits.

By this reasoning, the political mainstream cedes the politics of the local and vernacular to right-wing authoritarians. It focuses instead on the distant state, the brokering of power, and the usual *forms* of law and policy — but not on the ways in which ordinary people can find wholesome purpose and social connection in what they do. Anthropologist David Graeber has said that the problem of the left is that it has no credible alternative to bureaucracy.[45] He's right, and that's why empowering people to meet their needs more directly, in ways that engage their sense of local identity (without creating tribes of the righteous and resentful), deserves serious attention. The commons can address many of these challenges in constructive, democratic ways, and that is one compelling reason for politicians to embrace the commons. State support for the commons would take a fledgling agenda to an entirely new level. It would move beyond bureaucratic supervision to outright delegations of authority to commoners.

But a simple shift of legal authority is not enough. Any state support for commoning will require many novel forms of administrative coordination, legal support, infrastructure development, and public education. Four general types of support are needed.

1. Catalyze & Propagate

Imagine a town in which supermarkets are run as cooperatives, helping residents to buy higher-quality, local food produced under fair and eco-responsible conditions. The local taxi service and tourist lodgings

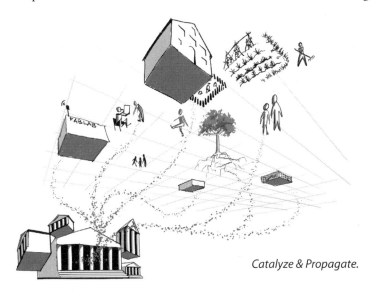

Catalyze & Propagate.

are managed by platform cooperatives, letting households and the community share the benefits. Nursing services are run by a neighborhood home care venture such as Buurtzorg (Chapter One). Electricity generated by rooftop solar panels is pooled and shared via distributed ledger technology software,[46] which is reducing high electric bills and allowing public divestment from fossil fuels and nuclear power. The state at all levels is providing infrastructures, technical advice, and funding that let people launch their own makerspaces, CSA farms, energy cooperatives, tool-sharing commons, repair cafés, and time-banking exchanges.[47]

This scenario may seem laughably utopian, but that is only because the state already has so many deep, often-invisible commitments to supporting the market system. Contrary to its ideological pretensions, the market system depends on countless state expenditures and interventions: subsidies to entire industries, special tax breaks, legal privileges, research funding, regulation to bolster consumer trust, trade treaties to facilitate exports, potential military support for overseas market assets, and much else. To spur market activity and growth, the state routinely uses its standard powers to build and finance infrastructure, create and oversee finance systems, and establish bodies of law to assist commerce.

Yet the benefits of this model of economic development flow primarily to a narrow class of investors and corporations, not taxpayers and ordinary people except in trickle down ways. Given the enormous costs and inequities — and dwindling returns — of this approach, the stewards of state power, or at least the shrewder ones, may find some genuine appeal in the commons. They could leverage the passions and imaginations of countless people while meeting their needs in fairer, more efficient, lower-cost ways. Why can't the state's capacity for building infrastructure, supporting finance, and drafting new bodies of law — now used primarily to support markets — be deployed in an analogous fashion to support commoning? One can imagine using state law to encourage free and open licensing, relationalized property rights in land, chartering regimes that authorize commons, cooperative finance, and technical assistance programs. In short, state institutions could do a great deal to Catalyze & Propagate the commons.

Functionaries for Commons?

Imagine if commons seeking to deal with city agencies could deal with a one-stop process rather than having to approach numerous public agencies one by one! For many projects, that would be like winning the lottery. The designated contact persons would have to be very knowledgeable in order to help commoners find their way through the thicket of rules and regulations they are confronted with. They would also need to have the authority to act independently, perhaps by being an organizational arm of the mayor's office, and have the competencies to grant permits and funding.

Amsterdam has taken a step in this direction with regional liaisons known as *gebieds-makelaars*. The "area brokers" maintain relationships with citizens' groups and share knowledge and information about public agencies with the citizenry. However, they lack an independent status within the municipal bureaucracy as well as the power and the personnel which would make them true clearinghouses for commons.[48]

The challenge is huge, because so much of it is cultural, in making commoning more publicly visible and developing a larger narrative about cooperation and sharing. State-supported institutions could serve as clearinghouses for technical, legal, and financial guidance about peer governance and commons-based provisioning in diverse contexts (agriculture, social services, energy, alternative currencies, etc.). A national office for timebanking could greatly expand that social system for meeting needs. Government support could be of immeasurable help in establishing community supported agriculture, acquiring land for housing commons, funding neighborhood services, providing technical guidance in getting Fab Labs started, and nurturing little-known innovations on the fringe.

2. Establish Commons at the Macroscale

One reason that state institutions are so indispensable to helping foster commons is the scale and coordination they can provide for managing large-scale resources. Forests, waterways, grazing lands, and underground mineral deposits often traverse large landscapes and cross political boundaries. Legal and administrative coordination at a macro-scale is therefore required to figure out how multiple claims to a given landscape or resource will be resolved, and how various individual commons should be defined and delimited. One example is a Dutch project called King of the Meadows.[49] Many people became alarmed at the disappearance of the once-common Black-tailed Godwit, due to agricultural practices that have wiped out its meadow habitat. The King of the Meadows project brought together citizens, farmers, musicians, artists, scientists, dairy producers, and others to reconnect people to the landscape and promote "nature-inclusive agriculture" to help restore the godwit and celebrate the connection between biological and cultural diversity. The initiative is now a robust regional, networked collaboration.

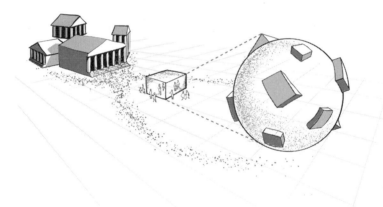

Establish Commons at the Macroscale.

In cases such as this, state power can play a useful role in providing "macroplatforms" to facilitate action that may exceed the capacities of individual commons to solve. State agents have an obvious role in serving as an honest broker among factions in conflict resolution and cross-border negotiations. Of course, the political chemistry of serving such a role effectively depends upon many circumstantial factors. But a state role is entirely plausible and should not be dismissed. Demonstrable public support can persuade the state to try new approaches.

Following a long-running controversy over the management of the Siuslaw National Forest in Oregon in the 1990s, the US Forest Service decided to abandon the standard bureaucratic processes driven by congressional politics and industry lobbying. Instead, it invited anyone with an interest in the forest to attend open roundtable meetings to discuss how forest policy might reconcile the competing interests of timber companies, environmentalists, recreational fishers, local communities, hikers, and others. The agency established a watershed council, which helped warring factions overcome mutual distrust and come up with durable consensus resolutions to jurisdictional conflicts (e.g., salmon spawn in one area of the watershed and later swim hundreds of miles to the ocean). The state's mediation also encouraged people to entertain flexible, long-term plans that would not otherwise have emerged through the bureaucracy or litigation.[50]

A remarkable number of innovative legal vehicles have been created in recent years to protect commoning. The government of New Zealand has granted legal personality to the Whanganui River, as sought by the Maori, recognizing it as "a living and organic whole … from the mountains to the sea, incorporating all of its physical and metaphysical elements."[51] The legislation means that the Whanganui iwi (people), as the designated guardians of the river, can continue their ancient commoning practices with the official sanction of state law. In Peru, the Quechua people have established the Indigenous Biocultural Heritage Area, or Potato Park, to protect the biodiversity of potatoes managed by Quechua people.[52] By having a legal instrument that can be recognized by Peruvian courts, the Quechua have greater assurance that they can live in intimate reciprocal relationship with the land, each other, and the spirit world. Most notably, the Quechua's legal protections help them protect their commons against attempted acts of biopiracy when biotech corporations try to patent the genetic information of rare potatoes.

3. Provide Infrastructures for Commoning

States have a special capacity to help disparate enterprises grow more rapidly by building infrastructures and requiring technical standards that allow for easy interoperability and safety. Infrastructures designed with commons in mind — or even better, designed to be stewarded by commoners themselves — can make it easier and cheaper for people to initiate their own self-organized systems. The classic example is the US Government's development of technical protocols known as TCP/IP, which enable diverse computing networks to interconnect into a single, integrated internet. The state could do similar things today by recognizing open technical standards that limit proprietary control, while taking steps to ensure that the largest, wealthiest businesses do not simply use open standards to capture the innovation space. We need open but protected commons (see pp. 69–72) to assure interoperability and nondiscriminatory access (as platform neutrality does).

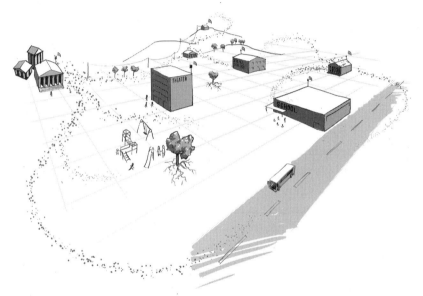

Provide Infrastructures for Commoning.

Open technical standards for government procurement could be issued to make free and open source software a default infrastructure in government agencies, especially in schools. Instead of being familiar with proprietary software, students would graduate from school with extensive skills in working GNU/Linux and other open source software. Schools would not be degraded by becoming quasi-captive extensions of large software corporations' marketing departments. This would have spinoff benefits for general education, higher education, municipal governments, and the general public. State-endorsed protocols for word processing, database, and email software and APIs (application protocol interfaces, which are the technical linkages between software programs and operating systems), could foster greater open source innovation, avoiding the walled gardens owned by Apple and Google. Cities might more easily develop platform cooperatives for housing, ride-hailing services, and information services to benefit local residents instead of Silicon Valley investors. Open design protocols for energy grids could replicate the success of the internet by using open standards to encourage bottom-up innovation by smaller, creative players and preventing proprietary lock-ins by larger companies.

The point of state support for commons-based infrastructures is to neutralize private aggregations of power and shift it to commoners. For infrastructures used by society in general, it is critical that they be discrimination-free, so that no class of users can be arbitrarily excluded from access.[53] This is one reason that the US National Institutes of Health now mandates open-access publishing protocols for taxpayer-funded research: it assures that state funds are used in open, accountable ways.[54] The guiding principle is simple: that which has been publicly financed needs to remain in public hands.

Direct spending on infrastructure to support commoning is always an attractive option. Local governments could directly install Wi-Fi in public squares, as many cities around the world, such as Tel Aviv and Mexico City, have done. Others even provide free server space for websites, email, and data. This is what the city of Linz, Austria, has done with its Open Commons Linz initiative.[55] Or states could support commons initiatives such as Freifunk, a network of German commoners that has built a free Wi-Fi network involving about 400 local communities and over 41,000 access points.[56]

4. Create New Types of Finance for the Commons

State agencies could provide essential support for all sorts of commoning by establishing commons-friendly finance systems. Even though most commons are nonmarket systems of provisioning, they operate within a larger world of market capitalism. They often need credit to build their own facilities and infrastructure, and to pay staff and buy goods and services. But unlike businesses or nonprofit organizations, commons seek to avoid types of debt that suck them into the world of competition, growth, and subordination to banks. They prefer to reject financial support linked to conditions beyond the scope and mission of the commons because debt entails a loss of freedom. Commoners also dismiss financing schemes that would allow private players to appropriate the value created (for example, through an equity stake that entitles investors or banks to skim off profits or to claim shared assets). Here, too, the very same logic seen in public settings applies: what has been created in the commons needs to stay in the commons.

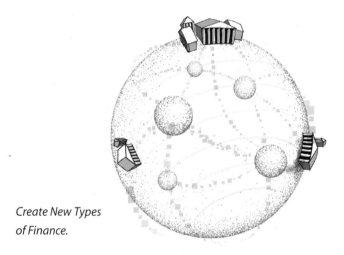

Create New Types of Finance.

At the moment, this is a field of experimentation and innovation. Some familiar progressive forms of credit such as public banks, cooperative banks, community development finance, and social and ethical banks, often support worthy social enterprises. But most of these finance schemes are geared toward providing less burdensome terms of credit (lower interest rates, easier approval, etc.) for enterprises facing the market. They do not seek to escape the force field of markets and conventional credit itself (competition, profit, growth), nor do they seek to support commons *as* commons.

Why not establish forms of credit that allow commons to function well on their own terms, not as ethically minded junior players in the great market system? What might this look like? The administrative barriers to accessing credit would have to be kept low, beginning with a noncompetitive approach in the granting of funds. Granting public funds and granting private credit is not just about approving the financials. It should be an open, trust-building conversation designed as a learning process for all actors involved, not just a dismal ritual of needy applicants begging an imperious loan committee for approval or satisfying empty metrics and superficial indicators of "success."

There are even better options: commoners themselves could be the source of credit — lend to each other, or to the collective — as old-time mutual credit societies in the nineteenth century used to do. Monitoring the repayment of funds could be managed by commoners themselves, along the lines of microcredit systems, but without the need to pay onerous sums of interest to external sources of capital. Of course, in all such schemes, there must be effective internal tools to monitor and assure transparency.

There is a great deal of promise in such forms of self-financing, and pay-it-forward schemes as ways to help commoners secure greater long-term independence from the market/state. We saw how this works in Mietshäuser Syndikat's pooling of funds from members, which is then used to buy additional rental housing. The Drugs for Neglected Diseases Initiative is another example in which donor governments and international organizations jointly finance basic research and development into new drugs for neglected diseases. (More about DNDi in Chapter Ten).

Commons and Subsidiarity

A key factor in advancing any of these initiatives is organizing political support — and then ensuring that state power does not overwhelm or debase the commons with its own interventions. This is complicated territory. While some form of state entanglement with commons is unavoidable, if only to decriminalize them and provide legal stability, active state involvement can introduce a range of messy political dilemmas. There is a fine line between *facilitation* and *interference*.

For this reason, it is important that the state's role be minimal and general. This allows commoners to have maximum discretion and authority in devising their own rules and governance, consistent with the principle of subsidiarity. This principle is widely mentioned in Ostrom scholarship, Catholic social thought, and even in the Lisbon Treaty, which provides the constitutional basis for the European Union. In actual practice, unfortunately, subsidiarity is more often

314 Free, Fair and Alive

celebrated than practiced. That's because, in most circumstances, Governing-through-Money and top-down management are allowed to override local empowerment. The dismaying history of subsidiarity as a grand aspiration, but rarely achieved reality, prompts us to conclude: *there is no real subsidiarity without commons!* The two have the same scope, the same boundaries; they are coextensive because commoning is inherently a distributed form of governance, and provisioning is not beholden to outside sources of power. The same cannot be said of traditional, hierarchical tiers of government (federal, provincial or state, and local).

If we are serious about subsidiarity, then commoners must have the legal authority and protected space to devise their own rules, consistent with the general principles of a state polity. This virtually requires that commoners first organize themselves, then federate at the meso-level (the spaces among individual commons) to support each other in building commons despite the looming presence and meddling of state power. This is how they can become a political force to defend true subsidiarity. While such an agenda will initially be seen as political because it challenges the status quo, over time the goal is to make acts of commoning utterly normal.

What about Fundamental Rights Guaranteed by the State?

To talk about rights is to look to state power as ultimately guaranteeing those rights. While the assertion of human rights, due process, and various civil rights represents an enormous advance in human history, the actual enforcement of these rights, and therefore their lived reality, remains a more problematic issue.

One reason that lawyers had to come up with a second generation of human rights (access to food, shelter, human care, and education),[57] and then a third generation (the right to a healthy environment, to participate in one's cultural heritage, and intergenerational equity),[58] was to prod states and international bodies to meet these ideals. Admirable as this is, it skirts the question of whether state bureaucracies are *structurally capable* of fulfilling these rights, not just as a matter of law in a given case, but as a society-wide reality. It is not uncommon for law to be used as a vehicle for aspirations and symbolism, in the way that the United Nations Sustainable Development Goals and the Paris climate agreement set certain targets for performance at a national level. However, given the limited ability and interest of states to transform themselves, one should not put too much faith in the effectiveness of treaties or national laws. Such enactments can be mere gestures; enforcement can be problematic; and organized industries and investors in practice are usually granted a veto.

Commoners do not generally speak about "rights" because rights depend on some external institution guaranteeing them. They imply an alien political and social order, one of isolated-I's petitioning a remote, powerful Leviathan. And yet, in assuring access to basic means of subsistence, many commons are arguably achieving much more than the high-minded goals nominally embraced by states and asserted in legal documents.[59] While fundamental rights do not truly provide everyone with access to the means of subsistence, most commons consider subsistence their core priority. At the same time, it is clear that many traditional commons in rural India or Asia do not embrace the worldview of individual rights, aspire to gender and ethnic inclusion, or even the adjudicatory authority of the modern liberal state. In short, the commons and the modern state represent an unresolved clash of worldviews and systems of governance. It is beyond our capacities here to prescribe a grand reconciliation of the different philosophical approaches. It is enough to say, for now, that the state retains the upper hand, if only because of its coercive power.

But as numerous states are discovering, there are functional legal means by which state sovereignty can be blended with the sovereignty of commons. Indeed, some states accommodate (at least in part) the demands of Indigenous peoples — the Maori, the First Nations of Canada, Native Americans. Other states recognize the power of open source communities and social networking. Still others, India or states in Africa, acknowledge the ecological and social appeal of traditional subsistence commons. Many possibilities exist; they just haven't been actively explored.

*   *   *

We now have a much clearer sense of the relationship between state power and commoning. But we also have a greater sense of the opportunities that may exist for state institutions to strengthen commons. Opportunities may arise unexpectedly through the vagaries of cultural moments when a specific initiative unexpectedly unleashes new energies among people for change.

While there can obviously be no omnibus, master strategy for gaining state support for commoning, there are some highly promising ways that commoners can build their capabilities and power and, in the process, become significant forces in the mainstream political economy. In Chapter Ten, we explore some of them.

10

Take Commoning to Scale

S INCE COMMONING IS SO ASSOCIATED WITH small-scale provisioning and governance, skeptics often wonder how a commons can possibly function at larger scales and have transformational effects. In this chapter we explore this question. The premise is that commons cannot play a significant role in addressing climate breakdown and other ecological problems, Peak Oil, poverty, inequality, and countless other problems because they are too small. Massive global problems require massive solutions, goes the thinking, which then requires nation-states to come up with something. By this logic commons have very little to offer.

This framing is precisely part of the problem, however, because it fails to consider that all kinds of solutions, big or small, may be failing precisely *because* their foundational parts are flawed. A building with an inadequate foundation for its size is destined to crumble. A society based on unfettered individual freedom should not be surprised if its citizens eventually over-exploit the Earth and destroy necessary social norms. The truth is that large systems often cannot be fixed at scale; repairing them may require revisiting and reinventing the system's smaller component parts and sub-assemblies. In addressing the pathologies of the modern market/state, that is our theory of social and political change.

To be sure, there are many worthwhile reforms that one can attempt by working within the system at scale. That is essentially the approach that social democrats and progressives pursue. They focus on creating new institutions like co-operatives, for-benefit corporations, land trusts, and public banks, or on creating new programs such as universal basic income, environmental regulation, and income-redistribution schemes. Such reforms may or may not lead to larger transformation — and that is our point. We wish to suggest how commoning can be transformational in positive, durable ways by protecting its structural and cultural integrity even as it expands its reach.

On too many occasions, progressive initiatives have been captured or co-opted by investors and corporations, among other forces, preventing them from inducing systemic change. We have seen, for example, how the Couchsurfing website, a gift economy of lodging for travelers, morphed from a hospitality commons into a commercial travel service several years ago. Its managers concluded that the website needed more funds to maintain itself, and so they accepted venture capital funding and the shifts in priorities that entailed. Similarly, we have seen how Silicon Valley has co-opted other websites dedicated to sharing and collaboration, turning them into lucrative micro-rental markets (for lodging, transport, and piecemeal labor, among other things). The state itself, working with influential industries, has often made it more difficult for commons-friendly systems to grow. This has been the experience of organic farming, open source software, and open-access scholarly publishing, for example.

The future demands that we break these patterns of co-optation and resistance. Commons need the means to grow, individually and as federations, on their own terms, and to be able to flourish even within the mainstream economy. This requires that they have a hardy internal culture and governance that can function as a fierce immune system to protect them from external invaders (figurative viruses, bacteria, and parasites). Imagine if commons had the benefits of state support in meeting this challenge — funding, technical assistance, public outreach, and policy support. Imagine if commons enjoyed full legal recognition and financial resources to support their work.

We see great promise in three distinct strategies for expanding commons as a social form in societies otherwise designed for the market/state. It is important to: 1) Develop community charters as tools for constituting commoning; 2) Build and use distributed ledger platforms that can provide remarkable new affordances for cooperation on digital networks; and 3) Design commons-public partnerships that can leverage state power for the commons. Our vision for building out the Commonsverse through these means is necessarily speculative. Many approaches are still fairly new, and so there is not an extensive track record to study and learn from. Still, we believe that commons

charters, distributed ledger technologies, and commons-public partnerships offer great potential for helping commons thrive despite their
immersion in the dominant political culture.

Charters for Commoning

One of the most powerful tools for BRINGING DIVERSITY INTO SHARED
PURPOSE and constituting a community of commoners is a charter
for commoning. Sometimes known as social charters and community
charters, these documents set forth the founding goals, practices, and
principles of their particular commons. In a way, the charter functions
as a constitution. Prepared after extensive discussions, negotiation, and
reflection, a charter articulates foundational commitments. It serves as
a touchstone for a group as it encounters novel opportunities, choices,
and setbacks. A charter is also an aspirational institutional statement
that declares how commoners wish to govern themselves and what
kind of culture they wish to create.

Charters are not meant to be fuzzy mission statements filled with
fancy rhetoric. They are fairly specific about the identity and operational
practices of the group. The WikiHouse open source design community
(see pp. 21–22) declares in its charter that its participants share design
globally and manufacture locally, use open standards and modular
design, and design for the whole life cycle of the house, including the
ability to make repairs.[1] The permaculture world has embraced a set of
twelve ethical and design principles such as "produce no waste," "use
small and slow solutions," and "use and value diversity."[2] Members of
the French stewardship organization Terre de Liens, which acquires
land to preserve for agriculture, are committed to "decommodify land
in perpetuity," "enhance the development of grassroots farming," and
"foster collaboration around land use as well as pool together tools,
funds, and experiences."[3]

"Given the uniqueness of every commons," writes James Quilligan,
"there is no universal template for social charters — but a baseline is
emerging." He argues that a social charter "should include, at minimum,
a summary of traditional or emerging claims to legitimacy; a declaration
of the rights and entitlements of users and producers; a code of ethics;
elaboration of common values and standards; a statement of benefits; a
notice of claims to reparations or re-territorialization of boundaries; and

a practical framework for cooperation." Of course, the elements in such a checklist could vary (should a code of ethics mean a statement of values or specific operational patterns?), but the point of a charter is to help peers align themselves in grappling with recurrent problems. Most charters do mention the nature of their Peer Governance as a form of democratic participation and transparent decision-making. There is often an attempt to ensure that administrative power is decentralized, which helps a community ensure its access to, and sovereignty over, its shared wealth.[4]

The Charter for Building a Data Commons, developed by a group of digital mappers of alternative economies, advises its network of participants to "reflect your ambition together," "separate commons and commerce," "design for interoperability," and "document [working processes] transparently," among other things.[5] It may be debatable whether the guiding principles for the annual Burning Man festival constitute a commons charter, but its ten principles function in much the same way. The 60,000 participants who trek to the Nevada desert every November define their ethos and culture through a commitment to "radical inclusion," acts of gift-giving, decommodification of culture, radical self-expression, and immediacy of experience as core values. The charter not only clarifies the identity of the massive pop-up community that is Burning Man, it guides the year-round work of the "Burners" network in the Bay Area.

Commoners do not generally seek to secure state recognition for their charters because, in truth, most states offer no legal means for doing so. (A nonprofit may resemble a commons in its actual functioning and ethos, but legally and organizationally it is quite different.) In any case, commoners generally do not want courts or government agencies to enforce the terms of a charter. They look to each other. The charter functions as a social compact. Its authority derives from members' explicit declaration of mutual intent and ongoing commitment to fulfill the terms of the charter. Its power derives from the breadth and depth of support that a charter commands in everyday practices. When such vernacular practices and social loyalties reach a sufficient intensity, they give rise to what James Quilligan calls "commons rights" based on natural law:

> Commons rights differ from human rights and civil rights
> because they arise, not through the legislation of a state,

but through a customary or emerging identification with an ecology, a cultural resource area, a social need, or a form of collective labor ... Social charters generate an entirely new context for collective action. Instead of seeking individual and human rights from the state, people may claim long-term authority over resources, governance, and social value as their planetary birthrights — whether at a community or global level.[6]

Commons rights may indirectly challenge state sovereignty and "the divine right of capital" (Marjorie Kelly), and thereby be seen as politically contestable. When people step up to take direct responsibility for a piece of land, a river, or urban spaces, they will ruffle the feathers of state and corporate authorities. So even though a charter is an important tool for conscious self-organization, it may prove equally useful for getting the attention of unresponsive government bodies and forcing them into a more serious political dialogue,

In this spirit, commoners embrace charters as a way to take action on problems the market/state is ignoring, as Scottish activist Isabel Carlisle notes. A number of movements — especially fights against mining and hydraulic gas fracking — are using charters as a focal point for political action. These movements include Carlisle's own Community Chartering Network in the UK, Lock the Gate in Australia, the Community Bill of Rights effort in the US, the global peasant farmers network La Via Campesina, and the Transition movement. Charter movements typically try to assert a positive, long-term vision. Carlisle writes:

> What communities lack is a way of convening around a rights-based vision of what their communities are *for* [in terms of] sustainable agricultural systems, sustainable energy systems, sustainable economies, real environmental protection, and improvement of health, safety, and welfare in the community. People on the ground are the ones best placed to understand systematically what is beneficial to their local economies and ecologies.[7]

When mining interests in Scotland moved into Falkirk and surrounding towns to extract coal bed methane (a process similar to fracking), people in the region came together in 2013 to develop the first community charter. The document states: "We declare our Cultural Heritage to be the sum total of the local tangible and intangible assets we have collectively agreed to be fundamental to the health and well-being of our present and future generations."[8] People refer to a clean environment, food security, and what they call "a healthy economy" as key priorities for their community. The Falkirk Charter helped persuade the Scottish government to declare a moratorium on drilling for unconventional gas. Other British communities — Glasgow, Edinburgh, Dartington Parish in Devon, St. Ives in Cornwall — have also developed charters as a way to host a genuine community dialogue, mobilize citizens, and set forth a vision for local self-determination.

But aren't municipal governments the more appropriate hosts for community charters? After all, isn't that the very role of government? In theory, yes. But even though municipal governments are smaller and closer to their citizens than, say, regional or national governments, they too are prone to the perils of centralized administration and politically driven behaviors. Community charters introduce an independent social energy "from the street" that can foster distributed decision-making. Initiatives can unfold on their own terms, with established grassroots engagement and leadership — i.e., as commons.

There are some interesting experiments using charters to reinvigorate municipal governance. After helping elect an activist mayor in May 2015, the organization Barcelona en Comú (Barcelona in Common) created a series of documents that set forth a new vision of municipal politics, governance, and ethics. While not formally a charter, the four documents — a code of ethics, "shock plan" (for assuring basic social rights), administrative program, and citizen participation process[9] — outline bold ambitions to "do politics differently." The documents were written to have a similar impact as community charters: to open up a new space for the "co-production of politics" among participants — in this case, between the city government and residents.

A number of large governmental bodies have developed what they call social charters. Regional blocs such as the European Union, the South Asia Association for Regional Cooperation, and ASEAN have actually developed charters on behalf of their national citizens. But these approaches tend to be problematic, as James Quilligan has noted.

National or regional charters "are typically generated by clusters of individual governments in consultation with a narrow cross-section of interest groups. Social charters generated by states often disempower those who use and manage a local commons. State-written social charters put the locus of power in government and function more as a complaint mechanism or quality control procedure than as a means of honoring the rights of people to their commons."[10] State-drafted charters also mean that the judiciary becomes the locus for resolving disputes about the commons — and thus state judges and legal experts assume greater authority than commoners.

Distributed Ledgers as a Platform for Commoning

There is a long history of hobbyists and tinkerers pioneering the development of new information technologies as amateurs. Once the potential has been demonstrated, major corporations then step in and take control of the systems to turn them into lucrative markets. Law scholar Tim Wu has called this "The Cycle."[11] Passionate visionaries attempt to usher in a grand social emancipation through a new technology — radio, television, cable TV, the web, open source software, the blogosphere, WiFi, wikis — but each time capitalists generally succeed in domesticating the technology to serve their market interests. The technology is revamped so that businesses can attract and retain an audience, monetize that audience through advertising or data mining, and then lock in the profit stream. In Wu's reckoning, business retains "exclusive custody of the master switch."[12] In our time, this has meant that a handful of corporate leviathans — Google, Facebook, YouTube, Twitter, Amazon — has used their centralized commercial platforms to manipulate the news we each see, host the spread of lies and disinformation, force-feed more advertising into the public sphere, and make us more vulnerable to identity theft.

We are now on the cusp of another turn of The Cycle, this time driven by a powerful networking software known as the blockchain. While the blockchain and Bitcoin are closely associated in the public mind, and even confused as the same thing, the blockchain is in fact just one version of what is sometimes called distributed ledger technology. Distributed ledgers are significant for the commons because they have the potential for providing a powerful software architecture to support commoning on open networks, going well beyond the limited modes of cooperation and security that are currently possible on the web. Distributed ledgers could be vehicles for enabling social emancipation.

As the first significant version of this technology, the blockchain has been hailed as a breakthrough because it has proved the feasibility of secure peer-to-peer communications on the internet. This was an epic achievement because it enabled the invention of a secure, wholly digital currency that can be exchanged on vulnerable open networks without the backing of a state or banks. In the jargon of the tech world, Bitcoin is "self-sovereign" because it autonomously verifies the integrity of any individual bitcoin used in a transaction. When someone uses a bitcoin to make a purchase, the specific bitcoin used is recorded on a single digital accounting ledger (the blockchain), which exists on thousands of computers at the same time. This peer-to-peer methodology is remarkably effective because, while it may be possible for a counterfeiter or thief to attack one bank's computer, it is impossible to attack and alter the same accounting ledger on thousands of computers. The network itself becomes a robust authentication system for any bitcoin transaction, without the need for a third-party guarantor.

One proof of the power of the blockchain is that by late 2018, ten years after the introduction of Bitcoin, the aggregate value of all bitcoins was more than $65 billion — and yet no one has succeeded in hacking the bitcoin code. (There have been hacks of commercial brokers who exchange bitcoins for dollars, euros, and other currencies, but Bitcoin itself has not been counterfeited.) Oddly enough, while Bitcoin is utterly secure as a store of value, its renown stems from its value as an object of speculation. The price of a bitcoin has gyrated wildly over the years, with investors making or losing enormous sums of money in short periods of time. Naturally, this has discouraged most people from using bitcoins as a way to actually buy or create things of value, let alone build a new community of shared purpose.

Inspired by the success of Bitcoin, software programmers have been trying throughout the 2010s to adapt digital ledger systems for a variety of other purposes, mostly commercially motivated. Some ventures are selling their own "tokens" through a so-called ICO process, or Initial Coin Offering, to finance new businesses and products. Others are trying to develop legal contracts that can be automatically implemented on digital networks — "smart contracts" — as a way to make market transactions more versatile and efficient than those using conventional money.[13] The general point of ledger systems is to use peer-to-peer networks to verify the authenticity of a unique digital object. Community members can then rely on that object as a token of value (money), an indicator of personal reputation, a recognized legal agreement among parties or a group, or a tool for voting and other decision-making.

Why are distributed ledger technologies important for commoning? Because they potentially offer a way for commoners to wrest control of the "master switch" in digital technologies away from capital, and instead empower and protect collective action. The technology creates new affordances that can, with the right design, greatly facilitate commoning in the digital age. Distributed ledgers can enable the creation of community currencies that enable people to coordinate the terms of their cooperation at scale, without the threat of enclosure. The technology does not automate or supplant the need for a group to common, but it does help people cooperate in more creative, flexible ways than are possible under conventional property law, money systems, and analogue organizational structures (nonprofits, trusts, cooperatives). Instead of making decisions through rigid hierarchies with centralized direction and relying on property rights vested in a few people, a peer-to-peer (P2P) platform can make it easier for people to cooperate and evolve the social system.

Although Bitcoin has captured a lot of attention as a drama of capitalist speculation, the more important story here is the role that distributed ledger technologies will play in the future. One of the most ambitious, potentially transformative suites of software platforms and institutions is being built around a novel set of networking protocols called Holochain. The technical details can quickly overwhelm the layperson, so we won't dwell on them, but they matter because they affect the future affordances and scalability of the platform. Unlike Bitcoin and Ethereum (the two most prominent digital ledger technologies), Holochain is far more energy efficient and flexible in the way that it authenticates digital objects on networks. Rather than relying on a single ledger — a "heavy" solution that requires the work of countless computers on the network — Holochain is a simpler, lightweight approach that lets every user have his or her own secure ledger and distributed storage system to store their personal data and digital identities. Its P2P architecture brings to mind the Federated Wiki platform described in Chapter Eight; both are based on a relational ontology, but Holochain has much greater versatility. As with Bitcoin, no one using Holochain need rely on a centralized source of authentication of data and digital identity, such as a Facebook or Google. This agent-centric approach means that users are far less vulnerable to identity theft because their data is strewn (or "sharded," in tech lingo) across multiple servers on a network, and not consolidated on a single, centralized database that represents a tempting data treasure house for hackers. The distributed architecture of data on Holochain networks prevents tech giants and third parties like Cambridge Analytica from controlling (and abusing) our data.

As importantly, the Holochain architecture of protocols aims to provide the framework for building a new generation of distributed, privacy-respecting apps and services. It is a lighter, more versatile set of software protocols than the blockchain. By preventing any company from owning your data by default, the Holochain protocols are designed to enable multiple types of service providers to arise and co-exist within the same economy. Having open source infrastructure with customizable adaptations of the Holochain is critical. On the web, a single set of proprietary protocols tends to result in a winner-take-all marketplace dominated in each sector by a handful of large companies like Amazon, Uber, and Airbnb. By contrast, Holochain protocols are part of an open data architecture, and so they can be adapted for specific purposes by different players.

A Brief Explanation of Hash and Hashchain, Blockchain, and Holochain

To encrypt data, programmers often create a *hash* (to hash = to chop), which is the value ("hash-value") created when large amounts of data are entered into a computing system and sent through a so-called "hash function" that makes the output digitally readable and greatly shortened. Data in different forms such as full-length names are to some extent chopped up and "cooked down," i.e., reduced to a short value in a uniform format. The result is a kind of digital fingerprint, an almost unambiguous identification that makes a digital object identifiable. A good hash function ensures that two different inputs reliably produce two different output values, and that no outputs can be inverted to obtain input data.

A *hashchain* is a sequential computing process that applies a cryptographic hash function to data again and again, generating one-time keys to unlock encrypted data and allow them to be validated quickly. After several passes, a kind of "digital fingerprint" for a specific entry is created.

A *blockchain* is a computing process that encrypts data by creating a series of "blocks" containing cryptographic hashes of preceding blocks, with a timestamp on all transactions between parties. A long string of blocks constitutes a record of all prior transactions and provides a very secure way to verify the identity of a digital object (such as a bitcoin). This is why blockchain technology is popular as a way to develop currencies that can be safely traded on open networks.

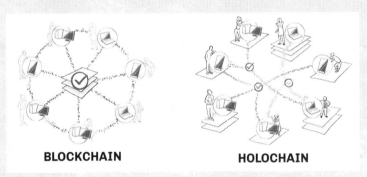

BLOCKCHAIN   **HOLOCHAIN**

Holochain is a set of network-based computing protocols that lets people create their own customized, distributed records for keeping track of value. Because there is no single ledger (as in blockchains), Holochain enables a richer diversity of systems for representing value. In this sense, Holochain is a tool based on a differentiated relational ontology (each user can express value in different, particular ways when interacting with people) while blockchain as a tool ultimately reflects an undifferentiated ontology (each user must accept the prevailing standard of the system). (See Chapter 2).

Holochain could thus be used by people to create both monetary and non-monetary currencies that embody new patterns of coordination for social organisms. Instead of privileging market valuations through prices and income, for example, Holochain could make visible reputation, skills, performance levels, or other flows of value within a community. This would enable distributed, peer-to-peer communities to build and share productive value on their own terms, including models that Relationalize Property and limit capital accumulation. Arthur Brock, one of the cofounders of the MetaCurrency Project, which has developed Holochain, explains that the real purpose of a currency should be to *make the flow of value visible*, as in a "current-see." Conventional money, as designed and used, cannot express important types of value, which Brock and his associates regard as a profound problem of the modern age. Dollars, euros, and other state currencies don't let us see the flows of value that matter most — ecological flows, the social relationships of gift economies, people's contributions to commons. It is envisioned that Holochain-based currencies will be used by communities to make visible the community-minded acts that build a reputation, for example, and to create mutual credit monetary systems, without simply establishing new forms of speculative, profit-seeking trade. The capital accumulation and Governing-through-Money that is routine in the capitalist economy could be re-engineered to set community limits on private accumulation and assure basic fairness in economic exchange. Holochain-based currencies are more equipped to actualize commons-friendly types of systems because they are based on a principle of mutual sovereignty — shared control by both the individual and the communities to which they belong. This means that very idea of the Nested-I and Ubuntu Rationality, interdependence, and mutual accountability are built into the system.

For more than ten years, Brock and the Holochain development team have been imagining and building out the open-ended Holochain protocols as an infrastructure upon which an alternative, autonomous social economy and currencies might be built. This is obviously a formidable, complicated, and uncertain proposition, since Holochain is not intended as a business model but as a vehicle for enabling social transformation. Still, the Holochain visionaries have persuaded an impressive number of tech developers, investors, and others to build not only Holochain applications, but a suite of initiatives — that is, a group of different players using the same software protocols to interact.

A 2019 release of the Holochain code aimed to demonstrate the feasibility of agent-centric control of data and identity, which means that individuals would directly manage the security and authenticity of their personal data without any need for third-party intermediaries. Holochain coders also aim to let app developers create their own distributed sets of protocols, and not rely on a single set of protocols controlled centrally by a given tech company. This means that P2P communities can control their own apps and data without needing to rely on data-sucking corporate giants like Google, Apple, and Facebook.

A key vehicle for launching the Holochain system is a business called Holo, a distributed hosting cooperative that will oversee the first large-scale use of the Holochain. The goal of Holo is to enable anyone with a computer to "rent out" their unused computing capacity using Holochain-based software, and in return, receive Holo Fuel currency. Holo Fuel, in turn, will allow people to make exchanges with others within the network and kick-start a new parallel economy of services based exclusively on the currency. (People can also buy special Holo Ports that make it easier to rent out computing hosting capacity to users — in other words, a device expressly designed to earn Holo Fuel for a person.)

Unlike many currencies, Holo Fuel is backed by a productive asset, the computing/hosting power of participating computers. One's acquisition of Holo Fuel is linked to the amount of engagement one has with the community, so it functions as a "proof of service" token — a confirmation that one has contributed a certain unit of computing power to the network. Technically, Holo Fuel is a mutual credit system[14] in which debtors and creditors are essentially the same people, albeit within a large, multilateral system. Although Holo Fuel could in principle be exchanged for dollars, euros, and other conventional currencies — potentially making it an object of speculation, as is Bitcoin — a mutual credit currency backed by an asset (computing power contributed to the community) is more likely to be treated as a stable token of value over time, and therefore actually used for exchange and a store of value.

The Holochain team hopes that similar mutual credit currencies will be created based on the productive capacities of growing food (such as CSA farms), providing transport (ride-sharing among peers), generating energy (solar), or eldercare services. As more enterprises come to use Holo Fuel and back its value with actual assets and services, a commons-based economy will emerge. To help this process along, the Holochain group is developing a Commons Engine that aims to contribute to the rise of a commons-based culture from which thriving economies can emerge. The goal is to help communities and organizations develop Holochain-based apps ("hApps"), design currencies, undertake open source and cryptoeconomics projects, and advance the social norms of commoning. The Commons Engine has a special focus on projects involving water, energy, food, land, knowledge, and community building.

In this process, it is envisioned that Holochain will be used to build decentralized applications for diverse types of cooperation — "governance, collaboration, organizational tools, social networks, social media, vendor relationship management, platform cooperatives, sharing economy apps, supply chain solutions, community resource management, as well as tokenless mutual-credit cryptocurrencies and reputation systems."[15] All of the elements of this alternative economy would rely on shared currencies and function in synergistic ways, while remaining independent of conventional banks and investors. As this quick tour of the envisioned Holochain universe suggests, a distributed ledger system along these lines would have far more versatile applications than the blockchain on Bitcoin or Ethereum.

For Eric Harris-Braun, executive engineer of Holochain, the ultimate purpose of Holo Fuel and other Holochain-based currencies is to help people "actually see and represent all different types of value inside of a commons framework, and to have a stable language to develop that value, at scale." In other words, the Holochain protocols would function as a grammar for the system, or language for building apps that name flows of value within a community, such as social contributions, reputation, work performed, care work, even community sentiment. Harris-Braun claims that Holo Fuel will not simply be a substitute form of money that will end up replicating capitalism, but will instead propagate a "different grammatics of value." Just as a different grammatical structure in a human language helps us to articulate different ideas and realities, the Holochain grammar is intended as a tool to express social forms of value — flows — that market prices are incapable of representing. Instead of market-exchange being the dominant form of value, it is envisioned that Holochain-based apps will enable other forms of value to be expressed and circulated within networked communities — in other words, not just the money values represented by prices. Instead of seeing the isolated individual as the only source of agency and value, Holochain makes the OntoShift and in effect embraces the "Nested-I." Harris-Braun told us:

Our model is built on "mutual sovereignty" in which the mutuality is between the individual and collective. Neither is put aside from the other. The actor or agent can say whatever he wants, but the collective [using the Holochain "grammar"] checks to see what is sent, or sees that the "move in the game" matches the collective rules. So there are all these linkages between the individual to the collective, and from the collective to the individual, to assure the social coherence of the group.

> In the real world in which we live, everything is actually "agent-centric" in that reality is always informed by perspective. What we do is create a shared reality by taking on a shared grammar with which to interpret reality — and then we check each other and hold each other to account in light of that shared grammar. That's what Holochain is designed to do.

By recognizing the mutual sovereignty of agents within a system, Holochain aspires to enact a "living systems of wealth" model that is committed to "the integrity of flows." "As a society, we have a pretty good understanding of objects and how to manipulate them, but we're not as good with flows," says MetaCurrency project founder Arthur Brock.[16] Holochain is about using different "patterns, principles, and protocols for how we use currencies (think 'current-sees') to share, measure, and enable all kinds of currents." Key ideas in this vision are "distributed, equitable, and regenerative." Harris-Braun told us, "I'm not at all interested in the monetization of value! For me, I am building toward a post-monetary world. I'm very interested in the formalization of embodied systems that allow us to 'see value.' But that is not the same thing as monetization."[17] The goal is to try to use alternative "current-sees" to avoid the pathologies of extractivism, private accumulation, and the disruption of ecosystems.

This commitment to seeing value in new ways is apparent in Holo's self-capitalization strategy. The business was initially financed through an Initial Community Offering that gave investors Holo Fuel in exchange for their dollars, with all returns on investment also made in Holo Fuel. The idea behind this is for the value of the investment returns to grow in tandem with the value of the Holo web-hosting network and the larger Holo ecosystem. "It's all about growing this pattern of self-replication of productive capacity into a commons," said Harris-Braun — meaning, the community will invest in its own infrastructure and economy, and recirculate the value it creates. It is an intoxicating vision, the idea of self-capitalization and development of commons, at scale, without the extractive imperatives of the conventional market/state system! But there is persuasive evidence — working code, strong early investment, app developer interest in Holochain, and potential participants in the Holo Fuel economy such as CSA farmers and cooperatives — that this vision will be able to grow without being compromised by the usual capitalist pressures.

Of course, in the end, any number of problems could intervene to derail Holochain's progress. It may or may not unfold as its tech sponsors hope. That is partly because Holochain technology can also be used to serve the ever-evolving purposes of corporate capitalism and its thirst for ever-more private control and profit, as Fernanda Ibarra, co-director of the Commons Engine at Holo has noted.[18] The invention of the printing press enabled the Bible and great literature to be widely distributed, but it also made possible tabloid journalism and propaganda. What matters about distributed ledger technology is the new and different affordances that it enables. It's an open question who will be first and most influential in leveraging those affordances.

But one thing is certain: the world is inexorably moving to distributed ledger systems because they are likely to overcome the many problems associated with centralized corporate data systems — the lack of user freedom, serious privacy violations, security risks, and the withering of creativity because people do not have individual or collective agency. So it is imperative that commoners develop this tech architecture to facilitate *their* goals — the creation of protectable commons — and to limit the ability of capital to marginalize commoning on these systems, as capital so brilliantly did in commandeering open source software, the web, and social networking to serve corporate purposes.

Holochain is an attempt to secure an important beachhead for commoners, even if it will also be used, inevitably, for less elevated purposes. The appeal of ledger technologies, whether Holochain or others still in the works, is their potential to create durable new affordances for commoning.

Commons-Public Partnerships

Given the state's close alliance with the corporate sector, it should not be surprising that the two often enter into so-called public-private partnerships, or PPPs. These are often good-faith attempts to address pressing social problems through contract-based collaborations between businesses and government. PPPs are typically vehicles for developing infrastructure for water supply or sewage management, or building roads, bridges, schools, hospitals, prisons, or public facilities such as swimming pools and playing fields. Through a separate legal entity (which can take different legal forms), state agencies and businesses negotiate the terms for financing, construction, and/or management of a project over a specific period of time.

Public-private partnerships are typically portrayed as win-win scenarios that address social needs, strengthen the economy, and reduce state expenditures in one fell swoop. Businesses supposedly provide public services at lower costs than the state because of more flexible work rules and efficiencies, and therefore the state is presumed to save money. However, this scenario often does not play out in practice because PPPs are based on fundamentally incompatible objectives — the state's obligation to protect the public good and private businesses' desire to maximize profits. In practice, many public-private collaborations function less as partnerships than as disguised giveaways.

In effect, a PPP can let a company acquire equity ownership of public infrastructure such as roads, bridges, and public facilities for a long period — fifteen, thirty, even ninety-nine years — and then manage them as a private market asset. In Chicago, for example, the city government actually sold the management of its thousands of parking meters to a private company, resulting in higher parking fees, worse service, and public outrage. In many PPPs, the government reaps a big one-time payment, which makes politicians look good for keeping a lid on government spending and avoiding public debt. But the hidden, long-term costs make many PPPs a bad deal. Businesses usually raise fees or charge for what was previously financed more efficiently through taxes. They cut corners on public safety and quality, and reduce upkeep and maintenance.[19] The state and the corporate sector both pretend that PPPs are a healthy, wholesome arrangement that benefits everyone and solves the lack of public funds. In truth, a great many PPPs amount to a marketization of the public sector that extracts more money from citizens, surrenders taxpayer assets to businesses, and neutralizes public accountability and control.

PPPs are not the only feasible way to build infrastructure and manage projects, however. But before we can consider alternatives and outline a different vision, some different questions must be asked, such as *who* needs what services and infrastructures in the first place? And for *what purpose*? Are new infrastructures needed to boost economic growth and transport-intensive international trade, whose benefits chiefly accrue to the investor class? Are the partnerships a way for companies to minimize risk and maximize revenue without competition? Consideration of any partnership must always ask: What is really needed on the ground? What really ensures quality service and quality of life without a loss of control to investors and volatile global markets? Couldn't we build a commons-friendly infrastructure that escapes the traps of economic growth, footloose international capital, and centralized administration?

The answer is yes! It is entirely possible to meet essential needs through a constellation of localized, distributed commons-public partnerships. Consider the way that firefighting is organized in Germany, where a remarkable ninety-seven percent of all firefighters are volunteers, not professionals. Nearly one million ordinary people — teachers, farmers, shopkeepers, craftsmen, drivers (mostly men) — are ready to step up if the need arises to join with other community members to fight fires. All over Germany there are only 107 *Berufsfeuerwehren* — professional firefighting brigades — exclusively in mid-size and large cities. Everywhere else, in Germany as well as Austria and Poland, volunteer brigades are the norm. Even in the bastion of global market culture, the United States, an impressive sixty-seven percent of the country's 1.1 million firefighters, or about 815,000, are volunteers.

Firefighting is, of course, part of the basic obligation of the state to protect public safety. But unlike in so many other areas of public need, the German state does not hire state employees or contract with businesses to fight fires. It has organized systems to enlist citizens to do the work themselves. Thus, the term "voluntary" is a bit misleading because it is not completely voluntary that people come together as fire brigades. It is a federal legal obligation for each community to organize them. If this is not successful on a voluntary basis, the municipal government can recruit citizens on a mandatory basis, much as US courts mandate participation on a jury. The whole system is structured to support citizens in taking responsibility to organize themselves. State authority is ingeniously blended with peer mobilization and management. "Every community or municipality is obliged to provide, maintain, and finance a fire department that meets the needs of the local situation," as the Law of Fire Fighting in the State of Baden Württemberg states. The state provides firefighting equipment, fire-extinguishing foam, training, communication infrastructure, education, work space, insurance for firefighters, and financial support, among other things — but the community members themselves manage the fire department.

One might call this a "public-civic" contract or partnership. The state creates a legal and administrative framework to bring into being a vast corps of volunteer firefighters. Besides supplying resources, the state makes volunteering possible by prohibiting employers from cutting an employee's paycheck while doing fire department work. Once assembled, fire departments self-organize to teach firefighting and medical skills, assign job tasks, and in other ways serve as an effective emergency team.

Let's note that this is not really a partnership with a commons, but a limited delegation of state power and responsibility to citizens that they cannot reject. In a limited sense, this kind of volunteering for firefighting *resembles* a commons. But volunteering is different from commoning. While both involve individuals choosing to participate, volunteers work under terms set by a sponsoring organization whereas commoners initiate and manage a project themselves, on their own terms. What we call "volunteering" usually occurs after work and often has a charitable character, whereas commoners generally choose to do something for its own sake or to meet needs outside of the market in a process that they control.

If you take the success of volunteer fire departments as an inspiration, you can imagine possibilities for meeting needs if the state's structural support and delegation of authority were made broader and less conditional. If, in addition, you let commoners actually instigate, manage, and steer the project, then you would have a *commons-public* partnership. Sounds utopian? This is what we could have said 150 years ago about the modern organization of firefighting.

When founded in Berlin in 1851, the German fire department was comprised of professionals. But by the 1920s, the tradition of volunteer brigades had taken root. A century later, there are more than 22,000 volunteer fire departments in Germany. Collectively they provide fire protection for virtually the entire country. In 2017 — and this is more than remarkable — there were only four instances in all of Germany in which enough volunteers could not be recruited. In such cases, the county government mandates the formation of "compulsory fire departments."

While the modern mind tends to see "mandatory" and "voluntary" as binary opposites, these polarities become blurry as soon as a concern is connected with intrinsic motivations and existential questions, as in this case. The state may require local communities to have fire departments, but at the same time local communities have significant autonomy to organize themselves. Actually, citizens freely volunteer; they usually don't feel pressured to join. When people experience freedom-in-connectedness, "free choice" versus "required" is an inappropriate framing of the situation. Responsible parents don't think about "choosing" to take care of their children or not; it is both a pleasure and a responsibility. Similarly, able-bodied community members don't regard "volunteering" as an imposition. It is just what needs to be done. Participants often take pride in doing what is important for the well-being of the community — and explicit acknowledgement is always welcome. People generally enjoy belonging to the fire department just as commoners enjoy the sense of belonging that comes from commoning. They RITUALIZE TOGETHERNESS through dinners and show off their firefighting equipment at open houses for the community. Volunteer fire departments are such a community tradition in

Germany that some 250,000 young people belong to youth fire brigades that supplement the fire departments' work and serve as a source of new participants.

It is precisely this multifunctionality stemming from its self-organized character that makes volunteer firefighting so effective and pleasurable. Market-based approaches cannot elicit such commitment and provide such satisfaction. Another advantage is that the tasks are not formally defined by rigid, enforceable job descriptions. Duties can be therefore more flexible and adapted to circumstances. While professionals generally bring skills and experience that volunteers don't have, hiring professionals for the entire country would be unthinkable. It would cost about 24 billion euro per year if everyone were paid the starting wage of a soldier in the German army. Even at minimal wages, a professional force would be very costly because full-time firefighters spend a lot of time just waiting for fires to happen. They are paid for their readiness, and their skills can be overly specialized (and thus more expensive) relative to the many basic tasks that must be done.

What interests us here is the potential of public-commons partnerships as an important alternative to public-private partnerships. A public-commons partnership is not about *commanding* people to do *x* or *y*. It is about *creating conditions* so that people *want* to contribute their personal energies and talents. This is critical in enabling commons at scale. Governments can achieve this only by aligning collective needs, the common good, and individual interests in addressing on-the-ground realities. The key is not offering the "right incentives" or salaries. It is about giving people real authority to manage their own operations — and supporting them with the right infrastructure, equipment, and funds. People are willing to participate so generously as volunteer firefighters because they are given the freedom to organize themselves and proper tools to meet an important community challenge.

A more conventional policy approach is to treat public services as line items in a government budget and the service providers as employees. This mindset misses the point. It fails to recognize that a volunteer fire department can elicit many energies and talents precisely *because* there is no formal employer-employee relationship here. To rely on the power of self-organization to fight fires not only serves an essential public need, it produces a special sort of social glue among people.

Firefighters, relatives, friends, rescued fire victims, and community members are brought together by the process. To be sure, volunteer firefighters endure some serious hardships — mobilizing at any hour of the day or night; clearing fallen trees from roads after storms; dealing with medical emergencies. But these sacrifices are tolerable and even satisfying amidst the camaraderie of doing important work. It is even a point of pride as the news media and fellow citizens express their gratitude.

To be clear, this volunteer firefighting is not entirely a matter of commoning. The state remains the senior partner facilitating participation and supplying resources. But on the other hand, neither is this a classic case of "citizen participation" in a government process, either. The state is not asking citizens to show up to join *its* process and render its outcomes legitimate. The state has delegated significant authority and committed resources — with few strings attached — to empower citizens to fight fires and manage themselves, as commoners.

The success of volunteer fire departments suggests the great potential of commons-public partnerships driven by the needs of people, not business interests. A *commons-public partnership* (CPP) is an agreement of long-term cooperation between commoners and state institutions around specific functions. It is about providing stable, secure ways for people to work together, often locally, to provide services to each other and to the broader public through commoning. A CPP is also about creating the infrastructures, spaces, and conditions for self-organization to occur. With modest support, people can be empowered to make their own decisions and customize solutions for their own needs and circumstances. For example, Guifi.net, the commons-based regional Wi-Fi network, does not need — nor want — to cater to outside investors or maximize returns at the expense of its users. As a commons, it can stay focused on long-term stability and service rather than get lost in the financial gamesmanship (mergers and acquisitions, creative financial instruments, etc.) that investors often favor. For these reasons, CPPs should be immensely appealing to regional and local governments: commoners are far more likely to "stand and deliver" than fickle investors whose loyalties are shallowly focused on the highest investment returns, not necessarily regional well-being.

In other words, a CPP pivots away from the approach of PPPs, which tend to shovel money, financing, subsidies, and legal privileges at businesses and markets. It can be designed instead to cultivate creative state collaborations with commoners in providing essential services and building open, nondiscriminatory infrastructure. CPP solutions tend to be less expensive than PPPs because they are not profit-driven and therefore can have a more flexible institutional logic and distributed social participation. A CPP can avoid the immense costs and complexities of administering a centralized system because it can leverage bottom-up contributions and creativity, open source-style. There are all sorts of self-organized peer communities that are currently meeting urgent human needs for a fraction of the cost of conventional bureaucratic "service delivery" systems, and they do this work with great human care and attention. What if governments were to provide basic infrastructure and support to the community-based insurance system Artabana, for example, whose small groups generate pools of money to self-insure each others' social and medical well-being? What if there were minimal infrastructure support for peer-governed networks such as Vipassana, whose work provides a vehicle for self-healing for thousands of people in highly effective ways — based on FREELY CONTRIBUTED, decommodified work? It would not only lower the costs for healthcare, it would, at the same time, co-create communities and a sense of belonging.

A key threshold challenge for any commons-public partnership is getting the state to recognize a group of commoners as a legitimate partner. State bureaucracies are accustomed to dealing with conventional legal entities — corporations, nonprofits, universities — that have presidents and hierarchical governance structures. A group of commoners may be seen as too unstable and loosely organized to be a worthy partner. But as we have seen with the Buurtzorg homecare organization, which provides peer-organized nursing care on a neighborhood scale (pp. 20–21), it is entirely possible for governments to enter into binding agreements with self-organized groups of commoners. Another innovative CPP is the Bologna Regulation for the Care and Regeneration of Urban Commons, which established a system whereby the city bureaucracy provides legal, financial, and technical support of specific projects initiated by commoners. This innovation has been further developed by the Co-City Protocols, a methodology developed by the Italian think tank LabGov for guiding co-governance initiatives.[20] The protocols are based on five design principles: "collective governance, enabling state, pooling economies, experimentalism, and technological justice."

Organizational development expert Fréderic Laloux has argued that every new stage in human consciousness has been accompanied by breakthroughs in our ability to collaborate, which is reflected in new organizational forms. As human economies moved from horticulture to agriculture to industrialization, for example — and as tribes became kingdoms and nation-states — different worldviews gave rise to novel, unexpected organizational paradigms. In his book *Reinventing Organizations*, Laloux sees the stage of human consciousness now emerging — and therefore the new breed of organization — as based on the search for wholeness and "self-management for evolutionary purpose."[21] This means that, unlike fixed, hierarchical forms of the past, organizations in the future will function as living entities driven by distributed leadership and "inner rightness and purpose as a primary motivator and yardstick." Based on his color-coding of stages of consciousness in organizations over time, Laloux calls the emerging stage of organizations "Teal."

There are striking parallels between Teal organizations and commons-based ones. Teal organizations are characterized by self-management that "operates effectively, even at a large scale, with a system based on peer relationships, without the need for either hierarchy or consensus." Such organizations strive for "wholeness" through "practices that invite us to reclaim our inner wholeness and bring all of who we are to work, instead of with a narrow 'professional' self." Teal organizations also have "a life and sense of direction of their own. Instead of trying to predict and control the future, members of the organization are invited to listen in and understand what the organization wants to become, what purpose it wants to serve." Teal self-management practices include such things as fluid and granular work roles for people, ad hoc coordination and meetings as needs arise, transparent real-time information-sharing, radically simplified project management with minimum plans and budgets, and formal, multi-step conflict resolution processes. Organizations that embody Teal principles include the Buurtzorg neighborhood nursing enterprise, Patagonia sportswear, Sounds True media, and the Heiligenfeld mental health hospitals in Germany.

Many lessons of Teal organizations lie at the heart of commons-state partnerships. The only real problem seems to be that CPPs are not a familiar archetype with known protocols. If state agencies were to open their imaginations, they could realize that the internal governance and social life of commons are not liabilities, but a potential source of creative, bottom-up energy. To learn more, the City of Ghent, Belgium, commissioned an intensive study in 2017 of scores of commons-based projects within its borders. It wanted to learn how it might augment the work of a neighborhood-managed church building, a renewable energy co-op, and a temporary urban commons lab that provides space to many different community projects.[22]

In developing a CPP, it is not enough for the state to explicitly authorize a commons; state bureaucracies must have a genuine commitment to the power of commoning. The Indian government made a bold attempt to assist village forest commons when it enacted the Forest Rights Act in 2006. The law explicitly restored the autonomy of forest dwellers to govern their community forests in traditional ways, with decentralized, democratic participation.[23] Implementation of this policy shift has been complicated, but in general it has strengthened livelihoods, regional food security, and ecological stewardship. Unfortunately, the entrenched bureaucracy has often resisted the law and not truly helped tribal communities.

Even though CPPs seem especially appropriate for the municipal/local level, their use need not be confined to small-scale or local endeavors. They can be achieved at the global level by states interacting with commons federations or coordinating bodies. A good example is the Drugs for Neglected Diseases Initiative (DNDi), a nonprofit organization that works in cooperation with various states, research institutes, and donors to overcome the broken drug development system.[24] Technically, DNDi is a commons-public-private partnership (CPPP) because it works closely with a variety of players — governments, private research enterprises, communities affected by diseases, and all types of donors. The partnership works because it BRINGS DIVERSITY INTO SHARED PURPOSE and guarantees everyone's involvement throughout all stages of the research and development (R&D) process. This "shared purpose" consists in banning commercial interests from controlling the drug research and production process, and aligning research priorities with human need.

This is vital for treating diseases that afflict the poor; tropical diseases, for example, mainly afflict people with low purchasing power. Large multinational drugmakers consider the potential "consumer demand" too weak to justify significant research investments into sleeping sickness; mycetoma (a disfiguring disease that results in deformities and amputations); leishmaniasis (a parasitic disease of the tropics); malaria (a mosquito-borne infectious disease); and pediatric HIV.

Focusing drug R&D on human need is not just important in tackling common diseases in the Global South, however. DNDi-style research about cancer, heart diseases, and diabetes can get us beyond Big Pharma's tendency to conduct intensive research into superficial variations of existing drugs rather than riskier, more medically significant basic research. DNDi points out that between 2000 and 2011, there were 850 new therapeutic products approved worldwide, but only four percent targeted neglected diseases, and only one percent were "new chemical entities" (NCEs) offering novel treatment possibilities.[25] DNDi aims to overcome these problems by sponsoring drug research and development that the drug industry has declined to pursue.

Based in Geneva, Switzerland, and with nine offices around the world, DNDi forges creative partnerships with governments, research institutes, health organizations, and the pharmaceutical industry to raise funds, conduct medical research, and administer clinical trials of new drugs. In 2015, DNDi delivered six new treatments and raised 350 million euro. By 2023, it hopes to develop sixteen to eighteen treatments on its total budget of 650 million euro.[26] This R&D work with over 160 partners worldwide means that an HIV positive mother in South Africa, a young woman with Chagas disease in Bolivia, and a working man with malaria can get affordable treatment. DNDi can save one life for $1, as the title of a film about DNDi puts it,[27] because no single company or research body is allowed to own any drug developed through DNDi. This means that drugs can be produced at minimal cost in locations where the diseases are prevalent, which in turn makes it easier to reach more people with the drugs they need.

As a CPPP, DNDi helps states avoid spending money on wasteful subsidies and "incentives" to induce businesses to produce what is needed. Instead, by sharing risks and infrastructure development, commons-public partnerships can radically reduce overall costs while meeting needs that markets would otherwise ignore. For example, based on a recommendation by the World Health Organization, and working with many partners, DNDi developed an affordable, fixed-dose drug that simplifies the treatment of malaria. It worked with the drugmaker Sanofi to put two active ingredients, artesunate and amodiaquine, into a single pill known as ASAQ. Then, working with Doctors Without Borders and others, DNDi oversaw pharmacological and clinical development of ASAQ in Europe, Africa, and Asia, and tested its effectiveness and tolerability in children. By 2010, the World Health Organization approved ASAQ, opening the door for production and distribution. The development and implementation costs over eight years were a relatively small twelve million euros. Distribution costs were greatly reduced because ASAQ cannot be patented. A single treatment is available at the cost of production, or less than US$1 for an adult, and less than US50¢ per child. In its first four years of availability, some 500 million treatments of ASAQ were administered to more than 250 million people in over thirty African countries.[28]

DNDi is able to achieve such radical efficiencies by assuring that the drugs it develops and licenses will be perpetually royalty free and non-exclusive. (Drugs are available to many producers, with the option of sublicensing rights for specific areas where a disease is prevalent.) Worldwide research and manufacturing rights are guaranteed. These provisions help make technology transfer and production less expensive. Instead of relying on just one factory, there can be multiple sources of production, which can help make drugs more accessible in regions where they are needed. Partners commit to making the final product available at cost, plus a minimal margin, in all endemic countries regardless of their income levels.

Reaping the benefits of a CPP (or CPPP) requires a structural rethinking of the policy process and administrative mindset. It first requires an understanding of the values and dynamics of commoning, and an appreciation for the potential of federating diverse cooperating partners. In real life, people's needs are local and specific; a national apparatus that seeks to impose a standard delivery mechanism in every locality will inevitably be cumbersome, inefficient, and rigid. A CPP can meet needs in more human-scale, localized, and distributed ways, with respect for the generativity of a commons. A CPP addresses elemental needs over institutional or power imperatives. It respects the need to organically grow a commons over time, and to rely on distributed infrastructures that invite multiple uses. Adaptation is easier because production and assembly revolve around modular elements. The proper role of the state in supporting CPPs, then, is to help bring together potential partners and federate CPPs, accelerating co-learning and translocal collaboration.

This obviously poses new challenges for state institutions. Bureaucracies are accustomed to directing other people's activities, not deferring to them. While it may be difficult for state institutions to accept the value of commoning, this recognition will have benefits: State bodies will earn greater trust from the populace. They will be able to address needs through money-lite commoning. And they will be able to mobilize creative energies, citizen commitment, and the use of situated and embedded knowledge that would otherwise remain dormant.

Commoning at Scale

Taking the practices of commoning to scale is a new frontier, but not an impossible goal. There are many real-life examples of commons, of course, but no standard template for developing them at large scales. A standard template cannot exist because each commons must be organically connected to its specific context. Passing a new law or implementing a new regulation might be helpful, but it will not be enough to "scale the commons." Policy solutions have very limited impact if they do not engage with real people and support their intrinsic motivations and self-determined initiatives. In short, policy cannot be divorced from commoning itself.

What is most needed, therefore, is a bold rethinking of the design and structures of policymaking itself and the premises of majority-rule politics. As currently structured, party politics is a competitive scramble to win 51 percent of the votes as the condition for wielding power. This means that the majority can largely ignore or minimize the concerns of the minority until the next election, effectively disenfranchising the minority of 49 percent. Commoning is an attempt to assert a different ethos for politics in which ideological posturing and political power plays are replaced by dialogue and negotiation about practical solutions. More to the point, commoners seek to develop new institutional forms that can honor and support the practices of commoning — a shift that over time can create a new framework for politics. The goal must be to reorient political activity so that it can nourish new types of institutions and intercommoning. Organic structures integrating the micro, meso, and macro (rather than having them collide with each other) can be built, based on the ideas outlined in Part I. This idea is illustrated by our image of the OntoSeed (p. 50), which attempts to show how our understanding of being itself affects how we imagine and build the world. This insight lies at the heart of the debate. From a core ethos and sensibility, a commons ethic branches and sends out shoots that grow outward in unpredictable, adaptive ways. The living process of commoning brings its operational and ethical logic to every level that it reaches.

We have come to the conclusion, after much research in this area, that there is really very little that cannot be reimagined, redesigned, and rebuilt from a commons perspective. So many of the commons that we have encountered in this book were, at first encounter, absolute surprises! A commons for neighborhood nursing? Buurtzorg. For regional fresh produce? Cecosesola, Park Slope Food Coop, CSAs. For housing? Mietshäuser Syndikat. For the intergenerational protection of farmland? Terre de Liens. For new house construction? WikiHouse. For machines? Open Source Ecology and Atelier Paysan. For textbooks and teaching materials? Open Educational Resources. For project financing? Goteo. A commons-friendly alternative to the blockchain? Holochain. And so on.

How have all these commons been realized? By people taking seriously the idea that their collaborations must be free, fair, and alive. Rather than clinging to ideology or mechanical blueprints for what supposedly must be done, they were brave enough to plunge into the messy realities of a situation and take the views of everyone into account. Rather than blindly adopting centralized systems of power and organization, or getting hooked on self-deluding notions of "rationality" and efficiency, the organizers of a commons have been able to see that everyone could potentially contribute to a solution, and help sustain it over time. They *enacted* a culture of commoning. Words and intentions are not enough.

We have tried to distill the core dimensions of commoning in our Triad of social life, peer governance, and provisioning — the universe of patterns through which the commons culture is built and made alive, even at large scales. While law, tech protocols, infrastructure, and other structures can play valuable roles in guiding the energies of commoning, ultimately it is our imagination and commoning itself that drive everything. This is precisely why, if you think like a commoner, it will be hard to align yourself wholeheartedly with a political party, especially in a context in which politics itself is conceived as a competition. In this kind of politics, parties are too deeply committed to their own programmatic and ideological principles (selectively applied and abandoned, of course!) to embrace the commons. Politicians and parties in today's world are generally more oriented to political power itself and to the concerns of the professional political class, than to those of us who question the capacity of representative, majority-rule democracy to bring about transformational change.

After reading this volume, you may still regard commoning as unlikely to achieve our grandest ambitions for change. Maybe you still think commons are too small, too disaggregated, too unorthodox, or too marginal to make a difference. Or maybe you think a commons asks too much of us to truly work, or takes too much time for results to emerge. But the insurgent power of the commons — the desire for a world that is free, fair, and alive — is no quixotic dream, as the preceding pages have shown. This power is quite real. Its achievements are substantial. It's just that the political mainstream and general culture have other priorities for now, as they cling to their imploding fantasies. Making the jump to the Commonsverse requires that we learn to see the world through new lenses and describe this reality with new terms. This is how we begin to enter into commoning, this is how we build an Ubuntu culture. The journey ahead may mean leaving our familiar political homes. But it also means joining a movement to build a new world, and worldview, that can actually work for centuries to come.

Acknowledgments

N O BOOK IS A SOLITARY ACHIEVEMENT because it can only grow from within a rich network of friends and colleagues, benefactors, critics, advisors, test readers, research sources, and indulgent family members. In a sense, a virtual commons must arise. That's what enabled the research, reflection, debate, writing, and revision that produced this book. One of the joys of finishing a book is saluting the many people who were indispensable in making it happen.

The Heinrich Böll Stiftung (hbs) is clearly our closest, most enduring partner. The earliest commitment to exploring the commons came from Barbara Unmussig, president of hbs, and Heike Löschmann, then head of the Department of International Politics, in 2009. Both of them have been steadfast champions of the commons and our work. Since this book got underway in 2016, we have been blessed by the intense care and support of Joanna Barelkowska at hbs, who kept everything on track, including our spirits, and by Jörg Haas, the incoming head of the Department of International Politics, who has been a strong champion of this book.

David Bollier is grateful to Peter Buffett and Jennifer Buffett, co-presidents of the NoVo Foundation, for their stalwart support of work on the commons, including this book. He also wishes to thank Susan Witt, Director of the Schumacher Center for a New Economics, for her collegiality, advice, and enthusiastic commitment to reinventing the commons. Once again, David wishes to thank Norman Lear for his steadfast, inspirational role over many years in supporting his research and activism on the commons.

Silke Helfrich is deeply grateful to colleagues at the Institute of Advanced Studies on Sustainability (IASS) in Potsdam, for providing a caring, co-creative environment for several weeks in 2018. She especially wishes to thank the AMA team (A Mindset for the Anthropocene), Jessica Böhme, Man Fang, Carolin Fraude, Zachary Walsh, and Thomas

Bruhn, who opened up a space to discuss how the commons might be at the center of creating a better mindset for the Anthropocene, and suggested improvements in the German version of the manuscript.

Because so much of our thinking about the commons strikes off in new directions, we have relied upon the insights and wisdom of a diverse array of test readers — practitioners, academics, activists, and others with a deep familiarity with various dimensions of commoning. Three especially dedicated, conscientious readers — Joanna Barelkowska, Julia Petzold, and Wolfgang Sachs — read most of the manuscript in advance, rooting out errors and gently urging us to reconsider this thought and that wording. In similar ways, we also benefited from thoughtful comments by Saki Bailey, Adelheid Biesecker, Bruce Caron, Jonathan Dawson, Gustavo Esteva Figueroa, Sheila Foster, Claudia Gómez-Portugal M., Samar Hassan, Bob Jessop, Alexandros Kioupkiolis, Kris Krois, Miguel Martinez, Silvia Maria Díaz Molina, Janelle Orsi, Jorge Rath, David Rozas, Neera Singh, Johann Steudle, Orsan Senalp, Simon Sutterlütti, John Thackara, Stacco Troncoso, Carlos Uriona, Ann Marie Utratel, and Andreas Weber.

Because so much of the commons remains underexplored in the academic literature, we often turned to people with personal experience in one or another specific topic, context, or commons. We are grateful to Laura Valentukeviciute and Katrin Kusche for sharing their knowledge on public-private partnerships and helping to imagine alternatives. Paula Segal's personal tour of the Park Slope Food Coop, including its General Assembly, helped us understand that venture with greater insight. Dina Hestad shared with us many hard-won nuggets of wisdom about transformational movements. We also learned a great deal about the messy realities and the solutions commoners come up with when interviewing Rainer Kippe on the SSM organization in Cologne; Peter Kolbe on Klimaschutz+; Amanda Huron, Sara Mewes, Johannes Euler, and Jochen Schmidt on housing commons; Siri and Oscar Kjellberg on Baskemölla Ekoby; Natalia-Rozalia Avlona on the Sarantoporo Community Network; Bettina Weber and Tom Hansing on Offene Werkstätten (Open Workshops); and Izabela Glowinska and Paul Adrian Schulz on Vivihouse.

On many occasions, our self-education about the commons was greatly advanced simply by being in the presence of active communities of practice. Ward Cunningham, Jon Richter, and the Federated Wiki community opened our eyes to the enormous possibilities of that tech platform. Similarly, Eric Harris-Braun, Ferananda Ibarra, and Jean Russell were patient and brilliant in explaining the Holochain protocols for commoning. Over the years, the Commons Strategies Group (of which we are cofounders) hosted a number of Deep Dive workshops that exposed us to some remarkable thinkers, activists, and fields of experimentation. We are grateful to Michel Bauwens for his invaluable collaboration and insights in these many discussions. A big thanks, too, to the dozens of participants in those gatherings for so freely sharing their knowledge and helping us think through vexing questions involving the commons.

The German Commons Summer School, and especially Heike Pourian, were among the first group of commoners to react to early versions of our patterns of commoning. They helped us confirm that we were on the right track, prodded us to clarify the field of inquiry for each pattern, and helped refine the names for many of our final patterns of commoning in German (especially Julia Petzold and Sandra Lustig). Needless to say, none of these people bear any responsibility for any errors or misinterpretations that may have crept into the text.

Because Silke lives in Germany and David in the US, we had to find creative ways to orchestrate in-person meetings to make sense of our research and develop our ideas. Fortunately, we had a number of gracious friends and colleagues who helped us find, or actually offered, wonderful spaces in which to work. At a critical stage in our thinking, Tilman Santarius and his family lent us their gracious house in Berlin as a hothouse for a week-long discussion. In Florence, Jason Nardi arranged for a lovely hillside retreat for us to work in while hosting us at several wonderful meals as well. Carlos Uriona and Matthew Glassman offered space and rich discussion at Double Edge Theatre in Ashfield, Massachusetts.

A small team of talented artists and designers were responsible for the beautiful appearance of this book and its illustrations. Two design students at Bozen University — Chiara Rovescala and Federica di Pietro, guided by their professors, Kris Krois and Lisa Borgenheimer — came up with some graphic illustrations of our early patterns. Some of those ideas later germinated and found richer development in the illustrations made by Mercè M. Tarrés, who gave the various patterns stunning, intuitive interpretations. The cover design, by Mireia Juan Cuco, conveys the spirit of our book with great elegance and energy as well. Overseeing the entire design work has been Stacco Troncoso and Ann Marie Utratel of the Guerrilla Media Collective, which will also manage the forthcoming Spanish translation of *Free, Fair, and Alive*. Their steadfast, supportive presence has meant so much to us over the past several years!

Readers of this English edition of *Free, Fair, and Alive* may not be aware that a German translation was produced immediately as we completed each chapter of the book. For this remarkable achievement, we thank our dedicated translator Sandra Lustig, whose painstaking translation of our manuscript was quite an accomplishment in light of the many novel terms we invented. Insights derived from the translation often fed back into improvements in the English manuscript. (The German translation was published by transcript Verlag in spring 2019.)

Finding a publisher who understands the commons and is willing to walk the talk by using a Creative Commons license, is difficult. We feel lucky to have found transcript Verlag in Germany and New Society Publishers in British Columbia, Canada, each committed to greater access to knowledge in a challenging commercial context.

Finally, we each have debts to acknowledge to our loved ones.

Silke: Jacques, throughout the long marathon of this book, when diving into deep intellectual waters or exhausted by too many hours in front of my computer screen, you have always been there with patience and encouragement to get me back on track, as only you can. You have allowed me to watch what happens when a person discovers "the commoner in oneself."

David: Thanks once again, dear Ellen, for your unstinting support during my many travels, research benders, and the prolonged writing marathon that was necessary to produce this book!

David Bollier, *Amherst, Massachusetts, USA*

Silke Helfrich, *Neudenau, Baden-Württemberg, Germany*
January 2019

Appendix A: Notes on the Methodology for Identifying Patterns of Commoning

W E HAVE BEEN CONDUCTING RESEARCH on commons for years outside the confines of academia, so in this section, we will outline *how* we developed our framework — the Triad of Commoning.[1]

You will recall that our purpose is not to *define* commons. That would not do justice to the topic or our concept of research. Because commons are living systems, they are not fixed entities that can simply be nailed down. Our purpose therefore has been to describe more precisely the dynamics of commons as a specific kind of behavior, and a way to satisfy needs and shape one's surroundings and society. We did so by tracking down the *recurring* basic features that characterize behaviors in *different* commons. In other words, we posed the question whether logics of action exist that are typical of commoning.

The starting point is the idea that the order of the world is reflected in patterns, a philosophical and empirical concept developed by mathematician, architect, and philosopher Christopher Alexander in his famous pattern theory and methodology. These ideas are described in detail in his four-volume work *The Nature of Order*.[2] We applied the patterns approach to commons in our 2015 anthology *Patterns of Commoning*.[3]

Patterns are identified, not invented. Identifying them is meant to make something latent visible. This is an important insight from patterns research. Pattern-mining requires patient observation, practice, and a combination of various steps. Methodologically, when attempting to make *living* processes comprehensible, one must not separate rationality from emotion or cognitive insights based on concrete experiences.[4] Patterning avoids these problems by assessing phenomena holistically. It recognizes that pure abstraction does not do justice to the rich complexity of life. Patterning is valuable, too, because it is capable of taking full measure of a layperson's tacit knowledge, which is often patronized or ignored by "experts."[5] In developing the patterns of commoning, therefore, we could TRUST SITUATED KNOWLEDGE.

Patterning requires focusing on *connections*, on what things have in common, rather than focusing on differences. In the process of doing this, a phenomenon or problem is not viewed as delimited or isolated; instead, it acquires its meaning only when viewed in its full context. Accordingly, a pattern applies only in a given context or in similar circumstances. There is no such thing as a context-free pattern.[6] In patterns of social phenomena, the purpose is to identify which behaviors (or, in more abstract terms, "logics of action") can help interactions succeed and strengthen relationships. Since relationships are multi-directional — i.e., they can have *both* positive effects on one aspect of a situation and negative effects on another — *formal* notation of patterns requires specifying related patterns. This makes the linkages between the patterns clearer, but we decided against using formal pattern notation in this book; we can only hint at those formalities. In any case, readers can easily imagine how various individual patterns are connected to other ones. In all their connections, they form a (yet-to-be-formulated) pattern language.

At the epistemological level, a pattern language approach ensures that the spirit and the body remain connected as tools of cognition. In the process of coining a pattern name, as we come to understand concepts, deliberately and through language — as we perceive what has been obscure but not yet put into words — we simultaneously experience moments of resonance in our bodies.[7] We experience resonance when a special energy emerges and we reflexively nod our heads in recognition of the congruence between experiencing, sensing, and discerning. When enough interviewees, workshop participants, readers, and other people experience this same resonance upon hearing a pattern, and their reactions align with each other, so to speak, we can feel confident that a high-quality pattern has been formulated. And still, the resulting pattern is in principle open and adaptable, if only because living systems are always changing and evolving. (See the section on validation below.) No pattern is a "once and forever" truth.

Beyond general pattern-mining methodology, we should address the methods used to construct the Triad of Commoning. They too can be presented only very briefly. Between June 2014 and December 2017, a total of nine pattern-mining workshops were held with participants of ages twenty to seventy, from a variety of contexts and cultures.

The workshops themselves were structured to introduce participants to the logic of the pattern approach by inviting them to ask, for each pattern:

- What is the context?
- What exactly, in this context, is the essence of a recurring problem?
- What solutions exist for this problem?
- What is the common essence of successful solutions?
- How can this common essence be put into words to form a pattern name?

A strong pattern name (in terms of accurately describing a pattern of social practices) is first of all short and succinct. It is free of punctuation, may use easy-to-understand abbreviations (such as FAQ, for example) and neologisms, relies on a verb to emphasize the process (or practice), and avoids vague clichés. A good pattern name is adaptable, too, meaning that it can be changed later. So exceptions from these naming criteria are commonplace.

In addition to the workshops, twelve semi-structured interviews were conducted with one to four people at a time. Most of these were university graduates who have been active in commons projects for a long time — some for fifty years. Two interviews were particularly extensive. As in the workshops, the purpose was to find out to what extent various practices are present in different patterns when they are used to address similar problems and whether common patterns of behavior can be discerned in successful solutions. The setting and character of the interviews as well as the kinds of questions asked are described in detail in Silke Helfrich's masters thesis (see note 1). Interviewees were asked *what was actually done* in the commons projects, not what they were *thinking*. After all, the purpose was to identify and document descriptions of actions, not gather opinions. The interviews were structured in advance by the three areas of our pattern-mining — social life, peer-governance, and provisioning (Chapters 4-6). Questions focused on typical problems within these areas, and were refined with each iteration. When we began to test the patterns already identified, we also asked interviewees whether the patterns felt right (resonance test).

Interview Questions

Since the purpose was to ask about behavior, not attitudes, it was important to avoid asking simple yes-no questions as well as questions that would force respondents to rationalize behaviors.[8] Most of the questions concerned *how* things were done. Questions sought to narrow down the problem area, to be as concrete as possible, and not use leading questions to suggest any particular answers. The questions referred to often-observed problems arising in social interactions in a commons context. The questions about peer governance were derived from the eight design principles developed by Elinor Ostrom as well as our own observations. When we developed the questions concerning commons provisioning, our starting point was the basic elements required for any creative/productive process (e.g., natural resources, knowledge, information, human activities, labor, etc.).

Questions About Social Interactions

- How do you succeed in finding a shared purpose? What is the role of values?
- How do you obtain the necessary contributions?
- How do you shape the relationship between giving and taking?
- How do you maintain quality in social relations? Do certain customs, practices, and conventions exist?
- What kinds of knowledge do you rely upon?
- How do you live your relationship to nature?
- How do you deal with conflicts?
- Through which mechanisms do rules and structures remain appropriate and adaptable?

Questions Concerning Governance

- How do you negotiate the tension between the pressure to exploit all kinds of resources commercially on the one hand and commoning on the other? How do you protect commons from being entirely governed or directed by money?
- How do you bring together purposes and values?
- Do you set boundaries? How permeable are they?
- How are your decisions made?
- How do you handle information, knowledge, code, and design?

- How are your organizational structures structured? Do they provide protection from abuse of power?
- How is your property governed?
- How do you enable that your actions are transparent?
- Which forms of finance do you use? Are they themselves expressions of commoning? Do flows of money strengthen commons?
- How do you monitor that rules are observed?
- How do you deal with violations of rules?

Questions Concerning Commons Production

- Who bears the production risk?
- Is there a separation between producers and users? How are the roles defined and fulfilled?
- How is that which is available allocated?
  - Referring to things that increase as more people use them (e.g., knowledge, software)?
  - Referring to things that are used up as more people use them (e.g., land, food, money)?
- How is that which is available allocated?
  - In a social context that is usually interpersonal and in which it is easy to get an overview of the situation?
  - In an anonymous, transpersonal context in which it is difficult to get an overview of the situation?
- Who determines the price, and on which basis, in market-like transactions?
- How do you conceive of your work? How do you allocate tasks, and how do you value and appreciate all activities?
- Who benefits from your tools and instruments? What purposes do they serve?
- Which of the existing infrastructures do you use, and why? Do they serve your purposes?
- How do you create new material and immaterial things?

Drawing on these interviews, on our prior knowledge, commons literature, and the workshops, we began to "verbalize" — to find appropriate pattern names. After that, the feedback process began. Even though this process was somewhat different for each of the generic patterns that we developed,[9] there were at least six systematic rounds for each pattern. We consulted with people with different qualifications — from a sustainability scholar to a student working with patterns, and from an educator who herself is a driving force behind a commons community to participants in the sixth German-language Commons Summer School. The two of us also discussed the pattern names ourselves time and time again. Each round surfaced ideas about needed corrections, shifts, additions, and deletions, leading to a large number of adaptations. We believe that these iterations as well as the combination of methods have yielded robust results.

Below is an example of the typical proceeding. We wish to make clear *how* we combined the methods, which was somewhat different in each case, depending on the number and type of critical decision situations. To illustrate our process of work, we have selected the pattern BRING DIVERSITY INTO SHARED PURPOSE, which is in the sphere of Peer Governance. It is not only illustrative of the many iterations each pattern went through, it also points to the relative importance of common values, which many people might assume that commoners must share in advance of commoning. When we began to probe this topic, we were interested in the role that common goals and values *actually* play in successful commons, as opposed to the scenario of diverse people growing together to share outlooks (which raises questions about how this is achieved).

Brief Description of the Steps.

This description reconstructs the research process used to coin the pattern name in German. It was similar but not the same as the English-language versions. You will therefore find the German pattern names in several iterations along with their respective English translations. The starting point for the German and the English process, however, was the same. We, as authors, deduced that the pattern would be:

GEMEINSAMEN ZWECK & GEMEINSAME
WERTE ERKLÄREN |
DECLARE SHARED PURPOSE & VALUES

and then we went on for several rounds of testing, correction, and adaptation.

1. Describe the problem: *Identifying the roles of common purposes and values.*

2. Derive a pattern name (first iteration, in this case by deduction). The goal is for the name to express that common purposes and values should be clear when people common:

   DECLARE SHARED PURPOSE & VALUES

3. Embed the pattern name in the context; give reasons for it, using examples in order to bring to mind its practical relevance; prepare a textual description and send it to experts (test readers) and interviewees. Be alert to any dissonant feedback among participants in the process, and look for consensus about the pattern name.

4. Conduct semi-structured telephone interview with a social scientist and commons practitioner, George E. on December 4, 2017. When a conflict arises in the experience of the interviewee, common purposes and values cannot be *presupposed*. Also, for common action to work, it is not decisive that such purposes exist or are declared. It is a social fact that any commons has to deal with a diversity of perspectives and values. People may share motivations and reasons for coming together, but we cannot presume any long-term shared purposes and values. As the interviewee put it: "We may assume specific short-term goals or purposes. For example, collecting signatures for a petition [...] before the second week of February. But these 'goals' or 'purposes' are not ends in themselves. We have motives, compelling forces pushing us in a certain direction that we can express those 'motives' as reasons. Instead of asking 'What for?' we ask 'Why?'"

5. Authors jointly reflect to derive the pattern name (a second iteration)

   VIELFALT FÜR COMMONS-ZWECKE AUFGREIFEN
   BRING DIVERSITY INTO SHARED PURPOSE

6. Discuss with an expert and reflect on the wording (a third iteration of pattern name).

   VIELFALT ZU COMMONS-ZWECKEN NUTZEN
   USING DIVERSITY FOR COMMONS PURPOSES

7. Discuss with another expert (June 15, 2018) and resonance test. A conflict arises. This version of the pattern name "doesn't feel right" or doesn't get to the heart of what needs to be expressed (a fourth iteration of pattern name).

> VIELFALT ZUM GEMEINSAMEN VERWEBEN
> INTERWEAVE DIVERSITY TO FORM WHAT IS COMMON

8. Review of all pattern names by an expert/social scientist (March 26, 2018)

    There is feedback on other patterns, but not this one. However, step 7 points to the fact that another round of review is needed.

9. Collective reflection by participants in the summer school, late June 2018, about resonance of the pattern name. Group discussion with practitioners and theoreticians; inductive elements are strengthened (fifth iteration of pattern name).

> SICH IN VIELFALT GEMEINSAM AUSRICHTEN
> BRING DIVERSITY INTO SHARED PURPOSE

This fifth version of the pattern name corresponds to the knowledge and experiences brought forward in the various steps and feedback loops *and* feels right. The pattern name is published (cf. Chapter 5).

The processes for identifying patterns were similar in all cases. The steps and the procedures for gaining insight are shown once again in the following diagram. Let us review the procedure for the pattern BRING DIVERSITY INTO SHARED PURPOSE as an example:

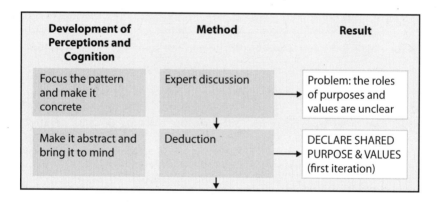

Development of Perceptions and Cognition	Method	Result
Focus the pattern and make it concrete	Expert discussion	Problem: the roles of purposes and values are unclear
Make it abstract and bring it to mind	Deduction	DECLARE SHARED PURPOSE & VALUES (first iteration)

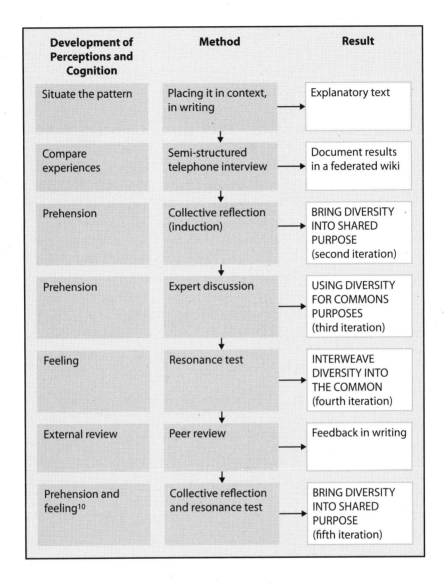

Development of Perceptions and Cognition	Method	Result
Situate the pattern	Placing it in context, in writing	Explanatory text
Compare experiences	Semi-structured telephone interview	Document results in a federated wiki
Prehension	Collective reflection (induction)	BRING DIVERSITY INTO SHARED PURPOSE (second iteration)
Prehension	Expert discussion	USING DIVERSITY FOR COMMONS PURPOSES (third iteration)
Feeling	Resonance test	INTERWEAVE DIVERSITY INTO THE COMMON (fourth iteration)
External review	Peer review	Feedback in writing
Prehension and feeling[10]	Collective reflection and resonance test	BRING DIVERSITY INTO SHARED PURPOSE (fifth iteration)

Validation and Procedure for Deriving the Pattern

When people identify patterns through this process, they usually assess the accuracy and validity of the pattern name subjectively since "some are more *true*, more profound, more *certain* than others," according to Christopher Alexander and his colleagues.[11] They sought to identify the "more true" patterns by assigning two, one, or no asterisks to each pattern, indicating a ranking of likely success in identifying whether a solution names "a true invariant." Using this process, we undertook an assessment of the pattern names identified in Chapters 4–6. You will find the result in the next table. In the case of a pattern name without an asterisk (see first column), we believe that we found something that, as Alexander put it, "summarizes a *property* common to *all possible ways* of solving the stated problem." That means it is basically impossible to solve the stated problem properly without "shaping the environment in one way" or another according to the respective pattern (ibid., emphasis in the original).

In the case of patterns with only one asterisk, we assume, with Alexander, "that *we have made* some progress towards identifying such an invariant: but that with careful work it will certainly be possible to improve on the solution." (ibid., xiv). Patterns with two asterisks signify that further examination is recommended in order to improve the pattern. The second column indicates most important procedures for deriving the patterns as well as the abstract concepts from which the patterns were deduced (in those cases where deduction was the primary methodology).

Social interaction	Procedure for deriving patterns (in the order of their predominance)
Cultivate Shared Purpose & Values	Inductive and deductive
Contribute Freely	Inductive
Practice Gentle Reciprocity	Inductive and deductive (from the concept of reciprocity)
Ritualize Togetherness	Inductive
Trust Situated Knowledge	Deductive (from the concept of situated knowledge) and inductive
Deepen Communion with Nature**	Deductive (from the basic understanding of the relationships between humans and nature) and inductive
Preserve Relationships in Addressing Conflicts*	Inductive
Reflect on Your Peer Governance*	Inductive

Peer Governance	
Keep Commons & Commerce Distinct	Inductive
Bring Diversity into Shared Purpose	Inductive and deductive (from the participant's assumptions about "human nature")
Create Semi-Permeable Membranes*	Deductive (from Elinor Ostrom's first design principle) and inductive
Assure Consent in Decision Making*	Inductive and deductive (from Ostrom's third design principle)
Share Knowledge Generously	Inductive
Rely on Heterarchy*	Deductive (from governance theory, critique of hierarchy) and inductive
Relationalize Property	Inductive
Honor Transparency in a Sphere of Trust	Inductive
Finance Commons Provisioning*	Deductive and inductive
Peer Monitor & Use Graduated Sanctions	Inductive and deductive (from Ostrom's fourth and fifth design principles)

Creating Commons	
Share the Risks of Provisioning	Inductive
Make & Use Together	Inductive
Pool & Share	Inductive
Pool, Cap & Divide Up	Inductive
Pool, Cap & Mutualize	Inductive
Trade With Price Sovereignty*	Inductive
Honor Care & Decommodify Work*	Deductive (from the concept of care, critique of wage labor) and inductive
Use Convivial Tools*	Deductive (from the concept of conviviality[12] and convivial tools following Ivan Illich and Andrea Vetter,)[13] and inductive
Rely on Distributed Structures	Inductive
Produce Cosmo-locally*[14]	Inductive and deductive (from the concept of cosmo-local production)
Creatively Adapt & Renew	Inductive

The Research Process

Finally, a flow chart shows the decisions that had to be made during the research process. It begins with the identification of a recurring problem in a commons context and ends with an evaluation as described just above. This flowchart was prepared, once more, for the example BRING DIVERSITY INTO SHARED PURPOSE, yet its approach applies to all patterns.

Each step was documented promptly and in various forms: as complete documentation of workshop discussions, individual documentation of workshop results including formal notation of the patterns, documentation of the interviews (on file with the authors), and notes from workshops, expert discussions, and editorial discussions.

From an Understanding of Being to Methods

As we can see from this explanation, the entire procedure of pattern mining has a theoretical foundation that incorporates and reflects a relational and procedural ontology. The methodology therefore takes into account a phenomenon's relationship to its context and its concrete existence in actual lifeworlds. The methodology is also open ended and adaptable, thereby enabling individual and collective self-reflection about its accuracy and further revision.

- **Onto-Epistemology:** Differentiated relational processes, evolutionary epistemology of living, generative processes
- **Theories:** Commons / pattern theory
- **Methodology:** pattern mining / methodological holism
- **Methods:** patterns workshops, semistructured interviews, peer review, "resonance test," conversations with experts, collective reflection
- **Results:** Patterns of Commoning

This methodology also suggests that patterns are not like Lego bricks that fit together only in predetermined ways. The ways to combine individual elements into successful solutions are not prestructured. That is why creative combinations of ideas can bring about new results that were not part of the individual solutions.

Decision Process in the Research Process

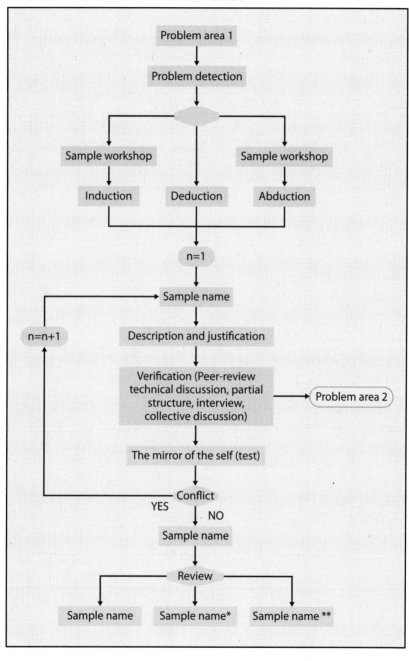

On Working with Patterns

The process of coining patterns enables one to discern order in the diversity of commoning processes, thus identifying the essential dynamics of commoning. It also provides a shared vocabulary and methodology, thereby enabling commoners to *create* that order. This is why linking patterns and commons is so fruitful for researchers and others in advancing both theory and practice. Practitioners can use patterns to:

- find a vocabulary and philosophical rationale for the collaborations they have been doing all along
- structure processes of self-reflection and identify their own strengths and weaknesses
- take up good ideas and use them to solve their own problems — in other words, apply patterns in a form adapted to their own context
- develop specific patterns tailored to their own context

Researchers can also use patterns to:
- review and then further develop them, in order to contribute to the conceptualization of commoning
- design interviews and research questions for research in the field
- apply all generic patterns together as a research framework.

The result can enable researchers to identify and analyze social, institutional, and economic processes in a concrete context from a commons perspective, similar to the way in which Elinor Ostrom's design principles have been used to compare institutional rules.

Silke Helfrich
Neudenau, February 4, 2019

Appendix B: Visual Grammar for the Pattern Illustrations

Visual Grammar

- Each illustration contains two layers of information.
- The first layer is the sphere around which the dots and squares move, representing the context of commoning.
- The dynamic layer contains the dots and squares that wrap around or move through the sphere, representing the subject/agent and predicate/action.

*   *   *

Layer 1: Sphere

Action takes place inside, between, and around one or more semitransparent spheres.

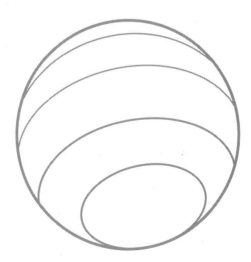

Our sphere is the commons, shaped and represented by a dynamic texture of dots and squares: a diversity of realities, commoners participating in interdependent relationships with the world outside the commons.

Commons

- *"They are COMPLEX, ADAPTIVE, LIVING PROCESSES that generate wealth and meet people's needs."*
- In contrast, the capitalist system (or its elements) is represented by squares without hue, gradient or texture.

*   *   *

Commoning

Inside

- People devising and enacting situation-specific systems of PROVISIONING and PEER GOVERNANCE
- Within a single commons
- Local

*   *   *

Outside

- People, things, or ideas interacting with the outside (e.g., the market system)
- Among various commons
- Global / network / federation

*   *   *

The sphere and the dot are abstract representations of the individual and the commons. Both are dynamic (non-static) and represented as circular. Both exist in (relational) singularity and plurality.

"'I am because we are and, since we are, therefore I am.'

The individual is part of a 'we' — and in fact, of many 'we's'. The two are deeply intertwined."

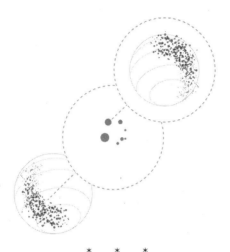

*   *   *

Layer 2: Dots and Squares, Flows and Areas

Commoners

"An identity and social role that people acquire as they practice COMMONING."

Communion

"The process through which COMMONERS participate in interdependent relationships with the more than human world."

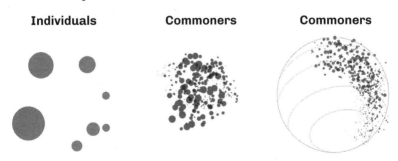

| Individuals | Commoners | Commoners |

*   *   *

Dots and squares come together as flows and areas, suggesting spaces inside and outside the spheres.

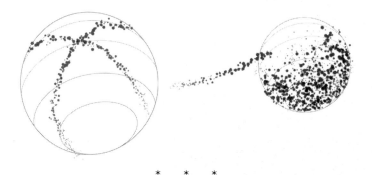

*   *   *

Flows of dots and squares represent connections, relations, directions, concrete actions, and spaces. Flows diffuse into wider areas.

Areas of dots and squares wrap around or move through the sphere, creating dynamic shapes.

*   *   *

Size = diverse realities

The size of the elements expresses different realities. Dots and squares, flows and areas behave in different manners.

Density = power

Density is achieved by increasing the volume of the elements, overlapping and reducing the space between them.

Movement/shift = aliveness

"Comets" = direction. Direction is achieved through flows of dots progressively decreasing in size. The "head" of the "comet" is formed by larger dots and higher density.

Organic vs. ordered configurations = Free vs. ruled activities/relations

*   *   *

All of these elements graphically depict relational dynamics.
"Since each is constantly evolving and affected by multiple influences, the world has no singular definition or representation ... It [is] a pluriverse — a diversity of living, dynamic social organisms that are conjoined by our common humanity and interdependence on other life-forms and the Earth."

*   *   *

Types of relational dynamics expressed by patterns and their graphic translation.

Convergent dynamics are expressed through spiral configurations.

Analysis/reflection dynamics are expressed through concentric circles/ eye configurations.

Making together and provisioning dynamics are expressed through braided configurations.

Sharing/dividing-up dynamics are expressed through wave configurations.

Dynamics related to love (trust, care ...) are expressed through concave configurations (as a nesting/nurturing reference).

Mercè M. Tarrés, from an initial graphic proposal suggested by Frederica Di Pietri and Chiara Rovescala

Barcelona, Spain
January 2019

Appendix C: Commons and Commoning Tools Mentioned in This Book

Acequias (Mexico, American Southwest). Community-based water irrigation systems in Mexico, New Mexico, and Colorado. pp. 105 and 194.

Artabana (Switzerland, Germany, Austria). A federation of community-based health insurance projects that is a kind of commons-public partnership. pp. 160–161.

Atelier Paysan (France, worldwide). A French-language group of engineers, farmers, and others who build convivial tools and open source machinery for small-scale farming. p. 176.

Bangla Pesa (Kenya). A neighborhood-owned and -controlled currency in Kenya, part of the larger Sarafu Credit system. p. 161

Bisses du Valais (Switzerland). A centuries-old network of canals in the Swiss Alps, managed as a commons, which brings water from the mountains to farmers' fields. p. 128.

Buurtzorg (Netherlands and worldwide). A peer-run organization that provides nursing homecare in a neighborhood scale. p. 20–21.

Cecosesola (Venezuela). An "omni-commons" federation of about thirty urban and rural cooperatives in the state of Lara, providing food, care, transportation, and communal burial services to hundreds of thousands of people. pp. 185–187.

Charters for Commoning. Documents created by people to constitute a commons by setting forth core goals, practices, and principles that will guide the group. pp. 319–323.

CoBudget (internet). A collaborative platform by which members of a group can keep track of a shared budget and allocate funds among proposals made. p. 129.

Commons-public partnerships. Agreements initiated by commoners in cooperation with state bodies to work together on specific problems over the long term. pp. 333–344.

Community currencies (worldwide). The Bangla Pesa and Lida Pesa, two neighborhood currencies in Kenya, are among six thousand alternative currencies worldwide. p. 161.

Community Land Trust (USA, Canada). An organizational form that allows a trust to acquire land and take it off the market in perpetuity, thereby reducing the costs of housing and small enterprises. p. 159.

Community Supported Agriculture (CSA) (worldwide). A form of collective farming in which families share the risks of production with farmers by buying shares of the harvest at the beginning of the growing season. pp. 22–24. See also Solidarische Landwirtschaft (Germany), p. 202, and Teikei, p. 23.

Community Supported Industry. An expansion of the CSA model that aims to strengthen regional economics by replacing imported goods with ones produced by local businesses that provide living wages and employ sustainable manufacturing processes. p. 23.

Cosmo-local Production Projects (worldwide). Collaborative efforts based on open source philosophy that share designs and knowledge globally and produce locally. Examples: Open Desk, p. 176, Open Building Institute, p. 196, Open SPIM, p. 196; Wikispeed, p. 197.

Creative Commons Licenses (worldwide). A suite of no-cost licenses that copyright holders may use to make their creative works and information legally available for copying, sharing, and re-use at no cost. p. 259.

Crowdfunding. A popular form of collaborative financing of commons projects, as in Goteo. pp. 159–160.

Data Commons for a Free, Fair, and Sustainable World. A commons charter for programmers dedicated to building shareable mapping databases. p. 320.

Drugs for Neglected Diseases Initiative (DNDi) (worldwide). A collaborative project for needs-based drug research and development that works with governments, research institutes, and communities affected by disease. pp. 341–343.

EnCommuns (France). A commons-based network of database programmers. pp. 164–165.

Enspiral (New Zealand and worldwide). A networked guild of hundreds of social entrepreneurs and activists that has built open source platforms such as Loomio and CoBudget, and experiments with new forms of peer governance. pp. 105 and 129.

Fab Labs (worldwide). Open workshops in which scientists, engineers, digital artists, and amateurs use computer tools to experiment and produce prototype processes and machines. pp. 168–169.

Federated Wiki (internet). A network of creators whose content on personal wikis can be easily and legally shared with other federated wiki users, avoiding the editorial and interpersonal problems of curating centralized wikis. pp. 246–252.

Free/Libre and Open Source Software (FLOSS). Software that can be freely shared, copied, and modified because of licenses such as the GPL (see below). "Free/Libre" does not refer to price but to a philosophical commitment to freedom. "Open source" is focused on practical benefits. pp. 80 and 258–259.

Freifunk (Germany). A network of free Wi-Fi access points in over four hundred communities. p. 311.

General Public License (GPL). A standard license that the copyright holders of software programs can use to authorize the sharing, copying, and modification of their programs. pp. 258–259.

GNU/Linus (internet). The computer operating system developed by a commons of programmers associated with Linux Torvalds' adaptation of Unix and free software pioneer Richard Stallman's GNU programs. pp. 80 and 90.

Goteo (Spain, Europe, and Latin America). A crowdfunding platform dedicated to the commons that has raised more than 7.3 million euros for more than 900 commons projects (2018). pp. 159–160.

Guerrilla Media Collective (worldwide). A socially minded group of translators, designers, and media workers. p. 165.

guifi.net (Catalonia). A commons-based Wifi infrastructure providing internet access to tens of thousands of people. pp. 24–25.

Hackerspaces (worldwide). Physical spaces in which hackers of all types meet, co-learn, and work together on various projects as a loose peer-organized network. p. 304.

Haenyeo (South Korea). An integenerational community of women divers who combine diving skills, spiritual traditions, and community commitment in harvesting shellfish off the island of Jeju. p. 128.

Helsinki Timeback (Finland). A timebank that enables more than three thousand members to exchange their skills and services. p. 2.

Iriaiken (Japan). A traditional philosophy (*iriai*) and practice of commoning in Japan that refers to collective ownership of nonarable areas such as mountains, forests, marshes, and offshore fisheries. pp. 266–273.

King of the Meadows (Netherlands and adjacent countries). A Dutch commons project to steward biodiversity connected with cultural heritage. p. 308.

Lake District (Scotland/UK). A commons of grazing rights for sheep that relies on high plots of grassland shared by many farmers. p. 147.

Lida Pesa (Kenya). A neighborhood-owned and -controlled currency in Kenya, part of the larger Sarafu Credit system. p. 161.

Loomio (internet). A software platform designed by the Enspiral community to facilitate online deliberation and decision-making. pp. 138–139.

Mietshäuser Syndikat (Germany and Austria). A federation of around 140 rental housing buildings that have been removed from the real estate market, each of which is permanently affordable and peer-managed. pp. 252–257.

Minga (Andean countries). Well-organized mobilizations of friends and neighbors to tackle shared challenges such as harvesting food or fixing a road. p. 270.

Movimento Sem Terra, Brazilian Landless Rural Worker Movement (MST) (Brazil). A movement to redistribute land to rural workers for small-scale farming, which has created occupied land settlements for hundreds of thousands of families. p. 150.

NextCloud (Internet). A global open space community of programmers developing shareable file hosting software. pp. 157–158.

Nidiaci Community Garden (Italy). A neighborhood-managed garden and playground in the heart of downtown Florence. pp. 207–209.

Oberallmeindkorporationen (Switzerland). Independent corporations authorized by Swiss cantonal law for over 1,100 years to govern common lands; similar to the Iriaiken in Japan. p. 223.

Obştea (Romania). Traditional community-owned and -managed forests. p. 223.

Open Commons Linz (Austria). A project that provides free Wi-Fi hotspots, a "municipal cloud" available to all citizens, open data produced by government agencies, among other digital provisions. p. 311.

Open Educational Resources (OER). Books, essays, curricula, syllabi, lesson plans, datasets, and other materials that can be freely used, shared, and modified. p. 202.

Open Prosthetics Project (USA). A network of users, designers, and funders dedicated to making public domain prosthetics available to anyone. p. 176.

Open Source Ecology (USA, worldwide). A global community of farmers designing and building non-proprietary, modular, and locally sourceable farm equipment using open source principles. p. 196.

Open Source Seed Initiative (USA, worldwide). A community of farmers and seed breeders committed to sharing seeds and derivative improvements as alternatives to proprietary seed. p. 265.

Open Source Seed License (Germany, Switzerland, international). A license that grants seed users the right to share breeding improvements if made available for public use and if follow-on users are required to do the same. p. 264.

OpenSPIM. An open source collaboration among scientists and engineers in building Selective Plane Illumination Microscopy (SPIM), a specialized technology used in biological research. p. 196.

Park Slope Food Coop (Brooklyn, New York). A large food cooperative started in 1973 that relies on unpaid, decommodified labor as a way to Pool & Share the benefits of a supermarket to more than 17,000 members. p. 238–241.

Peer Production License. A license that grants free use of licensed material to anyone belonging to the commons, except commercial users, who must pay. p. 402 #16.

Permaculture (worldwide). A integrated set of design principles for agricultural practices that reflect the holistic dynamics of ecosystems. p. 319.

Potato Park (Peru). A sociolegal stewardship system for the biodiversity of potatoes in lands north of Cusco, overseen by Indigenous Quechua people. p. 309.

Public Library of Science (Internet). A series of high-quality, peer reviewed open access journals on a variety of scientific topics, each available under Creative Commons licenses for free. p. 188.

Sarafu Credit System (Kenya). A network of neighborhood currencies in Kenya. p. 161. See also Bangla Pesa, Lida Pesa.

Sociocracy. A system of peer governance that seeks to secure maximum participation and transparency in group deliberation and decision making, chiefly by seeking consent, not consensus, for group decisions. pp. 140–141.

Sozialistische Selbsthilfe Mühlheim (SSM) (Germany). A self-organized work and residential project dedicated to dignifying life for everyone, including the unskilled and mentally ill. p. 348.

Subak (Bali). An effective peasant-run system of irrigation for rice crops that synchronizes social and religious practices with planting and harvesting times. p. 137.

Teikei (Japan). The system of community-supported agriculture in Japan. p. 23.

Terre de Liens (France). An organization that buys arable land to take it off the market permanently, hold it in trust, and make it available to farmers. p. 160.

Traditional Knowledge Digital Library (India, internet). A database assembled to document traditional medicinal knowledge and thereby thwart inappropriate international patents. p. 261.

Transition Town Movement (worldwide). A movement of pragmatically minded people seeking to build more resilient local provisioning systems in anticipation of the problems that Peak Oil and climate breakdown will bring. pp. 109 and 193.

Unitierra, or Universidad de la Tierra en Oaxaca (Mexico). A de-institutionalized university created by commons for commoners. pp. 126–127.

Water management commons (Zimbabwe). A cooperative water system in the Nkayi District in western Zimbabwe. p. 147.

Wikihouse (UK, worldwide). A community of architects, designers, and others who share designs for houses and the means to build them, with the help of eleven chapters around the world. p. 21–22.

Wikipedia (internet). The collaborative web encyclopedia that has about 72,000 active contributors working on more than 48 million articles in 302 languages. p. 246.

Wikispeed (internet, distributed locations). The global community of engineers designing open source motor vehicles such as racing cars, taxicabs, and mail delivery vehicles. p. 197.

Zanjeras (Philippines). A system of commons-based irrigation that uses social means to assure fair allocations of water and respect for community rules. p. 147.

Readers can find additional profiles of commons in Bollier and Helfrich, *Patterns of Commoning*, at www.patternsofcommoning.org.

Appendix D: Elinor Ostrom's Eight Design Principles for Successful Commons

THE LATE PROFESSOR ELINOR OSTROM identified eight key design principles for successful commons, which she set forth in her book, *Governing the Commons: The Evolution of Institutions for Collective Action* (1990).

1. Clearly defined boundaries

Individuals or households who have rights to withdraw resource units from the common-pool resource (CPR) must be clearly defined, as must the boundaries of the CPR itself.

2. Congruence between appropriation and provision rules and local conditions

Appropriation rules restricting time, place, technology, and/or quantity of resource units are related to local conditions and to provision rules requiring labor, material, and/or money.

3. Collective-choice arrangements

Most individuals affected by the operational rules can participate in modifying the operational rules.

4. Monitoring

Monitors, who actively audit CPR conditions and appropriator behavior, are accountable to the appropriators or are the appropriators.

5. Graduated sanctions

Appropriators who violate operational rules are likely to be assessed graduated sanctions (depending on the seriousness and context of the offense) by other appropriators, by officials accountable to these appropriators, or both.

6. Conflict resolution mechanisms.

Appropriators and their officials have rapid access to low-cost local arenas to resolve conflicts among appropriators or between appropriators and officials.

7. Minimal recognition of rights to organize

The rights of appropriators to devise their own institutions are not challenged by external governmental authorities.

For CPRs that are parts of larger systems:

8. Nested enterprises

Appropriation, provision, monitoring, enforcement, conflict resolution and governance activities, are organized in multiple layers of nested enterprises.

Notes

Introduction
1. George Monbiot, "Don't Let the Rich Get Even Richer on the Assets We All Share," *The Guardian*, September 27, 2017. theguardian.com/commentisfree/2017/sep/27/rich-assets-resources-prosperity-commons-george-monbiot

Chapter 1
1. Michael Tomasello, *Why We Cooperate*, MIT Press, 2009, p.4. See also Tomasello lectures, "What Makes Us Human?" youtube.com/watch?v=9vuI34zyjqU and "What Makes Human Beings Unique?" youtube.com/watch?v=RQiINQiAn4o
2. Samuel Bowles and Herbert Gintis, *The Cooperative Species: Human Reciprocity and Its Evolution*, Princeton University Press, 2011. Another useful book on social cooperation is Richard Sennett's *Together: The Rituals, Pleasures and Politics of Cooperation*, Yale University Press, 2012.
3. Garrett Hardin, "The Tragedy of the Commons." *Science* vol. 162, no. 3859, December 1968, pp. 1243–5.
4. Lewis Hyde, *Common as Air: Revolution, Art and Ownership*, Farrar, Straus and Giroux, 2010, p. 44.
5. Michael Kimmelman, "Refugee Camp for Syrians in Jordan Evolves as a Do-It-Yourself City," *New York Times*, July 4, 2014. nytimes.com/2014/07/05/world/middleeast/zaatari-refugee-camp-in-jordan-evolves-as-a-do-it-yourself-city.html
6. www.buurtzorg.com
7. Ernst & Young, "Business Case, Buurtzorg Nederland," 2009. transitiepraktijk.nl/files/maatschappelijke%20business%20case%20buurtzorg.pdf
8. "Home Care by Self-Governing Nursing Teams: The Netherlands' Buurtzorg Model," The Commonwealth Fund, May 29, 2015. commonwealthfund.org/publications/case-studies/2015/may/home-care-nursing-teams-netherlands
9. A good overview of literature assessing Buurtzorg can be found in Harri Kaloudis, "A First Attempt at a Systematic Overview of the Public Record in English on Buurtzorg Nederland (Part A – Buurtzorg's

Performance," August 25, 2016. medium.com/@Harri_Kaloudis/a-first-attempt-at-a-systematic-overview-of-the-public-record-on-buurtzorg-nederland-part-a-ff92e06e673d

10. See KPMG International "Value walks: Successful habits for improving workforce motivation and productivity," 2012. publicworld.co.uk/wp-content/uploads/2015/10/kpmg-buurtzorg.pdf

11. transitiepraktijk.nl/files/maatschappelijke%20business%20case%20buurtzorg.pdf

12. Alastair Parvin, "Architecture for the People by the People," TED Talk, May 23, 2013. youtube.com/watch?v=Mlt6kaNjoeI

13. Ivan Illich, *Tools for Conviviality*, Harper & Row, 1973, p. 23.

14. en.wikipedia.org/wiki/Teikei

15. Dan Gillmor, "Forget Comcast. Here's the DIY Approach to Internet Access," *Wired*, July 20, 2016. wired.com/2016/07/forget-comcast-heres-the-diy-approach-to-internet-access

16. Ibid.

17. Andreas Weber, *Enlivenment: Towards a Fundamental Shift in the Concepts of Nature, Culture and Politics,* Heinrich Böll Foundation, 2013. Heinrich Böll Foundation, 2013. boell.de/en/2013/02/01/enlivenment-towards-fundamental-shift-concepts-nature-culture-and-politics

18. Christopher Alexander, *The Nature of Order: An Essay on the Art of Building and the Nature of the Universe, Books 1–4,* Center for Environmental Structure, 2002-2012.

Chapter 2

1. Nancy Pick, *Curious Footprints: Professor Hitchcock's Dinosaur Tracks & Other Natural History Treasures at Amherst College*, Amherst College Press, 2006, p.2.

2. This quotation is often attributed to Judge Oliver Wendell Holmes, Jr., but also to others: quoteinvestigator.com/2012/04/13/taxes-civilize

3. Thurman Arnold, *The Folklore of Capitalism,* Yale University Press, 1937, p. 118.

4. See, e.g., Elisabeth Wehling: *Politisches Framing. Wie eine Nation sich ihr Denken einredet --- und daraus Politik macht,* Köln, 2016, p. 191: Frames haben einen ideologisch selektiven Charakter. See also George Lakoff, *Moral Politics: How Liberals and Conservatives Think,* University of Chicago Press, 2002, and *Don't Think of an Elephant: Know Your Values and Frame the Debate*, Chelsea Green Publishing, 2014.

5. John Maynard Keynes, *The General Theory of Employment, Interest and Money,* 1936. Reprint edition, Prometheus Books, 1997, p. viii.

6. E. P. Thompson, *Customs in Common*, Penguin Books, 1993, p. 159.

7. Uskali Mäki, *The Economic World View: Studies in the Ontology of Economics*, Cambridge University Press, 2001).

8. Margaret Stout, "Competing Ontologies: A Primer for Public Administration," *Public Administration Review*, 72(3), May/June 2012, pp. 388–398.

9. Feminist political theorists such as Carole Pateman, in her book *The Sexual Contract* (1988), have noted that the very idea of a social contract reflects patriarchal norms, such as the individual as autonomous, the supposed equality of everyone to bargain for a fair contract, the very idea of a contract as advancing freedom, and the supposed separateness and inferiority of the private sphere.

10. An excellent summary of the evolution of Western scientific and legal thought, and the implications of these for the commons, can be found in Fritjof Capra and Ugo Mattei, *The Ecology of Law: Toward a Legal System in Tune with Nature and Community*, Berrett-Koehler, 2015.

11. Carl Schmitt in *Political Theology: Four Chapters on the Concept of Sovereignty*, MIT Press, 1921/1985, p. 36: "All significant concepts of the modern theory of the state are secularized theological concepts, not only because of their historical development, in which they were transferred from theology to the theory of the state, whereby, for example, the omnipotent God became the omnipotent law-giver, but also because of their systematic structure." See medium.com/@csreader/sovereignty-and-the-miracle-ce4a4259c207

12. Stout, "Competing Ontologies," p. 393.

13. James Buchanan, *The Economics and the Ethics of Constitutional Order*, University of Michigan Press, 1991, p. 14.

14. Andreas Karitzis, "The Decline of Liberal Politics," in Anna Grear and David Bollier, editors, *The Great Awakening*, Punctum Press, 2019.

15. Arturo Escobar, *Designs for the Pluriverse: Radical Interdependence, Autonomy, and the Making of Worlds*, Duke University Press, 2018.

16. Stout, "Competing Ontologies," p. 389.

17. Sam Lavigne, "Taxonomy of Humans According to Twitter," *The New Inquiry*, July 7, 2017. thenewinquiry.com/taxonomy-of-humans-according-to-twitter

18. Cathy O'Neil, *Weapons of Math Destruction: How Big Data Increases Inequality and Threatens Democracy*, Crown, 2016.

19. Brian Massumi, *Ontopower: War, Powers and the State of Perception*, Duke University Press, 2015.

20. Anne Salmond, "The Fountain of Fish: Ontological Collisions at Sea," in Bollier and Helfrich, *Patterns of Commoning*, Off the Commons

Books, 2015, pp. 309–329. patternsofcommoning.org/the-fountain-of-fish-ontological-collisions-at-sea

21. Andrea J. Nightingale, "Commons and Alternative Rationalities: Subjectivity, Emotion and the (Non)rational Commons," in Bollier and Helfrich, *Patterns of Commoning*, pp. 297–308. patternsofcommoning.org/uncategorized/commons-and-alternative-rationalities-subjectivity-emotion-and-the-nonrational-commons

22. A metaphor used by Ludwig Wittgenstein when referring to ontologies.

23. See, e.g., Vijaya Nagarajan, "On the Multiple Languages of the Commons: A Theoretical View," *Worldviews* 21, 2017, pp. 41–60.

24. Marilyn Strathern, *The Gender of the Gift*, University of California Press, 1988, p. 13. We are indebted to Lewis Hyde for calling to our attention the work of Strathern, Marriott, and LiPuma.

25. Strathern, p. 340.

26. Strathern, p. 165.

27. Martha Woodmansee and Peter Jaszi, "The Law of Texts: Copyright and the Academia," *College English*, vol. 57, no. 7, November 1995, p. 769, cited in Lewis Hyde, *Common as Air*, Farrar, Straus Giroux, 2010, pp. 177–178.

28. John Swansburg, "The Self-Made Man: The Story of America's most pliable, pernicious, irrepressible myth," *Slate*, September 29, 2014. slate.com/articles/news_and_politics/history/2014/09/the_self_made_man_history_of_a_myth_from_ben_franklin_to_andrew_carnegie.html

29. Thomas Widlok, *Anthropology and the Economic of Sharing*, Routledge, 2016, p. 24.

30. Ecofeminist philosophers such as Donna Haraway and Val Plumwood, among others, have challenged the idea of the autonomous individual, emphasizing the deep interdependencies between humans and nature as well as situated communities. Plumwood writes: "To the extent that we hyper-separate ourselves from nature and reduce it conceptually in order to justify domination, we not only lose the ability to empathize and to see the non-human sphere in ethical terms, but also get a false sense of our own character and location that includes an illusory sense of autonomy." *Environmental Culture: The Ecological Crisis of Reason*, Routledge, 2002, p. 9.

31. See also Mike Telschow, *Townships and the Spirit of Ubuntu*, Clifton Publications, 2003.

32. John Mbeti, *African Religions and Philosophies*, Doubleday, 1970, p.141.

33. Author Pagan Kennedy writes: "According to Dr. Thomas Frieden, the former director of the U.S. Centers for Disease Control and Prevention, 'since 1900, the average life span in the United States has increased by more than 30 years; 25 years of this gain have been attributed to public

health advances.' That's why we should all fight for other people's health. Your decisions can affect when I die, and vice versa." *New York Times*, March 11, 2018. nytimes.com/2018/03/09/opinion/sunday/longevity-pritikin-atkins.html?rref=collection%2Fsectioncollection%2Fsunday

34. Rabindranath Tagore, *The Religion of Man*, Martino Fine Books, 2013, p. 1.
35. Martin Buber, *I and Thou*, Touchstone, 1971.
36. Martin Luther King, Jr., Letter from a Birmingham Jail," April 16, 1963. web.cn.edu/kwheeler/documents/Letter_Birmingham_Jail.pdf
37. Rachel Louise Carson, "Undersea," *The Atlantic,* September 1937, pp. 55-67, https://www.researchgate.net/publication/309354897_Undersea_-_Rachel_Carson.
38. See e.g., Massimo De Angelis, *Omnia Sunt Communia*, Zed Books, 2017; Daniel Christian Wahl, *Designing Regenerative Cultures*, Triarchy Press, 2016; and Wolfgang Hoeschele, *Wirtschaft neu erfinden: Grundlegung für ein Ökonomie der Lebensfülle*, Oekom Verlag, 2017.
39. Wesley J. Wildman, "An Introduction to Relational Ontology," May 15, 2006. wesleywildman.com/wordpress/wp-content/uploads/docs/2010-Wildman-Introduction-to-Relational-Ontology-final-author-version-Polkinghorne-ed.pdf
40. Eric D. Beinhocker, *The Origin of Wealth: Evolution, Complexity and the Radical Remaking of Economics*, Harvard University Press, 2006, pp. 167–168.
41. This idea has a deep kinship with the concept of patterns developed by Christopher Alexander, as explained in Chapter 1.
42. Stuart Kauffman, *The Origins of Order: Self-Organization and Selection in Evolution*, Oxford University Press, 1993. See also Wikipedia entry, at en.wikipedia.org/wiki/Stuart_Kauffman
43. The terms "self-organization" and "autopoiesis" may be problematic because they imply the autonomous agency of individuals, when in fact everything is embedded in larger contexts of interconnection and inter-dependency. That is why we use the term "peer governance" instead of "self-governance." However, if one takes a cue from philosopher Donna Haraway in her book *Staying with the Trouble*, autopoiesis is complemented by sympoiesis ("becoming-with"). The result is a generative friction between interactive and intra-active beings.
44. See, e.g., Terrence W. Deacon, *Incomplete Nature: How Mind Emerged from Matter*, W.W. Norton, 2012; summary at en.wikipedia.org/wiki/Incomplete_Nature. See also Andreas Weber, *Biology of Wonder: Aliveness, Feeling and the Metamorphosis of Science*, New Society Publishing, 2016.
45. Deacon, p. 310.

46. Kate Raworth, *Doughnut Economics: Seven Ways to Think Like a 21ˢᵗ Century Economist*, Chelsea Green Publishing, 2017.
47. Andreas Weber, *Matter and Desire: An Erotic Ecology*, Chelsea Green Publishing, 2017, p. 22.
48. Weber, *Matter and Desire*, p. 29.
49. Stacey Kerr, "Three-Minute Theory: What is Intra-Action?" November 19, 2014. youtube.com/watch?v=v0SnstJoEec

Chapter 3
1. Frank Seifart, "The Structure and Use of Shape-Based Noun Classes in Miraña [Northwest Amazon]," Phd Thesis, 2005. pubman.mpdl. mpg.de/pubman/item/escidoc:402010:3/component/escidoc:402009/ mirana_seifart2005_s.pdf
2. David Bollier, "The Rise of Netpolitik: How the Internet is Changing International Politics and Diplomacy," Aspen Institute Communications and Society Program, 2003, pp. 27–28. bollier.org/rise-netpolitik-how-in-ternet-changing-international-politics-and-diplomacy-2003
3. Thomas S. Kuhn, *The Structure of Scientific Revolutions*, Chicago, Illinois, University of Chicago Press, fourth edition, 1962/2012.
4. Ludwik Fleck, *Genesis and Development of a Scientific Fact*, University of Chicago Press, 1935/1979, p. 28.
5. Fleck, p. 27.
6. Fleck, pp. 38–39.
7. See the seminal work of Gary Becker in *Human Capital: A Theoretical and Empirical Analysis, with Special Reference to Education*, 3ʳᵈ edition, University of Chicago Press, 1964/1993.
8. Wibke Bergemann, "Last Words: What We Lose When a Language Dies," (German: Letzte worte Was wir verlieren, wenn eine Sprache stirbt), May 1, 2018. deutschlandfunk.de/letzte-worte-was-wir-verlieren-wenn-eine-sprache-stirbt.740.de.html?dram:article_id=416634
9. Robert Macfarlane, *Landmarks*, Penguin Books, 2015, p. 39.
10. Macfarlane, p. 311.
11. Macfarlane, p. 18.
12. Macfarlane, p. 20.
13. Jonathan Rowe, "It's All in a Name," January 26, 2006. jonathanrowe. org/its-all-in-a-name
14. Daniel Nettle and Suzanne Romaine, *Vanishing Voices: The Extinction of the World's Languages*, Oxford University Press, 2000.
15. Tim Dee, "Naming Names," *Caught by the River*, June 24, 2014. caught-bytheriver.net/2014/06/naming-names-tim-dee-robert-macfarlane/ cited by Macfarlane, p. 24.

16. See, e.g., George Lakoff, *Moral Politics: How Liberals and Conservatives Think*, 3rd edition, University of Chicago Press, 2016; Lakoff and Mark Johnson, *Metaphors We Live By*, University of Chicago Press, 2003; Lakoff, *The All New Don't Think of an Elephant: Know Your Values and Frame the Debate*, Chelsea Green Publishing, 2014.

17. Jeremy Lent, *The Patterning Instinct: A Cultural History of Humanity's Search for Meaning*, Prometheus Books, 2017, pp. 277–292.

18. Elisabeth Wehling, *Politisches Framing*, pp. 84–85.

19. Ludwik Fleck, *The Genesis and Development of a Scientific Fact*, p. 84.

20. Raymond Williams, *Keywords: A Vocabulary of Culture and Society*, Fontana, 1976.

21. John Patrick Leary, "Keywords for the Age of Austerity: Innovation," February 27, 2014. jpleary.tumblr.com/post/78022307136/keywords-for-the-age-of-austerity-innovation

22. Kate Reed Petty, "Is It Time to Retire the Word 'Citizen'?" *Los Angeles Review of Books*, April 22, 2017. blog.lareviewofbooks.org/essays/time-retire-word-citizen/

23. Wolfgang Sachs, "Development: The Rise and Decline of an Ideal" (article for the Encyclopedia of Global Environmental Change), Wuppertal Paper No. 108, Wuppertal Institute for Climate, Environment and Energy, August 2000. epub.wupperinst.org/frontdoor/deliver/index/docId/10 78/file/WP108.pdf

24. Miki Kashtan, *Reweaving Our Human Fabric: Working Together to Create a Nonviolent Future*, Fearless Heart Publications, 2015, p. 379.

25. Kashtan, p. 181.

26. sociocracyforall.org/sociocracy

27. Wikipedia entry, "Holacracy." en.wikipedia.org/wiki/Holacracy

28. C. Otto Scharmer, *The Essentials of Theory U.: Core Principles and Applications*, Berrett-Koehler, 2018.

29. See entry on "Scale" in David Fleming, *Lean Logic: A Dictionary for the Future and How to Survive It*, Chelsea Green Publishers, 2017, pp. 412–414.

30. See entries for "Intermediate Economy," "Regrettable Necessities," and "Intensification Paradox," in Fleming, *Lean Logic*, pp. 224–227, pp. 389–391, and pp. 219–220.

31. From Thomas Lomée's installation at the University of Ghent in solidarity with the Climate Summit in Paris, December 2015. arthistoryteachingresources.org.

32. Alan Rosenblith, "Scarcity Is an Illusion, No Reality," September 30, 2010. alanrosenblith.blogspot.com/2010/09/scarcity-is-illusion-no-really. html

33. James Suzman, *Affluence Without Abundance: The Disappearing World of the Bushmen*, Bloomsbury, 2017.

34. Arturo Escobar, "Commons in the Pluriverse," in Bollier and Helfrich, editors, *Patterns of Commoning*, Off the Common Books, 2015, pp. 348–360. patternsofcommoning.org/commons-in-the-pluriverse. See also Escobar, *Designs for the Pluriverse: Radical Interdependence, Autonomy, and the Making of Worlds*, Duke University Press, 2018.

35. The Directory of Open Access Journals listed 13,154 open access journals on May 9, 2019, containing more than 3.9 million articles. doaj.org

36. creativecommons.org/use-remix

37. The danger of focusing on openness and not commoning can be seen in the clever commercial strategies of certain academic publishers such as Elsevier and Sage. They often allow the publication of scholarly articles under Creative Commons licenses, but only after charging authors exorbitant upfront author fees or subscription rates. This is a degraded form of open access that exploits academic researchers as a way to maximize private profits without empowering them as commoners. Commons-based publishing, by contrast, seeks to minimize costs to all participants, maximize the benefits of no-cost/low-cost sharing, and therefore allow information to be widely shared.

38. A 2017 book by Paul Stacey and Sarah Hinchliff Pearson, *Made With Creative Commons,* examines diverse types of creative works that bear Creative Commons licenses and are successfully sold in the marketplace: creativecommons.org/use-remix/made-with-climate-change

39. Peter Barnes, *Capitalism 3.0: Guide to Reclaiming the Commons*, Berrett-Koehler, 2006.

40. Dardot and Laval, *Commun. Essai sur la révolution au XXIᵉ siècle*, 2015, p. 23. ("non seulement ce qui est 'mis *en commun,*' *mais aussi et surtout ceux que ont des 'charges en commun.*'").

41. Lynn Margulis, "Symbiogenesis and Symbionticism," in L. Margulis and R. Fester, *Symbiosis as a Source of Evolutionary Innovation: Speculation and Morphogenesis*, MIT Press, 1991, pp. 1–14.

42. openstreetmap.org

43 As cited by John M. Culkin, "A Schoolman's Guide to Marshall McLuhan," *The Saturday Review*, March 18, 1967, pp. 53 and 70.

44. See, e.g., cosmolocalism.eu

45. James C. Scott, *Against the Grain: A Deep History of the Earliest States,* Yale University Press, 2017).

46. "The pure cost-based process is … implicitly a life-destroying process," writes Christopher Alexander, because "it interferes with our freedom

to do what is right." Alexander, *The Nature of Order,* Book II, pp. 501–502.

47. Lewis Hyde, *Common as Air,* Farrar Straus Giroux, 2012, p. 35.

Part II: Introduction

1. John C. Thomas, "A Socio-Technical Pattern Language for Sustainability," IBM T.C. Watson Research, Vancouver, 2011.

2. Christopher Alexander, *The Nature of Order*, Book II, p.176.

3. en.wikipedia.org/wiki/Axiom

4. For more on universal patterns of social interaction, see David West, "Patterns of Humanity," Presentation at PurplSoc Conference, Krems 2017.

5. A pattern has a formal, structured description — which we don't use in this book — consisting of several elements: the pattern name, a description of the context and problem, an illustration, an example, mention of positive and negative forces, and related patterns, among other elements. Such structured descriptions vary according to the field of interest. But the first element of a full-fledged pattern description is always the same. It is the pattern name: the succinct expression of good solutions to a recurrent problem. In this book, we often use the word "pattern" as a shorthand for the formal pattern when in fact we are referring to the "pattern name."

6. For example (as we will see in coming chapters), the three patterns POOL & SHARE; POOL, CAP & DIVIDE UP; and POOL, CAP & MUTUALIZE that we describe in Chapter 6 each refers to the other and extends the others. Some patterns make existing tensions explicit, such as KEEP COMMONS AND COMMERCE DISTINCT and TRADE WITH PRICE SOVEREIGNTY. Other patterns complement each other, such as BRING DIVERSITY INTO SHARED PURPOSE and CULTIVATE SHARED PURPOSE AND VALUE. The point is, there is no such thing as a standalone pattern.

7. *International Journal of the Commons,* at thecommonsjournal.org

Chapter 4

1. Pascal Gielen, "Introduction: There's a Solution to the Crisis," in Pascal Gielen, editor, *No Culture, No Europe — On the Foundations of Politics,* Antennae Valiz), p. 22.

2. J.K. Gibson-Graham, *The End of Capitalism (As We Knew It): A Feminist Critique of Political Economy*, University of Minnesota Press, 1996/2006, p. xvi.

3. Gielen, p. 14.

4. Lewis Hyde, *The Gift: Imagination and the Erotic Life of Property,* Vintage Books, 1979, p. 16.

5. Elinor Ostrom, *Governing the Commons: The Evolution of Institutions for Collective Action*, Cambridge University Press, 1990, p. 44.
6. Michael Polanyi, *Personal Knowledge: Towards a Post-Critical Philosophy*, University of Chicago Press, 1958; and *The Tacit Dimension*, University of Chicago Press, 1966. See also en.wikipedia.org/wiki/Tacit_knowledge
7. Frank Fischer, *Citizens, Experts and the Environment: The Politics of Local Knowledge*, Duke University Press, 2000, back cover.
8. David Holmgren, *Permaculture: Principles and Pathways to Sustainability*, Holmgren Design Services, 2002.
9. Suzman, *Affluence Without Abundance*, p. 121.
10. M. Kat Anderson, *Taming the Wild: Native American Knowledge and the Management of California's Natural Resources*, University of California Press, 2002, p. xvi.
11. Donna Haraway, "Situated Knowledges: The Science Question in Feminism and the Privilege of Partial Perspective," *Feminist Studies* 14(3), August 1988, pp. 575–599.
12. M. Kat Anderson, p. xvi. This point is developed in a series of essays in *Reclaiming Nature: Environmental Justice and Ecological Restoration*, edited by James K. Boyce, Sunita Narain and Elizabeth A Stanton, Anthem Press, 2007.
13. Elizabeth Malkin, "In Guatemala, People Living Off Forests Are Tasked with Protecting Them," *New York Times*, November 25, 2015. nytimes.com/2015/11/26/world/americas/in-guatemala-people-living-off-forests-are-tasked-with-protecting-them.html
14. Shrikrishna Upadhyay, "Community Based Forest and Livelihood Management in Nepal," in *The Wealth of the Commons*, Levellers Press, 2013, pp. 265–270. wealthofthecommons.org/essay/community-based-forest-and-livelihood-management-nepal
15. Sim van der Ryn and Stuart Cowan, *Ecological Design*, Island Press, 1996.
16. David Abram, *The Spell of the Sensuous: Perception and Language in a More-than-Human World*, Vintage, 1997.
17. Andreas Weber, *The Biology of Wonder: Aliveness, Feeling and the Metamorphosis of Science*, New Society Publishers, 2016.
18. Siddhartha Mukherjee, "The Invasion Equation," *The New Yorker*, September 11, 2017, pp. 40–49. newyorker.com/magazine/2017/09/11/cancers-invasion-equation
19. In his book *Lean Logic*, about an envisioned post-capitalist culture, David Fleming noted the importance of carnival: "Celebrations of music, dance, torchlight, mime, games, feast and folly have been central to the life of community for all times other than those when the pretensions of large-scale civilization descended like a frost on public joy." He cited the importance

of enacting a "radical break" with "the normality of the working day," the need to express "the animal spirit of the heart of the tamed, domesticated citizen," and rituals of "sacrifice-and-succession" to symbolize the birth and renewal of the community despite the deaths of individuals in the community. David Fleming, *Lean Logic,* Chelsea Green Publishing, 2016, p. 30.

Chapter 5

1. Robert C. Ellickson, *Order Without Law: How Neighbors Settle Disputes,* Harvard University Press, 1994.
2. In the Grimm's fairy tale, Goldilocks, the little girl who walked into the Three Bears' house, rejected one bowl of porridge because it was "too hot," the other was "too cold," but the final one was "just right."
3. Elinor Ostrom, *Governing the Commons: The Evolution of Institutions of Collective Action*, Cambridge University Press, 1990, p. 90.
4. Christopher Alexander, *The Nature of Order*, Book II, pp.176–177.
5. This account comes from economics journalist Christian Schubert of the *Frankfurter Allgemeine Zeitung,* September 26, 2013. faz.net/aktuell/wirtschaft/wirtschaftswissen/3-prozent-defizitgrenze-wie-das-maastricht-kriterium-im-louvre-entstand-12591473.html
6. Luxembourg, Estonia, and Sweden, which is outside the Eurozone. nzz.ch/wirtschaft/europaeische-waehrungsunion-fuenf-antworten-zum-maastricht-vertrag-ld.133407
7. A designer of digital platforms, Simone Cicero, believes that online platforms will not succeed unless they provide people with "expanded opportunities to leverage their available potential (the assets and capabilities they have access to); respond to the continuous pressures they experience (in a techno-socially disrupted world); achieve their strategic goals; and provide them with relevant experience gains (easier, cheaper, faster ways to achieve their objectives …)." Simone Cicero, "Stories of Platform Design," at stories.platformdesigntoolkit.com
8. The official name of Unitierra (University of the Earth) is Centro de Encuentros y Diálogos Interculturales, A.C.
9. Interview with Gustavo Esteva, December 4, 2017.
10. Jukka Peltokoski, Niklas Toivakainen, Tero Toivanen, and Ruby van der Wekken, "Helsinki Timebank: Currency as a Commons," in David Bollier and Silke Helfrich, editors. *Patterns of Commoning,* Off the Commons Books, 2015, p. 195–198. patternsofcommoning.org/helsinki-timebank-currency-as-a-commons
11. Eric Nanchen and Muriel Borgeat, "Bisse de Savièse: A Journey Through Time to the Irrigation System in Valais, Switzerland," in Bollier and Silke, *Patterns of Commoning*, pp. 61–64. patternsofcommoning.org/

bisse-de-saviese-a-journey-through-time-to-the-irrigation-system-in-valais-switzerland

12. ich.unesco.org/en/RL/culture-of-jeju-haenyeo-women-divers-01068

13. cobudget.co

14. Arthur Brock, "Cryptocurrencies are Dead," *Medium,* September 15, 2016. medium.com/metacurrency-project/cryptocurrencies-are-dead-d4223154d783. See also Mike Hearn, "Why is Bitcoin Forking?" *Medium,* August 15, 2015. medium.com/faith-and-future/why-is-bitcoin-forking-d647312d22c1

15. Joline Blais, "Indigenous Domain: Pilgrim, Permaculture and Perl," *Intelligent Agent,* September 2006. researchgate.net/publication/2994 60968_Indigenous_Domain_Pilgrim_Permaculture_and_Perl

16. Stefan Brunnhuber, *Die Kunst der Transformation, Wie wir lernen, die Welt zu verändern,* 2016, p. 56.

17. Ibid. In German, *Komplexität müssen wir emotional aushalten können.*

18. Ostrom, *Governing the Commons,* pp. 93–94.

19. Christopher M. Kelty, *Two Bits: The Cultural Significance of Free Software,* Duke University Press, 2008, p. 118.

20. Ibid, p. 142.

21. Lewis Thomas, *The Lives of a Cell: Notes of a Biology Watcher,* Penguin, 1974, pp. 133–134.

22. Kate Chapman, "Commoning in Times of Disaster: The Humanitarian OpenStreetMap Team," in Bollier and Helfrich, *Patterns of Commoning,* pp.214–217. patternsofcommoning.org/commoning-in-times-of-disaster-the-humanitarian-openstreetmap-team

23. Ostrom, *Governing the Commons,* p. 93.

24. J. Stephen Lansing, *Perfect Order: Recognizing Complexity in Bali,* Princeton University Press, 2006.

25. Ibid.

26. Plurality and majority rule are different in that plurality makes the option with the most votes the winner, regardless of whether the fifty percent threshold is passed (equivalent to majority rule when there are three or more choices).

27. See Wikipedia entry for "Consensus Decision Making" at en.wikipedia.org/wiki/Consensus_decision-making. See also Ian Hughes, "QuakerDecision Making," February 2011. epoq.wikia.com/wiki/Quaker_Decision_Making

28. Richard Bartlett and Marco Deseriis, "Loomio and the Problem of Deliberation," *Open Democracy,* December 2, 2016. opendemocracy.net/digitaliberties/marco-deseriis-richard-bartlett/loomio-and-problem-of-deliberation

29. en.wikipedia.org/wiki/Consensus_decision-making

30. James Priest, March 9, 2015. jamespriest.org/sociocracy-consensus-decision-making-whats-the-difference

31. Ted J. Rau and Jerry Koch-Gonzalez, *Many Voices, One Song: Shared Power with Sociocracy,* Sociocracy for All, 2018. See sociocracyforall.org

32. For more on Sociocracy, see Wikipedia entry at en.wikipedia.org/wiki/Sociocracy

33. For more see sk-prinzip.eu

34. patternsofcommoning.org/we-are-one-big-conversation-commoning-in-venezuela

35. Ibid.

36. cell.com/trends/ecology-evolution/fulltext/S0169-5347(16)30043-X/html

37. Wikipedia entry, "Heterarchy." en.wikipedia.org/wiki/Heterarchy

38. Nicolas Kristof, "The Bankers and the Revolutionaries," *The New York Times,* October 1, 2011. nytimes.com/2011/10/02/opinion/sunday/kristof-the-bankers-and-the-revolutionaries.html?_r=1&partner=rssnyt&emc=rss

39. en.wikipedia.org/wiki/Heterarchy

40. Ostrom, *Governing the Commons,* p. 95.

41. F. Cleaver, "Moral Ecological Rationality, Institutions and the Management of Common Property Resources," *Development and Change,* 31(2): 374 (2000), in Michael Cox, Gwen Arnold, and Sergio Villamayor Tomás, "A Review of Design Principles of Community-Based Natural Resource Management," *Ecology & Society* 14(4): 38. ecologyandsociety.org/vol15/iss4/art38

42. Ostrom, *Governing the Commons,* p. 86.

43. Étienne Le Roy, "How I Have Been Conducting Research on the Commons for Thirty Years Without Knowing It," in Bollier and Helfrich, *Patterns of Commoning,* pp. 277-296. patternsofcommoning.org/how-i-have-been-conducting-research-on-the-commons-for-thirty-years-without-knowing-it

44. Franciscus W.M. Vera, *Grazing Ecology and Forest History,* Centre for Agriculture and Biosciences International, 2000, p. 386.

45. *Boyd v. United States,* 116 U.S. 616, 630 (1886).

46. According to Encyclopedia Britannica, the movement in 2014 has led more than 2,500 land occupations with about 370,000 families and has won ownership rights to nearly 18.75 million acres (7.5 million hectares) of land as a result of direct MST action.

47. This principle, developed during the nineteenth century, became Catholic doctrine with Pope Leo XIII's Rerum Novarum encyclical. Charles C. Geisler and Gail Daneker, eds. *Property and Values: Alternatives to Public and Private Ownership,* Island Press, 2000, p. 31.

48. International Co-operative Alliance, "World Co-operative Monitor," at monitor.coop

49. Benjamin Mako Hill, "Problems and Strategies in Financing Voluntary Free Software Projects," June 10, 2005. mako.cc/writing/funding_volunteers/funding_volunteers.html

50. Hill cites research by Bernard Enjolra at the Institute for Social Research in Oslo, Norway, who monitored the role and nature of voluntary labor in Norwegian sports organizations after money was introduced to deal with certain bookkeeping and organizational work. The result was that fewer people volunteered and those who did volunteer chose to work less. Bernard Enjolra, "Does the Commercialization of Voluntary Organizations 'Crowd Out' Voluntary Work?" *Annals of Public and Cooperative Economics* 73:3, 2002, pp. 375–398.

51. Simon Sarazin, "Separate Commons and Commerce to Make It Work for the Commons." discourse.transformap.co/t/separate-commons-and-commerce-to-make-it-work-for-the-commons/625. See also encommuns.com

52. wiki.guerrillamediacollective.org/index.php/Commons-Oriented_Open_Cooperative_Governance_Model_V_2.0

53. Karlitschek's resignation letter is at karlitschek.de/2016/06/nextcloud/?utm_content=bufferef6af&utm_medium=social&utm_source=twitter.com&utm_campaign=buffer. See also Steven J. Vaughan-Nichols, "OwnCloud Founder Resigns from His Cloud Company," ZDNet, April 28, 2016, at zdnet.com/article/owncloud-founder-resigns-from-cloud-company

54. Goteo.org. See also Enric Senabre Hidalgo, "Goteo: Crowdfunding to Build New Commons," in Bollier and Helfrich, *Patterns of Commoning*. patternsofcommoning.org/goteo-crowdfunding-to-build-new-commons

55. Sobiecki's currency listings can be found at quora.com/How-many-complementary-currency-systems-exist-worldwide. One of the biggest such lists is curated by the Complementary Currency Resource Center on its online map: complementarycurrency.org/cc-world-map

56. The proposal has been made by Philippe Aigrain, at paigrain.debatpublic.net/docs/internet_creation_1–3.pdf. See also Peter Barnes, *Capitalism 3.0: A Guide to Reclaiming the Commons*, Berrett-Kohler, 2006.

Chapter 6

1. en.wikipedia.org/wiki/Eating_your_own_dog_food

2. Donald E. Knuth, "The Errors of TeX," Software: Practice and Experience, 19(7), July 1989, p. 622.

3. openprosthetics.org
4. Thomas Berry, *Evening Thoughts: Reflecting on Earth as a Sacred Community,* Counterpoint, p. 17.
5. cedifa.de/wp-content/uploads/2013/08/04-FabLabs.pdf, page 14.
6. repaircafe.org/en/about; see the map: repaircafe.org/en/visit/
7. Neera Singh, "The Affective Labor of Growing Forests and the Becoming of Environmental Subjects: Rethinking Environmentality in Odisha, India," *Geoforum*, 2013 47:189-198. dx.doi.org/10.1016/j.geoforum.2013.01.010 and academia.edu/3106203/The_affective_labor_of_growing_forests_and_the_becoming_of_environmental_subjects_Rethinking_environmentality_in_Odisha_India
8. Silvia Federici's excellent collection of essays, *Re-Enchanting the World: Feminism and the Politics of the Commons*, PM Press, 2019, is illuminating on this point.
9. deutschlandfunkkultur.de/feministische-oekonomie-unbezahlte-arbeit-ist-milliarden.976.de.html?dram:article_id=331172
10. See e.g., feministeconomics.org
11. Samuel Bowles reviews many of these studies in his book *The Moral Economy: Why Good Incentives Are No Substitute for Good Citizens*, Yale University Press, 2016.
12. Richard M. Titmuss, *The Gift Relationship: From Human Blood to Social Policy*, Pantheon, 1971.
13. opensourceecology.org/wiki/LifeTrac
14. Rishab Aiyer Ghosh, "Cooking Pot Markets: An Economic Model for the Trade in Free Goods and Services on the Internet," *First Monday* 3(3). firstmonday.org/issues/issue3_3/ghosh/index.html
15. Hyde, *Common as Air,* p. 43.
16. Interview with Rainer Kippe of SSM, August 20, 2017.
17. Ibid. See also SSM website at ssm-koeln.org
18. Fred Pearce, "Common Ground: Securing Land Rights and Safeguarding the Earth," Land Rights Now, International Land Coalition, Oxfam, Rights + Resources, 2016. landcoalition.org/sites/default/files/documents/resources/bp-common-ground-land-rights-020316-en.pdf. The report concludes: "Up to 2.5 billion people depend on Indigenous and community lands, which make up over 50 percent of the land on the planet; they legally own just one-fifth. The remaining five billion hectares remain unprotected and vulnerable to land grabs from more powerful entities like governments and corporations. There is growing evidence of the vital role played by full legal ownership of land by Indigenous peoples and local communities in preserving cultural diversity and in combating poverty and hunger, political instability and climate change."

19. John T. Edge, "The Hidden Radicalism of Southern Food," *New York Times*, May 6, 2017, at nytimes.com/2017/05/06/opinion/sunday/the-hidden-radicalism-of-southern-food.html

20. Cecosesola's full name is Central Cooperativa de Servicios Sociales del Estado Lara (www.cecosesola.org). See profile, "We Are One Big Conversation: Commoning in Venezuela," in Bollier & Helfrich, *Patterns of Commoning*, pp. 258–264, at patternsofcommoning.org/we-are-one-big-conversation-commoning-in-venezuela

21. Ibid, p. 262. See also "Financing for the Commons."

22. Ivan Illich, *Tools for Conviviality*, Harper & Row, 1973, p. 23.

23. Ibid, p. 23.

24. Andrea Vetter offers criteria for convivial tools in Andrea Vetter, "The Matrix of Convivial Technologies: Assessing Technologies for Degrowth," *Journal of Cleaner Production* (2017), pp. 1–9. konvivialetechnologien. blogsport.de/images/Vetter_JcP2017_MatrixConvivialTechnology.pdf

25. A network involves individual people/nodes in episodic transactions with no ongoing social connections, whereas members of a federation have a shared goal and commitments.

26. Eric von Hippel, *Democratizing Innovation*, MIT Press, 2005. web.mit. edu/evhippel/www/books/DI/DemocInn.pdf

27. James K. Boyce, Peter Rosset and Elizabeth A. Stanton, "Land Reform and Sustainable Development," Chapter 5 in James K. Boyce et al., *Reclaiming Nature: Environmental Justice and Ecological Restoration*, Anthem Press, 2007), p. 140.

28. The idea has also been called "Indigenous innovation" and "informal innovation." See Peter Drahos and Pat Mooney, *Indigenous Peoples' Innovation: Intellectual Property Pathways to Development*, Australian National University Press, 2012. jstor.org/stable/j.ctt24hfgx. See also "Farmers' Rights," in Rural Advancement Fund International newsletter, May/June1989. etcgroup.org/sites/www.etcgroup.org/files/publication/555/01/raficom17farmersrights.pdf

29. Wikipedia entry, "Jugaad," at en.wikipedia.org/wiki/Jugaad

30. Campesino a Campesino, foodfirst.org/publication/campesino-a-campesino-voices-from-latin-americas-farmer-to-farmer-movement-for-sustainable-agriculture/

31. masipag.org

32. Open Source Ecology, opensourceecology.org

33. OpenSPIM, openspim.org. See also Jacques Paysan, "OpenSPIM: A High-Tech Commons for Research and Education," in Bollier and Helfrich, *Patterns of Commoning*, pp. 170–175. patternsofcommoning. org/openspim-a-high-tech-commons-for-research-and-education

34. scoutbots.com, also known as "Protei" hardware.
35. Wolfgang Sachs, *The Development Dictionary: A Guide to Knowledge as Power*, Zed Books, 2nd Edition, 2009, p.122.
36. Michael Bauwens, "The Emergence of Open Design and Open Manufacturing," We_magazine, 2009. snuproject.wordpress.com/2011/ 12/17/the-emergence-of-open-design-and-open-manufacturing-we_ magazine. See also Vasilis Kostakis et al., "Design Global, Manufacture Local: Exploring the Contours of an Emerging Productive Model," *Futures* 73, 2015, pp. 126–135; and P2P Foundation wiki entry, "Design Global, Manufacture Local" at wiki.p2pfoundation.net/ Design_Global,_Manufacture_Local
37. Celine Piques and Xavier Rizos, "Peer to Peer and the Commons: A Path Toward Transition: A Matter, Energy and Thermodynamic Perspective," P2P Foundation, 2017. commonstransition.org/wp-content/uploads/ 2017/10/Report-P2P-Thermodynamics-VOL_1-web_2.0.pdf

Part III: Introduction

1. Correspondence with Dina Hasted, December 2, 2018.
2. Shareable, *Sharing Cities: Activating the Urban Commons*, Tides Center/ Shareable, 2018. shareable.net/sharing-cities

Chapter 7

1. Eduardo Moisés Penalver and Sonia K. Katyal, *Property Outlaws: How Squatters, Pirates, and Protesters Improve the Law of Ownership*, Yale University Press, 2010.
2. E.P. Thompson, *Customs in Common: Studies in Traditional Popular Culture*, New Press, 1993, p. 162.
3. C.B. Macpherson, *Property, Mainstream and Critical Positions*, University of Toronto, 1978, pp. 199–200.
4. These themes are explored by scholars of institutional economics.
5. The person who is most cited for moving property from a concept of person object relations (Blackstone) to person-person relations (social relations) is Wesley N. Hohfeld. See Wesley N. Hohfeld, "Some Fundamental Legal Conceptions as Applied in Judicial Reasoning," 23 *Yale Law Journal* 16, (1913); Wesley N. Hohfeld, "Fundamental Legal Conceptions as Applied in Judicial Reasoning," 26 *Yale Law Journal* 710, (1917.)
6. Margaret Radin, *Reinterpreting Property*, University of Chicago Press, p. 35. Because property rights are generally focused on the right of alienation in a liberal market order, they privilege a kind of personhood based on absolute freedom in market relationships.

7. C.B. Macpherson, *The Political Theory of Possessive Individualism: Hobbes to Locke*, Clarendon Press, 1962, p. 3.
8. understandingsociety.blogspot.de/2011/08/possessive-individualism. html. Macpherson, p. 3.
9. Macpherson, *Political Theory*, p. 3.
10. William Blackstone "Of Property, in General", in George Sharswood, editor, *Sir William Blackstone, Commentaries on the Laws of England in Four Books* (J.B. Lippincott Co, Philadelphia, 1753/1893 reprint) Vol. 1, Book 2, Ch. 1. oll.libertyfund.org/titles/blackstone-commentaries-on-the-laws-of-england-in-four-books-vol-1
11. Cf. Gregory Alexander, *Commodity & Propriety: Competing Visions of Property in American Legal Thought 1776–1970*, University of Chicago Press, 1997, p. 321.
12. This is the conventional translation, but it can also be translated "To the common good."
13. John Locke, *Second Treatise of Government*. Edited by C.B. Macpherson, Hackett Publishing, 1980, p. 19.
14. There is a considerable scholarly commentary on the Lockean proviso, much of it kicked off when philosopher Robert Nozick coined the term in his book *Anarchy, State and Utopia*, Harper & Row, 1974, p. 178. See also the Wikipedia entry, "Lockean proviso." en.wikipedia.org/wiki/Lockean_proviso
15. Étienne Le Roy, "How I Have Been Conducting Research on the Commons for Thirty Years Without Knowing It," in Bollier and Helfrich, *Patterns of Commoning*, pp. 277–296. patternsofcommoning. org/how-i-have-been-conducting-research-on-the-commons-for-thirty-years-without-knowing-it
16. The idea of vernacular law is developed in Burns H. Weston and David Bollier, *Green Governance: Ecological Survival, Human Rights and the Law of the Commons*, Cambridge University Press, 2013, pp. 104–112.
17. Hohfeld as the founder of the social relations view of property is described by Syed Talha and Anna Di Robilant in "The Fundamental Building Blocks of Social Relations Regarding Resources: Hohfeld in Europe and Beyond," March 27, 2018. papers.ssrn.com/sol3/papers. cfm?abstract_id=3149768. Nonphysicalist understandings of the concept of property go back to the second half of the nineteenth century, however. See Gregory Alexander, *Commodity & Propriety*, p. 322, footnote 41.
18. Joseph Singer, "The Legal Rights Debate in Analytical Jurisprudence from Bentham to Hohfeld," *Wisconsin Law Review*, 1982, p. 987.
19. Alexander, *Commodity and Propriety*, p. 323.

20. Corporate property is often conflated with individual property, so that the significant differences between the two are not made salient. Individuals are misled into regarding corporate property as if it were personal property.

21. This account comes from Lewis Hyde, *Common as Air: Revolution, Art, and Ownership,* Farrar, Straus, and Giroux, 2010, pp. 169–173.

22. E.P. Thompson, *Customs in Common,* New Press, 1993, p 167.

23. A fascinating exploration of these issues can be found in Joseph L. Sax, *Playing Darts with a Rembrandt: Public and Private Rights in Cultural Treasures,* University of Michigan Press, 1999.

24. Hartmut Zückert, "The Commons — A Historical Concept of Property Rights," in Bollier and Helfrich, *The Wealth of the Commons,* Levellers Press, 2012, pp. 129. wealthofthecommons.org/essay/commons-%E2%80%93-historical-concept-property-rights.

25. More than 1,500 forest and pasture commons exist today in the Roman Carpathians alone. Monika Vasile, "Formalizing Commons, Registering Rights: The Making of the Forest and Pasture Commons in the Romanian Carpathians from the 19th Century to Post-Socialism," *International Journal of the Commons* 12(1), pp. 170–201. DOI: doi.org/10.18352/ijc.805. See also "The Role of Memory and Identity in the Obștea Forest Commons of Romania," in Bollier and Helfrich, *Patterns of Commoning,* pp. 65–70. patternsofcommoning.org/the-role-of-memory-and-identity-in-the-obstea-forest-commons-of-romania

26. oak-schwyz.ch

27. Trent Schroyer, *Beyond Western Economics: Remembering Other Economic Cultures,* Routledge, 2009, p. 69.

28. Oliver Wendell Holmes, Jr., *The Common Law* (1881). 1215.org/law notes/work-in-progress/holmes/index.html

29. Ibid.

30. One of the most extensive treatments of customary law is an anthology that shows how unwritten, informal law has flourished in a variety of contexts throughout history. Alison Dundes Rentln and Alan Dundes, editors, *Folk Law: Essays in the Theory and Practice of Lex Non Scripta,* University of Wisconsin Press, 1994.

31. Carol Rose, "Comedy of the Commons: Custom, Commerce, and Inherently Public Property," in her book *Property and Persuasion: Essays on the History, Theory, and Rhetoric of Ownership,* Westview Press, 1994, p. 134.

32. *Graham v. Walker* (1905), 62 Atlantic Reporter, at 99.

33. Rose, *Property and Persuasion,* pp. 123–24.

34. Land Rights Now. landrightsnow.org/en/home and pbs.twimg.com/media/DZXa7iCX4AAkgQI.jpg

35. Elinor Ostrom, *Governing the Commons: The Evolution of Institutions of Collective Action*, Cambridge University Press, 1990, p. 90.

36. Pierre Dardot and Christian Laval, *Commun: Essai sur la révolution au XXIe siècle,* Éditions La Découverte, 2014, p. 583.

37. Karl Polanyi, *The Great Transformation*, Beacon Press, 1944, pp. 132 and 252.

38. CBS Television interview with Salk, *See It Now* (April 12, 1955), quoted in Jon Cohen, *Shots in the Dark: The Wayward Search for an AIDS Vaccine*, W.W. Norton, 2001.

39. doc.govt.nz/parks-and-recreation/places-to-go/central-north-island/places/taupo-trout-fishery/licenses-access-rules-and-regulations/rules-and-regulations

40. "By the law of nature these things are common to mankind — the air, running water, the sea, and consequently the shores of the sea."

41. Inst. 2, 2 ap. Digest. 1, 8, 1: "Summa itaque rerum divisio in duos articulos diducitur: *nam aliae sunt divini iuris, aliae humani.* 'thus the highest division of things is reduced into two articles some belong to divine right, some to human right'."

42. See full list of World Heritage sites at en.wikipedia.org/wiki/World_Heritage_site

43. Usufruct is the civil law term for the right to reap the (renewable) benefit of a resource such as a plant or forest so long as the underlying resource itself is not diminished.

44. Theodore Steinberg, *Slide Mountain: Or, the Folly of Owning Nature*, University of California Press, 1995.

45. ejil.org/pdfs/16/1/289.pdf

46. In German, *Sache/Gegenstand, Streitfall, Angelegenheit.*

47. Yan Thomas, *La valeur des choses,* p.1449 and 1454; *Res* conveys more the meaning of the Greek *ta pragmata.*

48. The term "resource" as commonly used today, and also in the commons literature, including our own contributions, reflects a reified understanding of *res*, even though the two terms are etymologically different: "resource" as used in the seventeenth century denotes "means of supplying a want or deficiency," from the French *resource*, "a source, spring," and Latin *resurgere*, "rise again."

49. Silke Helfrich, "Common Goods Don't Simply Exist — They Are Created," in Bollier and Helfrich, *The Wealth of the Commons*, pp. 61–67. wealthofthecommons.org/essay/common-goods-don%E2%80%99t-simply-exist-%E2%80%93-they-are-created

50. Silke Helfrich, "Common Goods Don't Simply Exist — They Are Created," in Bollier and Helfrich, *The Wealth of the Commons*, p. 64. Saki Bailey, "The Architecture of Legal Institutions," in Mattei, Ugo and J. Haskell, editors, *Research Handbook on Political Economy and Law*, Edward Elgar Publishing, 2015, pp. 481–495.

Chapter 8

1. For details on workslots, see the Coop's membership manual at food-coop.com/manual/
2. Park Slope Food Coop website at foodcoop.com
3. Park Slope Food Coop Members Manual, p. 28.
4. Max Falkowitz, "Birth of the Kale," *Grub Street*, April 19, 2018. grub-street.com/2018/04/history-of-the-park-slope-food-coop.html
5. Cf. Karl Marx, Paris Manuscript, 1st Manuscript Nr. 4, "Estranged Labor," where Marx names four aspects of alienation (or objectification) of workers as a consequence of estranged labor: from the products of their own labor; from their own physical and mental energies (a self-estrangement); from their essential "species being" and spiritual nature; and from their own bodies. marxists.org/archive/marx/works/1844/manuscripts/labour.htm
6. Erich Fromm is instructive about self-reflection and the meaning of property, especially in his book *To Have or to Be? The Nature of the Psyche*, Harper & Row, 1976.
7. An idea promoted by futurist Stewart Brand and the Long Now Foundation, which was established "to foster long-term thinking and responsibility in the framework of the next 10,000 years." longnow.org
8. Thomas Berry, Evening *Thoughts: Reflecting on Earth as a Sacred Community*, Counterpoint, p. 17.
9. On Wikipedia, individual contributions can be traced back only in the article's history; they cannot be traced on the mainpage of the wiki entry.
10. This comparsion is inspired by Ward Cunningham's notes on the idea of ownership, at own.fed.wiki/view/welcome-visitors.
11. The one Achilles' heel: a large corporation could "suck out" content from a federation of Fedwikis and use it for its own purposes, and not share it, so long as it kept everything behind a firewall. But once published on the internet and available to a federation of Fedwiki sites, no one can assert copyright control over Fedwiki content. If a company keeps someone else's content on a website behind a firewall, the content would legally be considered private and not republished, and therefore not a violation of copyright law.

12. Civil law governs property systems in almost all Latin American countries. It was designed to deal with the overlap of written (codified) and unwritten (uncodified) approaches. Three sources of law had to be taken into account: *canonical law* (property that comes from God), *Spanish law* (property that comes from the King, the so-called regalian system whose core premises inform nation-states' management of property), and *Indigenous law* (property belongs to the respective monarch). See José Juan González: "Civil Law Treatment of the Subsurface in Latin American Countries," in *The Law of Energy Underground: Understanding New Developments in Subsurface Production, Transmission and Storage*, Oxford University Press, 2014, pp. 59–74. José Guadalupe Zúñiga Alegría, Juan Antonio Castillo López: Minería y propiedad del suelo y del subsuelo en México, in Alegatos, núm 87, México, May/August 2014, 132.248.9.34/hevila/Alegatos/2014/no87/7.pdf

13. In the US, infinite air rights based on ownership of land were formally rejected by the Supreme Court in 1946 in the case of *United States v. Causby*, 328 U.S. 256.

14. When the Napoleonic Code was drafted, article 552 declared that ownership of land included ownership of what is over and under it.

15. Blackstone's Commentaries Book 2, Chapter 2, p. 18. avalon.law.yale.edu/18th_century/blackstone_bk2ch2.asp

16 We focus here on the relationship between individual control of one's site with the collective right to make use of and take from it. We don't discuss the server ownership at this point.

17. While Creative Commons licenses can permit or restrict certain types of re-uses (e.g., commercial, derivative re-use if licensed for further re-use), copyright holders cannot easily differentiate among users in granting permission for re-use. One attempt to do that is the Peer Production License (PPL), a derivative of the CC licenses that permits only other commoners, cooperatives, and nonprofits to share and re-use the material, but not commercial entities intent on making profit through the commons without explicit reciprocity. See wiki.p2pfoundation.net/Peer_Production_License

18. syndikat.org

19. Stefan Rost, "Das Mietshäuser Syndikat," in Silke Helfrich und Heinrich Böll Stiftung, *Commons. Für eine neue Politik jenseits von Markt und Staat*, transcript Verlag, 2012, pp. 285–287. band1.dieweltder commons.de/essays/stefan-rost-das-mietshauser-syndikat. English version: patternsofcommoning.org/uncategorized/taking-housing-into-our-own-hands

20. Interview with Jochen Schmidt, May 15, 2018.

21. Rust, p. 285.
22. Essential legal ideas were derived from Matthias Neuling, "Rechtsformen für Alternative Betriebe," in Kritische Justiz, 1986), pp. 309–326, available at kj.nomos.de/fileadmin/kj/doc/1986/19863Neuling_S_309.pdf
23. Ibid.
24. Jochen Schmidt interview, May 15, 2018.
25. In the one case in which a building associated with Mietshäuser Syndikat was put back on the market, the reason was not a liquidation but inadequate financing to complete construction. For many reasons, the housing project never came into existence.
26. More details about solidarity transfers can be found at syndikat.org/en/solidarity_transfer
27. Eric Raymond, *The New Hacker's Dictionary*, 3rd Edition, MIT Press, 1996.
28. Chad Perrin, "Hacker vs. Cracker," *TechRepublic,* April 17, 2009. techrepublic.com/blog/it-security/hacker-vs-cracker
29. Free/open source software has often displaced proprietary software, decommodifying specific market segments, even as it has also served as the basis for new types of software and service markets.
30. Trebor Scholz, "Platform Cooperativism: Challenging the Sharing Economy," Rosa Luxemburg Stiftung, New York Office, January 2016. rosalux-nyc.org/wp-content/files_mf/scholz_platformcoop_5.9.2016.pdf. See also, Trebor Scholz and Nathan Schneider, *Ours to Hack and Own*, OR Books, 2017. orbooks.com/catalog/ours-to-hack-and-to-own
31. tkdl.res.in/tkdl
32. celdf.org
33. Professor Philip H. Howard, Michigan State University, tracks the concentration of the seed industry. See his 2018 account: philhoward.net/2018/12/31/global-seed-industry-changes-since-2013 and his chart, "Seed Industry Structure, 1996–2018."
34. Pat Mooney, "Blocking the Chain: Industrial Food Chain Concentration, Big Data Platforms, and Food Sovereignty Solutions," (ETC Group, October 2018). etcgroup.org/sites/www.etcgroup.org/files/files/blockingthechain_english_web.pdf
35. "Shrinkwrap" licenses and "click-through" licenses are one-sided contracts that the law regards as accepted by users when they break open the shrinkwrap around a software box or click on the website license for software.
36. Johannes Kotschi and Klaus Rapf, "Liberating Seeds with an Open Source Seed License," AGRECOL, July 2016. agrecol.de/files/OSS_Licence_AGRECOL_eng.pdf

37. Jack Kloppenburg, "Re-purposing The Master's Tools: The Open Source Seed Initiative and the Struggle for Seed Sovereignty," *Journal of Peasant Studies,* 2014.

38. The full title is Association for AgriCulture and Ecology in Africa, Asia, Latin America, and Eastern Europe.

39. opensourceseeds.org/en

40. osseeds.org

41. Maywa Montenegro de Wit, "Beating the Bounds: How does 'Open Source' Become a Seed Commons?" *Journal of Peasant Studies,* 2017, p. 15.

42. Jack Kloppenburg, "Enacting the New Commons: The Global Progress, Promise and Possibilities of Open Source Seed," public presentation at the International Association for the Study of Commons Workshop, "Conceptualizing the New Commons: The Examples of Knowledge Commons & Seed and Variety Commons," Oldenburg, Germany, June 6–8, 2018.

43. Hiroyuki Kurokochi et al., "Local-Level Genetic Diversity and Structure of Matsutake Mushroom (*Tricholoma matsutake*) Populations in Nagano Prefecture, Japan, Revealed by 15 Microsatellite Markers," J. Fungi, 2017 June, 3(2): 23. ncbi.nlm.nih.gov/pmc/articles/PMC5715919

44. Anna Lowenhaupt Tsing, *The Mushroom at the End of the World: On the Possibility of Life in Capitalist Ruins,* Princeton University Press, 2015, p. 270.

45. H. Saito and Gaku Mitsumata, "Reviving Lucrative Matsutake Mushroom Harvesting and Restoring the Commons in Contemporary Japan," paper presented at "Governing Shared Resources: Connecting Local Experience to Global Challenges," the Twelfth Biennial Conference of the International Association for the Study of Commons, Cheltenham, England, July 14-18, 2008. dlc.dlib.indiana.edu/dlc/bitstream/handle/10535/1552/Saito_155501.pdf?sequence=1&isAllowed=y

46. Tsing, *Mushroom,* p. 3.

47. Ibid, p. 14.

48. Saito and Mitsumata, p. 5.

49. Ibid, p 14.

50. Such auctioning systems also exist in China. Anthropologist Anna Lowenhaupt Tsing reports from the Chinese province Yunnan, in the mountains of Chuxiong Prefecture, where matsutake is the most valuable forest product, that the "money gained from the auction is distributed to each household and forms an important part of its cash income." Tsing, pp. 268–269.

51. Saito and Mitsumata.

52. Tsing, p. 271.
53. About this topic, see Ulrich Steinvorth, Natürliche Eigentumsrechte, Gemeineigentum und geistiges Eigentum. In: Deutsche Zeitschrift für Philosophie 52. 2004 (5), pp. 717–738.
54. Saito and Mitsumata.
55. Tsing, p. 16.
56. Ibid, p 8.
57. Ibid, p. 10.
58. Anatole France, *Le Lys Rouge* (The Red Lily)," 1894, Chapter 7.
59. Benedict Anderson, *Imagined Communities: Reflections on the Origin and Spread of Nationalism*, Verso, 2016.

Chapter 9
1. unoosa.org/pdf/gares/ARES_34_68E.pdf
2. It is also applied in the Convention on Biological Diversity (CBD).
3. CNBC Transcript: US Commerce Secretary Wilbur Ross Speaks with Joe Kernen and CNBC's 'Squawk Box' Today," February 23, 2018. cnbc.com/2018/02/22/cnbc-transcript-u-s-commerce-secretary-wilbur-ross-speaks-with-joe-kernen-on-cnbcs-squawk-box-today.html. See also Wilbur Ross, "The Moon Colony Will Be a Reality Sooner Than You Think," *The New York Times*, May 24, 2018. nytimes.com/2018/05/24/opinion/that-moon-colony-will-be-a-reality-sooner-than-you-think.html
4. Rich Hardy, "Trump, the Lunar Economy, and Who Owns the Moon," *New Atlas*, February 13, 2017. newatlas.com/who-owns-moon-trump-lunar-economy/47897
5. Prue Taylor, "Common Heritage of Mankind Principle," in Bosselmann, Klaus, Daniel S. Fogel and J. B. Ruhl, editors, *Berkshire Encyclopedia of Sustainability: The Law and Politics of Sustainability*, Berkshire Publishing Group, 2010, pp.64–69.
6. The Ecuadorian Government in 2007 proposed forgoing half of its anticipated oil revenues from twenty percent of its oil deposits, or $3.6 billion, if international partners contributed that sum to help Ecuador explore non-fossil fuel development strategies. The proposal was intended as a pioneering climate-change initiative among "less developed" nations. Juan Falconi Puig, "The World Failed Ecuador in its Yasuni Initiative," *The Guardian*, September 19, 2013. theguardian.com/global-development/poverty-matters/2013/sep/19/world-failed-ecuador-yasuni-initiative
7. Bob Jessop, as quoted in David Bollier, "State Power and Commoning: Transcending a Problematic Relationship," report on a workshop convened by the Commons Strategies Group in cooperation with the

Heinrich Böll Foundation, 2016, available at commonsstrategies.org/state-power-commoning-transcending-problematic-relationship.   See also Bob Jessop, *State Power: A Strategic-Relational Approach*, Polity, 2008, and Jessop, *The State: Past, Present, Future* (Key Concepts), Polity 2015.

8. This national identity is, of course, religious. Just as the Israeli government invokes the tenets of Judaism to justify its policy, state power strengthens the utterances and the influence of religious institutions and Halakha (the collective body of Jewish religious laws derived from the Written and Oral Torah).

9. swp-berlin.org/en/publication/israels-nation-state-law

10. Hannah Arendt, "Nationalstaat und Demokratie," transcribed remarks of a radio conversation with political scientist Eugen Kogon in Cologne, Germany, March 6, 1963, available at hannaharendt.net/index.php/han/article/view/94/154

11. Ramon Roca, "Landline Networks and the Commons," YouTube video of European Parliament Workshop on Community Networks and Telecom Regulation, October 17, 2017, at www.youtube.com/watch?v=9Cu88NnigBU

12. Geoff Mulgan, "Government With the People: The Outlines of a Relational State," in The *Relational State: How Recognising the Importance of Human Relationships Could Revolutionise the Role of the State*, Graeme Cooke and Rick Muir, editors, Institute for Public Policy Research, 2012.

13. Cooke and Muir, *The Relational State*. ippr.org/files/images/media/files/publication/2012/11/relational-state_Nov2012_9888.pdf?noredirect=1 (Jovell's short statement is on p. 61.)

14. See, e.g., Ivan Illich, *Medical Nemesis: The Expropriation of Health*, Pantheon, 1976; *Deschooling Society*, Harper & Row, 1971; and *Tools for Conviviality*, Harper & Row, 1973.

15. Marc Stears, "The Case for a State that Supports Relationships, not a Relational State," in Cooke and Muir, *The Relational State*.

16. Peer to Peer Foundation, "Commons Transition Primer," 2017. primer.commonstransition.org/archives/glossary/peak-hierarchy

17. James C. Scott, *Against the Grain: A Deep History of the Earliest States*, Yale University Press, 2017), especially pp. 93–115, 150–182, and 232.

18. *Leviathan* (1651) is a book written by Thomas Hobbes during the English Civil War. Hobbes theorizes about the structure of society and legitimate government, arguing for a social contract and rule by an absolute sovereign. *Leviathan* is regarded one of the most influential examples of social contract theory.

19. Shoshana Zuboff, *The Age of Surveillance Capitalism: The Right for a Human Future at the New Frontier of Power*, Public Affairs, 2019.

20. James C. Scott, *Seeing Like a State: How Certain Schemes to Improve the Human Condition Have Failed*, Yale University Press, 1998, p. 81–82.

21. Marc Stears, "The Case for a State," p. 39.

22. See, e.g., Benjamin Barber, *If Mayors Ruled the World: Dysfunctional Nations, Rising Cities*, Yale University Press, 2014; and Barber's TEDx Global Talk in 2013 at smart-csos.org/images/Documents/Systemic-Activism-in-a-Polarised-World.pdf

23. Murray Bookchin, "Libertarian Municipalism: An Overview," *Green Perspectives*, No. 24, October 1991. dwardmac.pitzer.edu/Anarchist_Archives/bookchin/gp/perspectives24.html

24. Kate Shea Baird, "A New International Municipalist Movement is on the Rise — From Small Victories to Global Alternatives," *OpenDemocracy*, June 7, 2017. opendemocracy.net/can-europe-make-it/kate-shea-baird/new-international-municipalist-movement-is-on-rise-from-small-vic

25. The term was coined by Italian designer Ezio Manzini and is explained at depth at the P2P Founation website at wiki.p2pfoundation.net/Small,_Local,_Open_and_Connected_As_Way_of_the_Future

26. Symbiosis Research Collective, "How Radical Municipalism Can Go Beyond the Local," *The Ecologist*, June 8, 2018. theecologist.org/2018/jun/08/how-radical-municipalism-can-go-beyond-local

27. Ibid.

28. Cf. walbei.wordpress.com/2015/06/15/was-bleibt-vier-jahre-nach-der-protestbewegung-15-m-in-spanien/

29. Cf.: Nikolai Huke: Politik der ersten Person. Chancen und Risiken am Beispiel der Bewegung 15-M in Spanien, in Sozial.Geschichte Online / Heft 21 / 2017, S. 226 https://duepublico.uni-duisburg-essen.de/servlets/DerivateServlet/Derivate-44168/10_Huke_Politik.pdf

30. David Bollier, "State Power and Commoning: Transcending a Problematic Relationship," workshop report, Commons Strategies Group and Heinrich Böll Foundation, 2016. commonsstrategies.org/state-power-commoning-transcending-problematic-relationship

31. Sutterlütti, Simon and Stefan Meretz: Kapitalismus aufheben. Eine Einladung, über Utopie und Transformation neu nachzudenken, Eine Veröffentlichung der Rosa-Luxemburg-Stiftung, VSA Verlag, 2018, p. 76.

32. Sutterlütti and Meretz, p. 80.

33. Hirsch, Joachim: Radikaler Reformismus, in Ulrich Brand, Bettina Lösch, Benjamin Opratko, Stefan Thimmel, editors, *ABC der Alternativen 2.0*, VSA Verlag, 2012, p. 182–183.

34. Ibid, p. 182–183.

35. Murray Bookchin, "Libertarian Municipalism: An Overview," opening epigraph.

36. Cf. Fabian Scheidler, *Das Ende der Megamaschine. Geschichten einer scheiternden Zivilisation*, Promedia Verlag, 2015.

37. J.K. Gibson-Graham, *The End of Capitalism (As We Knew It): A Feminist Critique of Political Economy*, University of Minnesota Press, 1996/2006, p. xvi.

38. Hannah Arendt, *The Human Condition*, University of Chicago Press, 1958, p. 200.

39. Bruno Latour, *Down to Earth: Politics in the new Climate Regime*, Polity, 2018.

40. A chilling account of this political history can be found in Nancy MacLean, *Democracy in Chains: A Deep History of the Radical Right's Stealth Plan for America*, Penguin, 2017.

41. Jose Luis Vivero Pol, "Transition Towards a Food Commons Regime: Re-commoning Food to Crowd-feed the World," Chapter 9 in Guido Ruivenkamp and Andy Hilton, editors, *Perspectives on Commoning: Autonomist Principles and Practices*, Zed Books, 2017. researchgate.net/publication/316877384_Transition_towards_a_Food_Commons_Regime_Re-commoning_Food_to_Crowd-feed_the_World

42. Ostrom, *Governing the Commons*, p. 90.

43. James C. Scott examines the highlands of five Southeast Asian nations, known as Zomia, as "the largest remaining region of the world whose peoples have not yet been fully incorporated into nation-states, in *The Art of Not Being Governed: An Anarchist History of Upland Southeast Asia*, Yale University Press, 2009, p. ix.

44. Scott, *Against the Grain*, pp 219–256.

45. David Graeber, *The Utopia of Rules: On Technology, Stupidity, and the Secret Joys of Bureaucracy*, Melville House, 2016.

46. Distributed ledger technologies consist of the many variations on the blockchain ledger pioneered by Bitcoin, but which now embody many different forms of social and political control over the resulting applications such as digital currencies. Examples include the Holochain, Ethereum, and Fairchain (fair-coin.org/en/fairchains). See Chapter 10.

47. Time-banking may appear to replicate market values and tit-for-tat reciprocal exchange, but in practice people use time-banking less as a transactional currency than as a vehicle for assisting neighbors in need and building community. They PRACTICE GENTLE RECIPROCITY.

48. Jens Kimmel, Till Gentzsch, and Sophie Bloemen, *Urban Commons Shared Spaces*, Commons Network & raumlaborberlin, November 2018.

commonsnetwork.org/wp-content/uploads/2018/11/SharedSpaces
CommonsNetwork.pdf

49. kingofthemeadows.eu/about-kening-fan-e-greide

50. For example, old logging roads were decommissioned, timber was harvested in more ecologically responsible ways, and fish habitat in streams was given greater attention. David Bollier, "New Film Documentary, 'Seeing the Forest," May 5, 2015. bollier.org/blog/new-film-documentary-%E2%80%9Cseeing-forest%E2%80%9D

51. David Bollier, "I Am the River, and the River is Me," June 29, 2017. bollier.org/blog/i-am-river-and-river-me

52. The Te Awa Tupua Act, signed on August 2014: parliament.nz/en/pb/bills-and-laws/bills-proposed-laws/document/00DBHOH_BILL68939_1/te-awa-tupua-whanganui-river-claims-settlement-bill. See also David Bollier, "The Potato Park of Peru," in *Patterns of Commoning*, 2015), pp. 103–107. patternsofcommoning.org/the-potato-park-of-peru.

53. For infrastructures created and managed by commoners, "openness" is less critical than the ability of commoners to protect and maintain their infrastructures (e.g., Wi-Fi systems, information collections, energy-sharing systems) in the face of businesses seeking to appropriate them and against vandals and other troublemakers.

54. US Department of Health and Human Services, National Institutes of Health Public Access Policy, at publicaccess.nih.gov

55. Open Commons Linz at opencommons.linz.at and cityofmediaarts.at/topic/open-commons_linz

56. Wikipedia entry, "Freifunk," at en.wikipedia.org/wiki/Freifunk

57. These rights are not only covered by the Universal Declaration of Human Rights (Articles 22 to 28) but also by the International Covenant on Economic, Social, and Cultural Rights. The ICESCR was adopted together with the Covenant on Civil and Political Rights as part of the International Bill of Human Rights in 1966.

58. This generation, even though difficult to enforce, is highly relevant to the commons as it includes group and collective rights, rights to self-determination, and communication rights.

59. Interestingly these documents stand in the legal tradition of the Magna Carta, into which the Charter of the Forest that guaranteed commoners' use rights was incorporated.

Chapter 10

1. wikihouse.cc/about and medium.com/wikihouse-stories/wikihouse-design-principles-47a49aec936d

2. permacultureprinciples.com/principles

3. terredeliens.org

4. kosmosjournal.org/article/people-sharing-resources-toward-a-new-multilateralism-of-the-global-commons/

5. blog.p2pfoundation.net/a-charter-for-how-to-build-effective-data-and-mapping-commons/2017/04/20

6. globalcommonstrust.org/?page_id=20

7. Isabel Carlisle, "Community Charters," *Stir* magazine, No. 9, Spring 2015, pp. 21–23.

8. Falkirk Community Charter. faug.org.uk/campaign/community-charter

9. For more about Barcelona en Comú, see wiki.p2pfoundation.net/Barcelona_en_Com%C3%BA. For Code of Ethics: https://barcelona encomu.cat/sites/default/files/pdf/codi-etic-eng.pdf. Shock Plan: https://barcelonaencomu.cat/sites/default/files/pla-xoc_eng.pdf

10. Ibid.

11. Tim Wu, *The Master Switch: The Rise and Fall of Information Empires*, Knopf, 2010.

12. Television critic Fred Friendly, cited by Wu, *Master Switch*.

13. Primavera de Filippi, "Blockchain Technology Toward a Decentralized Governance of Digital Platforms?" in Anna Grear and David Bollier, *The Great Awakening*, Punctum Books, 2020.

14. en.wikipedia.org/wiki/Mutual_credit

15. Trent Lapinski, "WTF is Holochain: The Revolution Will Be Distributed," *Hackernoon*, April 4, 2018. hackernoon.com/wtf-is-holochain-35f9dd8e5908

16. metacurrency.org/about

17. Interview with Eric Harris-Braun, October 30, 2018.

18. Interview with Fernanda Ibarra, November 30, 2018.

19. Two leading organizations that have documented the failures of public/private contracts are In the Public Interest (USA), at inthepublicinterest.org, and We Own It (UK), at weownit.org.uk/privatisation-fails. In addition, see the In the Public Interest guidebook, "Understanding and Evaluating Infrastructure Public-Private Partnerships," at inthepublicinterest.org/guide-understanding-and-evaluating-infrastructure-public-private-partnerships-p3s

20. The protocols are based on "field-experiments designed, analyzed and interpreted by LabGov in several Italian cities, together with 200+ global case studies and indepth investigations run in more than 100 cities from different geopolitical contexts." See labgov.city/co-city-protocol

21. Frederic Laloux, *Reinventing Organizations: Creating Organizations Inspired by the Next Stage of Human \ Consciousness,* Nelson Parker, 2016.

22. Michel Bauwens and Yurek Onzia, "Commons Transitie Plan voor de stad Gent" (in Dutch), Commons Transition, June, 2017. cdn8-blog.p2p foundation.net/wp-content/uploads/Commons-transitieplan.pdf

23. Soma K P and Richa Audichya, "Our Way of Knowing: Women Protect Common Forest Rights in Rajasthan," *Patterns of Commoning*, pp. 77–82. patternsofcommoning.org/our-ways-of-knowing-women-protect-common-forest-rights-in-rajasthan

24. DNDi website, dndi.org

25. dndi.org/diseases-projects

26. dndi.org/about-dndi/business-model

27. "$1 for 1 Life," documentary film by Frédéric Laffont, 2010. youtube.com/watch?time_continue=565&v=aSU4y-DFwt8

28. DNDi website, "Artesunate + amodiaquine (ASAQ) to treat malaria," at https://www.dndi.org/achievements/asaq (website last updated January 2019).

Appendix A

1. A detailed description, including an ontological rationale and foundation, is given in Silke Helfrich, *Lebensform Commons: Eine musterbasierte und ontologisch begründete Bestimmung,* thesis for masters degree, Cusanus University, institute for Economy, 2018.

2. Christopher Alexander, *The Nature of Order, Books 1–4, The Phenomenon of Life*, Routledge, 2001-2005.

3. See, especially, Helmut Leitner, "Working with Patterns — An Introduction," in David Bollier and Silke Helfrich, *Patterns of Commoning*, Levellers Press, 2015, pp. 15–25. patternsofcommoning.org/working-with-patterns-an-introduction.

4. In other words, the method has to overcome "methodological individualism," as described in Chapter 2.

5. Michael Polanyi, *The Tacit Dimension*, University of Chicago Press, 1966/2009.

6. A pattern of commoning that works in one context, for example, could be an "antipattern" within a capitalist economic context. In other words, a pattern that works in one context does not necessarily work in very different contexts.

7. In the diagram showing the process of gaining insight (p. 363), I call the moment of verbalization "prehension," following Alfred North Whitehead.

8. Questions that deviated from this rule such as, "Do you have rituals?" were immediately put in more precise forms, such as, "What rituals do you have? Please describe them."

9. Specific patterns are more concrete than generic patterns, but are incorporated into generic patterns. A pattern can be both specific and generic at the same time. This series of words may help illustrate this point: leaf → twig → branch → tree. A twig is specific in relation to the branch, and it is generic in relation to the leaf. The situation is similar with respect to patterns.

10. On "prehending" and "feeling" as epistemological concepts, following Alfred North Whitehead and Christopher Alexander, see Silke Helfrich's masters thesis, footnote 1.

11. Christopher Alexander, Sara Ishikawa, Murray Silverstein, Max Jacobson, Ingrid Fiksfahl-King, and Shlomo Angel, *A Pattern Language. Towns, Buildings, Construction*, Oxford University Press, 1977, p. xiv.

12. According to Ivan Illich, conviviality is individual freedom that is aware of its interdependency.

13. Ivan Illich, *Tools for Conviviality*, Harper and Row, 1973; and Andrea Vetter, "The Matrix of Convivial Technology: Assessing Technologies for Degrowth," *Journal of Cleaner Production*, 197(2), October 2018, pp. 1778–1786. researchgate.net/publication/314271426_The_Matrix_of_Convivial_Technology_-_Assessing_technologies_for_degrowth

14. This pattern may well be one level of abstraction above the other ones because it synthesizes them as a mode of production, cf. Chris Giotitsas and Jose Ramos, *A New Model of Production for a New Economy: Two Cases of Agricultural Communities*, Source Network / New Economics Foundation, 2017.

Index

community supported agriculture
(CSA)
  bidding round, 174
  defined, 374
  DIT and, 168
  as example of commons, 22–24
  in Germany, 202
  Peer Governance and, 136
  as power reallocation, 301
community supported industry,
  23–24, 374
complex adaptive systems, 47, 74,
  76, 366
complexity science, 46–48, 76,
  134
computer numerical control
  fabrication (CNC), 21
confirmation bias, 55–56
conflicts, 66, 85, 113–114, 215,
  231, 245, 276–277, 278, 308,
  340, 354, 380
  Peer Governance and, 278
  preserving relationships in
    addressing, 113–114
conscious design, 129
conscious self-organization, 64
consensus decision making, 137,
  139, 140
consent
  in decision making, 136–143
  explained, 139–140
constitutional framework, 33
consumer/producer binary, 67
Contribute & Share, 175–176
Contribute Freely, 62, 106–107
convivial tools, 193
  cosmopolitan localism and, 197
  defined, 77
  nature of, 22

provisioning through commons
  and, 189–191
relationalized property and, 244
cooperation, 8, 23, 40, 43, 50,
  66–67, 75, 102, 125, 127, 128,
  138, 154, 193, 201, 206, 320,
  324–325, 330. *see also* Cosmo-
  local Production
  in commons-public
    partnerships, 338
  in corporations and markets,
    145, 237
  graduated sanctions and, 147
  as human impulse, 13–14,
    276–277
  platform cooperatives, 260–261
  Pool, Cap & Divide Up,
    182–183
  Pool, Cap & Mutualize, 183
  property and, 242
cooperation/competition binary,
  66–67
cooperative innovation, 195
Copernicus, 55
copyright law, 65, 69–71, 80,
  166, 168, 197, 209, 210, 213,
  251, 258–259, 259, 375
corporate property, 275
corporation, as terminology, 64
Corpus Iuris Civilis (Justinian
  Code), 228
Cosmo-local Production
  defined, 77, 374
  emergent behaviors and, 78
  interoperability and, 82
  as money-lite commoning, 159
  rise of, 195
  stages of, 197
cosmopolitan localism, 197

About the Authors

D AVID BOLLIER is an activist, scholar, and blogger who is focused on the commons as a new/old paradigm for re-imagining economics, politics, and culture. He pursues his commons scholarship and activism as Director of the Reinventing the Commons Program at the Schumacher Center for a New Economics and as cofounder of the Commons Strategies Group, an international advocacy project. Author of *Think Like a Commoner* and other books, he blogs at www.Bollier.org, and lives in Amherst, Massachusetts.

CREDIT: THOMAS BOLLIER

S ILKE HELFRICH is an independent activist, author, scholar, and speaker. She cofounded the Commons Strategies Group and Commons-Institute, was former head of the regional office of Heinrich Böll Foundation for Central America, Cuba, and Mexico, and holds degrees in Romance languages/pedagogy and in social sciences. Helfrich is the editor and co-author of several books on the Commons, blogs at www. commons.blog, and lives in Neudenau, Germany.

CREDIT: MILPA FILMS/OLE
SCHWARZ, LICENSED UNDER
CREATIVE COMMONS BY SA LICENSE

A Note about the Publisher

NEW SOCIETY PUBLISHERS is an activist, solutions-oriented publisher focused on publishing books for a world of change. Our books offer tips, tools, and insights from leading experts in sustainable building, homesteading, climate change, environment, conscientious commerce, renewable energy, and more — positive solutions for troubled times.

We're proud to hold to the highest environmental and social standards of any publisher in North America. This is why some of our books might cost a little more. We think it's worth it!

- We print all our books in North America, never overseas
- All our books are printed on **100% post-consumer recycled paper,** processed chlorine free, with low-VOC vegetable-based inks (since 2002)*
- Our corporate structure is an innovative employee shareholder agreement, so we're one-third employee-owned (since 2015)
- We're carbon-neutral (since 2006)
- We're certified as a B Corporation (since 2016)

At New Society Publishers, we care deeply about *what* we publish – but also about *how* we do business.

Download our catalogue at https://newsociety.com/Our-Catalog, or for a printed copy please email info@newsocietypub.com or call 1-800-567-6772 ext 111.

New Society Publishers
ENVIRONMENTAL BENEFITS STATEMENT

*By Using 100% post-consumer recycled paper vs virgin paper stock, New Society Publishers saves the following resources:[1] (per every 5,000 copies printed)

44	Trees
3,988	Pounds of Solid Waste
4,388	Gallons of Water
5,724	Kilowatt Hours of Electricity
7,250	Pounds of Greenhouse Gases
31	Pounds of HAPs, VOCs, and AOX Combined
11	Cubic Yards of Landfill Space

[1]Environmental benefits are calculated based on research done by the Environmental Defense Fund and other members of the Paper Task Force who study the environmental impacts of the paper industry.

MIX
Paper from
responsible sources
FSC
www.fsc.org   FSC® C016245